ALSO BY BOB WOODWARD

State of Denial

The Secret Man
(with a Reporter's Assessment by Carl Bernstein)

Plan of Attack

Bush at War

Maestro: Greenspan's Fed and the American Boom

Shadow: Five Presidents and the Legacy of Watergate

The Choice

The Agenda: Inside the Clinton White House

The Commanders

Veil: The Secret Wars of the CIA 1981–1987

Wired: The Short Life and Fast Times of John Belushi

The Brethren
(with Scott Armstrong)

The Final Days
(with Carl Bernstein)

All the President's Men
(with Carl Bernstein)

THE WAR

SIMON & SCHUSTER

WITHIN

A Secret White House History 2006–2008

Bob Woodward

NEW YORK · LONDON · TORONTO · SYDNEY

 SIMON & SCHUSTER
Rockefeller Center
1230 Avenue of the Americas
New York, NY 10020

For information about special discounts for bulk purchases,
please contact Simon & Schuster Special Sales at
1-800-456-6798 or business@simonandschuster.com.

Designed by Paul Dippolito

Manufactured in the United States of America

10 9 8 7 6 5 4 3 2 1

Library of Congress Cataloging-in-Publication Data is available.

ISBN-13: 978-1-4165-5897-2
ISBN-10:   1-4165-5897-7

Photography credits appear on page 469.

To Elsa

CONTENTS

———————

AUTHOR'S NOTE

Two extraordinary people helped me with the conception, reporting, writing, and editing of this book:

Brady Dennis, a 2000 graduate of the University of North Carolina at Chapel Hill and a veteran reporter for the *St. Petersburg Times,* agreed in early 2007 to work for me full-time. He is that rare combination of gifted writer and great newshound, an exceptional journalist with both narrative and investigative skills. Furiously independent, wise and resourceful in every way, he is an engine of good sense and sound judgment, a tireless worker who insists on fairness and accuracy. He is a tough and tenacious reporter, and a decent and genuine soul. His generosity, calm nature and constant good humor have made the longest days seem shorter, the largest obstacles surmountable. As we worked together, I came to rely on him heavily and trust him completely. Always positive, he reminds me of what Ben Bradlee, my mentor at *The Washington Post,* must have been like in his youth. I can think of no higher compliment to either of them. Brady has been a partner and a confidant, and there would be no book without him. I hope he realizes that.

Evelyn M. Duffy, a 2007 English and Creative Writing graduate of George Washington University, is a young wizard of old and new media. She can track down anything and anyone. In the space of a year, she gained an extensive understanding of the U.S. government and the Iraq War. She has transcribed hundreds of hours of recorded interviews with people from President Bush to cabinet officers, from White House aides to military and intelligence officials. Diligent, caring, and learned, she added value to every page of every draft. Anyone who thinks the younger generation doesn't appreciate literature, history, and current events has not met Evelyn. At 23, she already has written and produced a one-act play called *Nighthawks,* based on Edward Hopper's famous painting of four lonely souls in a late-night diner. It is raw and modern and wonderfully mysterious. I know that much more fine writing lies ahead for her. Evelyn is a terrific editor, full of stamina and intellectual curiosity. I consider her my friend for life. You get only a handful of those.

CAST OF CHARACTERS

THE PRESIDENT OF THE UNITED STATES
George W. Bush

VICE PRESIDENT OF THE UNITED STATES
Dick Cheney

SECRETARY OF STATE

Condoleezza Rice	January 26, 2005–
Colin Powell	January 20, 2001–January 26, 2005

SECRETARY OF DEFENSE

Robert Gates	December 18, 2006–
Donald H. Rumsfeld	January 20, 2001–December 18, 2006

NATIONAL SECURITY ADVISER

Stephen J. Hadley	January 26, 2005–
Condoleezza Rice	January 22, 2001–January 26, 2005

U.S. MILITARY

Commanding General, Multi-National Force—Iraq

General David H. Petraeus	February 10, 2007–
General George Casey	July 1, 2004–February 10, 2007

Commander, United States Central Command

Admiral William J. Fallon   March 16, 2007–March 11, 2008

General John Abizaid   July 7, 2003–March 16, 2007

Commander, Multi-National Corps—Iraq

Lieutenant General
    Raymond T. Odierno   December 14, 2006–February 8, 2008

Lieutenant General
    Peter Chiarelli   January 19, 2006–December 14, 2006

Chief of Staff of the Army

General George W. Casey Jr.   April 10, 2007–

General Peter J. Schoomaker   August 1, 2003–April 10, 2007

Chairman of the Joint Chiefs of Staff

Admiral Michael Mullen   October 1, 2007–

General Peter Pace   September 30, 2005–October 1, 2007

Defense Intelligence Agency

Derek Harvey

Former Vice Chief of Staff of the Army

Retired General Jack Keane   June 25, 1999–October 2, 2003

STATE DEPARTMENT

Counselor of the Department of State

Philip Zelikow   February 1, 2005–December 19, 2006

Senior Adviser to the Department of State / Coordinator for Iraq

David Satterfield   August 1, 2006–

United States Ambassador to Iraq

Ryan Crocker   March 29, 2007–

Zalmay Khalilzad   June 22, 2005–March 29, 2007

John D. Negroponte   June 28, 2004–April 21, 2005

NATIONAL SECURITY COUNCIL

Deputy National Security Adviser

J. D. Crouch   January 31, 2005–May 4, 2007

Deputy National Security Adviser on Iraq and Afghanistan

Meghan L. O'Sullivan   November 3, 2005–April 2, 2007

IRAQ STUDY GROUP

Democrats

Lee Hamilton, co-chair

Vernon Jordan

Leon Panetta

William J. Perry

Charles Robb

Republicans

James A. Baker III, co-chair

Lawrence S. Eagleburger

Robert Gates

Edwin Meese III

Sandra Day O'Connor

Alan Simpson

IRAQIS

Prime Minister of Iraq

Nouri al-Maliki   May 20, 2006–

Ibrahim al-Jafari   May 3, 2005–May 20, 2006

Ayad Allawi   June 28, 2004–May 3, 2005

Shia Leaders

Vice President Adil Abd al-Mahdi

Mowaffak al-Rubaie, national security adviser

Abdul Aziz al-Hakim, leader of the Supreme Council for the
    Islamic Revolution in Iraq

Sunni Leaders

Vice President Tariq al-Hashimi

Adnan al-Dulaimi, leader of the Iraqi Accordance Front

Sheikh Ahmed Abu Risha, President of the Iraqi Awakening Council

Kurdish Leaders

President of Iraq Jalal Talabani

President of Kurdistan Massoud Barzani

Deputy Prime Minister Barham Salih

Leader of the Jaish al Mahdi (JAM)

Moqtada al-Sadr

Founding Leader of al Qaeda in Iraq

Abu Musab al-Zarqawi   Killed June 7, 2006

Former President of Iraq and Leader of the Baath Party

Saddam Hussein   July 16, 1979–April 9, 2003

                                  Executed December 30, 2006

BOOK ONE

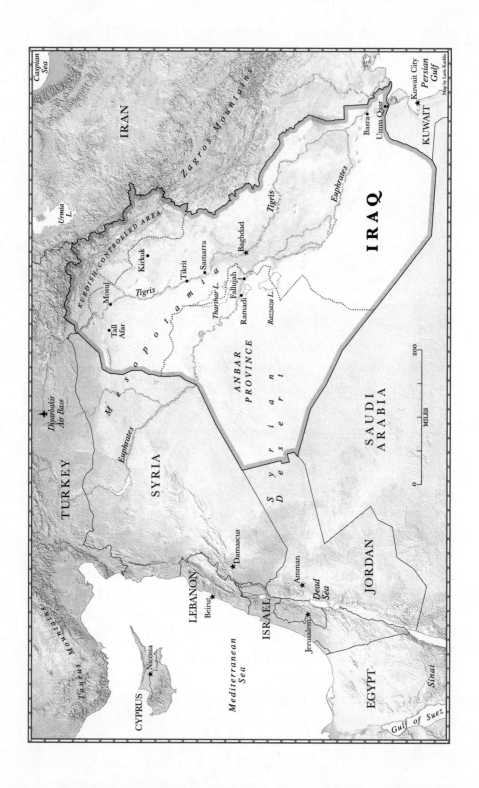

Caspian
Sea

IRAN

Zagros Mountains

KURDISH-CONTROLLED AREA

Urmia
L.

Kirkuk

Mosul

Tall
Afar

Tigris

Tikrit

Samarra

M e s o p o t a m i a

Tharthar L.

Fallujah

Ramadi

Razzaza L.

S y r i a n

D e s e r t

Baghdad

Tigris

Euphrates

IRAQ

Basra

Umm Qasr

KUWAIT

Kuwait City

Persian
Gulf

Map by Lars Karlis

ANBAR
PROVINCE

SAUDI
ARABIA

Diyarbakir
Air Base

Euphrates

TURKEY

SYRIA

Taurus Mountains

Damascus

LEBANON

Beirut

ISRAEL

Jerusalem

Amman

Dead
Sea

JORDAN

EGYPT

Sinai

Gulf of Suez

CYPRUS

Nicosia

Mediterranean
Sea

200

MILES

0

PROLOGUE

On June 13, 2006, halfway through the sixth year of his presidency and more than three years into the Iraq War, George W. Bush stood on a veranda of the American embassy compound in Baghdad. He had flown through the night for a surprise visit to the new Iraqi prime minister. With so much at stake in Iraq, where success or failure had become the core of his legacy, Bush had been anxious to meet the man he had, in many ways, been waiting for since the invasion.

It was now evening. A hazy sunset had descended over the sweltering, violent capital. The president stepped aside for a private conversation with Army General George W. Casey Jr., the 57-year-old commander of the 150,000 U.S. forces in the country. A 5-foot-8, four-star general with wire-rim glasses, closely cropped graying hair and a soft voice, Casey had been the commander in Iraq for two years. As American military units rotated in and out, rarely serving more than a year, Casey had remained the one constant, seeing it all, trying to understand—and end—this maddening war in this maddening land.

Recently, there had been some positive news in Iraq. A week earlier, U.S. forces had killed Abu Musab al-Zarqawi, the man Osama bin Laden had declared the "Prince of al Qaeda in Iraq" and the terrorist organization's in-country operational commander. And the previous month, after three elections and months of delay, Nouri al-Maliki finally had taken office as the country's first permanent prime minister.

Now, in the warm Baghdad dusk, the president and the general lit thin cigars.

"We have to win," Bush insisted, repeating his public and private mantra. Casey had heard the president's line dozens of times.

"I'm with you," he replied. "I understand that. But to win, we have to draw down. We have to bring our force levels down to ones that are sustainable both for them and for us."

Casey felt that the Iraqis, a proud people and resistant to the Western occupation, needed to take over. The large, visible U.S. force was ultimately a sign of disrespect. Worse, the prolonged occupation was making the Iraqis dependent. Each time additional U.S. troops arrived, they soon seemed indispensable. The Iraqis needed to take back their country and their self-respect, so central to Arab culture. They needed to fight their own war and run their own government; they were doing neither.

Casey studied Bush's face, now wrinkled and showing its 59 years, the right eye slightly more closed than the left under graying, full eyebrows. The general had pushed for a drawdown for two years. And while the president had always approved the strategy, he no longer seemed to buy Casey's argument.

"I know I've got work to do to convince you of that," the general said, "but I firmly believe that."

Bush looked skeptical.

"I need to do a better job explaining to you" why winning means getting out, Casey said.

"You do," Bush replied.

Casey had long concluded that one big problem with the war was the president himself. He later told a colleague in private that he had the impression that Bush reflected the "radical wing of the Republican Party that kept saying, 'Kill the bastards! Kill the bastards! And you'll succeed.'" Since the beginning, the president had viewed the war in conventional terms, repeatedly asking how many of the various enemies had been captured or killed.

The real battle, Casey believed, was to prepare the Iraqis to protect and govern themselves. He often paraphrased British Lieutenant Colonel T. E. Lawrence, the early-20th-century innovative godfather of

irregular warfare, known as Lawrence of Arabia: "Better they do it im-
perfectly with their own hands than you do it perfectly with your own."
In *Seven Pillars of Wisdom,* Lawrence had written, "For it is their war and
their country, and your time here is limited."

The year before, Casey had had a list of 11 rules printed on lami-
nated cards and posters to distribute to his troops. The most important
was: "Help the Iraqis win—don't win it for them."

This isn't a conventional war, Casey told every U.S. brigade that
came to Iraq. He emphasized that the job was to gradually shift counterinsurgency tasks to the Iraqi security forces while continuing to
conduct counterinsurgency operations themselves. On a scale of 1 to
10, he told the troops, "This is degree of difficulty 12."

"These guys are primarily Arabs. They're never going to like us," he
said, "We're going to do it, or they're going to do it. And I don't believe
we will ever succeed in Iraq by us doing it for them."

In weekly secure videoconferences with the president, Casey had
tried to drum home the point that they needed to reduce forces.
Casey's boss up the chain of command, General John Abizaid, the head
of U.S. Central Command, who sat in on the conferences, shared
Casey's view. Though video didn't have the intimacy of face-to-face
meetings, Abizaid watched Bush carefully—the nods, the expressions,
the president's impatient dance in his chair as he listened. After the
videoconferences, Casey and Abizaid, both students of Bush's body
language, often compared notes.

"What do you think?" Casey asked more than once. "Did we get
through today?"

"Oh, no, I don't think so," Abizaid would reply. "I think the body
language was bad on that one."

Casey and Abizaid had been one-star generals together in Bosnia in
1996 and had seen that the various ethnic groups in the Balkans didn't
reconcile until the violence got totally out of hand.

Abizaid had concluded that the United States' armed presence in
Iraq on such a large scale for so many years was doing more harm than
good. In private, he put it bluntly: "We need to get the fuck out."

Casey was troubled by the thought that the president simply didn't
get it, didn't understand the war and the nature of the fight they were

in. The large, heavily armed Western force was on borrowed time, he believed. And worse, the president never really understood how the economy and the politics of Iraq must be rebuilt if military gains were to be sustained.

The president often paid lip service to the importance of these political and economic elements, and winning over the people. But then he would lean in with greater interest and ask about raids and military operations, grilling Casey about killings and captures. Months earlier, during one of the videoconferences, he had told Casey that it looked as if he weren't doing enough militarily. "George, we're not playing for a tie. I want to make sure we all understand this, don't we?" Later in the videoconference Bush emphasized it again: "I want everybody to know we're not playing for a tie. Is that right?"

In Baghdad, Casey's knuckles whitened on the table. The very suggestion was an affront to his dignity that he would long remember, a statement just short of an outright provocation.

"Mr. President," Casey had said bluntly, "we are *not* playing for a tie."

After the screen went blank in Baghdad, David Satterfield, the deputy chief of mission in the embassy, who had been sitting in on the session, turned to Casey.

"George," Satterfield said, "I don't know how you manage to contain yourself."

"I'm disciplined," Casey replied.

Not so disciplined that General Abizaid, who was also on the videoconference, hadn't noticed. He called Casey. "You shouldn't yell at the president," he advised.

But Casey was boiling. The president repeatedly questioned his commander about whacking the bad guys, as if everything would be okay if they just whacked enough. He summed up Bush's approach for a colleague: "If you're not out there hooking and jabbing with American forces every day, you're not fighting the right fight."

The president's persistent questions suggested to Casey that the commander in chief believed in an attrition strategy of simply eliminating the bad guys. The Vietnam War had established that that wouldn't work. No matter how many insurgents they killed or arrested, more would follow. The United States had killed tens of thousands of Iraqis. The classified operational summaries showed that 1,000 AIF, meaning "anti-Iraqi forces," defined as al Qaeda, insurgents or other violent extremists, were being killed each month. It was pure body count, one more echo of Vietnam.

In 2005, after Hurricane Katrina had devastated New Orleans and the Gulf region, Bush praised Federal Emergency Management Agency Director Michael D. Brown. "Brownie, you're doing a heck of a job," he said, in one of the more memorable lines of his presidency. Within a week, Brownie had been relieved for bungling the disaster response.

At the end of one secure videoconference with Casey soon after the Katrina debacle, Bush told the crew in Iraq, "Guys, you're doing a heck of a job." He paused and added, "But then, I said the same thing to Brownie."

In Baghdad, when the video screen went blank seconds later, nervous laughter filled the room. Bush had seemed serious. It was a clear reminder for Casey that his neck was on the line.

Adding to the frustration was the fact that the president had approved Casey's strategy, which explicitly stated that the goal was to transition the security mission to the Iraqis.

The day before Bush's conversation with Casey on the veranda in Baghdad, the president and his war cabinet had met at Camp David and unanimously approved Casey's Joint Campaign Plan. The plan, classified SECRET, stated, "This strategy is shaped by a central tenet: Enduring, strategic success in Iraq will be achieved by Iraqis." The concept was broken down into three phases—"stabilization" to early 2007, "restoration of civil authority" to mid-2008, and "support to self-reliance" through 2009.

But Casey never felt he had broken through to Bush. "I never cracked it," he said later.

The private battle between president and general had been simmering for too long. Casey could feel their mounting mutual resistance, and he saw no way to lessen the intensity of their differences. Bush always insisted that he had confidence in Casey, but over time, each man had silently lost confidence in the other.

And now their bond seemed unrecoverable. Both men hoped the same wasn't true of the war.

Also on the veranda that evening in Baghdad was Stephen J. Hadley, the president's national security adviser. Hadley, 59, was the most deferential, perhaps the hardest working, and certainly the least visible to the public of the president's senior advisers. He watched from a distance as the president and Casey shared a smoke and a private chat.

Since World War I, presidents have had a central coordinator in the White House to act as their eyes and ears—and enforcer if need be—on foreign policy and war. Presidents Dwight D. Eisenhower and John F. Kennedy formalized roles for an assistant to the president for national security. President Richard Nixon raised it to new heights with Henry Kissinger. Some national security advisers, like the strong-willed and opinionated Kissinger, have dominated foreign affairs, while others have acted merely as referees.

Hadley believed he had developed as close a relationship with his president as any national security adviser in history. He was ever present, so much so that the joke around the White House was that the only time President Bush was alone was when he went to the washroom, and even then Hadley would be waiting outside with a fresh towel. Hadley said of their relationship, "If I feel it, he feels it. If he feels it, I feel it."

I later read Hadley's statement to the president during an interview in the Oval Office.

"Yes," Bush agreed.

"I'm watching him all the time," added Hadley, seated nearby.

"I'm watching him watch me all the time," Bush said.

The president lavished praise on his national security adviser. He said Hadley didn't need permission to walk into the Oval Office. He could stop by or call anytime.

Traditionally, the National Security Council provides a setting to present all his advisers' points of view to the president. But Hadley didn't believe the NSC should be an arena for contentious and divisive debate. He believed his task was to ascertain Bush's wishes, and then bring the secretary of state, secretary of defense, the chief of intelligence and others into line. He believed that consensus was not only possible in the quarrelsome world of national security policy, but necessary. "It is truth: A group of smart people looking at the same facts," he said once, "generally come to the same conclusions over time." In scientific discovery, brilliant people might suddenly see what nobody else sees, he said. But "you can't patent ideas in this policy world."

Bush's vision for Iraq relied heavily on the country developing a viable political system. Almost from the beginning, he had asked, "Who's going to run this country?" Under one of the first Iraqi plans, the presidency would have rotated each month. Both Bush and Hadley had been flabbergasted. During three elections over the past 18 months, the Iraqis had finally chosen Nouri al-Maliki, a little-known former spokesman for a small Shia party, as their first permanent prime minister. U.S. intelligence and most Iraq experts knew virtually nothing about Maliki, 55, whose unshaven look made him faintly resemble a Hollywood mogul.

"I need to go meet this guy," Bush had told Hadley, "look him in the eye, make an assessment of him, but also make a commitment to him that I'm going to work with him and support him. He's never been the head of a country before. He's going to have to learn. And I'm going to have to engage with him personally to help him learn. I can help him figure out how to be prime minister, because this guy has a lot of learning he's going to have to do."

And so they had planned the president's secret June 13 trip to Baghdad.

For months, Hadley had been trying to force a review of the Iraq strategy. In his special file that contained items for the president's attention, marked "GWB," he carried a SECRET chart showing that violence in Iraq was growing continuously worse and bloodier.

The president himself, despite his public statements, could see the war deteriorating. "If this is not working," Bush told Hadley, Secretary of State Condoleezza Rice and other close advisers in the spring and early summer of 2006, "you people need to tell me. Because I cannot in good faith send more people who might die in Iraq unless it is working."

"I meet with families of the deceased," Bush said later. "I have got to be able to tell them, one, the mission is worthwhile, and we can succeed."

It clearly wasn't working. As a first step to find out why, Hadley had prepared an agenda for the president's meeting with his war cabinet the day before his trip to Baghdad, June 12, at Camp David. He wanted the group to evaluate the assumptions and ask the hard questions— "the what, who, when, where and why," as he called it, of what they were doing.

The gathering was to be the curtain-raiser on a strategy review. The plan had been for the president to lead a conversation among his principals—Rice, Defense Secretary Donald H. Rumsfeld, Director of National Intelligence John D. Negroponte, Chairman of the Joint Chiefs of Staff General Peter Pace and Hadley. The SECRET agenda included big-picture questions, such as "What is fueling the current levels of violence?" Ninety minutes in the morning were to be devoted to "Examination of core issues and strategic assumptions" such as "Is our political strategy working?"

The morning had begun with a PowerPoint briefing on the campaign plan by General Casey from Baghdad, including this SECRET chart—a crazy quilt of circles, arrows, boxes and phrases with an undated end point called "Securing strategic victory." (See opposite page.)

In addition to stating, "This strategy is shaped by a central tenet: Enduring, strategic success in Iraq will be achieved by Iraqis," Casey added, "Completion of political process and recent operations have positioned us for a decisive action over the next year."

He listed nine risks, ranging from a loss of willpower, to increasing sectarian violence, to rampant corruption, to a strategic surprise.

Rice's State Department briefing at Camp David that day asserted that the "situation in Iraq is not improving." It recommended that the administration "prepare [the] U.S. public for a long struggle," and said that changing the governing culture of Iraq would "require a generation."

But it turned out to be impossible to manage the Camp David event since the president had decided to go to Iraq the next day to see the

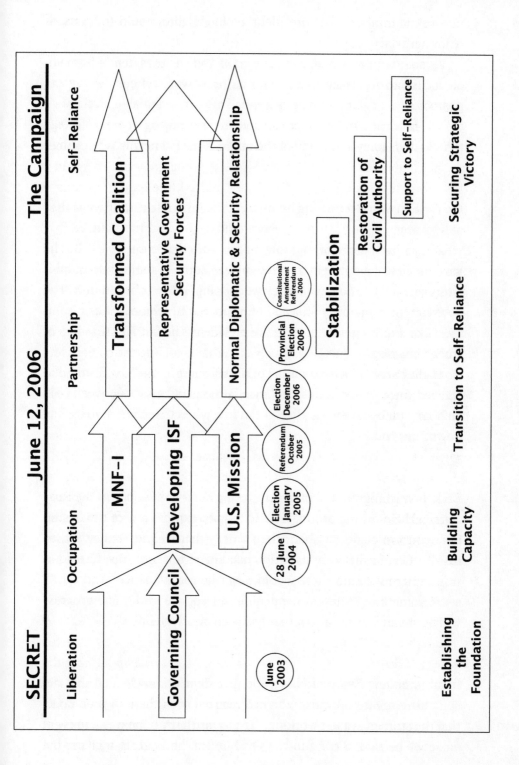

new prime minister. The president's mind, Hadley could tell, was already halfway to Baghdad.

As so often happened, the daily tasks and the president's immediate focus had overtaken all else, and the process of strategic review was postponed yet again. As Iraq descended into unimaginable levels of violence, more and more American soldiers were dying under a strategy that Bush, Hadley and many of the others already knew was faltering.

On Air Force One returning home from the June 13 meeting, Bush had at first been euphoric. It had been a good day, a great moment, exactly what they had been working toward for more than three years. But he gave the new government a mixed review. Some of the new Iraqi ministers seemed to know what they were doing, while others didn't. The government of majority Shia and minority Sunni seemed plausible. "It feels like a unity government," the president said, adding that lots of work remained.

Hadley stayed focused on the SECRET chart in his "GWB" file that showed the ever-increasing violence, a thousand attacks a week—six an hour. "I'll believe we got it right in Iraq when that chart starts going down," he said.

Back in Washington, the president held a news conference in the Rose Garden the morning of June 14. He did not express any of the hesitation, concern or doubt about the strategy that he and Hadley and so many others in the administration had begun to share. Yes, he said, it was a tough war and there would never be zero violence. And yet, "I sense something different happening in Iraq," he said. "The progress will be steady toward a goal that has been clearly defined."

In an interview two years later, the president acknowledged that despite his outward optimism, he had realized even then, in June 2006, that the strategy wasn't working. "Underneath my hope was a sense of anxiety," he said. Sitting in the Oval Office, he held up a chart that showed the spiking violence during the first half of that year. "I'm beginning to see" about this time, he said, hitting the chart twice with his hand, that the situation had taken a perilous turn. The strategy in place was one "that everybody hoped would work. And it did not. And therefore, the question is, when you're in my position: If it's not working, what do you do?"

Bush insisted he understood the nature of the war, whatever Casey might have thought. "I mean, of all people to understand that, it's me," he said.

But several of his on-the-record comments in the interview lend credence to Casey's concern that the president was overly focused on the number of enemy killed.

"What frustrated me is that from my perspective," the president said, "it looked like we were taking casualties without fighting back because our commanders are loath to talk about our battlefield victories."

Sure, periodically he had asked about how many enemy fighters had been eliminated. "That's one of many questions I asked. I asked that on occasion to find out whether or not we're fighting back. Because the perception is that our guys are dying and they're not. Because we don't put out numbers. We don't have a tally." He knew the military opposed body counts, which echoed the Vietnam-era practice of publishing the number of enemy killed as a measure of progress.

"On the other hand, if I'm sitting here watching the casualties come in, I'd at least like to know whether or not our soldiers are fighting," he said. "You've got a constant barrage of news basically saying, 'Lost three guys here. Five guys there. Seven guys lost.' You know, 'Twelve, twenty-eight for the week.'" The president simply wanted to know that the other side was suffering too.

So maybe Casey had hit upon a valid question. Did the commander in chief truly understand the war that he had started? Then again, did Casey himself understand the war? Did Rumsfeld? Or Rice? Or Hadley? Did anyone in the administration have a vision for how to succeed?

And most important, could anyone answer the president's own question, which loomed large and bright and inescapable:

"If it's not working, what do you do?"

1

Two Years Earlier

One weekday afternoon in May 2004, General George Casey bounded up the stairs to the third floor of his government-furnished quarters, a beautiful old brick mansion on the Potomac River at Fort McNair in Washington, D.C. His wife, Sheila, was packing for a move across the river to Fort Myer, in Virginia, the designated quarters of the Army's vice chief of staff.

"Please, sit down," Casey said.

In 34 years of marriage, he had never made such a request.

President Bush, Secretary of Defense Donald Rumsfeld and the Army chief of staff had asked him to become the top U.S. commander in Iraq, he said.

Sheila Casey burst into tears. Like any military spouse, she dreaded the long absences and endless anxieties of separation, the strains of a marriage carried out half a world apart. But she also recognized it was an incredible opportunity for her husband. Casey saw the Iraq War as a pivot point, one of history's hinges, a conflict that would likely define America's future standing in the world, Bush's legacy and his own reputation as a general.

"This is going to be hard," Casey said, but he felt as qualified as anyone else.

Casey's climb to four-star status had been unusual. Instead of graduating from West Point, he had studied international relations at Georgetown University. He'd been there during the Vietnam War and was a member of ROTC, the Reserve Officers' Training Corps. He remembered how some students had spit on him and hurled things when he crossed campus in uniform. In 1970, after his graduation and commissioning as an Army second lieutenant, his father and namesake, a two-star Army general commanding the celebrated 1st Cavalry Division, was killed in Vietnam when his helicopter crashed en route to visit wounded soldiers.

Casey had never intended to make the Army his career. And yet he fell in love with the sense of total responsibility that even a young second lieutenant was given for the well-being of his men. Now, after 34 years in the Army, he was going to be the commander on the ground, as General William Westmoreland had been in Vietnam from 1965 to 1968. Casey had no intention of ending up like Westmoreland, whom history had judged as that era's poster boy for quagmire and failure.

Casey had never been in combat. His most relevant experience was in the Balkans—Bosnia and Kosovo—where irregular warfare had been the order of the day. He had held some of the most visible "thinker" positions in the Pentagon—head of the Joint Staff strategic plans and policy directorate, J-5, and then the prestigious directorship of the Joint Staff, which served the chiefs. But aside from a 1981 stint in Cairo as a United Nations military observer, he had spent little time in the Middle East.

After getting Sheila's blessing, Casey met with Rumsfeld. The two sat at a small table in the center of the secretary's office. "Attitude" was important, Rumsfeld explained—Casey must instill a frame of mind among the soldiers to let the Iraqis grow and do what they needed to do themselves. The general attitude in the U.S. military was "We can do this. Get out of our way. We'll take care of it. You guys stand over there." That would not spell success in Iraq, Rumsfeld explained. As he often would describe it later, the task in Iraq was to remove the training wheels and get American hands off the back of the Iraqi bicycle seat.

For the most part, Casey agreed.

"Take about 30 days, and then give me your assessment," Rumsfeld directed.

Casey was heartened that Rumsfeld and he shared a common vision. But he was surprised that the secretary of defense had devoted only about 10 minutes for a meeting with the man about to take over the most important assignment in the U.S. military.

The president held a small dinner at the White House for Casey and John Negroponte, the newly designated ambassador to Iraq, their spouses and a few friends. It was a social event, a way to say good luck.

Casey went to see Secretary of State Colin Powell, who had served in the Army for 35 years and been the chairman of the Joint Chiefs of Staff during the 1991 Gulf War. Powell did not conceal his bitterness. Rumsfeld is screwing it all up, he told Casey. Marc Grossman, one of Powell's senior deputies and an old friend of Casey's, put it more pointedly. "These guys at DOD are just assholes," he said, "and I don't have any more patience for them."

Casey concluded that there was no clear direction on Iraq, so he invited Negroponte to his office at the Pentagon.

Negroponte, then the U.S. ambassador to the United Nations, had volunteered for the Iraq ambassadorship. At 64, he was a 40-year veteran of the Foreign Service. He believed that an ambassador was the executor of policy made in Washington. He and Casey agreed that they weren't getting much guidance from above.

"What are we going to accomplish when we get over there?" Casey asked, and they started to hammer out a brief statement of purpose. The goal was a country at peace with its neighbors, with a representative government, which respected human rights for all Iraqis and would not become a safe haven for terrorists.

The general and the ambassador were pleased with their draft. They had laid out mostly political goals, despite the fact that the United States' main leverage was its nearly 150,000 troops on the ground.

•   •   •

In Iraq, Casey relieved Lieutenant General Ricardo Sanchez, who had been the junior three-star in the Army when he had taken command of the forces the previous year. Casey asked him to stick around for a while after the change of command ceremony. Over dinner, Sanchez unloaded his bitterness about the lack of support he felt he had received from the Army, the Pentagon and Washington. "This is ten times harder than Kosovo," he said.

Casey could relate. He was familiar with the deep, irrational hatred that had driven the ethnic cleansing and other violence in the Balkans.

He met with officers from the CIA station in Baghdad. They posed ominous questions: Could the whole enterprise work? What was the relationship between the political and military goals? Casey and Negroponte had settled on the political goals, but how would Casey achieve the military goal of keeping Iraq from becoming a safe haven for terrorists? As he was briefed and as he read the intelligence, he saw that terrorists had safe havens in at least four Iraq cities—Fallujah, Najaf, Samarra and, for all practical purposes, the Sadr City neighborhood in Baghdad.

As Casey had passed through neighboring Kuwait on his way to Baghdad, the Third Army officers had a message for him: "If you want to understand this, you need to talk to Derek Harvey."

Harvey, a 49-year-old retired Army colonel and Middle East specialist who worked for the Defense Intelligence Agency, was a controversial figure within the U.S. intelligence world. He believed in immersion intelligence work, spending months at a time gathering information in the field rather than relying solely on reports and statistics.

In the late 1980s, Harvey traveled throughout Iraq by taxicab—500 miles, village to village—interviewing locals, sleeping on mud floors with a shower curtain for a door. He resembled the television detective Columbo—full of questions, intensely curious and entirely nonthreatening. After the 1991 Gulf War, when the CIA was predicting the inevitable fall of Iraqi dictator Saddam Hussein, Harvey, then a major, insisted that Hussein would survive because members of the Sunni community knew their fortunes were tied to his. He was right. Months before the 9/11 terrorist attacks, Harvey wrote an intelligence paper declaring that al Qaeda and the Taliban leadership in Afghanistan posed a strategic threat to the United States.

After the 2003 invasion of Iraq, Harvey had intermittent Army assignments in the country, traveling quietly, talking to insurgents, sitting in interrogation rooms.

One of his approaches was so-called DOCEX—document exploitation. He spent hours poring over files found in safe houses and financial data discovered in Saddam's briefcases. It was clear to him early on that a vacuum existed in Baghdad. Where was political power?

Harvey made scouting missions into the provinces in an SUV, making contact with tribes, learning that former Baathist regime leaders, generals and other former officers were reuniting. He studied documents and letters found in buildings that U.S. forces had raided. Together with his interviews, they told a story: The old regime elements had plans to create a violent, hostile environment.

Within U.S. intelligence agencies, a debate was taking place about how much real organization existed among the insurgents. Who was really in control? Harvey found that the insurgency was based on the old trust networks of professional, tribal and family relationships connected with the mosques. Guidance, instructions and exhortation—even the planning documents for operations—were often written in the religious language of holy war.

Harvey found that U.S. units had reported a lot of attacks when they first arrived, but the longer they stayed in Iraq, the fewer they reported. It wasn't because the troops had appeased or vanquished the insurgents. Rather, near the end of their tours, they ventured out into the population less and less—sometimes never. He also concluded that only 22 to 26 percent of the violence directed at U.S. forces was being reported.

General Sanchez never bought into Harvey's conclusions about the insurgency, even as officially measured violence in the classified SECRET reports kept rising. During one four-month period in mid-2004, the attacks doubled from about 1,000 a month to 2,000.

• • •

Casey summoned Harvey to a meeting in early July 2004. Harvey found the general on a balcony at his new headquarters at Camp Victory, gazing out over Baghdad. Casey held up two cigars.

"Do you smoke?"

Harvey nodded.

"Okay, come with me."

What's really going on in Iraq? Casey asked.

The Sunni insurgency is growing and getting worse, Harvey explained. It's organized. It's coherent. And its members have a strategy. They are gaining popular support. They believe they are doing well, and by any measurement they are—the number of attacks, their logistics, their financing, their external support, freedom of movement, ability to recruit. Every trend line was going up. Way up.

The insurgency is not a guerrilla war designed to win political power, he said. "It's all about wearing you out, getting you to leave and subverting the existing order, and infiltrating and co-opting the emerging Iraqi institutions."

The Iraqi government was weak, he added. It needed to be stronger, much stronger, but the United States was not going to change the attitudes or the culture. "We have to work around them," he said. "You're not going to force them to make decisions that they're not comfortable with. We don't have the leverage. We really don't."

Harvey said the Americans must learn to operate with humility, because there was so much they didn't understand about how and why the Iraqis made decisions. We think we know, but we're delusional. We get these glimpses, and we extrapolate. But if you really dig, what's it all really based on? Only whispers of the truth. "We don't understand the fight we're in," he said.

Harvey said the revelations about abuse of prisoners at Abu Ghraib months earlier had inflamed Iraqis. Photographs of smiling U.S. soldiers alongside naked, hooded, manacled and leashed inmates had flooded newspapers, television screens and the Internet. They had spread like a lightning bolt through Iraqi society and sent a devastating message: The U.S. occupation was the new oppressor.

As their cigars burned down and their conversation drew to a close,

Harvey fixed his gaze on the new commanding general. "We're in trouble."

In Washington, infighting over the war had gone from bad to worse within the administration since the 2003 invasion.

"Control is what politics is all about," legendary journalist Theodore H. White wrote. War is also about control—both on the battlefield and in Washington, where the strategy and policy are supposed to be set. But from the start, no one in the administration had control over Iraq policy.

In the early days of the war, the president's national security adviser, Condoleezza Rice, and Hadley, her deputy at the time, had worked on Iraq nonstop and yet they never got control over the policy making. They were no match for Rumsfeld. The president had signed a directive before the invasion, giving the authority for an occupation to the Defense Department.

Bush and Rumsfeld's selection of L. Paul Bremer, a career diplomat, to act as the viceroy of Iraq further diminished the role of Rice and Hadley, as well as Powell at the State Department. Bremer all but ignored the National Security Council.

"We're all told to stay out of it," Hadley complained to a colleague. "This is Don Rumsfeld's thing."

Bremer, who as a presidential envoy had a direct reporting line to the president, bypassed even Rumsfeld and made important decisions unilaterally and abruptly. Some of those decisions proved disastrous, such as disbanding the Iraqi army and excluding from government service tens of thousands of former members of Saddam's Baath Party.

Rumsfeld had his own view of how the U.S. should proceed. He would send out one of his "snowflakes," brief documents asking questions, looking for details, demanding answers, when it was unclear to him what had happened. Though unsigned, everyone knew they represented his orders or questions. But if a snowflake leaked, it provided deniability.

The snowflake sent on October 28, 2003, was two pages long and classified SECRET: "Subject: Risk and the way ahead in Iraq. In discussing the way ahead in Iraq, all agree that we should give Iraqis more authority more quickly."

Powell had a different view. Control was about security. In the first year after the invasion, Bush and Rice repeatedly expressed worry that the oil production in Iraq and availability of electricity were dropping—visible signs that conditions were worse in Iraq than prior to the invasion.

"Petroleum is interesting. Electricity is interesting," Powell said, but added, "Mr. President, none of this makes any difference unless there's security . . . Security is all that counts right now."

2

As Casey set off in July 2004 to decipher the puzzles of Iraq, Hadley worked the problem in Washington. At a meeting with NSC staff members on September 7, 2004, he told the group they had to find a way to measure success. "We need a framework," he said, "to think about or use to determine how we know if we are winning or losing."

Everyone, it seemed, had a different focus. Rumsfeld wanted to hand off to the Iraqis and get out as soon as possible. Powell believed the United States now owned Iraq and must protect its citizens. Rice and Hadley were intent on getting a functioning government in place.

Some suggested measurements included: how many countries were withdrawing their troops; how many companies were leaving Iraq, and which ones; recruitment rates in the Iraqi security forces; the number of flights that came under fire; assassination attempts.

The Pentagon's chief measure was how many Iraqi security forces were being trained and sent into the field. Quality control received little emphasis. Tens of thousands of Iraqis supposedly had been trained, but the Pentagon threw around numbers and cited so many increases that Powell could only laugh. An army could not be built in a matter of months or even a year. These numbers came from nowhere. Powell knew how the Pentagon worked: pumping up numbers that were guesses from the people on the ground.

And yet, some numbers seemed depressingly accurate. A SECRET analysis showed that in September 2004, about 50 percent of assassination attempts in Iraq were successful. By December, the success rate had jumped to 81 percent.

While the leaders in Washington wrestled one another for control, debated the strategy, and tried to determine how to measure progress, Iraq seemed to be blowing up. An epidemic of violence erupted around the end of October 2004, during the Muslim holy month of Ramadan. Daily attacks doubled from about 70 early in the month to nearly 140 at the end of the month. Derek Harvey's take on the insurgency now seemed prescient. Rumsfeld summoned the lone-wolf DIA intelligence analyst to brief him and other Pentagon intelligence brass. They sat around the conference table in the secretary's office.

The insurgency is gaining strength, Harvey said again. They have a strategy, they know what they need to do to win, and they are on the right trajectory. The insurgency continues to be driven by former beneficiaries of the old Saddam regime, motivated by both nationalist and religious messages, who fear the loss of power. Rumsfeld's pointed questions to Harvey suggested that he disagreed. The secretary viewed the insurgents as thugs.

They're not just thugs, insisted Harvey, who'd acquired the nickname "Grenade" when he served a tour in the State Department. "This is not a bunch of disenfranchised, decentralized, incoherent, local-generated insurrectionists going around." They are not just pissed-off Iraqis. They want power, influence and authority, and they're rejecting this forced change. The war had actually gone pretty well in the early part of 2004, but the dual catastrophes of Abu Ghraib and the botched coalition attack on Fallujah had added fuel and purpose to the insurgency. Recruitment and support are going up, Harvey told Rumsfeld.

"This is all very interesting," Rumsfeld replied, "but it's more opinion than fact."

"We've got good evidence," Harvey said. He cited documents, messages, interrogation reports. We are not doing the right things to check and thwart the insurgency, he said. One solution was tribal outreach.

"What underpins this?" Rumsfeld asked him. "Why are you saying that?"

Harvey reminded him that for years he had visited the tribes and their leaders. "We are constantly understating the violence." There was no good way to collect numbers, and the violence was much greater and more widespread than reported. He estimated that only about 25 percent of the attacks were being reported.

"Well," Rumsfeld said, "you can't count every bullet that's being fired."

Harvey didn't disagree.

"So you believe this?" Rumsfeld asked.

"Yes."

"We need to take this over to the White House," he said.

Harvey brought his briefing to the Situation Room, where Rice and Hadley listened to his description of an organized, powerful, well-honed insurgency.

"Well, this is the first time I've heard any of this," Rice said.

Hadley too was surprised. He opened a three-ring binder. "We've got all these programs," he said, describing the massive efforts to help with electricity, water and sewage treatment.

Harvey said he had been part of a team set up by General Casey to look at such programs, and it found that despite all the contracts, the money was being spent in the wrong places and sometimes not at all. Money needed to go to the areas of high unemployment where people felt most disenfranchised. But, he said, the response from those in command was "Well, it's not safe there."

Harvey next briefed Vice President Dick Cheney's chief of staff, I. Lewis "Scooter" Libby.

Libby had a different reaction from Rice and Hadley's. "I was worried that this was really what we're dealing with," he told Harvey.

In December 2004, Harvey came back to the Situation Room to brief President Bush. Rumsfeld, Rice, new CIA Director Porter Goss and CIA expert John Charles were present.

Bush had been warned that Harvey had an unorthodox view. The president asked three questions right off the bat: Who are you? What's your experience on Iraq? And why should I believe what you're saying?

"I've spent nearly 20 years working the Middle East" for the Army and DIA, Harvey answered. "I have advanced degrees. I've spent the last 18 months working, traveling, talking with insurgents, sitting in interrogation rooms." He described going into Fallujah, the epicenter of the insurgency, in the middle of the uprising when the city was walled off. He had entered the city without armed escort and spent the night talking with Abdullah al-Janabi, one of the clerics leading the insurgency. "We label him a religious extremist," Harvey said. "He's a Baathist who's very angry, has lost family members, okay? Drinks Johnnie Walker Black Label."

"Okay," Bush said, "let's go on."

You have a coherent enemy, Harvey said. They have a strategy. They're doing well by any measure. They're very well organized, and they're gaining popular support. All the measurements—the attack data, the logistics, the financing, external support, freedom of movement, ability to recruit—all these trend lines are going one way—up. This enemy is made up of the old Sunni power brokers, not a bunch of angry young men. Holding elections right now would be counterproductive. The Sunnis would boycott, thereby fueling the insurgency.

Harvey told the president that Syria was supplying support to the insurgents in Iraq, and though it was not absolutely crucial to the insurgency, it gave them strategic depth. Former senior members of Saddam's government were based in Damascus, the Syrian capital, and were providing direction, political guidance, coordination and money. Intelligence had traced at least $1.2 million a month of Syrian money going into Ramadi.

Charles, the CIA man, countered that the insurgency was fractious and very local, lacked coherence, and was made up of the angry, unemployed and disenfranchised. Nor did the Syrians have that much influence, he said.

Harvey began throwing out names, dates and amounts of money, saying that the intelligence showed that a certain man had left $300,000 in Ramadi, then another $250,000 in Diyala province.

"You're extrapolating too much," Charles retorted.

Harvey flashed some slides on the screen that named insurgency leaders in various provinces. "Here are their key leaders," he said.

"Here's where they assess they're doing well. Here's where they don't think they're doing well." The charts showed tribal, religious trust networks that Harvey had pieced together.

"We agree," Porter Goss, the CIA director, said unexpectedly, undercutting his own agency.

"Thank you," was all the president said, and the meeting adjourned.

In December 2004, Robert L. Grenier, the CIA's mission manager for Iraq since before the invasion, wrote a classified paper for the agency's new director, Porter Goss. Iraq was poised to hold its first election the next month, and President Bush was touting the event as a significant step on the road to democracy.

"With a month to go before elections, it's time to face facts," Grenier wrote. The Sunni insurgency was not going away, and elections were not going to fix things. The Sunnis had decided to boycott the elections. A new Shia-led government would only underscore that the Sunnis had lost power, doubtless fueling the insurgency. The result would be an increased likelihood of civil war. Already, the two branches of Islam had a violent history dating back centuries to the death of the Prophet Muhammad. The election could put them even more at odds.

Charles Allen, the CIA assistant director for intelligence collection, visited Iraq and issued a stark assessment. He said he had not been prepared for how the situation had deteriorated. He was stunned by the level of disorder and violence. Iraq was coming off the rails.

Rice summoned the NSC principals toward the end of the year to discuss both CIA reports.

But Bush would not budge. Postponement of the Iraqi elections, as the CIA was recommending, was not going to happen. "We're going to hold the election on January 30," he insisted.

On Saturday, January 8, 2005, Hadley was in his West Wing office. He was about to take over as national security adviser for Bush's second term. Rice, his former boss, was set to become secretary of state. Tall and calm, with a warm smile and large eyeglasses, Hadley had a studious, professorial look. He wore his dark suit jacket even in his own office. When he was summoned to the Oval Office about 75 paces away, jacket and tie were mandatory, even on weekends.

At the dawn of Bush's second term, so much seemed within reach. "The opportunity to spread freedom throughout the globe, and particularly in the broader Middle East and in the Muslim world," Hadley said that day, "that is, I think for the president, the defining idea of his presidency . . . it is not only a sort of moral duty, it's not only consistent with our principles, it's consistent with our interests, it's actually essential for our national security. . . . For liberty to be secure at home, liberty has to be on the march abroad. Big stuff. Not big. Huge."

That was the mission Hadley had signed on for. As for the president, he added, "The guy's really a visionary. . . . He defies the conventional wisdom by his boldness. He's unapologetic. He sits there and reaffirms it, and clearly almost relishes it. And, you know, it traumatizes people. And they think, 'What's he doing . . . this cowboy?'"

But it was different in the White House, Hadley said. "Those of us who are here believe in him. Believe in him and believe he has greatness in him. He has greatness in him and he could be a great president. We could use one right now."

Hadley would repeat his awe-inspired theme months later, on another Saturday morning in his office. "He's a remarkable guy," he said of Bush. He said there was a style of discourse at Cornell and Yale Law School, from which he had graduated in 1972, that was academic, long-winded and analytical, but Bush had "rejected all of that." Bush had adopted the style of Midland, Texas, and many people think "it's simplistic, it's two-dimensional, it's not subtle."

But what Cornell, Yale and most of the country had missed, Hadley believed he had discovered. "The guy is really strong," he said, and what "people don't recognize is, everybody else needs that strength. And he understands that. . . . And all the rest of us need it. We're strong because he's strong."

Hadley's acceptance of Bush's ways raises some basic questions.

When I interviewed the president on August 20, 2002 for my book

Bush at War, he mentioned a dozen times his "instincts" or his "instinctive" reactions as guides for his decisions. "I'm not a textbook player, I'm a gut player," he said. I wrote, "His instincts are almost his second religion."

National security decision making normally requires a rigorous process of examining alternative courses of action. But a "no doubt" president can swamp any process, not allowing much reconsideration. The president and his team had become marketers of Bush's certainty. Hadley had acceded not only to Bush's judgments but to his method. He had sidelined the analytical style of Cornell, Yale and his own experience.

A president so certain, so action-oriented, so hero-worshiped by his national security adviser, almost couldn't be halted. The administration lacked a process to examine consequences, alternatives and motives. There was no system to slow down the process so the right questions were asked and answered, or alternative courses of action seriously considered. The national security adviser has to be a negotiator and an arbiter, someone who tries to consider every angle to a problem. But Hadley had become the lawyer for the president's foreign policy, his unwavering advocate and a cheerleader for his greatness.

Throughout January 2005, the CIA kept up its dire warnings. A day before the Iraq elections, Bush slammed his briefing book shut at an Oval Office meeting when he was again warned that the outcome could be grim.

"Well," he said, "we'll see who's right."

When some 8 million Iraqis went to the polls, many waving their purple-inked fingers in the air to show they had voted, Bush hailed "the voice of freedom" coming from the Middle East. The CIA, in contrast, saw the seeds of deeper unrest and violence taking root.

On the evening of election day, January 30, 2005, Casey was about to meet with his staff in Baghdad when Rumsfeld called. He stepped into a hallway to take the call.

"George, the eyes of the world were upon you, and you stood and delivered," the secretary said.

"Well, thank you," Casey replied. "I'll pass that on to everybody."

It was a high moment, the icing on the most emotional day of Casey's time in Iraq. He felt encouraged and moved that so many Iraqis had stepped forward to take a stake in their future. He'd been saying in the run-up to the elections, "Look, millions of people are going to vote."

But Casey also felt a little disingenuous. Eighty percent of the country was Shia and Kurds. Of course they would turn out. It was the Sunnis, who had held power under Saddam and now made up the bulk of the insurgency, who had boycotted the election.

But for a fleeting moment, with his boss offering praise and the massive turnout dominating the airwaves, there was time to relax and wonder if this venture just might work.

3

In early 2005, Secretary of State Condoleezza Rice hired her old friend and colleague Philip Zelikow as counselor to the department. It was a normally low-profile but potentially powerful post. An intellectual with a law degree, a Ph.D. in history and a healthy ego, Zelikow had co-authored a book with Rice on German reunification after the Cold War and later served as executive director of the 9/11 Commission, which examined the terrorist attacks in detail and published a best-selling report that detailed their origins and execution.

Rice, who had little confidence that she was getting the straight story on Iraq from the military, dispatched Zelikow and a small team to assess the situation on the ground.

"If they want to send Zelikow over, he needs to look at the State stuff," Casey told Chairman of the Joint Chiefs of Staff General Peter Pace. "That's what's really screwed up."

Pace said it made sense that Zelikow look at everything.

"You can go anywhere you want," Casey told Zelikow when he arrived in Iraq, "and you can talk to anybody you want."

On February 10, 2005, Zelikow issued a 15-page report classified SECRET/NODIS—secret, no distribution—meaning that copies should go to no one other than Rice herself. It concluded, "Iraq remains a failed state shadowed by constant violence." Zelikow made two more under-the-radar visits to Iraq, carefully weaving in some good news with a heavy dose of realism.

Rice praised Zelikow for his memos, which offered a clear conclusion: The United States didn't know what it was doing in Iraq.

Rumsfeld always worried about surprises—"unknown unknowns," he called them. On October 11, 2005, he dashed off a SECRET snowflake to Pace, Abizaid and Casey, titled, "Intel piece on Iraq." He had read a CIA report discussing ways to preempt a possible Tet-like offensive by insurgents in Iraq.

The January 1968 Tet offensive in Vietnam had been a military defeat for communist forces but had provided an overwhelming psychological victory that shocked the American public and marked a major turning point in the war.

"What do you think?" Rumsfeld asked in a one-paragraph memo to General Casey. Could insurgents in Iraq pull off a similar attack?

Casey replied, "I believe this came from work I asked CIA to do on an Iraqi Tet. The conclusion was this insurgency couldn't mount a Tet. They don't have the organization or military formations, but they don't have to. They could create the perception of a Tet with far smaller numbers because of the increased media presence."

Congress was demanding a description of what the strategy was supposed to be. Rice made it the core of her testimony before the Senate Foreign Relations Committee on October 19, 2005. "Our political-military strategy," she said, "has to be clear, hold and build: to clear areas from insurgent control, to hold them securely and then build durable Iraqi institutions."

"What the hell is that?" asked Casey. He called Abizaid.

"I don't know," the central commander said.

"Did you agree to that?"

"No, I didn't agree to that."

When Rice next came to Iraq, Casey asked for a private meeting with her and U.S. Ambassador Zalmay Khalilzad.

"Excuse me, ma'am, what's 'clear, hold, build'?"

Rice looked a little surprised. "George, that's your strategy."

"Ma'am, if it's my strategy, don't you think someone should have had the courtesy to talk to me about it before you went public with it?"

"Oh, well, we told General Odierno." A bald, towering three-star general, Raymond T. Odierno had commanded the 4th Infantry Division during the invasion and now traveled with Rice as the liaison between the military and the State Department.

"Look, ma'am, as hard as I've worked to support the State Department in this thing, the fact that that went forward without anybody talking to me, I consider a foul."

Rice repeated that she had told General Odierno, and later she apologized to Casey.

To Casey, it wasn't a simple matter of miscommunication. He didn't see "clear, hold and build" as a viable strategy. It was a bumper sticker. His main goal was to build up all Iraqi institutions so American soldiers could go home. He called Rumsfeld.

"Mr. Secretary, what's this clear, hold and build thing?"

"Oh, goddamn State Department . . ." he grumbled.

Casey spoke with Zelikow. This was about more than just a slogan. "Look, Phil," he said, "this isn't professional. This is personal. I opened this up to you. You owed me the courtesy of a call."

"Well . . ." Zelikow began.

"Bullshit! This is man-to-man. We were dealing with each other as individuals here. You owed me a call."

"George," Zelikow replied, "how could I have called you?" They both knew how paranoid Rumsfeld would be. Rice's testimony had been sent to the Pentagon in advance and had been signed off on. But it had never found its way to Casey.

Casey's response to Zelikow was simple: "You can trust me."

Soon after Rice's statement of the strategy, Rumsfeld saw "clear, hold and build" in a draft of a speech that the president was going to give. He called Andrew Card, the White House chief of staff, about a half hour before Bush was to speak.

"Take it out," he insisted. "Take it out." The "clear" was fine because that was what the U.S. military was doing. "It's up to the Iraqis to hold. And the State Department's got to work with somebody on the build."

Rumsfeld lost. The president said in a speech on October 25, "As Secretary Rice explained last week, our strategy is to clear, hold and build."

Months earlier, Casey had commissioned a report to study counterinsurgency practices and how they were, or were not, being implemented across Iraq.

On November 12, he forwarded a 15-page summary to Rumsfeld. The third page laid out traits of both successful and unsuccessful counterinsurgencies. Successful ones, Casey noted, last an average of nine years. Unsuccessful ones average 13 years.

The characteristics of a successful counterinsurgency included an emphasis on intelligence, a focus on the needs and security of citizens, an ability to deny safe haven to insurgents and isolate them from the population, and a competent local police force.

It had become increasingly clear that the efforts in Iraq had too many characteristics of a failing counterinsurgency.

As Casey was trying to quell the insurgency and al Qaeda in Iraq, Rumsfeld was in his third-floor Pentagon office, trying to control the world through his snowflakes.

One minute he'd expound on issues as large as the war strategy; the next might inspire a memo on grammar. No detail was too large, and none was too small.

"I also note that on page two," Rumsfeld wrote to Pace in a SECRET memo November 17 about Iraqi security forces, "the third set of asterisks has four instead of three in the note, and that should be fixed.

"I particularly want to know why we cannot get any improvement at all between December 15 and June 1 in terms of color coding . . ."

•   •   •

On December 2, 2005, a snowflake came from Rumsfeld to Casey and Abizaid. "Subject: Insurgent infiltration in Anbar province."

Rumsfeld had seen a CIA intelligence paper assessing insurgent infiltration of Iraqi army units in that part of the country. The paper, which claimed to be based on multiple sources of human intelligence and other reporting, found that terrorists and foreign fighters "are active in western Iraq and have infiltrated some elements of the Iraqi army in al-Anbar province."

The secretary wanted answers.

"I am in general agreement with the thrust of the paper," Casey replied. "We are aware that insurgents and militia have infiltrated Iraqi security forces on a generally local basis with corruption [rather than] ideology as the primary motivation. The impact on the Iraqi army is low, but I remain concerned about the loyalty of some Iraqi police elements to a central government."

"Attached is a worrisome DIA report on coalition detention facilities and insurgent networks," Rumsfeld wrote on December 12 to Casey, Abizaid and Ambassador Zal Khalilzad.

The attached five-page SECRET report from the Defense Intelligence Agency brought more disturbing news from Iraq, suggesting that the aggressive detention program was creating more terrorists.

"Insurgents and terrorists use coalition detention facilities to trade information on successful tactics and techniques, teach detainees insurgent and terrorist skills, preach radical Islam and recruit new members into the insurgency," it stated.

At one detention facility, the report stated, detainees had an insurgent training program to prepare detainees for their release, in which they taught new recruits how to become suicide bombers, use IEDs—improvised explosive devices—and carry out kidnappings and torture.

That was especially troubling, considering that more than 75 percent of detainees were released within six months of their capture, including a substantial number of insurgents and terrorists.

"Many detainees are determined to be innocent of any involvement in the insurgency," the report continued. "Insurgent recruiters, however, exploit their feelings of humiliation, anger and fear to entice them to join the insurgency while in coalition custody or immediately after release."

The report concluded, "insurgents, terrorists, foreign fighters and insurgent leaders captured and released by coalition forces may be more dangerous than they were before being detained."

On Wednesday morning, February 22, 2006, Casey got a call from his second in command, Lieutenant General Peter Chiarelli. A bomb had gone off at a mosque in Samarra, a city on the Tigris River about 65 miles north of Baghdad.

Pictures began coming in showing that the golden dome of al-Askari Mosque, one of the holiest sites in Shia Islam, had been obliterated. With the help of the embassy, Casey had put together a list of possible catastrophic events, but the Samarra mosque hadn't been included and had been left unguarded.

Intelligence indicated that Abu Musab al-Zarqawi, the leader of the Sunni-based organization al Qaeda in Iraq, was behind the attack. It was a clear attempt to stoke sectarian tensions, and Casey realized right away it was one of the "unknown unknowns" that Rumsfeld so dreaded.

Within hours, Shia militias, particularly those associated with cleric Moqtada al-Sadr, poured into the streets, firing grenades and machine guns into dozens of Sunni mosques in Baghdad. Three Sunni imams were killed, and a fourth was kidnapped. Tens of thousands rioted. A daytime curfew was imposed in Baghdad. Bodies began turning up the next morning by the score.

Iraqi officials denounced the attack, and President Bush appealed for restraint. An anxious calm settled over the country after several days, and it seemed that perhaps the worst had passed.

"The interesting point here is what conclusions the communities draw from this difficult week. They've stared into the abyss a bit,"

Hadley said during a Sunday, February 26, appearance on CBS's *Face the Nation*. "And I think they've all concluded that further violence, further tension between the communities is not in their interest."

But to some, it now seemed more likely than ever that Iraq was on the brink of civil war.

On March 20, the president drew attention to the work of one of the most high-profile colonels in the U.S. Army. "I'm going to tell you the story of a northern Iraqi city called Tall Afar," he said, "which was once a key base of operations for al Qaeda and is today a free city that gives reason for hope for a free Iraq."

He explained how the 5,300 soldiers of the Army's 3rd Armored Cavalry Regiment, led by Colonel H. R. McMaster, had arrived the previous May in Tall Afar, 250 miles from Baghdad near the Syrian border. Insurgents and al Qaeda fighters had choked the life out of the city and filled its quarter million residents with fear of savage attacks against anyone who didn't cooperate. But over the coming months, McMaster and his regiment had methodically driven insurgents first from surrounding villages and later from Tall Afar itself. They had then begun to rebuild and restore basic services, reform the local police force, and establish a local government. The city had come back to life.

It had been a clear departure from so many past operations in Iraq, where American forces would sweep into an area, kicking in doors and rounding up many young Iraqis with no ties to the insurgency before moving on again, leaving no one to prevent insurgents from returning to terrorize the population. McMaster's focus on economic and political improvements in addition to the military operations, as well as providing basic public services to the people, had paid huge dividends.

McMaster was 43, a small, stout man at 5-foot-9 and 190 pounds—bald-headed, green-eyed and barrel-chested, a blur of energy and intensity. A 1984 West Point graduate, he was a bona fide combat hero of the first Gulf War, where in February 1991, he had led his soldiers in a decisive tank battle against an Iraqi Republican Guard brigade and earned a Silver Star for his leadership. Beyond the battlefield, he had forged a reputation as one of the Army's most outspoken and dynamic thinkers. Some superiors saw him as a handful, a renegade who too often did things his own way. But few questioned his competence and ingenuity.

McMaster spoke more like a surfer, or even a rock 'n' roll roadie, inserting the word "man" or sometimes "dude" into his profanity-laced sentences. After his Gulf War experience, he had earned a Ph.D. in military history at the University of North Carolina at Chapel Hill, where he researched and wrote a groundbreaking dissertation that became the 1997 book *Dereliction of Duty: Lyndon Johnson, Robert McNamara, the Joint Chiefs of Staff, and the Lies That Led to Vietnam.*

The book laid bare the culpability of military leaders for the failure in Vietnam. McMaster argued that the Joint Chiefs—the "five silent men," as he called them—had failed to adequately voice their reservations about the war. He concluded that the chiefs were weak and had failed to establish the essential personal rapport with the civilian leaders so they could speak their minds. The work struck a chord within the generation of military brass who had served in Vietnam and offered an enduring lesson about the responsibilities of leadership and candor.

Dereliction of Duty was in essence a field manual for avoiding another Vietnam, and it became required reading throughout the military. Even President Bush said he had read the book. It established McMaster as the voice of a new generation of military officers who were determined not to be silent or passive, especially before and during a war. McMaster had become a kind of barometer of the military's moral conscience and the fortitude of the officer corps to speak out.

His success in Tall Afar cemented his status.

"Tall Afar shows that when Iraqis can count on a basic level of safety and security, they can live together peacefully," Bush said during his March 20 speech. "The people of Tall Afar have shown why spreading liberty and democracy is at the heart of our strategy to defeat the terrorists." He added, "The strategy that worked so well in Tall Afar did not emerge overnight. It came only after much trial and error. It took time to understand and adjust to the brutality of the enemy in Iraq. Yet the strategy is working."

What Bush did not make clear that afternoon was that McMaster's success in Tall Afar wasn't part of a broader strategy, but rather a freelanced, almost rebellious undertaking by one Army colonel and his unit. It was further evidence that the greatest accomplishments in Iraq had come despite the administration's strategy, not because of it.

The next day, March 21, a SECRET CIA report stated that al Qaeda in Iraq was continuing to grow, undermining security and preventing legitimate political and economic development. The report asserted that even if the minority Sunnis were given a role in the Iraqi government, "It is likely that AQIZ [al Qaeda in Iraq] will continue to wage war against the Iraqi government for years to come."

Within days, Rumsfeld sent a snowflake down the chain of command. "Attached is a field commentary from CIA on al-Qaeda. I found it interesting," he wrote in perfect understatement. "If it is true, I wonder if we are properly focused on the al-Qaeda operations. I would like to discuss it with all of you."

It wasn't long before another disturbing CIA report crossed Rumsfeld's desk. Dated April 16, the SECRET report stated, "As of early April 2006, the Karbala Iraq chief of police, Brigadier General Razzaq Abid Ali al-Tai, hosted a meeting at his residence in Karbala to discuss forming an alliance between the Iraqi police major crimes unit, JAM"— the Jaish al Mahdi or Mahdi Army, a paramilitary force created by the Shia cleric Moqtada al-Sadr—"and the Iraqi national guard force in Karbala to fight the U.S. military if they attacked JAM forces. The meeting concluded after all parties agreed to fight jointly should U.S. military initiate an attack on Jaysh al-Mahdi."

The report went on to state that General Ali had provided JAM members with Iraqi police identification cards to allow them to travel in closer proximity to U.S. forces and to attack and inflict a greater number of casualties.

On April 17, the inevitable snowflake went out from Rumsfeld to Abizaid, Pace and Casey, with the CIA report attached. Though he didn't say so directly, the secretary seemed to realize the Catch-22 nature of speeding up transition to the Iraqis.

"The attached is worrisome," he wrote. "If it is true, we may want to think about the pace at which we equip and train the units that could be a problem in the future."

At a National Security Council meeting on May 5, with Rice, Rumsfeld, Khalilzad and others present, Bush wanted to know about Maliki, the man who had been selected as the new prime minister.

"How's he doing?" the president asked. "What's your broad assessment?"

"He knows what he wants," Khalilzad replied. "He's not so eloquent."

"Lay off that eloquence thing!" the president joked.

"He wants room to appoint good people," the ambassador continued. "Securing Baghdad, getting electricity from Baji to Baghdad using Ministry of Defense assets."

Rice, who had drawn up the agenda for the day, argued that three new efforts were necessary—a political launch, a security launch and a launch for an international compact. It was another in a line of down-in-the-weeds discussions of oil production, electricity and other infrastructure issues.

Bush said he wanted no action on the part of the United States that would cause disunity. "You want to avoid contention if things are going well," he said. "We don't want to trigger yet another Iraqi election."

On May 8, Rumsfeld composed a short SECRET snowflake to Hadley. The subject: "U.S. Casualties." The defense secretary noted that between the elections in December and the beginning of May, there had been "197 killed in action; 1,701 wounded."

"I think at some point, if you are working with the Iraqi leadership and you need an argument," Rumsfeld wrote, "you could tell them that the longer it takes them to get a government and the longer it takes them to start providing leadership, the more people are going to be killed. There has to be a limit."

For his part, Casey had a terrible feeling in the months after the

elections as he watched "the air go out of the balloon as they negotiated on the government."

On May 17, the NSC convened again with the president and vice president. In just three days, the new Iraqi government under Maliki would
formally be introduced at a ceremony in Baghdad. But the discussion
turned to the deteriorating security situation.

On video, Casey acknowledged that the situation in much of
Iraq was "turbulent," particularly in Baghdad. Attacks linked to sectarian violence were high and getting higher. He ticked off names and
numbers of recent executions, and the president's face flashed with
distress.

Casey mentioned a U.S. operation taking place in Baghdad named
Scales of Justice. It had had some effect, but they were short on Iraqi
police. The Sadr militias were operating as death squads and were responsible for much of the violence. Some Sadr militiamen had been
caught in Iraqi army uniforms.

Casey said Maliki seemed eager to help with the problems and had
offered to do what he could.

"Who are they going after?" Cheney asked, referring to the death
squads.

It's not random, Casey said. He had seen lists of targets, primarily
Sunnis being hunted down by Shia.

"This sounds political, not criminal," the president noted, and
Casey agreed.

The president asked about the persistent problem of IEDs, which
continued to kill and maim soldiers at an appalling rate. "Who is behind it?"

Casey emphasized that in recent months there had been an increase
in the use of EFPs—explosively formed projectiles—in the Shia areas.
He said the technology was coming from Iran and that it was especially
lethal.

What's the motive in planting the IEDs, the president asked.
What's the goal?

"Well, ultimately, for us to leave," Casey said, "although some of this is now violence for violence's sake to pressure the political process."

Bush said he was astonished by the volume of the attacks and wondered if there was any kind of command structure in which a few people could give the order to stop it. Casey said that if there was a structure, it was very loose.

Would the IED problem be as significant without the U.S. presence? Bush asked. Well, they would still want to hit Iraqi forces, Casey said. But at the moment, the Americans were the targets of two thirds of the attacks.

4

Frustrated by the lack of progress, Congress had created the bipartisan Iraq Study Group to assess independently the situation in Iraq and provide policy recommendations to the president. The White House offered reluctant support.

The group's members were the old set. Its co-chairs were Republican James A. Baker III, the 77-year-old former secretary of state and political consigliere for President George H. W. Bush, and Democrat Lee Hamilton, 76, who had served in the House for 34 years, chaired the House Committee on Foreign Affairs, and seemed to have been on every blue-ribbon commission since the Vietnam War.

Other Republicans included former Attorney General Edwin Meese III, President Ronald Reagan's top White House adviser, who had replaced presidential hopeful Rudy Giuliani; retired Supreme Court Justice Sandra Day O'Connor, the first woman to serve on the high court; Robert Gates, former CIA director for Bush senior; and former Senator Alan Simpson, the outspoken, cantankerous gadfly from Wyoming. The Democrats were Leon Panetta, the former California congressman and White House chief of staff for Bill Clinton; Vernon Jordan, civil rights attorney and Clinton confidant; William J. Perry, the reserved mathematics Ph.D. and military science expert who had served as Clinton's defense secretary; and former Virginia Governor and Senator

Charles Robb, a Marine in Vietnam and son-in-law of the late President Lyndon Johnson.

The group had met regularly to interview administration officials, Iraqi leaders, members of Congress, scholars and members of the military. On May 18, the last interview of the afternoon was reserved for Lieutenant General David H. Petraeus, head of the U.S. Army Combined Arms Center in Fort Leavenworth, Kansas, who was working on the military's first counterinsurgency field manual in 20 years.

I first met Petraeus in 1989, when he was a major and the aide-de-camp to General Carl Vuono, the Army chief of staff. I was working on a book on the Pentagon and invited him to dinner on January 31, 1990. The book was *The Commanders,* which focused on the 1989 invasion of Panama and the 1991 Gulf War during the administration of Bush senior. It was immediately apparent that Petraeus had an unusual, active intellect. He later sent me a copy of his 1987 Princeton Ph.D. dissertation, "The American Military and the Lessons of Vietnam." Its thesis, summarized in the introduction to the 317-page manuscript, was that "in no case since Vietnam has the military leadership proffered more aggressive recommendations than those of the most hawkish civilian advisers" to presidents.

"He's a small, academic-looking guy with glasses," begin the six pages of notes I typed after dinner. I've rarely spoken with anyone as intense. You could almost hear the gears in his brain whirring. Though only 5-foot-9 and 155 pounds, he was a fitness addict, having won all three prizes at the Army's Ranger School, a nine-week ordeal that grinds body and mind.

Petraeus at that point had served 17 years. He emphasized his belief that in the military, everything is "personality-driven, personality-dependent." Though he felt personal affection for his boss, Petraeus said that the chief was difficult. Vuono had told him early in his tenure as an aide, "One reason I hired you is I know you have enough self-confidence that if I chew your ass all day, you won't be destroyed by it." The slightest irregularity could set Vuono off. If the chief's black leather gloves were not instantly available, he would chew out Major Petraeus. If the schedule was not in order, Petraeus would get chewed. Before a speech the chief would sweat, get nervous and begin chewing out Petraeus. Once, when Vuono canceled a trip to buy shoes with his son, he suddenly had 30 minutes free. It was fidget city. Vuono couldn't deal with unscheduled time and had little inclination to read, which is what Petraeus would have done. His time with Vuono gave Petraeus an understanding of the impact a senior leader's personality can have on an entire organization.

Now, at 53, Petraeus remained a slim man with boyish features, famously smart, articulate and motivated. He had served two tours in Iraq, first as commander of the 101st Airborne Division in and around the northern city of Mosul, and later in charge of training the new Iraqi army and security forces as commander of the Multi-National Security Transition Command—Iraq.

The study group members wanted to talk to him because Petraeus had been lauded as a general who understood the situation on the ground and had a track record of pacifying the territory he controlled.

The meeting was supposed to take place by videoconference, but the United States Institute of Peace in downtown Washington, where the group had gathered, was having technical problems. Instead, a conference call was piped through speakers in every corner of the room, making Petraeus sound like the voice of God.

From the first moment, it sounded as though he were following a script.

"U.S. strategy over the last 18 months has been sound," he said. The ongoing violence had made the mission more difficult. "Nonetheless, no alternative strategy is better."

He said the United States had "terrific people" assigned to the war, endorsing Casey and Khalilzad and adding, "I would not break up the team of military and civilian leaders currently in Iraq."

What about the level of violence in Iraq? Hamilton asked. Petraeus acknowledged that it had increased, adding, "The violence and the insurgency are an independent variable," referring to the growing problem.

Panetta said the study group had been told it would be between 2009 and 2013 before Iraqis could take over security for their country. What did the general think about that?

That's a worst-case timeline, Petraeus said, though he added, "Iraq is the most challenging security environment I've seen in 31 years in the military." He did not offer his own timeline.

Petraeus also stressed national reconciliation. "You have to give Sunnis a reason to support the new Iraq," he said. "Iraq is a civil-military challenge."

He said, as he had often in public, that Iraq could not be solved militarily. It had to be solved politically.

The aging soldier showed up alone.

His hair had long ago turned gray and wrinkles had stolen the youth from his face, but Colin Powell still cut a striking figure as he arrived for his interview with the study group the next day, May 19. Though he had shed his general's uniform more than a dozen years earlier, he still marched perfectly erect, shoulders back, military bearing intact. He wore a dark suit, well-tailored shirt and tie and polished black shoes. He moved almost at quick time. But there was nothing careless or hurried about him.

Even in retirement, Powell, now 69, remained nearly as recognizable as the president of the United States. He might have held the job himself had he not declined to run a decade earlier when the polls had had him at the top. In the minds of many, including his own, he had possessed the tools needed to win the White House—a black Republican, former chairman of the Joint Chiefs of Staff, the nation's number one military man during the 1991 Gulf War, most trusted, most admired, the latest American version of The Great Man of Our Times.

Instead, he had taken a different path, a path that led him now to this small conference room inside the U.S. Institute of Peace in downtown Washington. It had been sixteen months since he had been pushed out as George W. Bush's secretary of state, a job that had turned out to be a rough ride. Powell had become an outsider in Bush's administration, seen as too much his own man, the Reluctant Warrior out of step with the fulsome muscularity of the post-9/11 Bush team.

Powell's path, of course, had also led to his role in the Iraq War. He didn't think it was a necessary war, and yet he had gone along in a hundred ways, large and small. He had resisted at times but had succumbed to the momentum and his own sense of deference—even obedience—to the president. During a mano a mano Oval Office session two months before the Iraq invasion, Bush had asked Powell for his support.

"Are you with me on this?" Bush had asked, in a personal request to join the commander in chief in battle. "I want you with me."

Believing the war decision belonged to the president—not to generals or secretaries of state—Powell had pledged his fidelity, perhaps halfheartedly, but unequivocally: "I'm with you, Mr. President."

Perhaps more than anyone in the administration, Powell had been the "closer" for the president's case for war. A month before the war, he appeared before the United Nations and the world to make the public case, displaying what he said were the "facts" proving that Iraq had threatening stockpiles of weapons of mass destruction (WMD). The 76-minute presentation had proven effective, too effective, with Powell displaying all his powers of persuasion.

Four years later, no WMD had been found, many saw the war as a catastrophe, and Powell's reputation was irretrievably linked to it, forever damaged. So the 10:30 A.M. meeting on this Friday was both a mission of accommodation and penance. He was going to have to confront the war and its aftermath for the rest of his life, and this was but another stop on the road to sort out his anguish.

As he entered the small conference room, Powell was greeted warmly by the members of the group. He gazed around the room. There must have been a jailbreak, he joked. The room erupted in laughter.

There was an obvious camaraderie between Powell and the group members, most of whom had dedicated much of their lives to building up American power and credibility, winning the last phase of the Cold War and shaping a world in which the United States was the only superpower. Now Iraq threatened to undermine all they had built.

Baker and Hamilton sat together at the head of a table, with Powell directly across from them. The other members lined the sides of the table, and staff sat along the wall.

Did Powell have something to say up front? Baker asked.

"I have no opening statement."

Okay, then why did we go into Iraq with so few troops? Baker asked.

It was an unusual starting point. The study group was supposed to focus on future remedies, not past troubles. But the question of troop levels seemed to be at the heart of the problem, and the relatively small invasion force of some 150,000 troops had contradicted Powell's philosophy of warfare—namely to send a large, decisive force that would guarantee success. For the 1991 Gulf War—a far simpler military task of ejecting the Iraqi army from its occupation of Kuwait—Powell, then JCS chairman, had insisted on a force of 500,000.

Baker's question sparked a monologue that went on for nearly 20 minutes.

"Colin just exploded at that point," Perry recalled later.

"He unloaded," Leon Panetta added. "He was angry. He was mad as hell."

Powell cited pages 393 to 395 from *American Soldier,* the memoir of General Tommy Franks, who was in charge of Central Command at the time of the Iraq invasion. Quoting from memory, he noted that Franks had faithfully reported a call that Powell had made on September 5, 2002, six months before the invasion. "I've got problems with force size and support of that force, given the long lines of communications" and supplies, Powell had warned Franks.

"Colin Powell was the free world's leading diplomat. But he no longer wore Army green," Franks had written. "He'd earned his right to an opinion, but had relinquished responsibility for the conduct of military operations when he retired as the Chairman of the Joint Chiefs of Staff in 1993.

"I picked up the Red Switch and spoke to Don Rumsfeld. 'I appreciate his call,' I said. 'But I wanted to tell him that the military has changed since he left.'"

Franks reported that "Rumsfeld chuckled," but wanted to make sure that Powell's doubts were aired. "I want him to get them on the table in front of the president and the NSC. Otherwise, we'll look like we're steamrolling," Franks quoted Rumsfeld as saying.

Again citing Franks's memoir, Powell noted that he had raised his concerns at an NSC meeting held at Camp David with the president two days later. According to Franks's account, "Soft-spoken and polite, ever the diplomat, he questioned the friendly-to-enemy force ratios, and made the point rather forcefully that the Coalition would have 'extremely long' supply lines."

Powell did not mention that two pages later, Franks wrote that he had outlined his war plan without objection. "Colin Powell didn't debate the brief I gave, and he didn't ask any more operational questions," Franks wrote, suggesting that Powell did not persist.

Powell acknowledged to the study group that he couldn't have predicted the insurgency or the chaos of post-invasion Iraq. But he did know that such a mission required plenty of troops. It was the Powell Doctrine: Go in big. Go in to win.

Seven months before the war, Powell had asked for a private meeting with President Bush to lay out what he felt were the consequences of an invasion of Iraq that the president and his team had failed to examine. Powell and his deputy, Richard Armitage, summed it up this way: "If you break it, you own it."

At the study group meeting, Panetta later recalled, Powell said he had warned the president. "I did make clear that once this happens, you're the one who is going to have to pick up the pieces and put it back together again. And it's not going to be easy to do." Or as he put it later: "We not only did not have enough troops to stabilize the country and act like an occupying force, we didn't *want* to act like an occupying force. But we *were* the occupying force. We *were* the government."

In the classic sense, Powell told the group, there had never been a "front" to this war. The insurgency had begun from behind.

After his recapitulation on force levels, Powell moved without pause to the lack of postwar planning. He said he was stunned that Rumsfeld, when asked publicly about rampant looting in Iraq, had said, "Stuff happens." At a Pentagon press conference three weeks after the invasion, Rumsfeld had said that freedom was "untidy" and the extensive looting was the result of "pent-up feelings" from decades of Saddam Hussein's oppression. Powell quoted the defense secretary's "stuff happens" with utter disdain, suggesting it was an absurd evaluation and an abdication of responsibility.

Throughout that spring of 2003, Powell said, he'd kept thinking to himself, "When are we going to get this together?" All the Pentagon would say was, "Chalabi is coming, Chalabi is coming," a reference to Ahmed Chalabi, the Iraqi exile with a checkered past who had long opposed Saddam Hussein. Chalabi had been the poster boy for a new democracy in Iraq, but Powell was dismissive.

"It was just Chalabi and 600 thugs," Powell said, noting that Chalabi failed to live up to the promise he'd made to the Pentagon to show up in Iraq with 10,000 men.

As secretary of state at the time of the invasion in 2003, Powell said he wasn't told about the decision to dissolve the Iraqi army until it happened. It was a monumental decision that disbanded the entire Iraqi army with the stroke of a pen, and its enactment was contrary to previous briefings that had been given to the president and to Powell. Nor was Powell told in advance about the sweeping de-Baathification order banning members of Saddam's Baath Party from many levels of government. It had effectively pulled the rug out from under the bureaucracy that made the country run, as many Iraqis had needed to be Baathists simply to get a job within Saddam's government.

Powell expressed astonishment that officials who lacked proper credentials had been sent to Iraq. He specifically mentioned Bernard Kerik, the troubled former New York City police commissioner, whom Bush had named to head the Iraqi national police and intelligence agency. "Bernie Kerik is in charge of police?" Powell asked, with a mixture of mock surprise and disgust. "Where did Bernie Kerik come from?"

Though he had been out of government for a year and a half, Powell's anger seemed fresh and raw. And now it had risen to the surface for them to see as he channeled years of accumulated resentments into his testimony.

Had it been anyone else, Baker and Hamilton probably would have interrupted. "We don't want any hand-wringing about the past," they were both fond of saying. But in this case, they let Powell unload without interruption. He was taking them on a journey inside the trauma and dysfunction of the war.

"This guy was speaking from the gut," Alan Simpson later recalled.

"He'd been through the fire, you know, and he had deep feelings about his situation."

Powell, who had been national security adviser to President Reagan for a year as a three-star general, complained about the NSC process, a not-so-subtle criticism of Rice. Huge issues were never brought to his—or the president's—attention, he said. The whole purpose of the NSC was to present issues and options for debate and decision to the national security team and the president. For instance, he said, when Bremer headed the Coalition Provisional Authority overseeing Iraq for more than a year, he operated outside anyone's control. Powell said he learned of Bremer's seven-point plan for Iraq in *The Washington Post*. In addition, Bremer had used the word "occupation"—a humiliating notion in any honor-bound Arab society—making it clear that he considered himself the sovereign authority.

The NSC had no apparatus to make sure things happened. Powell said the philosophy was "We're hoping things will improve. We say it'll happen. Therefore, we believe it will happen." There was no follow-through, no discipline.

To the essential question "Who are we fighting?," Powell said that the White House and Pentagon's answer would be Zarqawi, the al Qaeda leader in Iraq. That was too limited an answer, he said, but the Pentagon did not want to consider wider possibilities.

Powell singled out the handling of Army Chief of Staff General Eric Shinseki, who had argued for a larger force after the invasion. Rumsfeld had destroyed Shinseki's career, he said. No senior Defense official had attended Shinseki's retirement ceremony, he added with disgust. Dissent simply was not allowed at the Pentagon. Those who speak up get treated like Shinseki, he said.

"He revealed in very great detail his frustrations with Rumsfeld," Hamilton said later. "He felt like he'd lost every argument internally within the administration."

Speaking about the raging sectarian violence between the Shia and the Sunnis that was exploding in Iraq at the time, Powell told the group, "The American armed forces have little ability to understand what is happening and to react."

He said he felt the military was stuck, that the Americans had lost all authority. "We are no longer the occupier," he said. "We are watching the cabinet of 30 Iraqis sitting in the Green Zone"—the walled-off enclave in Baghdad that housed the Iraqi government and U.S. embassy. "We have little control over the events in Iraq."

Noting that the American public no longer supported the war, Powell added, "All we can do is hope that the Iraqi government pulls it together. . . . We are not driving this train anymore; the Iraqis are in charge."

How about sending more troops?

"Colonels will always ask for more troops and resources," Powell replied. "Generals should have asked for more troops when they had the chance to," meaning before the invasion. That opportunity had vanished, in his opinion. The Army and Marines were now stretched to their limits with multiple deployments and were cracking under the strains of perpetual war.

"You saw a very discouraged man when he talked to us," Hamilton said later. "And a very pessimistic man about the future. He really did not think that Iraq was salvageable at all."

What are the consequences of failure in Iraq? Hamilton asked.

The United States would be seen as impotent, Powell said, then quickly shifted to the present tense, as if that already were the case. "Mubarak"—the Egyptian president—"is putting people in jail. Putin is making sarcastic comments." The Chinese are listening politely, he said, but in reality they are ignoring us.

"Folks are tired of getting slapped around by the United States," Powell added. "They've stopped listening."

Throughout the interview, the temperature in the conference room kept rising and falling, and staff members kept slipping out to adjust the air-conditioning. But Powell himself stayed at a steady boil.

"All that we can do is to build up the army and the police to build a Humpty Dumpty," Powell said sarcastically. "An army isn't guys with five weeks training. An army is part and parcel of society."

What about the intelligence on the ground in Iraq?

"Station chiefs have been shooting up red cluster messages for years," Powell said, referring to the regular CIA reports of escalating violence and trouble. "We've got a mess here. Washington didn't want to hear it."

Is there any reasonable chance of getting help from the international community? Hamilton asked.

"No," Powell said sharply.

Any chance of getting help from Iraq's neighbors?

"No."

Several people in the room chuckled uncomfortably and shook their heads at the near hopelessness of what Powell was describing.

"He had a general view that the world, whole world, was down on us," Perry later recalled. "Which nobody argued with him about at the meeting."

"I thought of it very much as a therapy session," Panetta said later, "in that he felt he could sit down with people who were brothers in arms . . . people he related to from past experiences. And felt comfortable just kind of unloading."

The briefing, scheduled for an hour, had stretched longer, and the study group had an afternoon of interviews still to come.

"Well, Colin," Baker finally said, "you're going to have a great book."

Powell left as quietly as he had come, alone. Baker turned to Panetta and said solemnly, "He's the one guy who could have perhaps prevented this from happening."

5

In late spring, Bush met with his entire cabinet and made a strong pitch for everyone to participate in the war effort. Abizaid, Casey and Khalilzad all briefed, and the president gave an all-hands-on-deck speech. Several weeks later, at an NSC meeting on May 26, 2006, Rice, who was in charge of assembling personnel willing to go to Iraq from various departments and agencies, announced the final numbers: 48 people had signed on.

"Ma'am, that is a paltry number," blurted Casey, who was in the meeting by secure video from Iraq. To him, it proved that the civilians weren't contributing enough to the war—the most important undertaking of the Bush administration and a venture with so many U.S. interests at stake. He hoped the president would demand more action.

General, Rice replied tersely, you're out of line.

"On that happy note," the president said, "we will adjourn."

Rumsfeld immediately dashed off a SECRET snowflake to Casey: "My apologies to you for the comments that were made in the NSC meeting this morning. It is a pattern. There is not much anyone seems to be able to do about it. . . . Thanks for all you're doing out there and for your patience today as well."

Casey didn't feel at all patient. Neither Rice nor Hadley had come up with a national strategy for the Iraq War or found a way to make sure it was properly resourced. David Satterfield, the deputy chief of mission in the embassy, had told Rice on a visit to Iraq once, "Here's the most important mission for the country, and they have three linguists that can speak Arabic at the highest level from the State Department."

"I just took a look at the attached page 49 from the quarterly report to Congress," wrote Rumsfeld, focused on details as ever, in a May 30 snowflake to Casey about troop levels. "I noticed the gray area is coalition, and we are increasing the number of combat operations every month. I would have thought that the ISF [Iraqi security forces] would increase, the combined would increase, but the coalition would go down. It seems the opposite is happening. Let's talk about it and figure out why."

Now in the fourth year of the war, the defense secretary was still asking about the elusive numbers of exactly how many Iraqi soldiers were trained and ready for duty. And he was still pushing for a U.S. military less involved in Iraq, not more.

Jim Jeffrey, Rice's coordinator for Iraq policy, was a 6-foot-3 Bostonian and a career diplomat who had served as U.S. ambassador to Albania and later as deputy chief of mission in the U.S. embassy in Baghdad in 2004–05. He believed the United States could not abandon Iraq, as it had Vietnam in 1975. And like Zelikow, Jeffrey believed it was possible to devise a successful counterinsurgency strategy along the lines of what Colonel H. R. McMaster had done in Tall Afar.

On June 5, Zelikow and Jeffrey presented Rice with a SECRET 11-page memo titled "Possible political-military strategy for summer 2006." It reflected the sum of their frustrations.

They noted that Maliki and his new government continue "to roll out ill-prepared, ad hoc initiatives like last week's declaration of an emergency in Basra or this week's plan to announce a large-scale release of detainees" held by the U.S.

In bold letters, they wrote: "Likelihood of success for the proposed strategy is low."

This was still an American effort, and U.S. control was essential. "The argument that the U.S. should not strongly assert its preferences to the Iraqi government is wrong," they wrote, and saying "let-them-do-it-themselves" would be a cop-out.

"Maliki has never run a large organization," they noted. He had never even run a small one. A 56-year-old Shia, Maliki had been in exile for 23 years, apparently bouncing between Iran and Syria. His chief credential was that he had been a spokesman for the political party al Dawa (The Call), a relatively minor Shia party. The Iraqi parliament had selected him as the first permanent prime minister. He was a precarious compromise between the two real Shia forces in Iraq. The first was Moqtada al-Sadr, the young militant cleric and leader in Sadr City, the northeastern quadrant of Baghdad with more than 2 million people. The other was the Supreme Council for Islamic Revolution in Iraq, SCIRI, one of Iraq's most powerful political parties and the largest party in the Iraqi Council of Representatives, headed by Iraqi theologian and politician Abdul Aziz al-Hakim.

The SECRET memo offered three options: A) strong, B) medium and C) weak. Not surprisingly, Zelikow and Jeffrey encouraged the middle road.

Option A, which they rejected, was called "Full Counterinsurgency."

"This would apply a Tall Afar–like approach to all the major trouble spots, starting with Baghdad. It is very soldier-intensive. . . . It might require a significant additional infusion of American combat power— perhaps several additional brigades—to make it work."

The option was not presented as a surefire winning strategy, designed or guaranteed to achieve victory or to address the more important threshold question of whether victory was attainable. And it failed, like many other proposals, to address the problem of who would hold an area, assimilate the population, restore order, and demonstrate the benefits of signing up with the new Iraqi government and joining in the democratic process.

Option B was "Selective Counterinsurgency." It would include fighting in "a few selected areas" and "also could require some infusion of additional American forces in the short term, with the gamble that this strategy could produce a much better climate for withdrawal of American forces later this year or next." Calling an option they intended to recommend a "gamble" was highly unusual for the authors of an option paper.

Option C was described as a "keep-the-lid-on," "reactive" approach that would result in "increased chance of continued decay and security conditions." With little irony, they noted in recommending Option B that "our current policies seem most consistent with Option C."

They also said that Option B could result in a "significant drawdown of American forces, perhaps to below 100,000" within six months. In their analysis, "the latest Baghdad Security Plan does not appear sufficient to clear and hold the city, or even the most insecure neighborhoods in it."

Rice sent a copy of the memo to Hadley at the White House.

Given the obvious gravity of the situation, the remedies were modest, and the boundaries of Zelikow and Jeffrey's proposals were limited by what their superiors allowed on the table.

The CIA kept warning that sectarian violence was growing and that the new government did not have—and was not developing—roots. But the inner circle of the administration seemed to have shielded itself from bold new ideas, and those on the outside weren't breaking through.

Casey had the Special Operations units working day and night trying to locate Zarqawi, the leader of al Qaeda in Iraq. In early June, Lieutenant General Stanley McChrystal, the Joint Special Operations commander, called on a secure line and said he thought they had pinpointed Zarqawi in a small house that likely contained women and children.

"How sure are you that he's there?"

"I'm sure," McChrystal said, his voice cracking.

Not long afterward, McChrystal called to report that the planes had hit the target and that the body had been brought to his headquarters.

"We're going to wait on the fingerprints, but this is the guy," the

Special Operations commander said. "All my guys who've been working this for two years are convinced this is the guy."

"Mr. Secretary, listen," Casey said in a secure call to Rumsfeld, "I want to tell you something that I'm not 100 percent sure of, but I'm sure enough that you need to know this is happening."

Rumsfeld held his breath, expecting the worst.

"I think we got Zarqawi tonight."

"Oh, Jesus Christ!" Rumsfeld bellowed, unused to good news. "All I could say to myself was 'What the hell else could have gone wrong there?'"

Later, Rumsfeld dictated a personal snowflake to Casey: "Congratulations on finding, fixing and finishing Zarqawi. What a superb job you have done in Iraq—you make us all proud."

"I don't think you'll find that there is a lot of disagreement about the strategy," Rice said during a meeting on June 7, 2006. This was to be her public position—optimistic and unyielding. "I think you'll find that most people think we're on the only reasonable course." She and her staff were to keep up the appearance that widespread agreement existed on the current strategy.

But it was untrue. Most everyone inside and outside the administration was realizing that the current course seemed less and less reasonable. Rice had key staff members such as Zelikow examining the Iraq strategy and writing classified memos about their findings, and she knew only too well that the war effort was in serious trouble.

"It was pretty clear what we were doing wasn't working," she would say two years later, looking back on that time. "We were not going to succeed. We might not even be able to fight to a standstill if we just stayed on the course we were on."

"I've just returned from Baghdad," Bush said at a morning news conference in the Rose Garden on June 14, the day after his surprise visit to Maliki in Iraq, "and I was inspired."

He expressed no reservations about the strategy and gave no hint of the trouble they were in. Nor did he express doubt about Casey.

"I've got people who say, 'You need to increase the number of forces—now,'" Bush said. "I've gotten people that said, 'Well, the role of the United States ought to be more indirect than it has been,' in other words, in a supporting role. To those folks, I say, 'Look, I'm going to rely on General Casey.'"

He added, "I know there is a lot of discussion about troop levels. Those troop levels will be decided upon by General Casey. He will make the recommendations, in consultation with an Iraqi government. But whatever decision General Casey makes, the message is going to be, 'We'll stand with you.'"

That same afternoon, the president met privately with the 10 members of the bipartisan Iraq Study Group.

"It's going to work," he said, brimming with confidence. He said he never paid attention to public opinion polls and instead listened to General Casey.

He also seemed impressed with Maliki. "We know the problems," the president said. "He's going to solve them."

Bob Gates pressed. "We're putting a lot of chips on Maliki. Are we sure he's the right guy?"

Bush indicated that he had no doubts.

Alan Simpson insisted that the president find some way to talk with the governments of Iran and Syria. Not talking doesn't work, he said. Doesn't work in marriages, doesn't work between governments.

Throughout the meeting, the president offered little more than a reprise of his public statements.

Was this "the real deal"? Baker asked. Was the president serious about listening to the Iraq Study Group's recommendations, whatever they might be?

Bush insisted that he was and that he would order his administration to cooperate fully.

•   •   •

In Baghdad, Casey appreciated the president's repeated public votes of confidence. But he kept asking himself: What do civilian leaders bring to such a war? After all, neither the full capacity of the U.S. government nor the American people were ever mobilized. No one ever articulated a grand strategy about what the heck the United States was doing. Nearly everything fell to the military.

Casey was scheduled to return to Washington later in the month to see the president, Rumsfeld and the Joint Chiefs. So he sat down at breakfast with his senior commanders in Iraq. "Okay," he said, "does everybody have the troops they need?"

They all said yes.

On June 21, Casey was back in the United States, meeting with the Joint Chiefs in their secure conference room inside the Pentagon, known as the tank.

"Iraq Update and Way Ahead," read his SECRET briefing. Casey told them that all of Iraq would be ready for transition to Iraqi control within 18 months, with the exception of Anbar province. A colored map showed only Anbar as red, meaning not ready for transition. Everything else was green. Casey envisioned reducing the U.S. force from the current 15 combat brigades to as few as 10 within six months. Then, six months after that, it would be down to seven or eight brigades, and by December 2007 only five to six combat brigades would remain.

Currently, he said there were 69 U.S. bases in Iraq, but in a year and a half he intended to cut to 11 bases—an 84 percent reduction.

After the killing of Zarqawi, Casey felt optimistic. The war on the ground was nothing like Vietnam. They were not fighting organized units at all. As he put it, "Even the militias are just a bunch of ragbags in pickup trucks."

On Friday, June 23, Casey was at the White House residence, briefing the president.

"I think we can off-ramp a couple more brigades," he told the commander in chief, meaning about 5,000 troops would leave in September and not be replaced. He summarized his plan of continuing to draw down brigades for the next 18 months, leaving the United States with only five to six brigades by the end of 2007.

The president endorsed the concept but not necessarily the timetable. "We may not need to go that fast," he said.

On the third floor of the Eisenhower Executive Office Building next to the White House, Meghan L. O'Sullivan, the deputy national security adviser for Iraq and Afghanistan, was enduring a bout of soul-searching. A trim redhead with a Ph.D. in political science from Oxford, O'Sullivan was only 36. Her lack of military experience made her an unlikely deputy for coordinating two major wars. But she had attached herself to powerful patrons, first in the months before the invasion to former Army Lieutenant General Jay Garner, who had been chosen to oversee postwar reconstruction; then for more than a year on the staff of Garner's replacement, Jerry Bremer, the head of the Coalition Provisional Authority.

Afterward, O'Sullivan spent two years on the NSC staff working directly for Rice and then Hadley. She regularly reminded people that she worked 18-hour days, seven days a week, and hadn't had a date in years. O'Sullivan was bright, ambitious and persistent, and she thrived in the all-work, little-play environment. Five days a week, she wrote a highly classified Iraq Note, averaging three pages, which went directly to the president. The news covered casualties, bombings, military operations, and intelligence, providing Bush with a quick overview and summary of the day's events. Copies went to Cheney, new White House chief of staff Josh Bolten and Hadley. Day after day, the notes contained a lot of bad news. The president made clear to O'Sullivan and Hadley that he was not fully confident in the information and analysis he was receiving through the normal military, diplomatic and intelligence channels.

"Just so you know," the president later told me, "the environment is not one where I'm sitting here and occasionally a senior person pops in, takes 30 seconds of my time and pops out. There is a lot of action in here. Meghan O'Sullivan, she'd come in, and I'd say, 'Before you leave, I need to ask you something. What are you thinking, Meghan? How do you think? Give me your opinion.'

"I like to get information from a variety of sources."

As the violence had escalated throughout the spring, O'Sullivan went to talk privately with her boss, Steve Hadley, knowing that the national security adviser wanted important, sensitive communications delivered verbally rather than in memos that could leak.

"I'm really worried about where this is going," she said, referring to the latest spate of violence. "I don't feel good about it . . . I'm talking to my friends in Baghdad, and it's a different tone. They're scared." At the NSC meetings she attended, the president often showed his frustration, and it was unclear to her whether it was directed at Casey or at the overall lack of progress in Iraq. Now that Casey was recommending a drawdown of two brigades, she saw more trouble ahead.

"We have a huge problem on our hands," she told Hadley. "This is going to be a pretty significant move in the wrong direction. And it will be close to irreversible if it just accelerates the negative trends we have." Already, the negative trends were dominating Iraq. She said of the current situation, "This is broken."

She saw that Hadley shared her alarm. Unlike some in the administration, O'Sullivan still had faith in the CIA and other intelligence agencies' information and judgments. They briefed her on Iraq three or four days a week. And at least one of those days, she met with a half a dozen or more members of the CIA Iraq team to do what she called a "deep dive" into one aspect of Iraq for an hour and a half. She heard nothing that suggested it was all going to work out. O'Sullivan sensed an almost universal acknowledgment within the administration, even from the president, that things weren't going well and that the policy and approach were off track. And yet, nothing had changed.

What to do? And when? The upcoming congressional elections were five months off, and the Republicans' narrow control of both the House and the Senate were at stake. The mishandling of the Iraq War would be at the center of Democratic political attacks on Bush and the Republicans.

Hadley said he would try again to launch a strategy review.

6

In June 2006, David Satterfield, 51, a brainy foreign service officer fluent in Arabic, was wrapping up more than a year's service as the deputy chief of mission in Baghdad, the number two post in the embassy. The number two gets much of the difficult and dirty work, and it is traditionally known as the toughest job in an embassy.

Because of his penchant for listing his arguments in bullet point fashion, Satterfield was known affectionately around the State Department as "The Human Talking Point." Because of his willingness to serve in hardship posts such as Baghdad and take on difficult tasks, several of Rice's aides gave him the biblical nickname "The Job of the Foreign Service."

Satterfield was returning to Washington to become Rice's senior adviser and coordinator on Iraq. He had been in the foreign service for 25 years and had served in trusted positions in Democratic and Republican administrations. He had been a member of President Clinton's NSC staff and Clinton's ambassador to Lebanon. He wasn't ideological. He always asked: What are the interests of the United States?

On Iraq, Satterfield had grimly concluded that the current strategy and security posture were not working. The situation was spinning "decisively out of control." Sectarianism was rampant. The new prime minister was protecting Shia militias engaged in murders and torture of Sunnis. In turn, the Sunni leaders refused to condemn the violence of their militias and death squads.

Satterfield was skeptical that the United States could win in Iraq, at least in the sense that the president wanted. Instead, he was looking for ways to contain the damage and minimize the harm to U.S. interests. But he knew from attending NSC and other meetings that the environment would not be receptive to proposals for a dramatic change—whether it be withdrawing or adding U.S. forces. Either would go against the grain, and a foreign service officer could reach only so far.

From his perch at the embassy in Baghdad, Satterfield had concluded that Rumsfeld had mandated General Casey to draw down because the large U.S. military presence was a direct, visible challenge—even an insult—to the secretary's theory of a military defined by discrete lethal, quick successes. The prolonged and violent war was a refutation of Rumsfeld's theory and a fatal wound to his legacy, Satterfield believed, thus the urgency to begin getting out. The occupation, with 150,000 U.S. forces tied down in counterinsurgency, stabilization and civil affairs—everything from security at electrical generating stations to sewer repair—was not the role Rumsfeld envisioned for his lightning-fast, transformed military.

Satterfield had found the U.S. military's effort to train Iraqis largely bogus. Elaborate briefing charts showed how many Iraqis had been trained. But they never reflected the actual number of Iraqi soldiers available for duty. Because of desertion, injuries, illness and periodic leaves to take pay home, the Iraqi forces on duty were actually a small percentage of the number of those trained.

Satterfield tried many times to get accurate numbers, but had little success. He had spent the year in Baghdad attending the daily BUA— battlefield update assessment—in which cheerful briefers plotted in red, green and yellow PowerPoint slides an endless list of force levels, statistics, attacks and counterattacks. Numbers, numbers, always more numbers. But rarely were strategic outcomes defined, identified or assessed. Never talk of real progress.

So as he was about to assume his new duties as Rice's right-hand man on Iraq, Satterfield could not have been more concerned about where Bush and the administration were heading. He would be replacing Jeffrey, the career diplomat who had served a year as deputy chief of mission in Baghdad and a year as Rice's Iraq coordinator. Jeffrey was so worried about the increase in violence that he had remarked privately, "Sometimes I wonder, why did I ever take this job?"

At the end of June, Casey took a few days of leave but kept in touch with his staff in Baghdad by secure video teleconference. Al Qaeda launched some horrific attacks during his absence. A bicycle bomber in a central market north of Baghdad killed at least 18 people and wounded 43. Another bomb in Hilla, 60 miles south of Baghdad, killed six and wounded 56. Attacks on Iraqi police and army in Baghdad killed another 14.

Was it as bad as it looked on television from Washington? Casey asked.

No, his staff assured him.

A few days later, on Saturday, July 1, a truck bomb exploded in Sadr City, the Shiite enclave of 2 million people in Baghdad ruled by the radical cleric Moqtada al-Sadr. The death toll was at least 62 with 120 others wounded. A Sunni female member of the new parliament and eight of her bodyguards were kidnapped. By this time, Casey had returned to Baghdad, and the assessment had changed. The generals and colonels were painting a grim picture.

"Well, I'm glad I'm rested," Casey thought to himself, "because this is going to get a lot harder."

He spoke with Abizaid and finally with General Pace, telling the chairman he'd changed his mind about how quickly he could reduce troop levels. "Hey, look," he said, "I don't see us as off-ramping here. This is a security situation that has not gone in the direction I thought it was going to go in."

Pace was surprised but did not dispute the ground commander.

The next morning, Casey had his regular meeting with his number two, Lieutenant General Pete Chiarelli, the day-to-day commander in Iraq. Casey and Chiarelli had built a candid rapport after working closely together for more than six months.

"Last chance for the Strykers," Chiarelli said. The 172nd Stryker brigade combat team from Alaska, known as the "Arctic Wolves," was heading home after a yearlong deployment. The 3,800-member unit employed the Stryker armored vehicle—essentially an armored tank on eight giant conventional tires that can travel up to 60 miles per hour and is maneuverable in urban environments while providing armored protection for up to 11 soldiers. "I really need them," Chiarelli said.

Casey saw fear in his deputy's eyes. He pressed for his rationale to keep the unit. Chiarelli didn't really have one other than the increasing violence and his instincts.

"Okay," Casey finally said, acceding to Chiarelli's concern.

Later that day, Casey told Rumsfeld on the secure video, "You need to understand that I'm thinking about asking to extend the Strykers. I realize some of them have already gone home." About 300 soldiers had returned to Alaska, and another 300 had gone south to Kuwait, the staging area for the return home. He noted that the Strykers were the most capable force he had. "This can be hard, but right now, given what we have going on here, I think I have to keep that force here in Iraq. I need to think about it a little bit more, but that's where I'm headed."

"Okay," Rumsfeld said. "I have a meeting at the White House tomorrow, so if you think you really want to do something, let me know so I can tell the president."

The next day Casey called Rumsfeld to say he wanted to keep the Strykers. "I need to do this."

Rumsfeld didn't blink, and the president gave his approval.

All hell broke loose in Congress and in Alaska, where "Welcome Home" signs already hung at Fort Wainwright. One soldier's wife, Jennifer Davis, a member of Military Families Speak Out, an antiwar group, wrote on a Web site, "My husband called to let me know in the best way that he knows how, that the Army was extending his deployment four more months, mere hours before he was to board a flight home. I am totally frustrated, disappointed and heartbroken. Just when I thought we were going to be able to resume a 'normal' life. Just when I thought the nightmare was over, it was extended. . . . This war should never have started, and now I'm left wondering if it will ever end."

Rumsfeld sent a SECRET snowflake to Casey complaining, "We have to do a better job looking around corners to the extent it is humanly possible. We are facing some difficulties in Alaska and Congress because of it."

Casey waited a week to answer formally. "As the security situation in Baghdad continued to deteriorate, it became apparent to us in our planning that the Iraqi security forces and government did not have the ability to make a decisive impact on the Baghdad situation in the near term without more help from us. Extending the Strykers became an opportunity to make a decisive impact in Baghdad at a critical point in the government and in our mission." The 300 who had already returned to Alaska were being brought back to Iraq, he said.

"As always Mr. Secretary, I appreciate your courage and your continued support for our mission. George Casey."

Rumsfeld went to Fort Wainwright, Alaska, to meet with some 700 family members of the Arctic Wolves. The press was shut out of the meeting, but some of the wives videotaped the session and played the tapes for the media.

One woman asked why her husband was out on foot patrols clearing buildings and houses, and not in the well-armored Stryker, which could better defend against deadly IEDs. "My husband hasn't set foot in his Stryker since he arrived in Baghdad," she said.

"Over 90 percent of the house clearings are being handled by the Iraqis," Rumsfeld assured her.

Shouts of "No!" and "That's not true!" erupted from the audience.

"No?" Rumsfeld responded, caught off guard. "What do you mean? Don't say, 'No.' That's what I've been told. It's the task of the Iraqis to go through the buildings."

It was a tough session, and the family members had plenty of questions. Was it possible the Wolves would be extended beyond the 120 days? Would they be home for Christmas? Rumsfeld said he didn't have a magic wand, but he would do everything in his power.

And he did. In a SECRET snowflake to Pace, Army Chief of Staff General Peter Schoomaker and Generals Abizaid and Casey, he wrote, "It would be a wonderful thing if we could get them home for Thanksgiving instead of Christmas." He also wrote, "I need assurances in confidence that these folks are not going to be asked to extend again." The Strykers weren't home for Thanksgiving, but they made it by Christmas, and as the secretary of defense ordered, they were not extended again.

For some time, Casey came to expect two or three e-mails a night from spouses calling him every name in the book for extending the Strykers.

On July 7, President Bush answered a few questions from reporters after a speech in Chicago and once again voiced his confidence in his Iraq commander. "General Casey will make the decisions as to how many troops we have there," he said. "General Casey is a wise and smart man, who has spent a lot of time in Baghdad recently, obviously. And it's his judgment that I rely upon. He'll decide how best to achieve victory and the troop levels to do so. I spent a lot of time talking to him about troop levels and I told him this. I said, 'You decide, General. I want your judgment, your advice. I don't want these decisions being made by the political noise, by the political moment.'"

On July 19, Hadley called Rumsfeld to inquire about a new group that Casey, Ambassador Khalilzad and the Iraqi government were to form that supposedly was going to be called the "Joint Commission on Coalition Withdrawal."

Surely that couldn't be true, both agreed. That might be the intent, but they didn't want to be so explicit. Withdrawal was a dangerous word that smacked of "cut and run." Rumsfeld snowflaked Casey, saying, "Certainly, in the current environment, the title Steve Hadley believes has been decided on would not be good."

Casey answered that such a get-out-of-Iraq title had never been considered. Instead, Casey said, they had worked out with the Iraqis the title "Joint Committee for Achieving Iraqi Security Self-Reliance (JCAISSR)." The name would emphasize the "self-reliance" rather than the "withdrawal," though the two went hand in hand as far as Casey was concerned.

•   •   •

Casey questioned Prime Minister Maliki's efforts to get control of
the Shia militia that operated freely, especially in Baghdad. Under
an old order (CPA 91) from the Bremer era, the Iraqis were supposed to undertake what was called "disarmament, demobilization
and reintegration"—known as DDR—of the militias. Casey told the
president that Maliki might be deliberately dragging his feet so the
Shia militias could establish themselves around Baghdad. On the other
hand, he said, it was possible that it was just Iraqi ineffectiveness. He
leaned toward ineffectiveness. But his assessment of Maliki was harsh.

"He's got two biases that he's got to break through," Casey said.
"One, he absolutely believes that the Baathists are coming back. He's
scared to death of the Baathists, and Baathists equals Sunni, and so he
doesn't trust them at all. And second, he's sectarian. He's a Shia." Maliki's Dawa Party, a small Shia group, is deeply sectarian, Casey noted.

In her office adjacent to the White House, O'Sullivan kept a chart of
the violence in the 15 main neighborhoods of Baghdad. She had tried
to get everyone to focus on Ghazaliya, a Sunni Arab neighborhood in
west Baghdad with dramatically escalating violence. It vividly demonstrated that what the military was doing was not working. The picture
that the president was getting from Casey and Khalilzad was much better than the reality. Their strategy of training the Iraqis and getting out
did not fit. But she wondered how to get them to acknowledge that.
The weekly hour-long brief from Casey was not a forum to ask fundamental questions. But fundamental questions were exactly what
needed asking, the kind that would come only through a full strategy
review.

As far as O'Sullivan was concerned, Casey had a credibility problem. On July 19, she sent a long SECRET memo to Hadley and his
deputy, J. D. Crouch, titled, "Adjusting Our Security Strategy to the
New Realities in Iraq."

Two months into the new Maliki government, she noted delicately, "tangible signs of progress have been elusive as Maliki has struggled with limited tools at his disposal and a deteriorating security situation.

"Now is an opportune moment," she wrote, aware that the moment had existed for months, "to explore: 1) Whether our security strategy has been sufficiently adjusted to account for new realities (especially sectarian strife)." The use of the word "strife" implied tensions and difficulties rather than the bloodbath she knew was taking place. She continued: "2) Whether external constraints on available U.S. military resources through the end of 2007 limit our ability to respond adequately to these new realities." In other words, were there enough troops? "And 3) Whether we have strategic options for filling any gaps between available U.S. resources and what may be required to ensure long-term success in Iraq." Plainly stated, did the United States possess enough force?

On one level, O'Sullivan was asking the hardest and most basic question: Do we know what we are doing? But the memo's tentativeness and deference, its muted and conditional phrasing, reduced its sting.

"The current focus on drawing down coalition troops," she wrote, "is one of several factors suggesting that"—and here she switched to bold type—"we are executing a plan based on assumptions that are no longer valid."

She then proposed that before withdrawing any further troops, the security strategy be "reevaluated" because security was getting worse in some places and the "presence of MOI [Ministry of Interior] forces in Sunni areas may actually fuel sectarian violence."

She went on to note, again with understatement, "It would also be hard to characterize a decision to bring troops home at this point as a consequence of success or the result of an improvement in conditions.

"For all these reasons, we recommend a security review where the president considers asking the following series of questions." The questions focused on the sectarian violence, whether they had the right approach to Baghdad, and the impact of the Ministry of Interior on the Sunnis.

O'Sullivan then asked whether they should consider what she

called an "additive" strategy by providing more troops. To pump up the urgency, she suggested that the NSC meeting with the president that day be devoted to these questions.

But other events that Wednesday, July 19, swamped Bush. He issued his first veto in five years as president, rejecting a law passed by the Congress lifting restrictions on human embryonic stem cell research. It was a highly emotional issue, and the president staged a ceremony for the veto that afternoon in the East Room of the White House, attended by children who had developed from frozen embryos.

Also that day, Maliki broke publicly with Bush to strongly condemn Israeli attacks into Lebanon that Bush had said were justified as defenses against terrorism.

In the daily crush, the pressing questions about the U.S. strategy in Iraq were placed on hold again.

7

———————

Hadley and O'Sullivan realized that conducting an Iraq strategy review was risky, even under the greatest secrecy—swearing everyone involved to confidentiality and stamping all the paperwork with high classifications. The administration's public posture was that while the war was difficult, progress was being made. A leak that the White House was questioning its strategy could be devastating. The congressional elections were barely three months away. Iraq was likely to be the main issue, and the Republicans' thin margin in both the Senate and the House already was in jeopardy.

But O'Sullivan knew the current Iraq strategy was broken, and she wasn't about to give up. Perhaps there was a way to have a review without calling it that. She knew from her time in Baghdad that the relentless day-to-day operations made it hard, if not impossible, to step back and reevaluate fundamentals. There was never time to ask basic questions. So she proposed to Hadley that he send a series of broad questions to Rumsfeld, Casey and Khalilzad. In answering the questions, she hoped that they would wake up and realize, "Hey, this picture has changed."

Hadley was willing to try again. First, he recognized the painfully obvious disconnect between what was happening on the ground and the strategy of drawing down steadily. Casey's slides kept calling for a drawdown, even though he had himself decided not to off-ramp brigades in the coming fall and had extended the Stryker brigade's tour. It was not lost on Hadley, or the president, that Casey's plan to cut forces had been delayed again and again for more than a year. The Army had a SECRET graphic, known as the "Failed Assumptions Chart," showing the plans for drawing down brigades in Iraq—sometimes very dramatically—going back to 2003. On every occasion, the plans had not been realized, and the same number of about 15 brigades remained.

Hadley spoke with the president every day about Iraq, and both felt increasingly uneasy. They seemed to agree that every society has its own tolerable level of violence—a theme often stressed by Rumsfeld. For Iraq, the question was whether the violence was too overwhelming to allow the Iraqis some semblance of normal life. But the sectarian violence in and around Baghdad—now 50 to 150 bodies turning up each day—meant that everyday life remained extremely difficult and daunting. Hadley told Bush he wanted to plant the seed for a full strategy review by asking Rumsfeld, Casey and Khalilzad a series of tough, detailed questions. "I'm going to ask Don to do it," Hadley said. "I think he'll let me do it."

"Go to it," Bush said.

Bush later confirmed to me that he had okayed the question session. "In order for the SVTS [secure video] to go forward with the secretary of defense and main commander," he said, "it needed the blessing of the president."

On July 20, 2006, the president read his daily TOP SECRET/SCI Iraq update. SCI stands for Special Compartmented Information—the highest classification of the most sensitive intelligence data obtained from communications intercepts, human and other sources.

"The deteriorating security situation is outpacing the Iraqi government's ability to respond," the three-page memo said. The Sunni Arab insurgency was diminishing, an intelligence assessment said, "but spiraling sectarian violence by Sunni and Shia extremists, including some elements of the Iraqi Security Forces, is becoming the most immediate threat to Iraq's progress." Then the assessment reached its most dire conclusion: "Violence has acquired a momentum of its own and is now self-sustaining."

At the bottom of the third page was a chart the president saw each day, summarizing casualties since the 2003 invasion. On this day, as of 11 A.M. Eastrn Standard Time, the chart read:

"U.S. forces killed in action: 2,015

"Non-hostile deaths (not in combat): 532

"Wounded in action: 19,057."

"Don," Hadley told Rumsfeld, "there are some tough questions we need to ask about where we are."

Rumsfeld agreed.

Hadley was delighted because he knew that Rumsfeld could have told him to stuff it or simply could have ignored the request, as he often did.

So Hadley sent pages of questions to Rumsfeld, Casey and Khalilzad, and a secure video teleconference was scheduled for Saturday, July 22, which happened to be Casey's 58th birthday.

The general was flabbergasted. There were 14 major questions, each with a series of subquestions. He counted a total of 50 and presumed they must be of the kind the media, Congress or even the president was asking. These were questions Hadley couldn't answer. It didn't take much to see the list was a direct assault on the current strategy. One question was "What is the strategy for Baghdad?" and one of the main headings was "Grand Strategy." Casey and Khalilzad decided beforehand that they wouldn't go down the list and try to answer every question. It was demeaning, especially after the president's expansive and public vote of total confidence for Casey two weeks earlier in Chicago.

On July 22, Hadley called the secure video teleconference with Rumsfeld, Pace, Abizaid, Khalilzad and Casey to order. Other observers—including Meghan O'Sullivan and someone each from State, Defense and Cheney's office—watched.

Hoping to put off the questions, Casey and Khalilzad began the session with a routine update. But Hadley and O'Sullivan were determined to move past that.

"Who is behind the sectarian violence in Baghdad?" Hadley asked. "Al Qaeda terrorists? Baathists? Sunni rejectionists? Badr Corps? Mahdi Army? Criminal elements?"

Casey answered that it was increasingly "complex," with all of the above involved. In addition, Iranian support for violence was on the upswing. But he underscored that violence alone wasn't a good measure of success or failure when they were transitioning the security responsibility to the Iraqis. The main security challenge was the sectarian violence, which Casey and Khalilzad said was really a struggle between Iraqis for political and economic power.

"What is the role that Prime Minister Maliki plays in providing political guidance?" Hadley asked.

"Critic," Casey noted on his copy of the questions. He explained that Maliki was standing on the sidelines with his arms folded, offering criticism but not accepting responsibility for the situation. He said he tried to accommodate political guidance from Maliki but in limited quantities so as not to paralyze the system. The prime minister wanted to approve all U.S. military operations, and Casey would say no. But he had promised the prime minister, "I'll come to you on the big ones, the things that have big political impact." Casey said he had kept that promise.

Have there been disconnects about how to use the Iraqi security forces?

Casey said he didn't trust them. Maliki's forces did not react quickly. For example, Casey said, Maliki tried to exert direct control over the Iraqi Special Forces, the most competent element of the Iraqi army and a group that prided itself on working with the United States, going after anyone against the government, including the Shia militias. Casey said he had told Maliki, "You don't want these guys taking their instructions directly from you. You want them under the minister of defense, because if you task them to do something and they wind up killing a bunch of people by mistake, then you're the one that gets blamed for that." Maliki seemed to understand that that made good sense, but he still wanted control.

"Do security forces need to be more aggressive in Baghdad?" Hadley asked.

Eventually, yes, Casey said, noting on his sheet that the security forces were "not empowered" by Maliki to act on their own. The prime minister had to prove that he was on their side.

"Have we struck the right balance between one, not letting the Iraqis be overly dependent on us and two, putting too much responsibility on them too quickly?"

That's the question I wrestle with every day, Casey said. While that was always the question, the strategy was to give the Iraqis ultimate responsibility.

The next question was "Are additional resources, coalition and Iraqi, needed to bring greater security to Baghdad over a reasonable time frame, say six weeks?"

Casey said that whenever the U.S. forces established security in a given area and then turned it over to the Iraqis to build and hold, it would gradually break down. So the truth was that the U.S. forces never completely turned security over to the Iraqis but rather found a way to stay in the area. His implied answer was "yes," he might shift more U.S. forces to Baghdad, but he did not say it directly. He also made it clear he did not think he needed more U.S. forces overall.

How about the militias? "How long do the Iraqis think it will take before progress is tangible?"

"Eighteen months to two years," Casey said. Demobilizing the militias, each of which had anywhere from 20,000 to 100,000 members, was a large task.

"Is it part of the U.S. and coalition security mission to stem increasing levels of sectarian-fueled violence?"

That was the question that weighed constantly on Casey. He wrote on his list, "Protect the population?"

Classic counterinsurgency strategy held that the security of the population was the top priority. But the question mark reflected Casey's deep doubts. Undertaking that task would require more forces, and he was hesitant to ask for more because it was contrary to his overall strategy of preparing and training the Iraqis to take over. In addition, Maliki wasn't on board and had been putting restrictions on American operations in Baghdad. For example, the prime minister had canceled five U.S. and Iraqi Special Forces missions in Sadr City.

It was a complicated story. During his first days as prime minister, Maliki had given Casey a "don't touch" list of about 10 politically significant people and elicited a promise that Casey would call him before they were attacked. Sadr headed the list, and many of his lieutenants followed. All were suspected of shady activities, such as sectarian attacks or cooperation with al Qaeda. U.S. Special Forces and the intelligence people would work hard to get actionable intelligence, often risking their lives to do so.

Casey would then call Maliki or the Iraqi national security adviser, Mowaffak al-Rubaie, about going after the suspects, only to be told no on at least five occasions. "I understand that you're doing this for political reasons, but here's the impact on the military," Casey said he told them. The canceled operations were demoralizing and left his troops asking, quite openly and understandably, "What the fuck are we doing here?"

Casey had kept pressuring Maliki on the bad guys, and Maliki had offered progressively less resistance. Most were picked up or killed. On one occasion, Casey went ahead with an operation without telling Maliki and the prime minister said nothing.

Hadley continued. Under the heading, "Grand Strategy," he asked, "Is sectarian violence now self-sustaining and thus beyond the capacity of the political process meaningfully to influence?"

What the fuck? Casey thought. If the answer was yes, then they might as well give up. "No," he said, and wrote "No" on his page of questions.

"Are we convinced that Shia leaders in Baghdad are serious about reining in the JAM and Shia death squads?" JAM, the paramilitary force loyal to Shia cleric Moqtada al-Sadr, remained powerful in many neighborhoods.

"No," Casey said, scribbling the answer in big capital letters on his sheet. He still attributed the Iraqi foot-dragging to inefficiency and incompetence rather than active delay so the Shia militia could increase its hold on parts of Baghdad. But he was watching Maliki and the others as closely as possible. There was some evidence, accompanied by deep suspicion, that the delays were intentional and that there was a purpose behind their lack of action.

"Are we prepared and well positioned to address more confrontational issues with the Kurds this year (oil, federalism, Kirkuk)?"

"No," Casey said. The United States had no leverage over the Kurds, the large ethnic group that lived in relative autonomy in northern Iraq.

Overall, Khalilzad said, currently the Sunnis and Shia did not accept each other as credible partners and had not agreed on the terms of the partnership.

Hadley then launched into a long discussion of what was called "a Dayton-like process," referring to the celebrated and successful negotiation in 1995 when Richard Holbrooke, the chief Bosnia envoy in the Clinton administration, had called the leaders of the three warring parties in Bosnia to Dayton, Ohio. Shuttered away in private for weeks with the three, Holbrooke, a gifted and wildly self-confident negotiator, cajoled and threatened them until they agreed to a peace settlement. It would end years of killing. The price was a U.S. commitment of 20,000 troops, a small deployment in retrospect.

Casey felt there had not been a political strategy in Iraq since the December 2005 elections, and someone like Dick Holbrooke needed to be taken off the shelf to bring the Shia and Sunni leaders together, knock their heads together, and throw money at them to move the political process along. Back in the 1990s, Casey had been assigned to Holbrooke's team in the Balkans, and he considered Holbrooke a master. He had been there once when Holbrooke came out of the Belgrade office of Serbian President Slobodan Milošević, the notorious thug and war criminal. "Okay," Holbrooke had said, "I want the B-52s taken out from England and on TV now!" It was part of the theater of coercive diplomacy. Ten days later, a NATO bombing assault began.

On one of his many trips back to the States, Ambassador Khalilzad had looked for a building in which to hold a Dayton-like conference. He wanted to bring the Iraqi leaders to the United States and lock them in a room until they reached an agreement.

Casey said, "You can buy reconciliation. You put $2 billion to this thing in investment, and you could turn the south" of Iraq, which was dominated by Shia and was home to the richest oil supplies in the country.

But no Dayton-like conference was ever launched. Neither Holbrooke nor other Clinton officials involved in the Balkans issue were ever asked for advice or assistance.

Rumsfeld made it clear he was not happy with the session. Likewise, Casey left feeling it was an affront—Hadley's birthday present wrapped in 50 demeaning questions.

O'Sullivan prepared a SECRET summary of the July 22 discussion that was circulated to Hadley, Rumsfeld, Pace, Abizaid, Casey and Khalilzad. It began, "Overarching strategic question: What has changed about the situation in Iraq, and do these changes warrant alterations in our military and political strategies?"

It was an argumentative question, but she and Hadley had effectively sparked a strategy debate.

Hadley briefed the president about the results. The most pressing problem was that they didn't have a plan for securing Baghdad, where bodies were turning up each morning by the dozens.

In secure videoconferences during this period, the president asked whose job it was to bring security to Baghdad. Maliki would say Casey. Casey would say Maliki.

Asked later if this was accurate, Bush told me, "True," but added, "My mind works this way: If the responsibility is muddled, let's clear it. Ideally, the Iraqis would be in the lead. And, you know, Maliki wanted to be in the lead. And Casey wanted Maliki to be in the lead. We all wanted Maliki to be in the lead, but the problem was the strategy wasn't working. He wasn't ready to be in the lead. And [the goal] was clear, hold and build, except [the reality] was clear, and no build and no hold."

Bush said this showed "that the tactics are flawed, and we need to adjust. And that's what Steve's policy review was doing."

Rumsfeld had said over and over again that the United States needed to get its "hand off the Iraqi bicycle seat." Hadley told Rice and several others that he had come to disdain Rumsfeld's bicycle metaphor, in part because it triggered an unpleasant but relevant personal memory. In Hadley's telling, during the early 1950s, when he was in kindergarten in Toledo, Ohio, his father decided to teach him to ride a bike. Dutifully holding the bicycle seat, the father got his son going down the street at a fast clip.

"Great job!" his father yelled, as the young Hadley, wearing shorts and a short-sleeved shirt, pumped away at the pedals. But as his father's voice grew more distant, the boy realized he was on his own. He turned to look back and spilled right over, tearing up his knees and elbows. It would be two and a half years before he got back on a bicycle.

Now, when Rumsfeld said it was time to take the hand off the Iraqi bicycle seat, Hadley thought, "Well, there are costs and consequences of taking the hand off the bicycle if the lad falls over."

8

With the midterm congressional elections three months off, the Democrats stepped up their criticism of the war. A dozen top congressional Democrats, including House Minority Leader Nancy Pelosi and Senate Minority Leader Harry Reid, sent a letter to the president on July 30. "Far from implementing a comprehensive 'Strategy for Victory' as you promised months ago, your administration's strategy appears to be one of trying to avoid defeat," it read. "Meanwhile, U.S. troops and taxpayers continue to pay a high price as your Administration searches for a policy."

It concluded, "Mr. President, simply staying the course in Iraq is not working. We need to take a new direction."

They did not know that the president had reached the same conclusion, though he wasn't about to say so publicly.

On August 1, a roadside bomb detonated under a bus filled with Iraqi soldiers in northern Iraq, killing 23 and wounding 40. The next day, a suicide bomber killed 13 and wounded 26 in a well-to-do area of Baghdad, and two bombs placed in gym bags near a soccer field in a Shia area in west Baghdad exploded, killing 12 and wounding 14. Most of these victims were children. That was only a sampling of the extent and variety of the grisly slaughter.

In Steve Hadley's "GWB" file of pressing matters for the president's attention, the classified summary showed 150 attacks a day in Iraq, six an hour. The attacks included assaults on Iraqi facilities, bombs, IEDs, mines, sniper fire, ambushes, grenade and small arms, mortar, rocket and even surface-to-air fire.

DIA analyst Derek Harvey circulated a classified paper in August based on the latest intelligence. He forecast the inevitable fracturing of the country if the administration remained on the same course. The Iraqi government was failing; it had no chance of overcoming the violent Shia-Sunni hostilities. The Iraqi security forces had not changed or adjusted. The U.S. "catch-and-release" policy on insurgents who were picked up and detained was feeding them back into the population rather than removing them as a threat.

Harvey's paper soon acquired a nickname: "The Doomsday Paper."

The Baker-Hamilton Iraq Study Group continued its work behind closed doors. On Wednesday, August 2, members gathered in an ornate meeting room on Capitol Hill. Their first session was with a dejected Senate Republican leadership—Bill Frist of Tennessee, the majority leader, and Mitch McConnell of Kentucky, the number two. "It is pretty obvious," Frist said, "that hopes are falling in Iraq. There will be a real hard time unless things start to turn. A lot of big ifs have to go right to get to a safe and prosperous Iraq." McConnell said that Iraq needed at least reasonable stability. Referring to one of the largest, most notorious, authoritarian and repressive regimes in the Middle East, he said, "I'd settle for Egypt."

Nearly everyone laughed.

The next meeting was with the leadership of the Senate Armed Services Committee—Virginia Republican John Warner and Michigan Democrat Carl Levin. Levin, who would become committee chairman if the Democrats won control of the Senate, said that the Iraqis "think they have a security blanket. The bottom line is that right now patience is the watch word. The watch word should be that we're impatient. We're *damn* impatient."

Study group member Charles Robb thought that since the United

States had invaded Iraq, it had a moral obligation to stay until the Iraqis could restore order.

A conservative, hard-line, promilitary Democrat, Robb had been a young Marine captain during the mid-1960s when he was assigned as a military social aide to the White House. There, he met President Johnson's daughter Lynda Bird, and the two married at the White House on December 9, 1967. Robb went on to serve two tours in Vietnam, winning a Bronze Star as commander of a combat rifle company.

Robb had been pushing the idea of adding more troops on a temporary basis to stabilize Baghdad. "We have far too much skin in the game to just walk away on a fixed timetable," he argued. None of the other members seemed to agree.

Still active in Marine Corps matters, Robb knew General Pace and was proud that a Marine was finally chairman of the Joint Chiefs of Staff. So he floated his idea of adding forces to Pace. Was it possible? Was the military capable? In several conversations, Pace responded positively. But when the two exchanged e-mails, Pace seemed hesitant.

Robb was the only senator to serve simultaneously on all three national security committees—intelligence, armed services and foreign relations. During the session with Senators Warner and Levin, he inquired about a possible escalation, calling it a "surge," according to notes of the meeting. He picked the word out of the air because it reflected his view of a sudden increase that would eventually decrease. Was a "surge" possible?

Yes, said Senator Warner.

No, said Senator Levin.

But Robb had put the idea on the radar screen. As he said later, "Every river starts somewhere."

Lee Hamilton asked his favorite question: What should be the definition of success in Iraq?

"I would drop the word victory," Warner said. "Success is a stable Iraq that can take the reins of sovereignty."

Levin said, "Iraq will not have a democracy. The goal should be stability. But democracy should be mentioned."

Alan Simpson chimed in. "People are fed up with this war. Republicans are going to pay a huge price for this war in November. I think we're going to lose the election in November because of this war."

The study group members headed to the U.S. Institute of Peace in downtown Washington to meet with the commander of U.S. Central Command, General Abizaid, who appeared in uniform and handed out a PowerPoint presentation.

Here was the combatant commander responsible for Iraq before the group that was supposed to study the Iraq War, but Abizaid, as usual, talked about the entire region of his command—the Middle East, East Africa and Central Asia. He mentioned the problems of Pakistan with nuclear weapons and Saudi Arabia with its oil. He mentioned Sunni extremism in the Horn of Africa and the Shia revolutionary movement in Iran.

On intelligence, Abizaid said, "CentCom and CIA aim to be seamless on targeting data." Referring to human intelligence sources, he said, "Our HUMINT is at about 30 percent of what it should be, up about 10 percent from a few years ago. Now we get information from the Saudis based on a raid, it goes to the CIA, and the CIA gets us a target to hit in Iraq."

"What is the problem in Baghdad?" asked Panetta.

"To move a car bomb is not a problem," Abizaid said, "even with increased troops. The death squads have to be targeted. The insurgency has to be controlled. Both sides want civil war—al Qaeda because it serves Sunni extremism, the Shia militias because it will serve Shia extremism."

The general said he was "optimistic" that the violence would diminish before the holiday of Ramadan the next month. "Violence cannot be the measure of success," he said. His argument was an old one: the enemy—insurgents, al Qaeda or sectarian extremists—decided to launch attacks, and if the measurement of success was the level of violence, then the enemy was in charge.

Would a drawdown of U.S. forces be a signal of impatience? Robb asked. Or did the United States need to send more troops?

"We are trying to work ourselves out of a job in Iraq," Abizaid said. "The Iraqis do not believe that we are leaving. This is not a good dynamic, and it is the psychology of the region. We have to make clear to the Iraqis that 'It's your country. We'll help you to the extent possible, but it's your country.'"

What might be the sign of a tipping point in Iraq? Bob Gates asked.

"If the Iraq army dissolves," Abizaid replied, "if it becomes sectarian or quits serving the national government. Or if the Iranian government made a strategic decision to attack coalition forces and cause greater casualties. They might do that. You could end up with a Hezbollah-like situation in the south and a weak Iraq." Hezbollah is an Iranian-backed political and paramilitary extremist group based in Lebanon.

"We're putting a lot of chips on Maliki," Lee Hamilton remarked.

"We could lose Maliki," Abizaid said. "It would not, for instance, be as big a problem as if Karzai were to go"—a reference to Hamid Karzai, the president of Afghanistan.

Afterward, several members remarked how little Abizaid had talked about, or even seemed focused on, Iraq.

The next day, August 3, Abizaid testified before the Senate Armed Services Committee on Capitol Hill. Senator Levin asked the general if he believed that Iraq was sliding toward civil war.

"I believe that the sectarian violence is probably as bad as I've seen it, in Baghdad in particular," he replied, "and that if not stopped, it is possible that Iraq could move toward civil war."

His comments received prominent attention on that evening's national newscasts and landed the next morning on the front pages of *The New York Times* and *The Washington Post*.

Hadley had kept Rice informed of his efforts to get an internal strategy review going, and she was familiar with the 50-question grilling that he had meted out to Khalilzad and Casey. It was increasingly obvious to Rice that they didn't have a strategy. She wanted to reevaluate the strategy herself. But to be quite frank, she said, she didn't want "to do anything that would be above the radar screen in the heavy political breathing of the November elections." The administration did not need what she called "a hothouse story" that acknowledged Iraq had gotten so bad that they were considering a new approach. That would play into the hands of critics and antiwar Democrats.

On Friday, August 4, Rice appeared on an MSNBC cable news show for an interview with NBC White House correspondent David Gregory.

"I believe that we've made progress," she said. "No, I do not believe that it's failing."

"But," Gregory asked, "is there not some discussion about what happens if this doesn't work, a plan B?"

"David," she replied, "what you want to do is settle on a plan and then press as hard as you can to make that plan work. And that's where everyone's energies are at this point, and I think this plan is going to work."

The problem was that her statements weren't true. Plenty of energy was going into finding a new and better plan.

The next morning, Saturday, Rice left Washington for a weekend at the president's Crawford ranch, arriving about 11:30 A.M. She had lunch with the president and Hadley.

They had been hoping the sectarian violence would burn itself out, but it kept getting worse. The intelligence reports showed large-scale displacement of residents in Baghdad. Whole neighborhoods were being attacked by militias—both Shia and Sunni—and bodies continued to pile up at the average of 50 a day, some days far more. The violence was worse than at any other time during the war. Baghdad's neighborhoods had become a patchwork of self-protective enclaves. Burnt-out cars and trucks, barriers and walls created virtual forts dotting the vast city.

Rice told the president that she was worried that the very fabric of Iraqi society was rending. She held her hands in front of her and pulled them apart dramatically. The Iraqis, she said, weren't going to have anything to build on if they kept going at each other this way. The core of Iraqi civil society was in jeopardy.

"I think we all knew that that was the problem," Rice recalled.

In an interview two years later, the president acknowledged that Iraqi society indeed had been "rending."

"And the reason why is that, because in the absence of a government that is providing the average person security, they're choosing sides," he said. "If I might ask myself a question that you should be asking me here . . ."

"Please," I said.

"What caused you to believe that this was not inevitable?"

"Good question. And the answer?"

He said he believed people want to live in peace and eventually would reject the violence. But without an effective government, they weren't being given much chance. "They now found themselves in a situation where they had to rely on the local cat with the big gun."

The next day, Rice appeared on several of the Sunday morning talk shows. She voiced optimism and disagreed with negative assessments that Tim Russert quoted on NBC's *Meet the Press*. "Iraqis have made a choice for a unified government that can deliver for all Iraqis," she said. "And when I say Iraqis, I mean not just their leadership, which clearly has not made a choice for civil war, but their population."

On Monday, Bush and Rice held a joint press conference. The president cited Iraq as a "notable battleground in the advance of liberty," adding, "What the American people need to know is we've got a strategy."

By August 16, Bush was out on the campaign trail, stumping for Republicans in the upcoming November elections. At a political rally in Lancaster, Pennsylvania, he said that his war strategy was to keep on the offense. "The stakes are high," he declared to a crowd of 400 people at a Republican fund-raiser. "But I clearly see where we need to go."

•   •   •

That same week, Bush and Cheney, with Rumsfeld, Hadley and long-time adviser Dan Bartlett, had lunch at the Pentagon with four Iraq experts, including Reuel Gerecht, from the conservative American Enterprise Institute, and Eric Davis, a political scientist from Rutgers University.

Bush made it clear that he wished the United States got more credit for its efforts and sacrifice in Iraq.

The president noted the "mass psychology" that al Qaeda had inflicted in one solitary act—the February bombing of the Samarra mosque. Isn't there anything positive in Iraq? he asked.

Davis said that education was getting better and a civil society was beginning to emerge.

"Well, that won't matter if this cycle of revenge keeps accelerating," Gerecht said. "You need Americans monitoring the situation with a heavy American presence."

Exasperated, Bush said he was growing weary of the ingratitude on the part of the Iraqis. He said it was hard for him to understand.

9

On Thursday morning, August 17, the president gathered his war council in the windowless Roosevelt Room of the White House for a secret meeting on Iraq that Hadley had planned for nearly a month. The Situation Room, the normal venue for such an important meeting, was being renovated.

The temperature outside was headed toward 90 degrees, humid and muggy—vacation time for most anyone who could escape the summer doldrums of the nation's capital. Rice was away for a rare break—a five-day stay at the Greenbrier Resort in West Virginia. But in the West Wing, it was a time for reflection. Hadley had given the president special briefing material in advance, including the SECRET summary of the July 22 question-and-answer session with Casey and Khalilzad.

Above the mantel in the room, just a few steps from the Oval Office, hung a picture of Republican President Theodore Roosevelt, the Rough Rider himself, astride a great black horse. Solemn and determined, Roosevelt looks as if he and his horse might bound off the canvas.

"The situation seems to be deteriorating," the president began, acknowledging to his closest advisers a rebuttal of his public optimism. He said he was searching for a way to go. "I want to be able to say that I have a plan to punch back." He had to find a way to explain to the

American people what defeat might mean so they would understand the consequences. He recalled, as he often did, that Central Commander General John Abizaid had said that if the United States withdrew under pressure, the extremists and terrorists would follow to the United States. Defeat for the United States would embolden the enemy. They must "make it clear that we have a plan to defeat them," Bush said. "We need a clear way forward coming out of Labor Day." They had nothing close to a clear way forward that day, with less than three weeks to go.

The number of attacks in Iraq had risen to more than 900 each week. Bush was clearly unhappy, almost dejected. After nearly six years in office, the presidency—and the war—were wearing on him. He had turned 60 the previous month, and the photographs of the young Texas governor of the late 1990s contrasted with the gray-haired president who now sat before them. The high-octane optimism of the Bush persona was in remission.

"We get only rare glimpses of anything positive going on," he said, sounding disheartened. Mass bombings and killings in Iraq were the staple not only of the television news but often of the classified reports he received and the daily Iraq Note from the National Security Council staff. "Surely, something else is going on?" Bush asked.

At one point, trying to puncture the gloom, Rumsfeld interjected. "Terrific!" he said, referring to the president's opening remarks. "We need that leadership." Perhaps a new message, a new speech, could be used to "show that a defeat of the United States would amount to defeat of the Iraqi people," he proposed.

"We are constantly adjusting our tactics," the president said, repeating one of his favored lines, "but we're firm in our objectives." He cited Mosul, Iraq's second largest city, where the recent fighting had been brutal and slow. U.S. forces had fought hard, demonstrating a willingness to stay, he said.

"We have to fight off the impression that this is not winnable," the president said. Support for the war had plummeted. In a recent Gallup poll, 56 percent of Americans said the war was a mistake, as 41 percent said it was not. Bush's approval ratings hovered at about 37 percent.

"Can America succeed?" he asked, one of the few times he seemed to entertain the possibility that it might not. "If so, how? How do our commanders answer that?"

General Abizaid had joined the meeting through the secure video link, as had General Casey. Before they could answer, the president recounted his conversation with a widow of a soldier. The woman had said, according to the president, "Look, I trust you. But can you win?"

Then the president recited his goals—a free society that could defend, sustain and govern itself while becoming a reliable ally in the global war on terrorism. Then he added a dreary assessment, saying, "It seems Iraq is incapable of achieving that."

"The region is in a sour mood," General Abizaid said. "It seems like it's hitting an unseen tipping point." He said they needed to focus on and assist moderates such as Prime Minister Maliki, while always driving toward turning responsibility over to them. This was the theme Rumsfeld, Casey and he were still pushing. It was necessary to get the hand off the back of the bicycle seat, to take the training wheels off the Iraqi government.

Abizaid said he saw three big regional problems—conflict between the Muslim sects, the Shia and the Sunnis; the Israeli-Palestinian disputes; and the general undercurrents of extremism. Many others in the region were in the fight—the Pakistanis, the Afghans and the Iraqis. "The way we're focusing on this problem is too military. We need to help them help themselves." The political and economic elements needed more resources and attention. "We need to think about how to get a different message out," he said. The president was interested in a new message. Abizaid seemed to be missing the point the president was making: They had to consider a more fundamental change. Bush urged Abizaid to write his ideas and give them to Rumsfeld. The secretary reiterated his theme: "Help them help themselves."

"Senators," Bush said, "are now hearing intelligence briefings about the fact that Iraq is now in a civil war"—an idea that he had dismissed. "This is an important moment, and people are also looking at how things are going in Baghdad."

"We need a defining speech," said Khalilzad. It was another mind-bending moment. Bush had given dozens of speeches and public presentations on Iraq, many intended to be "defining." Like Abizaid, Khalilzad failed to recognize that the change the president was talking about meant more than rhetoric.

"We need to show how we deny a safe haven for terror," Casey said. That was one presumed accomplishment: Iraqis were not exporting terror to other countries. Terrorism was being imported into Iraq. "The plan is not unfolding fast enough for some people," Casey said. "Enduring success will only be achieved by Iraqis." The new Iraqi government of Prime Minister Maliki, in office less than four months, was still finding its legs. "It's moving forward at a better pace than the last government," Casey said. "There's steady progress, but it needs another four to six months. It's too soon to tell if the government will turn out good or bad."

Casey's forces were going to try to decrease the violence in Baghdad between then and Ramadan, the Muslim holiday barely a month away. Casey said they would try to increase local neighborhood efforts everywhere and try to transition Baghdad to the local security forces. Of the announced strategy of "clear, hold and build," he said, "Clearing is the easiest part. It is harder to hold. We're doing a transition of control to the Iraqi government in the provinces."

On the Iraqi security forces—army and police—Bush asked, "Is there a way to quantify how good they are?"

"The Iraqi army is in the fight. We're doing well," Casey answered, dodging half the question. He believed that the president still saw Iraq in terms of measuring how much damage was being inflicted on the enemy. Bush always asked about offensive operations. So Casey threw the commander in chief a bone. "We're killing 300 to 350 insurgents a month."

"We don't want to make this a body count," injected General Pete Pace. Pace hated body counts, the clear echoes of Vietnam; he knew it was a false measure, and that using numbers as a metric of success could be seen by the troops as encouragement to kill more. Because the mission in Iraq was to get out of the country, killing more did not necessarily help. But Pace submitted to the president's intent. "We've gotten thousands," he said.

Bush stated that the numbers were just for his personal comfort level, but for Casey it was another sign the president did not get it.

Casey and others knew three wars were raging in Iraq. First, there was the battle with the Sunni insurgency, including those from Saddam's Baath Party. Second, there was a fierce conflict with the terrorist al Qaeda network that had sprung up inside Iraq only after the invasion. Third, there was an increasingly violent sectarian war between the Sunni minority and the Shia majority.

"Ninety percent of the sectarian violence is within 30 miles of the center of Baghdad," Khalilzad said. "We need to get the different forces in Iraq to come together." He ran through the political priorities—equal distribution of oil and gas revenue, letting more of the lower-ranking former Baathists into the government, and curbing the role of the local militias, which were increasingly sectarian and violent. Another headache was the Ministry of Interior, which oversaw the sectarian and corrupt national police, and which needed drastic overhaul and reform.

"Folks are not in a compromising mood," Casey said. "We have to force action in this timeline." Two months earlier, in June, he had presented his SECRET three-phase timeline that would lead to Iraqi self-reliance in 2009.

Bush turned to the thorny problem of the Iraqi police and reminded General Casey somewhat sarcastically that the general had said 2006 would be "The Year of the Police." So, the president inquired, how's that going?

"We're doing a good job of building them up," Casey answered. "It will be completed in 2006." A new program to pull the police off-line for inspection and training was under way and would be complete by year's end. He was moving forward with an effort to bring American soldiers into Baghdad police stations.

Rumsfeld asked if there was anything that could be done to better advise Prime Minister Maliki to develop a plan, show if it were on track, and force dates for action.

"This is a critical issue," Khalilzad replied, "but it is hard to threaten the Iraqi government." The United States had little leverage. This flew in the face of the simple fact that the United States occupied the country. "You can only just drink tea with them," Khalilzad said, referring to his endless sessions with Iraqis that produced meager results.

The focus turned to Bush's statement that they needed a plan with concrete, measurable steps, rather than abstract goals.

Philip Zelikow, the State Department counselor who was sitting in for Rice, said there were four important conditions that were favorable for the coalition. The enemy was unpopular with the Iraqi people; the Iraqi government was getting better; the United States was growing more experienced; and most of the violence was not aimed at overthrowing the government.

Turning back to Baghdad, the president said, "It looks pretty bad."

"There's really a difference of views on the threat," Khalilzad said. The Shia majority, which controlled the government, wanted to go after al Qaeda and the Baathists. "To them, the Shia death squads are defensive. All their enemies are Baathists. On the Sunni side, the real problems are Shia militias and Iran," which was supporting the militias.

"How are we doing on al Qaeda?" Bush asked. "Do we have enough manpower to do Baghdad and keep taking on al Qaeda and the Baathists?"

"We have an effort against al Qaeda that is keeping a steady operational tempo," Casey answered.

"Lots of people being picked up," Rumsfeld said. "Lots of people being interrogated."

"Just uncovered a big car bomb network in Baghdad," Casey added. "We don't need more troops to do that. In Baghdad, we have enough for right now." He had just doubled the number of U.S. forces in Baghdad from about 7,000 to 14,000. The Iraqis would have to "hold" the areas that had been cleared, the general said, but he said he wasn't sure the Iraqis could deliver.

Bush had always maintained that he had to let the generals run the war. The problem during the Vietnam War, he told me in 2002, was that "the government micromanaged the war"—both the White House and Secretary of Defense Robert S. McNamara. During Vietnam, Bush had been a Texas Air National Guard F-102 pilot, though he had never served in combat. "I remember my pilot friends," he said, "telling me that over Thud Ridge"—the path American jets took to Hanoi—"they could only fly a certain time, and the enemy knew when they were coming."

Micromanaging the war from the White House had been a red line for Bush. The generals' words almost always were unchallenged gospel. He did not want to second-guess them. He would regularly ask if they had everything they needed.

All that was about to change.

"We must succeed," Bush said. "We will commit the resources to succeed. If they"—the Iraqis—"can't do it, we will." In a direct challenge to Rumsfeld, the president used the bicycle seat analogy. "If the bicycle teeters," he declared, "we're going to put the hand back on. We have to make damn sure we cannot fail. If they stumble, we have to have enough manpower to cope with that."

"I've got it," said Casey. "I understand your intent." What he didn't quite understand was just how much his world was about to change.

The president was not done. Did Casey need the permission of Prime Minister Maliki to deal with the Shia militia—especially those led by Moqtada al-Sadr?

Yes, Casey said, he did indeed need Maliki's approval to go after targets in the Sadr City enclave. "Maliki claims that he's working with [Moqtada al-]Sadr, that he may have a deal there." Maliki had refused to okay five missions against Shia death squad members in Sadr City and nearby areas, Casey said. "'If you're not going to let us go after them,' I tell Maliki, 'then ask Sadr to give these people to us.'" So, Casey said, "Maliki is exercising his sovereignty." The United States and the coalition had technically ended the occupation three years earlier, formally declaring that Iraq was a sovereign nation. As the president knew, Maliki didn't see the death squads as a threat. He himself had no political base and believed he needed the Shia extremists who supported him to one extent or another.

"If the Shia believe that we're hitting the Sunni extremists, that we're hitting al Qaeda, then won't that reassure them?" Bush asked.

"Well," Casey said, "70 percent of our effort—targeting—is against al Qaeda and the Baathists, 30 percent against the death squads." So he had a credible case to make to Maliki.

"How's Maliki doing?" Bush asked.

"He's a dramatic improvement over his predecessor," Khalilzad said, referring to the former interim prime minister Ibrahim al-Jafari, who was too close to the Iranians and Moqtada and was known as the "fog machine" because he talked endlessly and in circles. "He's decisive. He works at a faster pace, relatively speaking." But he was constrained by the bigger forces of Shia cleric Moqtada al-Sadr and Abdul Aziz al-Hakim, leader of the largest Shia political party in Iraq.

Casey agreed with that assessment. "Maliki's a little more like Allawi"—Ayad Allawi, the CIA-supported Shiite who was the first prime minister in 2004. "He's still getting his legs as prime minister." Though Maliki viewed the Baathists as the universal enemy, he had included some Sunnis in the government.

Bush reminded them that he had thought the Camp David conclave two months earlier would produce benchmarks for Iraqi political progress.

Khalilzad said he was trying to put something together, especially on fuel subsidies and a law on investments. But on political issues, the ambassador said, it was just very hard. The implication was that it was not doable.

"Every quarter," Pace said, "governments report to their populations on how they're doing. Maybe the Iraqi government ought to make a report to the Iraqi people quarterly on how it's doing."

That's a new idea, Khalilzad said charitably.

"You may need to consider it," the president said. But he wanted to go to larger issues. "Is there a normal life at all for the people of Iraq?" he asked. Since the invasion, he had asserted that the Iraqis, as all people did, craved freedom. Now his question was more basic. "Is there some matrix you can use to describe what life is like for the people in Iraq?"

"You can see at night, when you fly over, lights are on," Rumsfeld said. "Currency is relatively stable. Schools are open."

"More children in school," Bush said, "universities are full. More electricity. So life is relatively normal?" He paused. "We can make that case?"

"Vast areas are doing well," Khalilzad said. "Seven million people have cell phones. The whole of the north is stabilizing. There is a building boom there. And part of the south is also doing all right."

Zelikow, who had made a dozen trips to Iraq, could not contain himself. "Mr. President," he said, "Baghdad is in terrible shape, and that's one quarter of the population of the country. There's violence all over the place." There were more than 150 violent attacks a day in the country—IEDs, car bombs, suiciders wearing vests of explosives, small-arms fire, ambushes, mortar, artillery, as well as some surface-to-surface and surface-to-air missiles. Zelikow named major cities and provinces outside Baghdad that were experiencing substantial violence—in the north, Mosul, Kirkuk, Diyala; Basra in the south; and Anbar in the west. "The conditions there are not normal," he said. "For millions of Iraqis, they're in daily struggles to survive that we can only barely understand."

As a professor of history, Zelikow had written about presidential decision making and the dynamics of a national security team under stress in his book *The Kennedy Tapes: Inside the White House During the Cuban Missile Crisis*. So perhaps it was the pained look on Bush's face or the discomfort in his body language. Perhaps Zelikow didn't want to be entirely out of step with the optimism or didn't want to be seen as a naysayer. Perhaps he simply could not overcome the old cliché that advisers fold in front of the president. Whatever the reason, Zelikow quickly shifted ground. "But one of the inspiring things about the reason why we're there," he said, "and why we need to help these people, is the heroism of ordinary Iraqis—thousands of people we never ever hear of who are putting their lives on the line to try to make things work in a desperately difficult situation."

Casey said that extremism in its many forms was itself a major problem that transcended the sectarian divide between Sunni and Shia. The death squads on both sides were pushing people into one camp or another. It was a struggle for power among the Iraqis. "We have to deal with that," Casey said.

Are al Qaeda fighters still streaming in? Bush asked.

"They are trying," Casey said. Abu Ayyub al-Masri, the current al Qaeda leader in Iraq, was "trying to pull in foreign talent."

"Don't understate the sectarian problem," Abizaid said. "There is a sectarian line that divides the whole Arab world. It runs right through Iraq. Religion is a way of life, and so a sectarian divide is profound. And this struggle in Iraq could be one that is defining for the whole region." He spoke with an air of historical understanding: History itself might be against the kind of new order that Bush envisioned.

Do you think Iraqi nationalism trumps religious convictions? Bush asked him. The U.S. approach was based on the presence of Iraqi nationalism, or at least reconciliation between the Shia and Sunnis.

"The center may not hold," Abizaid replied. "It's tottering. The battle for moderation is hugely important."

Was coexistence possible? Bush asked. "Because if not, a fix would be impossible."

The question hung in the room.

The United States could help shape it, Abizaid said. "We must shape it in Iraq."

Josh Bolten, 51, who had been chief of staff for 16 months, had been quiet. His predecessor, Andrew Card, had told him that his job would be "Iraq, Iraq, Iraq," so Bolten had immersed himself in the policy debate. He was the former editor of the *Stanford Law Review* and a Goldman Sachs investment banker. "It's most important for the Iraqi government to reach accommodation on how to divide power and resources. If it gets worse," Bolten asked, "what radical measures can the team recommend?"

A long silence followed. "Radical" was a word rarely used in the Bush White House, where core principles and courses of action seemingly had long ago been settled: Taxes must be reduced. Presidential power must be increased. The Iraq War must be waged and won.

Rumsfeld finally attempted an answer. "That's the back side of my earlier point. What do we do? There are things we can preview now and say, 'Here's what we may do. We could close bases, borders . . .'" He even proposed fashioning some external event, but he was vague about it and it was not clear what he meant. It seemed he did not catch the weight and drift of Bolten's suggestion of something "radical."

For the third time, the president returned to Baghdad. Could it be calmed down?

"Yes," Casey said. Operation Together Forward was under way, with thousands more U.S. troops brought into Baghdad from other parts of Iraq.

Hadley also had been silent for most of the time. The 2006 congressional elections were only 10 weeks off, and the possibility of losing Republican control of both the House and Senate seemed likely. The last years of the Bush administration were going to be rough no matter what, but he knew that if the Congress were lost, an unbelievably difficult road lay ahead.

"Is the effort to seek reconciliation with the Sunnis a fool's errand?" Hadley asked. It was one of the harshest, most explicit questions he had ever posed. "And is there any chance that that strategy can succeed?" The mere posing of the question by the man who was supposed to remain neutral was surprising. Could the Shia and the Sunnis work together? Was the very idea of Iraq, as one nation, even possible?

Too soon to tell, Khalilzad answered, but he added that the elements of reconciliation were not in place. "Sunnis are not yet really in the political process." After three elections in Iraq and three and a half years of war, he said, "Their issues are not being addressed yet." The rivalries remained intense. "This will take time. You can't win this by killing enough people without having reconciliation. Seventy percent of the population are against the Sunnis. But we can continue and we can try to close a deal, and then make a judgment."

The president returned to his opening question: "Can we succeed? If the answer is maybe, if there's doubt, then maybe we need another posture."

"We definitely can," Khalilzad said. "We're making progress." Paying some attention, as he put it, to Iran and Syria could help with that progress.

Casey agreed. "As I keep reminding Steve Hadley, the Iraqis know they are not going back" to the old order, he said.

The president said he was planning to give a speech that would put any new analysis, information and strategy together in the larger context, including the Palestinian and Israeli issues.

Perhaps recognizing that the meeting had been both directly and indirectly critical of Khalilzad and Casey, Cheney offered praise for the hard work that both the men were doing.

"I support you guys 100 percent," Bush chimed in, taking the cue. "But we need to ask tough questions. I hope that Ambassador Khalilzad and General Casey understand that. So that we can be confident, I have to tell you folks what's on my mind. If you can't answer the questions, that makes me nervous. These are difficult times; we need to ask some difficult questions."

Casey said he appreciated the hard questions, and the president adjourned the session.

But the sense of doom and the dark insinuation remained. The declaration that the president and vice president supported the generals "100 percent," of course, carried the not-so-subtle suggestion that the opposite was true. Some of the hard questions remained unanswered. Bush later told me that he was intentionally sending a message to Rumsfeld and Casey: "If it's not working, let's do something different . . . I presume they took it as a message."

10

————————

Though Meghan O'Sullivan was writing the daily TOP SECRET Iraq Note for the president, Bush often peppered her with questions when he saw her during the day at briefings or meetings in the Oval Office with Cheney, Hadley, chief of staff Josh Bolten or others. Several times it was just Bush and O'Sullivan. Not only was she the deputy national security adviser for Iraq, but she also had extensive personal contacts in Iraq whom she had kept in touch with for more than three years.

In early May 2003, when she had gone to Baghdad to work first for Jay Garner and then for Jerry Bremer, her first political job was to get to know the largest Shia party, SCIRI, the Supreme Council for Islamic Revolution in Iraq, which was obviously going to have a major say in the new Iraq. SCIRI leaders, who had extremist and Iranian ties, were reticent to build relationships with the United States. So at 33, O'Sullivan had driven her beat-up Hyundai all over Baghdad, stopping when she saw a SCIRI party sign and asking people, "Do you know anyone from this party? Do you know where I could find them?" She went knocking on doors like a saleswoman or a journalist. She made the rounds for almost a year and got to know the party leaders—Abdul Aziz al-Hakim and Adil Abd al-Mahdi. From the White House, she kept in touch with these Iraqis by phone and e-mail. So when Bush quizzed her, she spoke with some authority. More than a dozen times, he asked her questions such as "What are you hearing from people in Baghdad? What's it like in Baghdad? What are people's daily lives like? Can they get around? Do they live a normal life?"

His queries were growing in number and variety that summer. He was also more insistent. O'Sullivan was determined not to mislead or lie to him. So her answer was often simple: "It's hell, Mr. President."

Her reports contradicted the happy talk and positive spin from the military and the Baghdad embassy. She thought it was smart of Bush that he kept asking, and she could see his deep frustration. Her job was to get him good information, but she did not know, or would not say, how—or whether—he squared what she told him with the other reports.

Bush later confirmed to me that O'Sullivan's reports contradicted a lot of what he was hearing from Rumsfeld, Casey and Khalilzad.

"The whole time I'm asking the question, 'Are people able to live peaceful lives?'" the president recalled. O'Sullivan was saying no, and he agreed. "The answer's also no from the number of deaths I'm seeing and the number of, you know, the famous attacks chart." Also, the reports of 50 bodies a day showing up bound, with bullets in the back of the head.

"It's a sign that the strategy's not working," Bush said. "It becomes apparent when you're picking up reports saying, 'Twenty-five people murdered here. Thirty people's throats slit here. Fifty-five here. Ethnic cleansing. Refugees. Neighborhoods that were once mixed are now pure.' I mean, it was beginning to accelerate."

He added, "The fundamental question at this point in time, during this period of time, one would ask, 'Why do you think it's possible to design a strategy that will work in the face of what you're seeing every day?'" The answer, he said, was "People want to live in peace."

I noted that a desire to live in peace does not itself provide the means to achieve peace.

"Correct," he said, then added that the U.S. military could win battles. "Remember, every time we show up, we whip these people." The question, he said, was whether the Iraqi government could provide security, help people find work, and improve the availability of basic services.

"So you're pretty hot during this period?" I asked him.

"You mean, meaning angry?" the president said. "No, no, no."

"No, not angry, no," I said.

"Well, that's what hot means."

"Well, wait a minute," I said. "We've got increasing violence, we've got somebody like Meghan [O'Sullivan] and some of the intel people . . ."

"I'm concerned it's not working," he said. "Period."

"Right, exactly," I said. "And so your usual line is, fix it."

"Yeah, but in this case, yeah," the president said. "But this case, the fix-it was Stephen J. Hadley." Looking toward Hadley, who was sitting on a couch in the Oval Office, he asked, "Is it 'J'?"

"It is 'J,'" said Hadley. He added, as if to give the president a talking point, "But it was *your* team responding to *your* direction."

"Well," the president replied, "that's what I said."

Of course, what he had really said, what he had stressed again and again in our interviews, was that Hadley was the engine driving a lot of this.

"Sure," I said. "Other words, he's the head man in terms of implementation."

"He's the guy," the president said. "Look, here's the thing. Hadley knows me well enough that we don't need a major seminar to figure out that we got to do something different. So he starts a very thorough process and keeps me posted."

Iraq was the most important issue in Bush's presidency. He was commander in chief, and he knew the war was essentially failing. By his own account, he was thinking about it all the time. So I asked, "Did you give them a deadline at this point?"

"I don't think I did," the president said. "This is nothing that you hurry."

But how could there be no deadline, no hurry, three and a half years into a failing war?

•   •   •

When David Satterfield considered the credibility of the military's reports from Iraq, he thought back to early 2001, after Ariel Sharon had taken office as Israeli prime minister. Satterfield, then 46 and deputy assistant secretary of state for the Near East, had met with the new prime minister after midnight at his residence. One of the most controversial figures in Israel's history, Sharon had been a military general and later defense minister. That night, Sharon devoured a huge platter of sushi while giving a lecture, repeatedly stubbing his finger on the table for emphasis. He predicted he would remain in power for years, because while he did not have the support of the extreme right and certainly not the left, he claimed he had the all-important center.

"I will tell you something else," Sharon insisted. "I was a general. I know the generals lie. They lie to themselves and they lie to the politicians. They will never be able to lie to me."

It was a great speech, Satterfield thought, and good advice. After a year of listening to General Casey's briefings in Iraq, which presented the prospects through the most rose-colored lens, Satterfield had asked him, "George, explain to us what's happening on the ground. How are you assessing what 'clear' means? What 'secure' means? We see these color charts of this neighborhood cleared. What does it mean? How are your metrics coming out? We want to see the tracking, day by day, week by week."

Casey's response was "It's tough. We're moving. We're succeeding." Satterfield didn't think Casey or the military were lying. That was just the way they did business, clinging to their optimism and can-do spirit. But he couldn't shake the memory of Sharon's edict: The generals lie to themselves and lie to the politicians.

"Senator, are we winning in Iraq?" NBC's David Gregory asked Arizona's John McCain on the Sunday, August 20, 2006, episode of *Meet the Press.*

"I don't think so," McCain replied, "but I'm not sure that it's turned into a civil war. . . . But it's a very difficult situation. We've got to win, we do—still do not have enough of the kind of troops we need over there, and it's going to be a very difficult process."

"The president has said repeatedly that he has a strategy to win," Gregory said, "that if his commanders want more forces, they will get them. Should more troops be sent?"

"Well, I think it's been well documented now that we didn't have enough there from the beginning, that we allowed the looting, that we did not have control," McCain replied. "We make mistakes in every war, and serious mistakes were made here. The question is, are we going to be able to bring the situation under control now? I still believe we can."

"Do you think military commanders on the ground are asking for more troops?" Gregory asked.

"I know that military commanders on the ground need more troops," McCain replied.

The next day, August 21, despite the criticisms that were now building from allies and opponents alike, with some like McCain calling for more troops and others demanding a timeline for withdrawal, the president passionately defended his Iraq policy in a news conference. He acknowledged that the increasing sectarian violence and growing U.S. casualties were "straining the psyche of our country," but he argued that withdrawing from Iraq too quickly would carry grave consequences.

"Leaving before the job was done would send a signal to our troops that the sacrifices they made were not worth it. Leaving before the job is done would be a disaster," Bush said.

"You know, it's an interesting debate we're having in America about how we ought to handle Iraq," he said, not mentioning the behind-the-scenes debate that was now under way within his own administration. "There's a lot of people—good, decent people—saying, 'Withdraw now.' They're absolutely wrong. It would be a huge mistake for this country."

He insisted that the war in Iraq was vital to the larger struggle against global terrorism. "If you think it's bad now, imagine what Iraq would look like if the United States leaves before this government can defend itself and sustain itself."

The president's once ambitious goals for Iraq seemed to have evaporated. No longer able to argue that the U.S. presence was making the
situation in Iraq better, he was left to argue only that leaving would
make it worse.

On Thursday, August 24, General Abizaid toured two of Baghdad's violent neighborhoods, accompanied by *Washington Post* columnist David
Ignatius and a CBS reporter. For several months, Casey had thrown
thousands of additional U.S. troops into the capital to restore security
under Together Forward, meaning that U.S. and Iraqi forces would
team up to regain control of the capital. As they tramped around in the
115-degree summer heat, Abizaid asked an Iraqi dressed in a white
knitted prayer cap and robe if security had improved. "Thank God,
yes!" he replied. Though somewhat skeptical, Ignatius reported that
the murder rate in Baghdad had dropped 41 percent that month, and
his column in the *Post* the next day was headlined, "Returning Some
Order to Iraq's Mean Streets."

The next day, Casey issued a SECRET commander's assessment.
"Baghdad security improving but still long way to go," he said, adding
optimistically, "On track to make noticeable impact by Ramadan"—the
next month.

The SECRET report contained statistics from Operation Together
Forward, phase two, and said precisely—the military was always
precise—that as of August 25, "buildings cleared: 33,009. Mosques
cleared: 25. Detainees: 70." That was an astounding amount of dangerous work for the troops, often going into buildings virtually blind,
never sure whether the place was rigged with explosives or full of
armed fighters. During this period, the report said, the military had
taken only 70 detainees. That meant that nearly 500 buildings had to
be cleared to apprehend each suspected insurgent, al Qaeda terrorist
or sectarian extremist.

I asked President Bush about this August 25 report and told him I
was astonished when I saw that they had cleared so many buildings and
captured only 70 detainees. It meant that the enemy was moving out
ahead of U.S. troops, waiting for them to leave before they returned.

"Oh, I can't remember my reaction to that meeting," the president said, before offering advice about how to write this book. "Look, use all this to paint the general environment of, it isn't working, Bush starts the process—"

But I wanted to know what he had said to his commanders. "Did you say to General Casey—"

"I can't remember."

"Or Rumsfeld, 'Don, General, this isn't working.'"

"I can't remember what I told them."

Hadley interrupted and said that Rumsfeld and Casey were "partly telling him it's not working" because the statistics showed the problems.

Yet Casey had mentioned the 33,000 buildings as an accomplishment.

"I can't give you the interface [with] these men," Bush said, "because I can't remember it."

But at the time, David Satterfield at the State Department was appalled when he saw the report. Just more numbers, he thought. It was a smoke screen. It made no sense. CIA reports and other intelligence showed that soon after the buildings were cleared, various extremist or violent elements—especially the Shia militias—moved right back in. The Iraqi forces that were supposed to join in and "hold" the neighborhoods and buildings had never arrived at full strength. And staying behind to "hold" was not part of the mission of the limited U.S. forces, despite what the clear-hold-and-build strategy said on paper.

Satterfield wished that the president, Cheney, Rice, Hadley, or Rumsfeld—somebody—had responded to Casey's reports along the lines of "George, this doesn't make sense to me." Instead, they had only nodded. Often, discussion at the NSC would descend into a Kabuki or formalized pantomime: Casey would give his report. The president would ask if Casey needed more forces. Casey would say he didn't, and General Pace, the JCS chairman, would remind the president that whatever was necessary could be made available.

At principals meetings—the NSC without the president—Rice on several occasions blasted Casey's optimistic reports in front of Cheney, Hadley, Pace and others. Once she said, "We've had years of over-confident briefs by the military, gliding past the emergent problem. The president needs to be focused on the skeptical case, not the best case."

She maintained to her senior staff that she thought Pace, Casey and the senior military officials were "honest guys" who just got caught up in meaningless numbers and metrics and were no longer measuring the real problem of sectarian violence.

She never brought her complaints directly to the president for two reasons. First, she was an optimist, as was the president. "Everybody has a tendency toward optimism," she said. In fact, the president almost demanded optimism. He didn't like pessimism, hand-wringing or doubt. Second, Rice claimed that as secretary of state, she didn't feel it was appropriate to criticize Rumsfeld or Casey to the president. The military was their realm, not hers, and the president should judge their information and advice on its merits. "It's not that they're trying to pull the wool over the president's eyes," she maintained. "It's not that they're trying to deceive him."

So there never was direct conversation, and the Kabuki went on.

"Unless you are pretty blind," Rice said, it was obvious "this just isn't going in the right direction."

When Rice returned from her five-day vacation in West Virginia that August, she asked her staff for copies of all the major cables from Baghdad, including intelligence reports and estimates. She took the paperwork and some computer discs back to her apartment in the Watergate complex and spent a few days alone reevaluating the past year and the road ahead—and addressing the question: What is going on in Iraq?

She found two especially distressing issues. First, bringing the minority Sunnis into the political process—the so-called political reconciliation—was supposed to stop the insurgency, but it hadn't. Second, the bombing of the Golden Mosque at Samarra had set off ethnic tensions and violence that had deeply infected the political process. How could reconciliation occur when government officials themselves were condoning and even inciting violence? The only slightly positive development was Anbar province, where it looked as if al Qaeda was wearing out its welcome and the population was turning against it.

On August 30, in Salt Lake City, Utah, Bush argued that leaving Iraq would be a total disaster.

"If we leave before Iraq can defend itself and govern itself and sustain itself, this will be a key defeat for the United States of America in this ideological struggle of the 21st century," he said.

"If we leave before the job is done, we'll help create a terrorist state in the heart of the Middle East that will have control of huge oil reserves. If we leave before the job is done, this country will have no credibility. People will look at our words as empty words. People will not trust the judgment and the leadership of the United States. Reformers will shrink from their deep desire to live in a free society. Moderates will wonder if their voice will ever be heard again. If we leave before the job will be done, those who sacrificed, those brave volunteers who sacrificed in our United States military will have died in vain. And as General Abizaid has said, if we leave before the job is done—if we leave the streets of Baghdad—the enemy will follow us to our own streets in America."

In the streets of Baghdad that day, the enemy had kept plenty busy. A string of explosions ripped through predominantly Shiite neighborhoods in the capital city, killing at least 43 people and capping a week in which more than 300 Iraqis and 18 American service members died violent deaths.

The next day, August 31, Casey's updated SECRET commander's assessment said, "Baghdad security continues to progress. Attacks up slightly as enemy challenges security plan. Buildings cleared in Operation Together Forward Phase II: 41,054."

So Casey had cleared another 8,000 buildings in six days, yielding another several dozen detainees. But the operation wasn't "together" in any sense because the Iraqis weren't showing up, and it was hardly "forward" because the violence was up—as usual.

Despite the 50 questions from Hadley that zeroed in on the essence of the strategy, the tough session with the president just two weeks before, and the increasing violence, Casey held firmly to his leave-to-win strategy. He continued to report that within the next 12 to 18 months, Iraqi security forces could take over the security responsibilities for the country with very little U.S. support.

The violence unfolding outside the fortified Green Zone told a different story. Just after ten that morning, a bomb inside a vendor's cart at a bustling Baghdad market killed at least 24 citizens and wounded 35 others. South of the capital, a bicycle rigged with explosives killed another dozen people near an army recruiting center. And a car bomb near a gas station in Baghdad killed two civilians and wounded 21, including five Iraqi policemen. *The New York Times* reported that scattered throughout the city authorities found another 13 bodies.

11

Seven members of the Iraq Study Group, including Baker and Hamilton, landed in Baghdad on August 31. They were given flak jackets and helmets and rushed onto attack helicopters for the five-minute flight to the Green Zone.

They flew over the sprawling brown, low-rise housing and burned-out blocks of the capital city, with the helicopters shooting flares as a precaution against shoulder-fired missiles and a gunner leaning out an open window to scope out any threats in the city below.

In the Green Zone, they were herded into a waiting fleet of armored Humvees, each with a medic seated in the back. The security measures, routine for most of the American occupation, were jarring to newcomers.

The group met with Prime Minister Maliki first. The meeting took place in an ornate, ceremonial room in one of Saddam's former palaces. They sat in wooden chairs and were served tea.

"It will be very useful for you to know that the Iraqi people are living in freedom," Maliki, surrounded by a large staff, said through an interpreter. "Never before in history have the Iraqi people lived in freedom. This is a treasure the Iraqi people will never give up. . . .

"Success has been achieved," he said, adding, "There is trouble. This is natural. It happens in every democracy. . . .

"There is progress, clearly seen in the decline in the number of explosions."

The study group members looked at one another.

"We have political stability," the prime minister continued. "Despite bloody scenes, progress is under way. . . .

"The terrorists used to be on the offensive. Now we are."

This triggered some stirring in the wooden chairs, but no one challenged the prime minister.

Asked about the security situation, Maliki said, "The real problem is Baathists. And we have steps that we will follow to weaken them further."

More shifting in the chairs.

Hamilton was taken aback. Maliki seemed seriously out of touch, or else he simply wouldn't acknowledge what was going on. He seemed programmed to say what he thought Americans would want to hear.

Maliki acknowledged that the Iraqi army was trained and equipped better than the police. "The problem with the police is the presence of the Mokhaberat [Saddam's former intelligence service] and former regime loyalists," he said.

It was a remarkable statement. He was referring to groups of Sunnis and Baathists, when the real problem with the police was its assistance to the Shia death squads.

What would be the outcome of a vote in Iraq on the U.S. presence? Panetta asked.

"We do not have public opinion polls in Iraq," Maliki said. "There are definitely those who talk about the Americans leaving. But it is the top-level people who will decide, and we want you to stay."

The prime minister asked only one question himself, and it came at the end of the hour-long interview.

"Are Americans—Republicans and Democrats—drawing close to withdrawal from Iraq?" he asked.

"You'll have your answer on November 7," Baker said.

Election day.

•   •   •

On September 1, the morning after their interview with Maliki, the members of the Iraq Study Group met with Iraqi National Security Adviser Mowaffak al-Rubaie. Rubaie, a Shia and a neurologist by training, had left Iraq in the early 1980s to study in Britain, returning after the American invasion.

Rubaie said the Sunni insurgency had to be pursued and crushed. Baker asked about the Shia militias, adding, "They have not renounced violence, either."

"Yes, but it's different. The militias are different," Rubaie said. "Moqtada al-Sadr is using violence, but he's using it to gain power *within* the government."

"But they just killed 100 Iraqis yesterday," Baker said.

"Yes, but this is different. He is expanding his power and authority in the government," Rubaie said.

Baker asked if he was making a distinction between those who want to overthrow the government and those who use violence to seek power within the government.

"Yes," Rubaie said.

The Iraqi government's national security adviser was essentially condoning the violence of the Shia militias. It was a very sobering moment.

Later that day, the group met with Barham Salih, a Kurd and deputy prime minister of Iraq. Salih was a balding man in his mid-40s, with a mustache, wire-rimmed glasses and an easy smile. After leaving Iraq in 1979, he had earned engineering and statistics degrees from universities in Wales and England. For years he represented the Patriotic Union of Kurdistan (PUK) in London and Washington. And even as he worked in the fledgling Iraqi government, his wife and two children remained at their home in Maryland.

Salih spoke almost flawless English and was a smooth operator. Many at the American embassy asked the study group members, "How's Barham?" They acted as though he were an American. The Kurd clearly had won over officials at the embassy.

Salih noted that Sunni and Kurdish leaders who didn't want the United States to leave tended to blame Iran for everything. They knew that argument would appeal to Americans.

"Iran doesn't want to break up Iraq," Salih said. "Iran wants a weak Iraq. It wants the U.S. stuck in a quagmire. When the world relied on Saddam to balance Iran, it led to polarization and genocide in Iraq. Now the Iranians are worried about a democratic, federal Iraq and its impact on their regime. Terrorism and all the problems we face can be resolved, but Iran and Syria continue to work to destabilize us.

"The source of the problem is Syria and Iran. The Syria-Iran alliance must be broken. Syria needs to be taken out of the equation. The Syrians are getting the Iraqis killed. They are allowing terrorists across their borders. They are allowing Baathists safe haven in Syria."

Salih was very at ease as he offered his advice, speaking almost as if he were a U.S. official. "If *we* win in Iraq, *we* transform the Middle East," he said. "The mission is doable, but it requires tough choices. Iraq is not Somalia. It is the epicenter of the Middle East. The United States has sufficient political and military allies in Iraq to prevail."

Salih was providing the narrative the Bush administration wanted to hear: We can do this. There's progress. But Iran is screwing everything up.

Still later that day came a session with Abdul Qader al-Obeidi, the Iraqi minister of defense. Obeidi, a Sunni Arab, had been a general in the Iraqi army under Saddam Hussein. He had once told parliament that he had been demoted for opposing the 1990 invasion of Kuwait. The study group members had heard repeatedly in advance what a great guy he was. Military officials said he was the take-charge type, no-nonsense, always professional. If there was any criticism of him, it was that he was too technocratic; he didn't play politics.

He was upbeat during the interview.

"We are in the first stages of the [Baghdad security] plan," Obeidi said. "The results are better than expected. Entering Sadr City will be a problem because they have lots of weapons there and clever leaders. Other regions of the city have similar problems. We will address them in the future. . . . I have faith that the security will be in place and that the minister of interior will be able to maintain security and develop the capacity of the police."

"Yesterday," Lee Hamilton said, "54 people were killed in Baghdad and 196 injured. Headlines in America will focus on this violence. That causes support among Americans to drop, and that support for the war has continued to drop in America."

"The main sources of violence are car bombs, explosive devices and indirect fire," Obeidi responded. "Since the end of 2004, terrorist attacks have dropped." This clearly was not true. "Terrorists have not been able to take on a police station. Terrorist operations are not quality operations. They tend to target civilians and innocent people."

Obeidi said he broke down al Qaeda into two groups—those from outside the country who do nothing but kill and those from inside the country, "whom we can come to an agreement with. The biggest source of violence in Iraq is disagreement over politics, because all politicians have armed groups."

He then joked that it would help if they killed more politicians. "The politicians are killing innocent people," he continued. "What happened yesterday—the 54 killed in Baghdad—is a response from one politician to another politician. It is not terrorism."

It was a startling observation. Much as Mowaffak al-Rubaie had seen no problem with Sadr's killing of people for political ends, the Iraqi defense minister saw the recent killings as just part of the political process.

Panetta had begun to sense a theme: Shias did the Shia thing. Sunnis did the Sunni thing. And they all had their militias to protect them. It became increasingly clear, not to mention entirely depressing, that many Iraqi leaders accepted violence as a legitimate and necessary tool of politics.

The next morning, September 2, the group headed to the heavily fortified U.S. embassy to hear an assessment from CIA officials. When asked about the Iraqi government, the operatives said it was remarkable and commendable that Iraqi government employees show up for work at all, given the threats and violence they faced.

The CIA station chief told them, "Maliki was nobody's pick. His name came up late. He has no real power base in the country or in parliament. We need not expect much from him. We continue to be amazed that the Iraqis accept such high levels of violence. Maliki thinks two car bombs a day, 100 dead a day, is okay. It's sustainable and his government is survivable."

The official also worried about the Ministry of Interior, which ran the national police: "The Ministry of Interior is uniformed death squads, overseers of jails and torture facilities. Their funds are constantly misappropriated."

The bottom-line judgment: "We won't lose so long as we are in Iraq, but how long are we willing to stay? For sure, it falls apart if we leave. By nature, I am an optimist," the station chief said, but then added he was not very optimistic about the situation.

Later that day, the group met with Bayan Jabr, Iraqi's minister of finance, who had a reputation as a malicious, underhanded sectarian leader. When he was asked about corruption within the government, Jabr brushed the question aside, saying, "Corruption used to be a problem in previous governments, but now it's under control. We have an audit board."

It was an absurd statement. The Americans knew it. The Iraqis knew it. Members of the study group certainly knew it.

The members gathered at the U.S. embassy the next morning, September 3, to meet with Lieutenant General Pete Chiarelli, Casey's deputy and the commander of all U.S. ground forces in Iraq.

Chiarelli, a Seattle native with two master's degrees, had served a year in Iraq as a two-star division commander. A total of 160 men and women in his division, the 1st Cavalry Division, had been killed. Chiarelli had long been a leading proponent of soldiers embracing the local people, helping rebuild, hooking up sewer lines and kicking down fewer doors. The "point of penetration," he argued, was armed social

work. Given the Iraqi culture of revenge and honor, killing and arrest-
ing Iraqis only made things worse, further alienating an already alienated population.

Most generals are monotone models of calm disconnect, speaking
in PowerPoint mode—cool and composed—using sterile statistics. But
Chiarelli was passionate, forceful, emphatic.

"We could go into Sadr City," he said right off the bat, "but the Iraqi
government has to make an unequivocal commitment to go after Sadr
City. We cannot do it alone." It was essential to understand the population, he added. "Iraqis care about security, electricity, water, sewage
and health care, in that order."

The current environment was too sectarian, he said. "When the
U.S. government changes, you don't worry whether or not your electricity will be cut off. Iraqis have to worry about that." Living conditions were appalling. "Trash in Sunni neighborhoods is waist high.
Electricity is less than two hours a day. Banks are closing because the
finance minister orders them to close. The government ministries, the
service providers, are contributing to the conditions that lead to violence." It was astonishing the many steps the Shia-led government
would take *not* to help certain people, he said.

"If this government doesn't get its act together to win the confidence of the people, it will fail," the general said. "Otherwise, you have
to create a security force" of army and police so big that we set up "the
creation of another strongman" like Saddam.

Well, Baker asked, isn't chaos worse than having a large security
force?

"We have taken the Iraqi army as far as it can go," Chiarelli said,
"without the support of its own government." The Shia and Sunnis
have to learn how to govern together, he added. Reconciliation held the
key to success.

Gates's question was one he asked frequently: What about the consequences of catastrophe in Iraq? Leading the witness, he said he
thought the geopolitical implications of failure in Iraq far exceeded
those of failure in Vietnam.

"The comparisons of strategic importance are not even close,"

Chiarelli agreed. "Iraq is a war of the future, and you have to under-stand the nonkinetic aspects, which are more important than the use of force."

Chiarelli reiterated the quality-of-life issues, which he felt were central to success. He had seen the practical benefits of "full-spectrum operations," meaning that his soldiers didn't stick only to typical in-fantry tasks but also worked on civil projects—water and sewer lines, restoring electricity, opening schools—that won favor with the popula-tion. The unemployment problem, perhaps as high as 40 percent, was a threat to his soldiers, Chiarelli said. Conversely, when his men had studied the municipal water supply systems and solved some of the water problems in Baghdad, it had a noticeable impact.

He said that Moqtada al-Sadr had built his support in part by controlling key ministries such as transportation, health and agricul-ture. Chiarelli knew that game well: Control the services, control the people.

After the general left, the members commented on how direct and impressive he had been. Baker and Hamilton wondered aloud if they should recommend to President Bush that Chiarelli be given a fourth star and Casey's job.

Bill Perry later took Chiarelli aside privately. The administration and Pentagon line was that they did not need more troops. But Perry wanted the straight scoop from a commander on the ground.

"This isn't working," Perry told Chiarelli, noting that the two To-gether Forward operations had failed to secure Baghdad.

Chiarelli agreed.

"If I were the secretary of defense," Perry said, "and I were to come over here and look at the situation, I would say this isn't working and we don't have much more time. Politically, time is running out on us. So I'm willing to give you another four or five brigades to secure Bagh-dad. First of all, would that help?"

"No," Chiarelli replied, Perry recalled.

"I'm prepared to do it. What's your answer?" Perry pressed.

"No," Chiarelli said. "Unequivocally, no."

"And then he gave me a long list of reasons," Perry said. The list boiled down to the fact that this was not a military problem but rather a political one, and it must be solved by the Iraqis—their people, their army and their police—and not by the U.S. military.

Leon Panetta recalled that Chiarelli told the group, "We're not going to win this thing militarily. We're only going to win it when we provide jobs to people, when we meet their basic needs, when we clean the trash up, when we deliver water, when we deliver electricity. Until we do that, we're fighting a losing war."

12

Next, the study group met with Lieutenant General Martin Dempsey, who was in charge of training the Iraq army, and Major General Joseph Peterson, who commanded the units training Iraqi police.

Dempsey said they had trained the targeted number of Iraqi military, but without national reconciliation it was useless. "If they don't make that progress by the end of the year," he said, "there are not enough troops in the world to provide security."

Peterson struck a different tone.

"The widespread pessimism about the police is unwarranted," he said. "So many people in the media and elsewhere emphasize the bad and overlook the good. Today in Iraq, the police are standing up and fighting. They are doing a lot of good in a lot of places."

This contradicted almost everything the group had heard about the police, including from the CIA station chief, who had told them the day before that their ministry ran death squads and torture facilities.

The study group members had come to the small conference room within the embassy dressed in suits, a show of respect toward Iraqis. As General Peterson was finishing, the door burst open, and in rushed Chuck Robb, in shirtsleeves. Normally reserved, Robb was steaming. He had ventured out into Baghdad and was dumbfounded by how much support the U.S. military had to provide to one of the Iraqi army's "showcase" units.

"Everything that is happening under the Baghdad security plan is because of the American military and the Iraqi army, not the police," Robb said. He said a full U.S. Army company made up of several hundred soldiers was assigned to each neighborhood. "The police are not the disciplined group we are looking for."

Robb said he had talked with several ordinary Iraqis on the street and asked: Who would you pass tips along to if you knew about insurgents or terrorists or wrongdoing? "They said, 'The Americans. Not the Iraqi police,'" Robb reported.

General Peterson, his positive tale of progress suddenly undermined, said that U.S. forces hadn't finished clearing that particular neighborhood. After the clearing, the Iraqis would stand and hold it.

Robb shook his head no. He wasn't buying it. This was the military's showcase neighborhood and its showcase Iraqi unit, and all he had seen were American soldiers leading the way.

The study group members headed across the Green Zone to interview Abdul Aziz al-Hakim.

Hakim, head of the powerful Shia party, the Supreme Council for Islamic Revolution in Iraq, had not been on the original interview list. But everyone kept mentioning how influential he was, how he and Moqtada al-Sadr were the real Shia power players, though neither had an official role in the government.

At Hakim's palace in the Green Zone, they found the cleric dressed in a black robe and black turban. He was serene and soft-spoken and served the group tea and orange juice. However, they did not feel welcomed as warmly as they had been by other Iraqis.

"Some want to return to the old regime," Hakim told the group. "They include Baathists, Saddamists and those who accuse us [Shia] of being infidels. The Baathists do not accept change. They resort to attacking the infrastructure. One of their first acts was to kill my brother." His older brother, Mohammed Baqir al-Hakim, a founder of SCIRI, had returned to Iraq after the invasion in 2003, only to be killed by a massive car bomb in August of that year. At least six of his other brothers had been killed under Saddam Hussein.

"Other states in the region want to turn back to the former regime," Hakim said. "They want the American project to fail.

"Some thought they could cure the violence by bringing the Sunnis into the political process. The problem is not the Sunnis. We want to live with them. The problem is the Saddamists"—those still loyal to the former dictator.

He added that "the steps adopted by America did not reduce, but increased, the terrorists."

Hakim clearly had little interest in national reconciliation, which the group had been told time and again was the key to success.

"The government is the strongest in the region," he insisted. "It has a wide popular base. Eighty percent of the people support it." He didn't mention that the 20 percent who didn't support it were the Sunnis. Essentially, he was saying that the Shia and Kurdish majorities supported the government, so who cared what the Sunnis thought?

"Even though we have problems, we are moving forward," Hakim said. "If one tenth of these problems had happened in Europe, the government would fall."

Hamilton pressed Hakim on national reconciliation.

"Of course we support this process," Hakim said. "But to speak frankly, we must ask, 'Reconciliation with whom?' With Saddamists, with Takfiri, or whom?"—by Takfiri, he was referring to a radical strain of jihadists who believe in taking action against those deemed to be infidels—"If it is with those who have killed us for 35 years, the Iraqi people will keep fighting them. . . . We have held a conference on national reconciliation. We will hold additional conferences. But will they stop the violence?"

Not only did Hakim display no sense of urgency, he seemed to see no problem with the sectarian rifts in the country—not entirely surprising for a man leading the majority party.

Hakim sat in a corner chair next to Hamilton and Baker. The vice president of Iraq, the finance minister and the national reconciliation minister sat next to him like quiet, subservient schoolchildren. It sent a clear message about who was in charge.

Also seated next to Hakim in robes and a turban was a man named Humam Hammoudi. He would oversee a committee reviewing the

Iraqi constitution, meaning Hakim would have a large say in the new constitution.

Baker asked Hakim if he stood by the Iraqi government. He said he did. Hammoudi interjected, "All Shias support the government." It was a clear swipe at the lack of Sunni participation.

Hamilton and Baker stopped asking questions and started offering advice to Hakim, almost scolding him, and urging him to embrace national unity.

"Eighty percent is an extraordinary political base," Hamilton told him. "As an American politician, what that says to me is that the government should move very rapidly on national reconciliation because you've got such a good political base."

"The moves of this government are very limited. That is just reality," Hakim replied.

"It is not hard to blow this country apart. To keep the country together takes extraordinary leadership," Hamilton said, hoping to appeal to Hakim's vanity.

Later, Hammoudi observed that the questions the group members were asking gave an impression that they believed national reconciliation was the most important step. He said, "The Shia are unified. The Shia have only one enemy"—repeating Hakim's line—"the Saddamists and the Takfiri." He said reconciliation would not stop the violence, implying that only eliminating the Sunnis would.

Baker didn't give up. He asked about the militias.

Hakim said there were four kinds of militias: 1) Those who had fought Saddam—the "good" militias. 2) The facilities protection service, a kind of private army for each ministry, which Bremer and the Americans had created. 3) Shia and Sunni militias that people had formed to defend themselves. He said those could be turned into "neighborhood defense committees." 4) Saddamists, Takfiri and the like. "Those, we must confront," Hakim said.

"Time is of the essence for the Iraqi people and the American people," Baker said. He called for movement on quelling the militias and on creating national reconciliation. "It is early in the new government, but we are at a critical time."

The group left the meeting despondent, less certain than ever that reconciliation could become reality. It was one of their last interviews in Iraq, a sour note on which to leave.

Hamilton looked around and thought, "There isn't an optimist among us."

On the long flight back, Gates and Panetta tried to address the question "Where are we headed?"

"I have a very real concern that the Iraqis may not have the ability to govern themselves, may not have the ability to implement the reforms that are necessary," Panetta said. "If they don't, if they can't, then what the hell is our option? What do we do? What's plan B?"

Baker said that he had recently talked to Egyptian President Hosni Mubarak, who said that Iraq—like Egypt—needed a strongman who could get things done. "Maybe," Baker joked darkly, "Plan B is bringing Saddam back."

The others pressed Baker on whether President Bush was going to listen to the group's recommendations.

"I wouldn't be doing this," Baker replied, "unless I thought he would be willing to listen and do it." The president might not agree with everything they would recommend, Baker added, but from a political point of view he might have to go along in order to save his ass.

"Where is the central authority for dealing with politics in Iraq?" Panetta asked. He knew from his experience as President Clinton's chief of staff that someone in the White House had to take charge of such issues. But the Bush administration seemed to have no such authority. "Who controls policy there? Is it Hadley? Is it Rice? Is it Rumsfeld? Is it the National Security Council?"

The others agreed it was an important question. Panetta tried to get an answer but never did.

On September 5, President Bush addressed the Military Officers Association of America. Hours earlier, the White House had released an updated version of the administration's "National Strategy for Combating Terrorism." The 29-page document described successes in the "war on terrorism" and warned that the nation faced evolving terrorist threats over the long term. It argued that Bush's idea of spreading freedom and democracy offered the best remedy for worldwide terrorism. The document was long on goals and vague on how to accomplish them.

"We're on the offense against the terrorists on every battlefront," Bush said that day, "and we'll accept nothing less than complete victory."

He cited the successful December 2005 elections in Iraq and the killing of Zarqawi in June. He said that the country's new unity government was another sign of progress.

"If we retreat from Iraq," he said, "if we don't uphold our duty to support those who are desirous to live in liberty, 50 years from now, history will look back at our time with unforgiving clarity and demand to know why we did not act."

On September 11, 2006, the fifth anniversary of the 9/11 terrorist attacks, the president gave an evening address to the nation. He cited the brutality of the attacks as the reason why leaving Iraq was not the right path. The events of 9/11 remained a guiding star for Bush—a constant reminder that the war in Iraq, with its immense political and security problems, was nevertheless a necessary and righteous endeavor.

"Our nation is being tested in a way that we have not been since the start of the Cold War. We saw what a handful of our enemies can do with box cutters and plane tickets," Bush said. "Whatever mistakes have been made in Iraq, the worst mistake would be to think that if we pulled out, the terrorists would leave us alone."

The next morning, September 12, Peter J. Schoomaker walked down the marble hallways of the Rayburn House Office Building and turned into office 2423.

Schoomaker was into his third year as Army chief of staff, a job that had taxed him emotionally and filled his days with frustration. A bear of a man, Schoomaker had served in Special Operations almost his entire career. He had been a captain in the legendary Delta Force during the ill-fated 1980 operation—named Desert One—to rescue the 53 Americans held hostage in Iran. The failed raid, in which eight American servicemen died, was another blow to the U.S. military on the heels of Vietnam, and it had essentially sunk the presidency of Jimmy Carter.

In the years that followed, Schoomaker had risen through the ranks and been involved in all the Army's major operations, including the 1991 Gulf War. He had retired in 2000 as a four-star general, after commanding all Special Operations forces.

But in the spring of 2003, just months after the Iraq invasion, he was driving through Wyoming, looking to buy a ranch, when a call came from Rumsfeld's office. Spurning all active duty generals, Rumsfeld put a full-court press on Schoomaker to return as Army chief of staff. Schoomaker flew to Washington and had dinner with Rumsfeld and his wife, Joyce. He also spent the better part of an afternoon getting a pitch from Cheney, who had been Schoomaker's congressman from Wyoming for a decade.

Rumsfeld wanted a more mobile, agile and lethal Army, and he told Schoomaker he would support him in re-creating the Army in the image of the Special Forces—smaller, self-contained units that could deploy rapidly into any situation.

Schoomaker took the job, though he didn't see any definitive winning or losing. The war simply looked like a long slog, for which Rumsfeld and the others had refused to plan. Schoomaker had spent years during the 1980s in Lebanon, where he had witnessed insane, illogical escalations of violence. He had come away believing that human beings possess a dark nature and that once emotions boil over into fighting, they are nearly impossible to quell.

Office 2423 was home to Congressman John Murtha of Pennsylvania. A framed picture of Marines raising the American flag at Iwo Jima hung on one wall. On another was a picture of Theodore Roosevelt. Near the entrance sat a bronze bust of George Marshall, who supervised the U.S. Army during World War II and later became President Harry Truman's secretary of state.

The surroundings served as a reminder to visitors that Murtha was a military man to the bone. He had earned a Bronze Star and two Purple Hearts for his service as a Marine officer during Vietnam.

He had voted to authorize the Iraq War in 2002 but had come to regret the decision. In November 2005, much to the dismay of the White House, he had publicly called for a redeployment of troops from Iraq and had been an irritant to the administration ever since.

Murtha, 74, was the ranking Democrat on the House Appropriations Defense Subcommittee, meaning he had a firm hand on the purse strings.

Which is precisely why Schoomaker had come to visit. Weeks earlier, he had taken the unprecedented step of refusing to submit the Army budget by the August 15 deadline. His protest followed a series of cuts in the service's funding requests by the White House and Congress. Rumsfeld wanted the Army to get by on $114 billion, $25 billion short of what Schoomaker said it needed.

For the better part of an hour, the two gray-haired warriors had a civil give-and-take. The conversation turned to the war and the future of the military. Schoomaker believed the biggest future threat was global terrorism. Murtha didn't agree. He felt China and other potentially hostile nations posed more significant threats.

Schoomaker argued that it was important to win in Iraq. Most people he had met out in the country, he said, wanted to see it through. It was important to succeed.

Murtha launched into a diatribe against the president and the Iraq War. You can be as enthusiastic about the war as you want, he said, but we simply don't have the troops to sustain it for much longer. Public opinion was strongly against the war. How could the president ignore the American people? This is a democracy, Murtha insisted, pounding the table, waving a copy of the Constitution in the air and claiming that Bush had become "a dictator."

Schoomaker suggested that if Murtha thought the president's approval rating was low, he ought to take a look at recent polls. You'll find that the military is the institution that people have the most confidence in, followed by police and firefighters, then organized religion, he said. All those were above or near 50 percent approval. The president was down in the 30s, and Congress was in the 20s or lower. "Congress is even lower than the president," Schoomaker said.

"This meeting's over!" Murtha shouted, red-faced and angry as hell.

Schoomaker left quietly.

Several days later, on September 15, Bush held a press conference in the Rose Garden at the White House.

The Washington Post's Peter Baker asked, "Mr. President, you've often used the phrase 'stand up, stand down,' to describe your policy when it comes to troop withdrawals from Iraq. . . . The Pentagon now says they've trained 294,000 Iraqi troops and expect to complete their program of training 325,000 by the end of the year. But American troops aren't coming home, and there are more there now than there were previously. Is the goalpost moving, sir?"

"No, no," Bush insisted. "The enemy is changing tactics, and we're adapting. That's what's happening. I asked General Casey today, 'Have you got what you need?' He said, 'Yes, I've got what I need.'"

Bush continued, "The reason why there are not fewer troops there but are more—you're right, it's gone from 135,000 to about 147,000, I think, or 140,000-something troops is because George Casey felt he needed them to help the Iraqis achieve their objective. And that's the way I will continue to conduct the war. I'll listen to generals. Maybe it's not the politically expedient thing to do, is to increase troops coming into an election, but we just can't—you can't make decisions based upon politics about how to win a war. And the fundamental question you have to ask . . . Can the President trust his commanders on the ground to tell him what is necessary? That's really one of the questions."

The president seemed almost to be having a debate with himself.

"In other words," he said, "if you say, 'I'm going to rely upon their judgment,' the next question is 'How good is their judgment; or is my judgment good enough to figure out whether or not they know what they're doing?' And I'm going to tell you, I've got great confidence in General John Abizaid and General George Casey. These are extraordinary men who understand the difficulties of the task, and understand there is a delicate relationship between self-sufficiency on the Iraqis' part, and U.S. presence.

"And so to answer your question, the policy still holds. The 'stand up, stand down' still holds, and so does the policy of me listening to our commanders to give me the judgment necessary for troop levels."

Of course, both the president and his advisers knew the stand up/stand down approach—as the Iraqis took charge, the Americans would reduce their role—wasn't working. Behind closed doors, they were searching ever more urgently for a strategy that would.

By mid-September, Chuck Robb realized that the Iraq Study Group was coalescing around a recommendation for a fixed early withdrawal from Iraq. The group was scheduled to meet the week of September 18, but Robb had a family vacation that had been planned for a year. So he wrote a memo to his fellow members. "Without being overly dramatic, I believe the Battle for Baghdad is the make-or-break element of whatever impact we're going to have on Iraq. . . . My sense is that we need, right away, a significant short-term surge in U.S. forces on the ground." Taking U.S. forces from elsewhere in Iraq would leave them playing "whack-a-mole," because new trouble would likely pop up in the places that they left behind. Robb added that "time is of the essence," and if Together Forward did not succeed by spring, "we lose." His memo said it was "time to let our military do what they're trained to do on offense—without being overly constrained by a zero casualties or collateral damage approach." The clock was running out, and the study group report needed to be "bold and consequential," he wrote, adding, "I'm very much aware of the difficulties inherent in this brief rant."

Baker and Hamilton wanted a unanimous report and a unanimous series of recommendations from the five Democrats and five Republicans. Without consensus, they knew they would have little or no impact, rendering their efforts meaningless. Robb believed he had sent a clear message—he would not sign on unless a "surge" option was included.

13

———————

The man who walked into the Pentagon on Tuesday, September 19, had a private appointment with Secretary Rumsfeld. On first glance, you might swear he worked with his large hands and measured his hours in sweat. At 6-foot-3 and 240 pounds, he had a boxer's face— red and ruddy and hard, framed by tightly cropped hair. He was retired Army General Jack Keane, a 37-year veteran and former vice chief of staff, the number two man in the U.S. Army.

At 63, though no longer on active duty, Keane couldn't shake the dread that accompanied his thoughts about the Iraq War. As a paratrooper in Vietnam, he had seen the multiple confusions of that war shatter his beloved Army and drain his country of spirit, resources and moral authority.

Few had more command experience than Keane. He had led a full corps of 50,000 soldiers. He'd become a Rumsfeld favorite among the generals—no small feat, given the mutual contempt between Rumsfeld and many of his military officers. In 2002, Keane had agreed to Rumsfeld's request to become the chief of staff of the Army, but he had later changed his mind and retired because his wife, Terry, was seriously ill with Parkinson's disease. Rumsfeld had shown him compassion and understanding.

Like many, Keane found Rumsfeld abrasive, dismissive and distrustful of the uniformed military leaders. But he believed Rumsfeld was right about the need for dramatic change within the military, especially in the Army. As a member of the Defense Policy Board, an outside group of advisers that received regular top secret briefings, Keane stayed up to date on Iraq. He shared his frustrations over the war with a fellow policy board member, former House Speaker Newt Gingrich, who urged him to lay out his concerns to the secretary.

When Keane got to Rumsfeld's office, he found General Peter Pace as well. The three men sat around a small conference table.

Keane said he had been reluctant to come. "I just don't want to be another critic. You have many of them," he began. "I don't want to be another burden. I hate armchair know-it-alls who believe they have a better idea than those who are actually doing it. That's not me. Newt Gingrich thought we should talk, and I think that's probably why you asked me to come in."

Rumsfeld nodded.

"I don't want to waste your time. Everybody is working so hard and sacrificing so much to get it done and do what is right. I'm here as a member of the team—the Defense Policy Board, which I take very seriously." He explained that he had attended many staff briefings, made trips to Iraq, and been involved in the assessments in 2004 and 2005.

"We're edging toward strategic failure," Keane said. "And I want to discuss some things to minimize and reduce that risk." It was a stark assessment, and he tried to soften it. "Strategic failure in the sense that the government is fractured and if it does fracture it'll lead to civil war." In 2003 and 2004, the U.S. military strategy was offensive. "Its principal purpose was to kill and capture insurgents. And we backed into that strategy, as you know, in the spring and summer of '03"—the months after the invasion.

Rumsfeld was taking notes.

"We were a conventional army. The preeminent land force in the world. Well trained for big wars but ill prepared for counterinsurgencies. And the commanders initially started off executing what they know, which was using conventional tactics against an unconventional enemy. . . . We also had no unifying strategy, no campaign plan, all through '03 and most of '04." This was the period when the junior three-star officer in the Army, Ricardo Sanchez, was the Iraq commander.

Then a campaign plan was developed and approved in 2004 and 2005, Keane said. "It has multiple lines of operation—security, governance, training the Iraqi security forces, economic recovery, infrastructure and information operations. But it is really a defensive strategy, and it's also a short-war strategy."

"What do you mean—short-war strategy?" Rumsfeld asked.

It was designed for us to get out as soon as possible, Keane said. "It relies heavily on establishing an effective government and franchising the Sunnis, isolating the insurgents and bringing them into . . . the political process. It makes sense. I believed it at the time."

The military approach focused on turning security over to the Iraqi security forces as quickly as possible, Keane said. "The other part is to protect ourselves in the process—the force protection of our own troops." Another part was to eliminate al Qaeda sanctuaries. "Despite these efforts and despite capturing Saddam and killing his two sons, and despite holding three elections, and despite writing a constitution and installing a permanent government and despite the improvement in the Iraqi security forces and also killing Zarqawi, the fact is, the harsh reality is, the level of violence has increased every year in the contested areas.

"Security and stability are worse. It threatens the survival of the government and the success of our mission. And what's wrong? What's wrong is our strategy. We never adopted a strategy to defeat the insurgency."

What do you mean? Rumsfeld asked.

"Well, we don't have a mission to defeat the insurgency. If we did, we should be protecting the population. And the fact that we're not protecting the population has exposed it to al Qaeda, to the Sunni insurgents and the Shia militia that take advantage of it. And that's why we have the bloodbath we have today." He said the Iraqis were not yet capable of handling security. "That's the problem," he said. "We put our money on that horse." And the horse had come up lame.

"That was Casey and Abizaid's strategy," Rumsfeld said.

"I understand that, Mr. Secretary," Keane said. "But I think your influence over this strategy was there." He reminded Rumsfeld that he disagreed with what he called the secretary's "minimalist ideology"—the desire to avoid creating an artificial dependence by doing everything for the Iraqis. Rumsfeld always had believed that the model from Bosnia-Kosovo in the 1990s was wrong, bloated by far too many people from U.S. agencies doing too many things that local governments should do for themselves. Reasonable logic, Keane said, but not in a situation with "somebody contesting you and conducting armed violence against you."

Rumsfeld kept putting it off on Abizaid and Casey.

But you influenced the environment with your strong views, Keane replied. You allowed this to happen. The effort to advise the Iraqi security forces needs to be beefed up considerably, he added. The U.S. forces doing the training of Iraqis are often National Guard and Reserve officers who don't have operational experience and on occasion are advising more experienced Iraqis. Some of it was embarrassing. "This needs to be the number one personnel management policy in the United States Army," Keane said.

"It is," Rumsfeld replied. "These guys have got it, and they're fixing it."

"No," Keane said gently. "I have too much anecdotal evidence to the contrary. The advisory program is far less than what it really needs to be, and we have to put a major emphasis on it."

Keane didn't think he was telling Rumsfeld anything he didn't know deep down. He offered some possible solutions.

The options on the table, as he saw them, included immediate withdrawal, gradual withdrawal, or staying where they were and increasing the number of advisers and trying to better the Iraqi security forces. "All those options leave the enemy with the initiative, leave the enemy with its momentum," Keane said. "And they will continue to exploit the vulnerabilities and push this government. It will fracture the government, force it to disintegrate and we have the potential of truly leading to a civil war, where you don't have to debate whether it is or not. It'd be obvious to everybody. There is no option remaining to us at this point other than to do what should be obvious to all of us now—

what we never did. And that is get security for the people. . . . It has become so obvious to me that security has become the necessary precondition for political progress, for economic development, and even for social progress in this country that's so fractured."

Keane saw that Rumsfeld didn't agree, but the secretary wasn't in his usual combative mode.

What was needed, Keane said, was an "escalation of forces to gain security." It would mean many more brigades—tens of thousands more troops.

At this, Rumsfeld's face sank. It was exactly what the man who had conceived of a small, agile force did not want.

"How do we attain victory?" Keane asked. "You cannot defeat the insurgents by destroying their forces, in other words by focusing on killing and capturing. The fact is they will be re-created." There was an almost limitless supply of discontented and angry young men in Iraq. While killing insurgents had a value, Keane said, killing alone was not an acceptable strategy. "Victory is attained by the permanent isolation of the insurgent from the population," he said. "You have to protect the population to get that kind of isolation. The bitter lesson learned: The insurgents, Sunni insurgents, control the population in the contested areas.

"We would concentrate our forces in an area to run out the insurgents, we would place static forces to control the population once that's done, and protect them and support [them]. And prevent the insurgents from coming back in to terrorize and intimidate and also to assassinate." We must live "with and among the people" 24/7, Keane said, "not returning to forward operating bases each night, as we have in the past. We're much too isolated from the people. We have to control the population in terms of movements—census, ID cards. Eventually we need to set up local elections and test leaders. And we have to drive out the remnants of the insurgents."

Keane cited a model from 2005. "You remember Tall Afar, for example, H. R. McMaster?"

"Yeah, yeah, I do," Rumsfeld said.

"Let me take you back to that," Keane said. It was a city of 250,000 people. The operation was carried out in three phases—drive the insurgents out, set up static patrol bases in the town, and win trust from the people so they'd help prevent insurgents from coming back in. Colonel McMaster then held local elections to empower the local officials and brought in economic recovery. He stabilized that city in about six to eight months, which is pretty remarkable, Keane said. "Anybody that's looked at it knows how remarkable it is."

Reading from notes he had jotted on yellow legal pages, Keane asked, "What else can we do? First of all, we have to decide if we *want* to win. And are we really serious about it? That's a major decision. And you have to recognize that the current strategy—if we don't change it, we will lose and we will fail.

"If we want to win, then we have to match our policies and our resources with our rhetoric." Then, aiming squarely at General Casey, Keane said, "We have to put somebody in charge who knows what he's doing. We have to demand victory from him and hold him and the other generals accountable. And tell them they are not coming home until they achieve it."

Also, he said, we must put the entire weight of the U.S. government behind this effort. "Recognize the limitations of good, conventional war commanders. Some do not make good counterinsurgency leaders—lack of intellectual flexibility, agility in dealing with a high degree of uncertainty." Conventional warfare leans heavily on satellites and upscale signals intelligence to help determine where the enemy is, he continued.

"In counterinsurgency or irregular warfare, you really don't know where the enemy is." In conventional warfare, the enemy has to move equipment, supplies and men, thus flagging his intentions. "Here, you can't see any of it. So every single day, you're dealing with a very high degree of uncertainty. And in my view, not everybody can deal with that if you are trained to deal" with conventional fighting. What a commander naturally does is to try to control uncertainties and develop measurements to assess performance. "But we were not doing it in the context of what the enemy was really doing to us," Keane said. He recommended that Rumsfeld assemble some people to examine the strategy, using the accelerating violence as a rationale for an outside study.

"This is a good time to make a change with Casey and Abizaid,"

Keane told Rumsfeld. Both generals already had been extended. "You put in a new strategy, in fairness to that strategy, we should put a new team in to execute it and not rely on the old team. It's much too much for them to make a dramatic change and reject their politics from the past. I don't believe you have to make a major announcement of the change, in the sense that you can give the generals a soft landing." It was an unwritten, and normally unspoken, military rule: Protect the generals.

As Rumsfeld listened, Keane pressed on with his notes. "Stop the ramp-down planning now," he said. Casey had put this in motion despite the rising level of violence. It was confusing everyone about U.S. intentions and commitment. How willing would troops on the ground be to risk their lives, knowing that withdrawal was imminent? "Stop pressuring to accelerate the training of Iraqis, and stop pressuring to accelerate the transition to Iraqis. Stop the plans to move to four megabases." Casey's plan was eventually to move entirely out of Baghdad. Defeating insurgencies required decentralization just like the insurgents, Keane said, and Casey was going to make everything more centralized to reduce casualties. Reducing casualties was essential, but not at the expense of the mission, he said.

Number eight, Keane said—he had listed his points—double the size of the planned Iraqi security force to 600,000 army and police.

Rumsfeld clearly didn't like that one, but he remained silent.

"We need to generate more U.S. forces," Keane said again, without suggesting how many more. "We need enough to secure Baghdad." More forces could be found many ways. "We don't have to do 12- and seven-month tours for the Army and Marine Corps, respectively. We can go to longer tours for each. We can go to indefinite tours. We have fought more of our wars based on indefinite tours."

Going back to his time as Army vice chief, Keane recalled, "I'm the one that recommended to you the one-year tour, if you remember, and then you asked me to go over and talk to the president about it a couple of days later. So I obviously believed in the value of a rotation.

"But this goes back to my original premise about 'Do we want to win, and how serious are we?' And if we are, then it's going to be at some sacrifice." Operations Together Forward I and II had failed miserably, Keane reminded the secretary, and primarily because there were not enough troops to protect the population.

"What we do right now is, we have forward operating bases. Big bases, highly protected, very Americanized inside." The largest bases had gyms for working out and movie theater complexes like those found in U.S. shopping malls. "And so, we go outside those bases on patrol. Patrols are overwhelmingly vehicle-borne patrols," which only invited the stepped-up IED attacks. "We call them presence patrols. They have very little value. They do not pick up much intelligence, and we're more targets than anything else."

As an alternative, Keane said, "We would move into a neighborhood and occupy some empty buildings that are not being used. Or, in some cases, we may take over some building that the Iraqis are using or living in, and we would work out a payment for them to do it." It had been done before. The soldiers would eat there, sleep there and patrol there. They would do foot patrols, and the IEDs don't work as well against such patrols, Keane said. "The advantage that that patrol has is its contact with the people, day in and day out. Talking to merchants, talking to citizens. And eventually, what happens is the people see that we're staying, not leaving. Trust begins to build up, and this is an important issue."

The soldiers and the Iraqis become mutually dependent. "And that takes a few weeks to happen, but it will happen because then they start to clue them on who the enemy is, and if there's a threat to them in the area, then they'll start reporting the threat. And we have evidence that that's what's happened in Tall Afar over and over again. . . . We know this can work in terms of the people becoming, really, an intelligence vehicle for us."

Keane said, "We have to fix the strategic and operational intelligence." Not enough people were working on Iraq. "The Central Intelligence Agency, reported to me from a reliable source, has 38 analysts that work exclusively on Iraq. We have more working on China than we have on Iraq, and yet Iraq is of emergency proportions and is a major threat in terms of our national security if we lose it."

Rumsfeld made some pejorative comments about the CIA, to which Keane agreed.

The Joint Chiefs' intelligence directorate, called J-2, and the Defense Intelligence Agency have 61 people who work Iraq exclusively, Keane said. They are supposed to have 156. So they're sitting below 50 percent strength in the entire Pentagon on Iraq intelligence.

"We are not mapping the networks," Keane said. "What I mean by that is, in the theater, in Iraq, we don't have enough analysts to actually try to determine the insurgent and al Qaeda network. What is it, and how do you map it? This is like detailed homicide work, detective work, putting the mosaic together." That entails tedious reading and sifting of interrogation reports, tactical operations, signals intercepts, other human intelligence reports, he said, along with captured documents.

Keane also had a laundry list for how to reconstitute the political and civil society in Iraq.

"We need to avoid triumphant rhetoric. It's caused credibility problems—the so-called Westmoreland 'light at the end of the tunnel.' Casey's been withdrawing forces twice now, based on successes. And what I'm telling you is obviously that hasn't worked, and what we have to do is increase forces. So if we're going to accept a change in strategy here, then as that strategy begins to work, which I think it will, we have to avoid being triumphant about it. Because the enemy has a vote here, and we've always underestimated our enemy."

Number 15 on Keane's list: "We have to win the battle of Baghdad. We have to absolutely stabilize Baghdad by control of the population, I know I've said that before, but I'm coming back to it for emphasis."

As if this were not enough, Keane had a reading assignment for Rumsfeld. "I think you and others should read, to understand this, a book called *Counterinsurgency Warfare: Theory and Practice* by David Galula. It's only about 100 pages, and if you don't want to read the whole hundred pages, read the foreword and the introduction, and then read chapters four through seven, which is really execution."

Galula, a former French military officer, had argued in the 1964 book that insurgencies are revolutionary wars that are won or lost based on who wins the support of the local population.

The defense secretary had taken notes, asked questions and probed. But it was a scaled-down version of the old, fiery Rumsfeld. As Keane left, he realized that the atmosphere within the office seemed different. Every aspect of Rumsfeld, from the tired look on his face to his body language, signaled a sense of resignation. Nothing Keane had said should have come as a surprise to Rumsfeld, Keane thought, other than the fact that a friend was saying it all so directly.

But something had to change. Between 50 and 75 U.S. service members were being killed each month, and that number was rising sharply.

14

Lieutenant General David Petraeus was a rising star in the Army and, in Jack Keane's view, the general most likely to solve the Iraq problem.

Petraeus also was like a little brother to Keane. They had first met back in the late 1980s, when Keane was a colonel at Fort Chaffee, Arkansas, and Petraeus was a major working as an aide to Army Chief of Staff Carl Vuono.

They soon crossed paths again at Fort Campbell, Kentucky. By then, Petraeus was a lieutenant colonel serving as a battalion commander in the 101st Airborne. Keane, a brigadier general, was the assistant division commander.

One Saturday morning in September 1991, Petraeus and Keane were standing together watching an infantry squad practice assaulting a bunker with live grenades and ammunition. A soldier tripped and fell about 40 yards away and accidentally squeezed the trigger on his rifle. The M-16 round tore through the "A" over the name tag on the right side of Petraeus's chest and left a golf-ball-sized exit wound in his back. If it had hit above the "A" in "U.S. Army" on his left side, he likely would have died on the spot.

"Dave, you've been shot," Keane said, as he leaned over his downed colleague. "You know what we're going to do here. First of all, you're going to make it, all right?" He kept talking to Petraeus, trying to keep him from slipping into shock. "I want you to stay focused," he said, clutching the lieutenant colonel's hand, aware that Petraeus was growing weaker.

"I'm gonna be okay. I'll stay with it," Petraeus said.

In the local emergency room, a trauma expert shoved a chest tube into Petraeus—an excruciating procedure that makes grown men scream and jolt off the table. Petraeus never moved and let out only a low grunt. "That is the toughest soldier I've ever had my hands on," the doctor told Keane.

A medevac helicopter flew Petraeus, with Keane by his side, 60 miles to Vanderbilt University Medical Center in Nashville. Keane had called ahead and requested the best thoracic surgeon available. When they landed on the roof of the hospital, Keane saw a man waiting for them dressed in golf clothes.

"I'm Bill Frist," said the man who would become majority leader of the U.S. Senate a decade later. "I'm the chief of thoracic surgery here."

"Were you on a golf course?" Keane asked.

"Yeah, I got a call. I understand you've got a seriously wounded soldier here."

"Yeah, I do," Keane said. "He means a lot to us."

"Stop wasting time," a barely conscious Petraeus ordered Frist. "Open my chest this very minute if you need to."

Frist operated on Petraeus for more than five hours. Petraeus recovered at the Fort Campbell hospital and drove the hospital commander crazy trying to persuade the doctors to discharge him. "I am not the norm," he told them. He pulled tubes out of his arm. He hopped out of bed and did 50 push-ups. Finally, they let him go home.

The incident marked a formative moment in Petraeus's life and his military career. Afterward, Petraeus would joke that he had taken the bullet for Keane. "It took fast reflexes to save you that day, General Keane," he would say. But he never forgot that Keane had been there holding his hand as he felt his life begin to ebb away. It sealed a bond between the two men. They became friends and confidants, remaining close years later as Keane rose to vice chief of staff of the Army and Petraeus led the 101st Airborne during the invasion of Iraq in 2003.

• • •

On September 19, the same day Keane went to see Rumsfeld, the president met privately with Jalal Talabani, the president of Iraq, a ceremonial but important post under the new Iraqi constitution. He was a large, grandfatherly figure with glasses and a mustache, an outgoing man who spoke fluent English.

Bush said that the Shia militias and their death squads were among the key problems.

A Kurd who believed in local autonomy, Talabani disagreed strongly. Let the local areas and local forces liberate themselves, as was happening in Anbar province, he said. Iraq did not need more U.S. troops. It needed fewer. A big problem, he said, was that the United States was not supplying the Iraqi forces with enough advanced weapons to fight the terrorists and extremists. The Iraqi defense minister had a list. Talabani said he knew the Americans didn't always trust the Iraqis, especially the police, and worried that the weapons would end up in the hands of the terrorists. But he wanted to give assurances.

Bush said the United States would try to do better.

It was one of the inconsistencies in the U.S. policy. While the overarching strategy was to train and prepare the Iraqi forces to fight and be self-sufficient, the Bush administration would not supply the weaponry that the Iraqis needed.

For example, during a State Department meeting the next day, September 20, Jim Jeffrey, Rice's Iraq coordinator, said the resources being given to the Iraqi army were so low, "It makes you want to cry."

Just three weeks earlier, Sadr's Mahdi Army, or JAM, had executed a dozen Iraqi soldiers who had run out of ammunition.

"JAM has more firepower than the Iraqi army," Jeffrey said. "Anybody has more firepower. The Washington SWAT team has more firepower than the Iraqi army, because we did not give them mortars, antitank weapons other than a few RPGs, and that took a lot of squeezing. And we still haven't gotten significant numbers of armored Humvees."

• • •

That same day, September 20, Rumsfeld received a sensitive intelligence document on Iraq:

TOP SECRET—HUMINT-COMINT CHANNELS
DEFENSE ANALYSIS REPORT: IRAQ
POTENTIAL FOR FRACTURE INCREASING.

It was a grim report, detailing a virtual sectarian collapse among Shia, Sunni and Kurd. The government was not providing sufficient infrastructure services and, most important, not providing security for its own people.

The report was based on human sources (HUMINT) recruited by the CIA and communications intercepts (COMINT) gathered by the National Security Agency. It showed that the lack of political progress by Maliki and other Iraqi politicians was due in part to their settling into sectarian camps rather than trying to come together.

Later, when I asked the president about this September 20 document and its warning that the potential for fracture in Iraq was increasing, he said, "What Condi has told me, they're now telling me. 'We'd better do something different.' I mean, it's just another data point." He added, "I'm not so sure that that's a relevant document. Just because you've got it doesn't mean it's relevant."

But apparently Rumsfeld had thought it was relevant. He forwarded copies of the report to Generals Abizaid, Pace and Casey. "Let's have a discussion about it at the earliest possible time," he wrote.

When they did, they asked the usual questions: Is Maliki the right guy? Was he going to make it? Would he survive? Their conclusion was a version of the old notion that in the land of the blind, the one-eyed man is king. Maliki was about as good as they were going to get—at least for the moment.

On September 22, three days after his meeting with Rumsfeld, General Keane went to see JCS Chairman Pete Pace. Pace, who had sat in on the earlier meeting, had asked Keane to come by his office for a private chat.

"I forgot how direct and frank you are," Pace said, flattering Keane for his blistering report card on Iraq. "I would like you to give me an assessment of how you think I'm doing as chairman after one year on the job."

Keane was surprised. On one hand, he thought, the gesture might reflect an unusual degree of self-confidence from Pace, a sign that the chairman wanted to get the straight story from a truth teller. On the other hand, it might reflect some insecurity, that there was an underground view of him that he had not heard. In the Pentagon, such "how do you think I'm doing" requests usually mean "flatter me."

"I would give you a failing grade," Keane said softly.

"Why?" Pace asked, pain evident on his Boy Scout face.

"Well, Pete, here's the answer. The number one priority facing the country is the war in Afghanistan and Iraq—particularly Iraq because it's not going the way we expected. It's the number one priority, therefore, under the Department of Defense. I'm a part-time guy working on the Defense Policy Board, and quite frankly, I know more about this than you do. You're not in this day in and day out. You are not intellectually, emotionally and passionately committed to this thing. The guys that are briefing me should be briefing you. I've seen what they send to you, which is trend analysis. It's somewhat superficial."

"What do you think I should be doing?" Pace asked.

"First of all, you should be immersed in this every day. Intellectually immersed in it," Keane said, adding that he was well aware that the chairman had other obligations. "There's congressional testimony. You have to think about the future of the military. You go into meetings and do all of that, and they're easier to go to because they have a predictability and a routine to them. And they're not that challenging. They're the bureaucratic process that it takes to do business." But Keane believed the chairman was drowning in the soothing, paint-by-numbers leadership, in which simply meeting a grueling daily schedule can make you feel as if you are accomplishing a great deal.

"But the real defining work of what you're here for as a four-star, and what Secretary Rumsfeld is here for, is to win this war," Keane said. "That's what the American people expect. They expect us to win this thing and continue to protect them as a result of it.

"What the chairman should be doing is taking the Joint Chiefs, rising them up over their service parochialism."

General Casey needed help desperately, Keane said. "George Casey is at this 24/7. He has nothing to nurture his life. He is completely immersed and isolated by one thing and only one thing. That's this war. It has completely captured everything he does. His capacity at times to see clearly is always going to be limited and defined by his day-in, day-out experience and the fatigue he suffers."

Keane said he thought the obsessive work ethic of the senior military men was self-defeating. "Our generals fight wars today almost at a frenetic pace that is counterproductive," he said. Compare that to World War II General Douglas MacArthur, who watched a movie every night, Keane said, or Army Chief of Staff George Marshall, who went home every night at a reasonable hour and "rode a horse, for crying out loud, and sometimes took a nap for an hour and a half during the day. And these guys were doing big, important things. You know what our guys are like? They're at their desks at 6:30 in the morning, and they stay up till midnight."

It was a manhood issue, Keane thought. Because the soldiers were out there 24/7, the generals thought they better do the same. But the core issue was fresh, clear thinking about the tasks of war. What you need to do is take the Joint Staff and the Joint Chiefs, and what you should be doing is challenging the premises and assumptions of both Casey and Abizaid, he said. "If there are things that are not working right, which I think we are aware of, we should be looking at alternative strategies. Not to run into your boss"—Rumsfeld or the president or the National Security Council—"but to help George and John. That's what you can be doing. You have this enormously talented Joint Staff here that's all handpicked, smart people . . . and they're rubber-stamping what George and John do. Why are they doing that? Because you want them to do it, implicitly, because you don't challenge it." Pace and the chiefs and the staff were not doing their job, Keane said, and "that's why I think this is a failing grade."

Keane said that Pace should meet with Derek Harvey, the intelligence analyst, and listen to him very closely. Harvey had understood the war from the very beginning. The CIA, the DIA and the chairman's own intelligence directorate, the J-2, had fought him but had now come around, Keane said.

Pace said he would get briefed by Harvey, and he added, "I should put together a task force of guys, pull them out of the staff, smart guys, people you can trust, people who are not going to run to the media," he said, "and have them validate what is working and what's not working in Iraq."

And to examine alternative strategies, Keane said.

"Who would you recommend for that?" Pace asked.

"Colonel H. R. McMaster," Keane said. McMaster, who had led the recent Tall Afar success, had accompanied Keane on two trips to Iraq earlier in the year.

"Anybody else?" Pace asked.

Not off the top of his head, Keane said, but McMaster was key—a handful, but essential. He also said that if the strategy was going to change, it was pretty obvious that the leaders had to change.

"Who should lead in Iraq?" Pace asked.

"Dave Petraeus," Keane said. "Unequivocally, there is no other candidate that would be as good." If Pace shopped around, there would probably be universal agreement that Petraeus was the general for the job, Keane maintained.

"There's some negative feedback about Dave out there," Pace noted. When Petraeus had been the executive officer for General Hugh Shelton in the 1990s, he had been tough to deal with—had worn his boss's stars and been a self-promoter. Some of the generals thought he was a "schemer." And when Petraeus had been appointed to head the training of Iraqis, he had appeared on the cover of *Newsweek* in July 2004 under the headline "Can This Man Save Iraq?" Rumsfeld and others in the Pentagon and Army resented what looked like a giant ego engaged in self-promotion.

"Yeah," Keane said. Ambitious, sure. Excessively, no. Ambitious generals were nothing new. "It shouldn't bother you. This is a very, very talented guy."

"Who should go to CentCom?" Pace inquired. Who should replace Abizaid?

"Fallon," Keane said, referring to Admiral William J. Fallon, the commander of U.S. Pacific Command.

"Fox Fallon?" Pace said with some surprise, using the admiral's nickname.

"He's smart and tough-minded. This command deserves somebody who has experience. He already has been out managing Pacific Command, the second most troubled neighborhood we have in the world." Fallon had been dealing with heads of state in the Pacific, defense ministers, and was "used to dealing with the congressional leadership in Washington, the administration and all the influencers."

"Boy," Pace said, "that's an interesting idea."

Fallon wasn't just a Navy guy, Keane said. Several years back, when Keane had been the vice chief of the Army, some whiz-bang Army electronic program had come up for approval before the Joint Requirements Oversight Council, one of the numerous layers that decide on Pentagon programs and budgets. Though it was small and not that expensive, everyone was dumping all over it. Fallon piped up, "Ground forces win wars. The rest of us support these ground guys. Give them their program, will you?"

The ground guys—Pace and Keane—found that very appealing.

The next day, Petraeus, head of the U.S. Army Combined Arms Center at Fort Leavenworth, called Keane to report that he had received a call from the Army chief's office. "They want to put together some smart guys to look at the strategy and what's working and what's not working in Iraq," Petraeus said.

Keane knew, of course. He called Admiral Fallon. "Fox, I've got to tell you something. I recommended you to become the CentCom commander."

"Goddamn it, Jack," Fallon said, coming through the phone loud and angry. "What are you doing to me?"

15

The same day that Keane met with Pace, Ken Adelman arrived in Rumsfeld's office for a 2:30 P.M. appointment. When a Rumsfeld aide had called a few days earlier to say the secretary wanted to meet, Adelman had wavered on whether to return the call. In the end, he decided he needed to face his old friend.

Adelman, an outspoken hawk with a Ph.D. in political theory, was 14 years Rumsfeld's junior. But the two men had a close political and personal relationship. Adelman had first worked for Rumsfeld 36 years earlier, in 1970, when Rumsfeld headed the Office of Economic Opportunity under President Nixon. He'd also served as Rumsfeld's civilian special assistant during his first tour as secretary of defense under President Gerald Ford. In 1986, when Rumsfeld briefly contemplated running for president, he made clear he would have wanted Adelman as campaign manager.

The Adelman and Rumsfeld families had shared countless vacations over the years. They visited each other's homes in Taos, Santa Fe, Chicago and the Dominican Republic. They often stayed up deep into the night discussing politics, literature and the weighty questions of life. In 2002, Adelman published an op-ed piece in *The Washington Post* declaring that an invasion of Iraq would be a "cakewalk" because Rumsfeld and other senior officials in the Bush administration were so competent.

Along with Jack Keane, Newt Gingrich and Henry Kissinger, Adelman was a member of Rumsfeld's Defense Policy Board, so he knew the many ways the Iraq War had turned sour. This Friday afternoon, as he sat alone with Rumsfeld at the small table inside the secretary's spacious office, with its dark navy carpet and heavy drapes, he felt at ease. He'd spent so much time in this room during the 1970s and so much time with the man across the table, it was familiar ground.

"I wanted to call you in," Rumsfeld began. We've been friends for most of our adult lives, he said, and "I personally hope that we remain friends for the rest of my life."

Rumsfeld, in all his gruffness and insensitivity, rarely revealed such emotion, and it caught Adelman by surprise.

"Don, I just want you to know that you've been a gigantic influence in my life and a very big presence. You've been wonderful to Carol," Adelman said, referring to his wife. "You've been wonderful to our daughters. And for 30-some years, I've loved you like a brother." I've loved you more than some of my brothers, he added.

"I know which ones," Rumsfeld said, cracking up. But then he turned serious. "It might be a good idea if you got off the Defense Policy Board," he said.

"Listen," Adelman told Rumsfeld, "if you want me off the Defense Policy Board, just tell me. It's not a big part of my life. It's not a big part of my identity. You put me on there; you can take me off."

"I'm not saying that I want you to get off," Rumsfeld replied, apparently not wanting to fire Adelman himself. "I'm saying it might be better if you got off."

If it were better for me, I would have gotten off, Adelman said. I'm on it because I enjoy it. "If it's better for you," he told Rumsfeld, "tell me, write me a letter, and I'll get off."

Rumsfeld tried to explain. As the war had progressed and grown grimmer, Adelman had begun asking more questions at briefings, interrupting more often, expressing more skepticism. "You are disruptive," he said. "You are negative."

The kind words from minutes earlier had evaporated.

"The disruptive part is bullshit, Don. It is just bullshit," Adelman said. "And the negative part is absolutely right."

Rumsfeld flashed with anger. "Let me tell you what I mean," he said. "When people are giving briefings, you sometimes interrupt those briefings. You don't let them finish."

"Well, if that's what you mean by disruptive," Adelman said, "I guess that's true. But let me tell you, you know where I learned all that? In this office. I learned it 30 years ago." He pointed to where Rumsfeld usually sat. "I learned it from the master."

Rumsfeld couldn't help but chuckle at that. Okay, he said. Okay. But they weren't finished.

"To tell you the truth," Adelman continued, "you are right on the negative thing. I'm extremely negative on two things, Don."

"What's that?"

"Your total lack of accountability," Adelman replied, and the "abysmal quality of your decisions."

"What do you mean by accountability? I'm accountable for everything," Rumsfeld said.

Adelman pointed out that Rumsfeld always blamed problems or screwups on others—the State Department, the commanders, the Iraqis. "I don't see you taking any responsibility in any of this," he said.

"Well, that's just wrong!" Rumsfeld fired back. "I take a lot of responsibility."

"I cannot understand the abysmal quality of your decisions," Adelman said again.

"Like what?" Rumsfeld asked.

Adelman said he could single out plenty of bad decisions, but two in particular troubled him most—Rumsfeld's "stuff happens" response to the widespread looting in Iraq after the invasion and the handling of the Abu Ghraib prison abuse scandal.

"I could not understand how you can go on at the podium of the Pentagon and say, 'Stuff happens. That's what free people do,'" he said. "That's not what free people do. That's what barbarians do."

"I don't remember saying that," Rumsfeld replied.

"Oh, c'mon, Don," Adelman said. It was likely the most quoted line Rumsfeld had ever uttered, a shoo-in entry to *Bartlett's Familiar Quotations*.

The 140,000 U.S. troops in Iraq hadn't done "jack shit" about the constant looting, Adelman said. Why hadn't anyone ordered them to put a stop to it?

They had been ordered to stop it, Rumsfeld said.

"Oh, did you give the order?" Adelman asked.

"I didn't give the order!" Rumsfeld shouted. "Somebody around here gave the order."

"Oh, well who gave the order, Don?"

"I don't know who gave the order."

"You didn't give the order. You don't know who gave the order. How do you know the order was given?"

"Because I know an order was given."

They argued the point for a few minutes. If the order was given, Adelman finally asked, "Tell me why 140,000 troops didn't obey the order."

"Well, I don't know that," Rumsfeld said.

They moved on to Adelman's other complaint—Abu Ghraib. Adelman made clear he didn't blame Rumsfeld for the abuse that had happened, but he did fault him for handling the situation poorly.

"You found out about this on January 14, and you didn't do jack shit about it till May," he said.

"Goddammit, that's just not fair!" said Rumsfeld, fuming. "I didn't know how serious it was."

If it was serious enough to tell the president about, Adelman said, it must have been a big deal. "Didn't you know there were pictures?" he asked.

Rumsfeld said he didn't know.

So, Adelman continued, there was nobody between January and May, when the story broke, who recognized what a bombshell this was?

"No," Rumsfeld said.

"Well, that's a pretty sad system, when no one goes and says, 'Holy cow, this is gigantic,'" Adelman said. "The way you handled that was just abysmal, and it just aggravated what was a serious blight."

Rumsfeld argued back that even as secretary there was only so much he legally could do, because he had to ensure the military criminal investigations were handled independently of any "command influ-ence" or meddling from the top.

Adelman didn't buy it one bit. He had gone on the Web and read the defense secretary's guidelines on interrogation. How could any young soldier interpret such mangled language? "I have a doctorate from Georgetown, majored in philosophy, and I couldn't understand what you were talking about," he told Rumsfeld. "I couldn't diagram one of those sentences. I doubt that you could understand it. You signed it, but it was all lawyerese. And it didn't tell you what you could or couldn't do. It was unintelligible." It was another example of hiding behind lawyers and vague language and not giving the troops on the front line meaningful instructions. As a result, he had let them down.

Rumsfeld had heard enough. "I got to go," he said.

"Thank you for doing this," Adelman said. "This was really very nice of you to do."

Rumsfeld walked his old friend out of the office and offered a quick good-bye. As Adelman walked away, their three decades of cama-raderie flashed through his mind. He thought about their trips around the world, the family get-togethers and the unusual intimacy, about their conversations that had probably numbered in the thousands. He thought, "This is going to be our last."

Adelman knew it was best to forgive others for their transgressions, and Rumsfeld had never done anything to hurt him. He'd been a kind and loyal friend. But Adelman simply could not forgive him for the havoc he had wreaked on the country. Even worse, like so many who enjoyed being on the inside and close to power, he couldn't forgive himself for not speaking his mind sooner.

A couple of weeks later, Adelman received a letter in the mail from the secretary of defense's office. It said the Pentagon would be reorga-nizing the Defense Policy Board and would soon name a replacement for Adelman.

It concluded, "Thank you for being so cooperative on this. Sin-cerely, Donald."

•   •   •

That same week, the phone rang inside an office at Arundel House, a centuries-old brick building overlooking the Thames River in London.

Colonel H. R. McMaster had recently moved his wife, Katie, and two of their three daughters—the third was away at college—across the Atlantic to begin a stint as a senior research fellow at the International Institute for Strategic Studies, a prestigious think tank focused on political-military conflicts. They were still unpacking boxes.

McMaster answered the call. It was a member of the Army chief of staff's office.

"Can you be in Washington tomorrow?"

"What's it about?" McMaster asked.

"We can't tell you."

"Well, how about two days, man?"

He wanted time to pack a few things and say good-bye once again to Katie and the girls.

Nearly 5,000 miles away, in Kansas, Colonel Pete Mansoor checked his e-mail and found a note from David Petraeus. It told him to be in Washington in two days to begin a three-month temporary assignment inside the Pentagon at the request of the Army chief of staff.

Mansoor, like Petraeus, had forged a reputation as one of the Army's foremost thinkers. He'd graduated at the top of his class from West Point in 1982 and gone on to earn a master's degree and a doctorate in military history from Ohio State University, as well as a master's in strategic studies from the Army War College. He'd written a book about World War II titled *The GI Offensive in Europe,* taught at West Point, and served a stint on the Joint Staff at the Pentagon, where he had worked on planning for operations in Bosnia and Kosovo during the late 1990s.

Mansoor wore wire-rimmed glasses. He looked more like a university professor than an officer who had commanded the 1st Brigade, 1st Armored Division in Iraq during 2003 and 2004.

Barely two months earlier, he had arrived with his family at Fort Leavenworth, Kansas—at Petraeus's request—to help establish the new U.S. Army and Marine Corps Counterinsurgency Center.

When the call came, Mansoor packed a bag and called a cousin in Silver Spring, Maryland, to ask if he could crash in the guest room.

Around the same time, the phone rang inside Marine Colonel Tom Greenwood's home in Virginia. An aide in the office of the chairman of the Joint Chiefs told Greenwood that he had been selected to be part of a secret group of colonels who would conduct an in-depth review of the Iraq War and related strategic issues. The assignment would last through Christmas, the aide said. And oh, by the way, could he report to the Pentagon tomorrow?

Greenwood, a modest, cerebral career officer who had served as an aide to the Marine commandant and worked on the Bush National Security Council staff during the invasion of Iraq, was delighted. He viewed it as an opportunity to use his years of Washington and policy experience to speak frankly to the top brass.

Greenwood had recently returned from a year in Iraq's Anbar province, where he had overseen the training of Iraqi security forces. He was 50, the son and grandson of military men, and had graduated with an economics degree from Washington and Lee University, a small liberal arts school in Virginia. He later earned a master's degree from Georgetown.

At 5-foot-10, with close-cropped hair and soft eyes, Greenwood looked and spoke like Andy Griffith without the accent, more small-town neighbor than a senior Marine. But he had commanded at every level up to brigade and had traversed the world in service to Uncle Sam—training at Camp Pendleton, tsunami relief in Asia, counter-insurgency in Iraq. After his recent stint in Iraq, he had been named director of the Marine Corps Command and Staff College in Quantico. But that would now be on hold during this secret Pentagon assignment.

During his time on the National Security Council staff years earlier, Greenwood had been a front-row witness to what he considered the alarming failures of the Bush White House, the Defense Department and the State Department to coordinate and communicate honestly with one other. One example came in the fall of 2002. Rumsfeld

had just gone through a presentation in the White House Situation Room on the latest version of the TOP SECRET plan for the invasion of Iraq.

Greenwood was sitting along a back wall, the "cheap seats," as he
called them. Rumsfeld and Rice were on either side of the president at
the main table. After the presentation, Rice reached for a copy of the
TOP SECRET PowerPoint packet of slides, code-named Polo Step,
which had been handed out during the briefing.

"You won't be needing that," Rumsfeld said, reaching across the
table to snatch the sensitive packet from the national security adviser.
He didn't want it left around—even in the White House—adding,
"This is highly secret and classified."

"Well," the president said sarcastically, "I think it's pretty safe
around here, but I'll let you two work it out." He turned and walked
out. Rice didn't leave with a copy of the slides.

Later that day, Frank Miller, his immediate boss and the senior
director for defense policy on the NSC staff, called Greenwood to his
office.

"Hey," said Miller, a 22-year veteran of sensitive Pentagon posts,
"come over here and see me."

"You're going to tell me to go over to the Pentagon," Greenwood
said, "and get those slides that they refused to leave over here."

Exactly right, Miller said.

Greenwood, who normally wore a civilian suit at the White House,
changed into his Marine uniform to improve his chances. He also
had an official courier identification and a briefcase. He didn't rate a car
and driver, so he took the underground Metro subway. At the Pentagon, he went to the office of a friend on the Joint Staff. It was way
too risky to approach the several people he knew well on the civilian
side—Rumsfeld's staff. They would surely feel compelled to inform
Rumsfeld.

"I need a favor," Greenwood said. "Isn't it a crazy world?"

The friend complied, knowing it would be reciprocated, most likely
in the form of a briefing from Miller or Greenwood on what happened
in NSC meetings. A formal "summary of conclusions"—a classified
document that outlined the decisions or conclusions from a meeting—

was circulated after the meetings but could take days or weeks to make its way to the Pentagon. Even then, they were often bleached-out versions of what had happened, making them bland and hardly useful.

To Greenwood, the subterfuge was symbolic of an administration infected with distrust.

Several months later, just before Christmas 2002, Greenwood had been in his office and was planning to leave about 1 P.M. to do some holiday shopping, excited about the prospect of time off.

Miller again summoned him. "What are you doing this afternoon?" he asked.

Greenwood's heart sank. It was code for "I've got a really lousy deal coming your way."

"I've got to go Christmas shopping," Greenwood said.

"You're not going to go Christmas shopping for a couple of hours because we've got to go on a little trip."

"Do I need my toothbrush?"

"No, but you need your map of Iraq and you need your brief on war preparations for the invasion. And bring all that stuff. We've got a car meeting us downstairs in 15 minutes." Rice was sending them to brief Secretary of State Colin Powell, Miller finally revealed.

Normally, Greenwood prepared for these briefs and rehearsed all day.

Greenwood gathered his material. Rice's instructions had been clear: "Keep this quiet because I don't think the Pentagon"—read Rumsfeld—"would appreciate my NSC staff going over to brief the secretary of state on war preparations."

A White House driver took Miller and Greenwood the 10 blocks to the State Department. Up on the seventh floor, the halls were quiet and empty. The holiday already had begun. Powell wore a casual windbreaker and was reading a newspaper. His deputy and best friend, Richard Armitage, the outspoken, barrel-chested former naval officer who had served three tours in Vietnam, also was there.

Greenwood pulled out his charts and descriptions of the war plan. They included a major multidivisional southern thrust from Kuwait north into Baghdad. The U.S. 4th Infantry Division was still on ships in the Mediterranean, waiting to strike into Iraq from the north.

"A two-front war would certainly make sense," said Powell, the former Army general. "How are they going to help, being on ships?"

"Well, sir," Greenwood said, "the idea is that they get diplomatic permission to cut in from the north, but that hasn't been achieved yet."

"It's getting late in the game for that," Powell said, turning to Armitage. He was skeptical that Turkey would give permission for a whole U.S. infantry division of 20,000 troops to march through it. Leaving the division on ships was "a stupid idea." It was important to get the 4th Infantry into the fight. He added, "That's one of a number of problems that I see with this plan."

As the other divisions move to Baghdad, Powell asked, how many U.S. forces will be left behind to stabilize the area and prevent attacks from the rear?

Greenwood said he didn't have a lot of information on that, but it would not be many because the concept was a lightning, blitzkrieg drive to Baghdad to topple Saddam.

That's a hell of a distance, Powell said, looking askance, noting that it was more than 300 miles, with some big cities along the route. "Can you believe what you're hearing here?" Powell said to Armitage. To lighten the moment, the former general started poking fun at Miller and Greenwood for coming up with such a plan.

"Sir," Greenwood said sheepishly, "I can't take full responsibility for this."

Powell made it clear he understood exactly where it had originated, namely, with Rumsfeld and General Tommy Franks.

Greenwood had witnessed midlevel battles within the Bush administration, but now he had seen the same dysfunction at the most senior levels. Near-catastrophic voids in cooperation and information flow existed at the top, even on the most basic matters. Given that Bush and his team were on the brink of starting a war, there was nothing comforting about this experience. For Greenwood, it was one of the lowest of lows in his decades as a Marine.

"You hit a home run!" Miller assured Greenwood as they descended in the State Department elevator.

"Frank, I don't feel like I hit a home run. What is a broke-dick colonel like me who works for you at the White House doing briefing the secretary of state on a war plan for which we get information third-hand, through hook and crook?"

Now, years later, he held out hope that his summons for the secret Pentagon group would give him another chance to help turn around a war that he felt had been mismanaged from the beginning.

16

One by one, 16 men whose lives had been placed on hold showed up at the Pentagon for their mystery assignment. Three were Marines, four were from the Army, four from the Navy and five from the Air Force. Some had logged significant time in Iraq or Afghanistan. Most had advanced degrees. But few knew the precise purpose behind their summons to the mother ship on the banks of the Potomac.

It was the last week of September, and they gathered in the National Military Command Center within the Joint Chiefs section of the Pentagon—the nerve center of worldwide crisis response.

Pace had assembled the brightest military minds to study what had become of Iraq and to examine the United States' broader global challenges. These were the star thinkers of the military, many of them destined to make up the next generation of admirals and generals. Now this windowless basement space would be their home for the rest of the year.

On September 27 and 28, Pace and the other chiefs, along with JCS staff director Lieutenant General Walter "Skip" Sharp, outlined the assignment the colonels would tackle for the next three months.

The group was to remain highly confidential. If anyone asked what the colonels were doing, they were to stick to a cover story—they were conducting research for a series of war games.

Pace told the men to think broadly and creatively. They had the freedom to follow their intellects, and they need not come to consensus. Dissenting opinions were welcomed, even encouraged, he said. The colonels should try to figure out what decisions America must make in order to win "the long war," he said, the global struggle against terrorism.

Pace and the other chiefs posed a range of questions for the group to consider. Among them: How can the United States best implement all the elements of national power? Does the country have the correct national security strategy? How can it outthink and overmatch its enemies? How can we tackle the Israeli-Palestinian problem? How do we improve the American image throughout the world?

Take a critical look at the way America has waged the global war on terrorism. Analyze the role of CentCom. Study the responsibilities and performance of the JCS. Research historical insurgencies. Bring in experts and critical thinkers. Challenge any and all assumptions. Help the decision makers figure out the fight we're in. Take on the 800-pound gorilla in the room—Iraq.

The group would report directly to Pace and the service chiefs every Friday afternoon, schedules permitting, from 2:30 to 4:30.

A tangible excitement surrounded the colonels. Greenwood felt his adrenaline rising with the thought of the mission ahead. It seemed weighty and important. Seldom did such a small group of officers get the chance to influence policy at the highest level and perhaps put the country—and the world—on a better footing.

The group would get face time with the chairman and the Joint Chiefs each week. The secretary of defense would be looking to them for wisdom, he thought, and perhaps the president would too.

In those first weeks, the colonels immersed themselves in their task like soldiers digging trenches on the front lines—motivated, determined and resolute. There was a sense within the group, a certain idealism, that they were going to fix the Iraq problem.

Half jokingly, they began referring to themselves as the Council of Colonels.

• • •

On September 30, General Casey presented his view on the nature of
the enemy to the NSC during a secure videoconference. "The enemy—
and the security situation—is much more complex than ever before,"
he told them. He outlined four major groups that must be confronted:
Sunni extremists, Shia extremists, those carrying out resistance attacks on the coalition, and the Iranians, who were covertly undermining stability.

"We're going to have to do this by the drink," Hadley told Bush, the
former heavy drinker. "We're going to have to buy American support
for continuing the war by the drink. We're going to have to have a new
strategy. We're going to have to show that the new strategy is succeeding. And if we can have a three-month period where we begin to show
some success, we can probably buy some support for another three-
month period."

The president said that sounded right.

"We're going to have to do this on the installment plan," Hadley
went on. They didn't have much time, certainly not the multiyear timelines General Casey was still using. They both knew they were getting
hammered from the left and the right, and as Hadley saw it the criticism was basically the same. The Democrats were saying, "It's not
working. Go home." The Republicans were saying, "It's not working.
Make it work or get out."

They both also knew that their most immediate vulnerability was
from their own party. Lindsey Graham, the South Carolina senator, had
told reporters, "We're on the verge of chaos, and the current plan is not
working." Virginia Senator George Allen said, "We cannot continue
doing the same things and expect different results. We have to adapt
our operations, adapt our tactics." Kay Bailey Hutchison of Texas,
Chuck Hagel of Nebraska, Lincoln Chafee of Rhode Island and
Olympia Snowe of Maine were among the high-profile Republican critics. But they were far from the only Republicans whose loyalty had
worn thin.

Hadley and the president realized they would have to convince their colleagues by the drink too.

On Sunday, October 1, Hadley sent his deputy, J. D. Crouch, to talk with former Navy Captain William J. Luti, the senior director for defense on the NSC staff.

"Would you put together a concept, operational concept—a plan—on a new direction in Iraq?" Crouch asked. "Steve wants you to do this."

Luti, who previously had worked for Cheney and former Speaker Newt Gingrich, was known on the NSC staff for his hard-line views. He had strongly supported the Iraq War. He jumped at the chance to help turn it around.

Hadley knew that other reviews were under way within the government—Rice's at State, another at the Pentagon—not to mention the Iraq Study Group. But he was unsure whether a surge option would emerge from any of them, and he wanted to make sure it got on the table. He had already concluded that a surge was the way to go, and he knew the president would want it as an option. The Luti assignment was essentially an insurance policy for the surge and a chance to assess the feasibility of adding more troops.

"Give it to me when you're done," Crouch told Luti. Work quickly. Work quietly. Highest classification. No leaks. The House and Senate elections were only five weeks away.

In early October, the president set out campaigning for Republicans across the country. In Reno, Nevada, on October 2, he said, "If you listen closely to some of the leaders of the Democrat Party, it sounds like they think the best way to protect the American people is, wait until we're attacked again." But then he added, "What you're seeing is the beginning of a victory against an ideology of extremists." In Arizona, on October 4, he said the nature of warfare had changed since World War II and the Korean War. "This is a different kind of war," he said. "It's a war that depends upon our capacity to find individuals and bring them to justice before they strike again." It was the kind of round-'em-up-and-kill-'em mentality that General Casey felt reflected the president's basic misunderstanding of the war.

Condi Rice's worries were escalating. She had not been to Iraq for five months. "I'm going out," she told the president and Hadley. "I think I need to have a firsthand look."

Rice arrived unannounced in Baghdad on Thursday evening, October 5. After a brief meeting with Maliki and a 20-minute press conference, Rice met with the Sunni leaders in Ambassador Khalilzad's large, open living room around 8 P.M. The Iraqis lined the chairs and sofas in the room in an almost perfect square around the secretary. Khalilzad and Satterfield also sat in.

"Why don't you tell me how you see things here?" Rice began.

Dr. Adnan al-Dulaimi, the elderly head of the largest bloc of Sunnis in the parliament, said sectarian violence was paralyzing Iraqi society, especially in Baghdad. "The school year has started," he said, "but no one—teachers or students—can go to class." Trade was on the verge of collapse because Iraqis were too afraid to leave their homes.

We're victims, he and his fellow Sunnis insisted. Nobody's doing anything to protect us. The leaders presented Rice with eight-by-ten glossy photographs, some in color, showing Sunni victims of torture—decapitations and bodies with holes drilled into their heads and hands—a gruesome portfolio. They insisted that the killings and torture were the work of Shia death squads linked to people in the highest ranks of the government.

Rice knew that these pictures conformed with recent intelligence reports that sometimes showed 150 bodies turning up overnight in Baghdad.

The Sunnis' message was simple: We need to be protected. The leaders provided details and names from the Ministry of Interior, which ran the national police. Most of it involved crimes of omission, looking the other way, but there were clear acts of barbarism. On the political side, they claimed, Moqtada al-Sadr was trying to force a resolution on a timetable for U.S. withdrawal, in their view an item on

Iran's agenda. They complained that the Shia had not followed through on promises made during the formation of the government and that they viewed their Sunni counterparts as adversaries, not partners. Those Sunnis who had been given roles in the government were regularly circumvented by officials from the prime minister's office. In their eyes, all the political and security troubles were traceable to the Shia.

On a scale of 1 to 10, with 10 a devastating earthquake, Rice concluded the situation warranted a 9.

After an hour with these Sunni leaders, she met with the Shia leadership, most notably Abdul Aziz al-Hakim.

"We tried to do this the right way" by accommodating the Sunnis, who used to rule Iraq, Hakim said. "We could have said, 'They killed our fathers. They killed our brothers. They destroyed our families and our villages. They gassed our people, and therefore we're going to do the same thing to them.' There were those among us who thought that's exactly what we should do. But we didn't. We've tried to bring them into the government. We tried to work with them. They don't want to work with us." He added in frustration, "Don't you see that they don't really want to be a part?" They wanted everything as in the old days of Saddam. They want to be in power again, he said.

The Shia narrative was the mirror image of the Sunni narrative. Each saw the other as the enemy.

Rice, who listened intently for more than an hour, finally said she wanted them to understand how Americans looked at Iraq. "Americans understand that there are people who lost their standing—Saddamists who are fighting us. And they understand al Qaeda" because of the brutality of the 9/11 attacks. "Americans understand that there might be some people who think we're occupiers, and they're fighting us. But Iraqis killing Iraqis—they don't get that. And Americans are not going to stay with you if you're asking us to be in the middle of your centuries-old fights. And so what is going to happen is we're going to leave, because we won't be able to stay, and within six months you'll all be swinging from lampposts."

Afterward, Rice realized that the "swinging from lampposts" description might have been a touch indelicate. But it had gotten their attention. Rice asked her translator how it had gone over.

"It translated just fine," he replied.

Around 10:15 P.M., weary from her trip and consecutive frustrating meetings, Rice met again with Prime Minister Maliki, with only their interpreters in the room.

No matter what we do, she told him, this will not work if the Iraqis are not resolved to bring about some kind of reconciliation. "I don't mean by reconciliation that you all have to love each other," she said. After years of bitter internal warfare, she understood the tensions. She had heard the awful stories from both sides. "I have reason to believe that these stories are true—that when the army or the police want to defend a neighborhood, they're either called off or they're punished if they're going after Shia who are killing Sunnis. Innocent people are innocent people. And I need to know, do you believe that?"

Yes, he said, he believed it.

"This is our problem," she said. "We don't see it." Your words do not match your actions, and the United States would not keep its troops in Iraq if it was not fixed. She repeated the warning she had given the others: "In six months, you'll all be swinging from lampposts."

Rice left Baghdad the next morning, realizing that she had miscalculated. She had thought that some political deal was possible, a kind of grand bargain whereby the Kurds, Shia and Sunnis would all opt for a place in the sun and compromise on the division of power, oil and money. But the sectarian violence was all-consuming—especially with the Maliki government sanctioning and even abetting killings. It was tearing the country apart.

Back in Washington, Rice quickly beat a path to the White House. She met with the president in the Oval Office. Cheney and Hadley came to listen.

"What we're doing isn't working," Rice told the president. She said she thought there hadn't been an adequate response to the deteriorating situation since the Samarra bombing. And as she had in August, she again raised with Bush the image of an Iraqi society that was "rending," stretched to the breaking point and on the precipice of coming apart.

She recounted her conversations with the Iraqi leaders and told the president that Maliki wasn't the main problem. It was bigger than that. The problems seemed systemic. For example, no one trusted the police.

"We have a Bull Connor problem," she said, recalling her childhood during the turbulent 1960s in Birmingham, Alabama. Bull Connor, the notorious commissioner of public safety, had made his own law. He was a member of the Ku Klux Klan and a rabid segregationist, a law-man who ignored the law and fought integration with fire hoses, attack dogs and intimidation. "If the police came into my neighborhood, it wasn't for good," Rice said, adding that Iraq had a similar problem. "And until they find a way to make people think that the police or the army or somebody is there to evenly protect the population, this isn't going to work."

"You really think it's gotten to that point?" Bush asked.

"Yes," she said. The Iraqis had a lot to prove to their own people. Maliki had to prove he would not countenance, participate in or ignore organized violence. "And, frankly, they have a lot to prove to us."

She said she was worried that the effort the United States was making was no longer relating to the reality on the ground. Bush, usually given to a back-and-forth, mostly listened.

"How do you know that?" he finally asked. "How do you know that they aren't making the tough choices? What is it that you see?"

There are certain metrics to watch, indicators that would make it clear one way or another, Rice said. Most important, the Shia-led government must not act in a sectarian way. It must take on the Shia militias.

The average Iraqi has nobody to trust, she said. Not the government, not us. We are losing the population. Life is far from normal in Iraq. "It's not approaching normal," she said. "And it's not going to be normal unless the security situation is better."

They eventually got around to the obvious questions: What do we do about it? How do we fix it?

"Mr. President, I can't give you any easy answers," Rice said. "I want to go think about it. I want to go think about what we can do about it."

She had gotten off the plane from Iraq only hours earlier. She needed time to contemplate what she had seen, and more important, to figure out what must come next.

Rice and Hadley talked about which direction to head. "Obviously, we're going to need some way to think through this," Rice said. Maybe it was time to get people together and study the situation in a more formal, aboveboard way.

But they both were worried about the upcoming elections and wanted to avoid drawing attention in the charged political environment.

So the reviews continued under the radar.

17

_____

On Friday afternoon, October 6, the Council of Colonels headed to their first full session with the Joint Chiefs. They descended into the secure conference room known as the tank, a World War II moniker from when the chiefs had met in a basement room of the Public Health Service Building on Constitution Avenue. The entrance to the room was down a flight of stairs and through an arched doorway, giving the impression of entering a tank.

Officially known as the JSC conference room, or the "gold room," the current room in the Pentagon is trimmed in gold carpet, heavy gold drapes and dark wood paneling, much like a down-at-the-heels men's club. The tank is the military's secret society, a sacrosanct place where candid debates take place and what's said is not supposed to be reported to outsiders.

Chairman Pace and the service chiefs were seated in dark leather chairs around a long wooden conference table. The 12 colonels and four Navy captains sat along the walls.

For any military officer, participating in a tank session is a heady experience. But for Colonel McMaster, it qualified as downright surreal. His 1997 book, _Dereliction of Duty_, had blasted the Vietnam era chiefs who had met in this same room as "five silent men," meek and indecisive, utterly failing to be forceful and honest with President Johnson and Secretary of Defense McNamara.

The day's session was to focus on the so-called long war against terrorism. Was the goal spreading democracy or simply stabilizing a country or a region like the Middle East? First up from the colonels was "Issue 1: Stability vs. Democratization," an indirect shot at President Bush, the most outspoken advocate for spreading democracy around the globe.

The chiefs took the bait.

"Some folks are frenetic about us shoving Jeffersonian democracy down people's throats," said Air Force Chief of Staff General Michael Moseley, who had joined the Air Force in 1971 during the height of the Vietnam War.

Pace said he had told the president that "'democracy' is not as effective a term or concept as 'representative government.'"

Admiral Michael Mullen, the chief of naval operations, a 1968 graduate of the Naval Academy at Annapolis, cautiously inquired, "How far beyond military advice can we go on this point?"

"Can't avoid it," said General Peter Schoomaker, the Army chief of staff, noting that they had to examine all elements of national power—not just the military but diplomacy, and the economic and financial impact.

"I am comfortable taking anything to the president that negatively impacts our troops on the ground," Pace said.

The agenda then called for a discussion of America's "strategic vulnerability."

"We should be looking at how our current preoccupation with insurgents and terrorists in Afghanistan and Iraq reduces our ability to deter other potential hostile actors," General Schoomaker said.

"We have forgotten how to use the other elements of national power except for the military," complained General Moseley. "We have at least one arm tied behind our back. That is why we are losing ground . . . and our military is coming apart."

"We are not overstretched," Pace shot back testily. "Only a fraction of the nation has been mobilized, if that . . . General Moseley, what do you mean we are coming apart?"

"By all standards of measurement we have lost standing in the world," Moseley replied. "Politically, our reputation and stature, the national treasure we are spending on the war . . . all of it . . . we are in a downward spiral. I attended a NATO conference recently where they questioned our ability to sustain the fight and meet our global commitments." Then he added, trying to lighten the mood, "On the bright side, I think the Poles are with us."

There were a few muted chuckles.

"Our ground forces are stretched to the breaking point," Schoomaker added.

"We must be a learning organization," Pace said, falling back on an old military cliché. They needed to adapt, he said, and the American public would adjust. "We need to help them turn the corner. They are waiting for us to do this."

Some of the colonels were dismayed by the aimless discussion. Here were the senior military advisers to the president, in the middle of wartime, more or less adrift. It was clear the chiefs were angry and shockingly disconnected from policy making. Worse, they had no plan of their own and no unified voice. It resembled a late night barroom chat.

Colonel Greenwood turned to Colonel McMaster at one point. "Doesn't this make you think no one read your first book?" he asked.

"Yeah," McMaster said.

At 10:45 A.M. on October 10, Rumsfeld dispatched a SECRET snowflake to Pace and Eric Edelman, his policy undersecretary. The subject was "New construct for Iraq."

"Two months ago I told you I wanted to change the construct for Iraq," he wrote. His proposal was not radical: "Establish a public plan (benchmarks) to turn over responsibility for governance and security to the Iraqis and thereby permit reduction of Coalition forces." He said the president agreed with his proposal. Rumsfeld claimed this would be a "forecast," not a rigid "timetable," that could be carefully qualified by saying "we don't know if the Iraqis can meet the targets." It was little more than a public relations baby step.

But Rice saw it as something more. To her, it was Rumsfeld's way of speeding up a drawdown and shifting blame and responsibility to the State Department.

"I'm sick of hearing this line from the DOD," she told colleagues in private. "I'm sick of hearing that State's not in the fight, civilians aren't in the fight. I'm sick of hearing it. That's just wrong."

Meanwhile, Bill Luti on the NSC staff had spent 11 intense days working on the new operational concept for Iraq that Hadley wanted. Three months earlier, he had been to Iraq with Rumsfeld and noticed what he called "a subterranean burning." The Shia militias had launched their bloody campaign of reprisals, changing the nature of the war. The Abizaid-Casey strategy of turning the war over to the Iraqis might work if Americans were patient. But there was no more patience, Luti concluded.

On October 11, Luti took his new operational concept to Hadley's deputy, J. D. Crouch. He was proposing a giant step. His 10 classified slides, titled "Changing the Dynamic in Iraq," recommended a "surge" in U.S. forces to "secure and hold" and "to provide enhanced security in Baghdad and other insurgent" hotspots such as Anbar and Diyala. Luti urged greater reliance on the Iraqi army rather than on the police force. One slide urged a near doubling of the size of the Iraqi army, from 10 to 18 divisions. The military operations should emphasize eradicating the Shia militias as much as al Qaeda, with a new effort to quell Iranian meddling. To mollify the U.S. military, Luti also recommended increasing the overall size of the Army and Marine Corps.

Crouch accepted Luti's ideas and gave a copy to Hadley.

So while in mid-October the secretary of defense was advocating a plan that would accelerate America's departure from Iraq, a lone NSC staffer was proposing a surge that would recommit the country to the war.

The Luti paper presented a couple of problems for Hadley. First, he hadn't told O'Sullivan that he had requested it. Second, he knew that the White House and the NSC staff were not supposed to undertake military planning strategies. So Hadley decided, more or less, to hide it in plain sight. He called in General Pace.

"These are ideas from our staff," Hadley said, handing Pace a copy of Luti's paper. "You're the military planners. You're running your own process"—the Council of Colonels. "All I'd ask is to consider this in your process."

"Thank you very much," Pace said.

The result, Hadley hoped, was that the military would pitch the surge as its own idea. Though he felt a surge was the best option, he believed it was important that he not become an advocate too early and openly.

At 11 A.M. on October 11, the same day Luti took his surge paper to Crouch, the president held a news conference in the Rose Garden. He had just met with Casey in Washington.

"The situation is difficult in Iraq, no question about it," Bush acknowledged. Americans were seeing "unspeakable violence" on their television screens. The president said that attacks and casualties were up because U.S. and Iraqi forces "are confronting the enemy," engaging illegal militias. "The reason I bring this up is that we're on the move. We're taking action."

Steve Holland of Reuters asked: "Senator Warner says Iraq appears to be drifting sideways, and James Baker says a change in strategy may be needed. Are you willing to acknowledge that a change may be needed?"

"Steve, we're constantly changing tactics to achieve a strategic goal," the president said, dodging the question. "Our strategic goal is a country which can defend itself, sustain itself, and govern itself. The strategic goal is to help this young democracy succeed in a world in which extremists are trying to intimidate rational people in order to topple moderate governments and to extend a caliphate."

He added, "And I appreciate Senator Warner going over there and taking a look. I want you to notice, what he did say is, if the plan is now not working—the plan that's in place isn't working—America needs to adjust. I completely agree. That's what I talked to General Casey about. I said, 'General, the Baghdad security plan is in its early implementation. I support you strongly, but if you come into this office and say we need to do something differently, I support you. If you need more troops, I support you. If you're going to devise a new strategy, we're with you,' because I trust General Casey."

But behind the scenes, the Iraq strategy reviews were gaining steam, and Casey wasn't included.

That same day, Rice held a private meeting by secure video with Satterfield, Zelikow, Jeffrey and Khalilzad in Baghdad. Satterfield reported that the number of deaths had increased since the Baghdad security plan had gone into effect. "How can this plan be a success when the number of people dying is greater?" he asked. That wasn't a sign of success. That was a sign of failure.

"What does that tell us about the Baghdad security plan?" Rice asked rhetorically.

Khalilzad said U.S. military officials were saying they did not have enough forces to do the job.

"Can the Iraqi army beat the JAM?" Rice asked, referring to Moqtada al-Sadr's Mahdi Army.

No way, Jim Jeffrey thought.

"It's not working, Zal," Rice said. "Baghdad seems to have descended into mob rule."

Pace requested a private meeting with Rice. On October 12 at 2:45 P.M., he arrived on the seventh floor of the State Department and was ushered into her small inner office, with a desk in one corner, a couch and a handful of chairs arranged around a small, low coffee table.

The two had shared a cordial relationship dating to the early days of the Bush administration but had rarely met one-on-one.

Pace, even-keeled and rarely dramatic, seemed unsettled. He had brought along two classified charts to show the secretary. One was a version of the chart Hadley kept in his "GWB" file, showing the number of attacks in Iraq going up and up. The second showed the number of Iraqi security forces—army and police—a figure that also kept rising steadily. Together, they revealed a disheartening paradox.

"How do you explain this to people?" Pace asked. "The number of forces in the country is clearly going up, and the violence is still going up."

"Yeah, that isn't a very pretty picture, is it?" Rice replied. She didn't know what more she could say. Both security and the training of the Iraqi forces fell under his purview.

Pace explained that he had set up the Council of Colonels. He said that along with the chiefs, the group would be asking some fundamental questions about the current strategy.

Rice had heard about it "through the ether," as she liked to say—meaning from Hadley. She said she too had her staff conducting a similar examination of the overall mission and what they were trying to accomplish politically.

Rice saw no way she and Pace could join their efforts at the moment, because it might leak and generate "hothouse" news stories about an administration second-guessing its strategy. It would reveal a secret debate inconsistent with the president's public assurances that the United States was winning.

The Council of Colonels met with the Joint Chiefs again on Friday, October 13.

"The immediate center of gravity is the U.S. public," Pace said at one point, suggesting that the problem was a failure to make an adequate public relations case. Referring to General Casey, he said, "George had a four-year timeline, and the American people are going to give us about 90 days." They needed "to articulate that 'the U.S. is coming home' does not mean that 'the war stops.' If not Iraq, then Afghanistan or somewhere else."

"What is the long war?" Schoomaker asked. "Is it 30 years? How do we set up for reasonable expectations and deal with a 30-year problem while keeping flare-ups in the box? . . . The enemy won't quit after two years."

"How do we prepare the American people for the long haul?" Admiral Mullen asked.

"We don't," said General Michael Hagee, the Marine Corps commandant. "They continue to be spectators unwilling to change their habits."

"The American public," Schoomaker added, "does not want to do anything different."

"Their end state is: The troops simply come home," Hagee said.

But the public, Pace protested, holds the key to future success. "We need to better articulate the long war," he said. "Ask them to sacrifice."

"The problem is in this building," Schoomaker said, pointing up at the ceiling, toward Rumsfeld's third-floor office.

The Marine commandant had a suggestion that President Bush would not have liked. "We should have asked the American people to sacrifice by imposing a 5-cent gas tax on every gallon of gas or something like that right after 9/11," Hagee said.

"The nation needs to mobilize," Schoomaker agreed. "Most of the country is in spectator mode."

They turned to the Israeli-Palestinian situation and the peace process.

"U.S. policy is naturally biased toward Israel," Pace said.

Admiral Mullen said that the United States needed more active, visible diplomacy on the issue. "Poll after poll cites this as the central problem unifying the world against America."

"Almost anything would be better than what we have now," Moseley said, then summed up his sentiments about the Israelis and Palestinians. "Pack of assholes on both sides!" he declared.

Though Hadley was almost eight years older than Rice, he had served as her deputy in the White House for the first Bush term. Now, in the second term, he had taken over her old job as national security adviser when she moved to the State Department. They had formed a genuine friendship and exchanged all information freely. They spoke many times each day—in person at the White House, before and after meetings, on the secure phone, and on the regular phone.

One day, Rice raised the question of the various reviews being conducted in what she called an "atomized fashion."

"If I feel it, he feels it. If he feels it, I feel it," National Security Adviser Stephen J. Hadley said of his relationship with President George W. Bush. The president gave Hadley responsibility for the 2006 Iraq strategy review. "Let's just cut to the chase here," Bush said. "Hadley drove a lot of this."

"We have to win," Bush told General George Casey on June 13, 2006, in Baghdad. "I'm with you," Casey replied. "I understand that. But to win, we have to draw down." Despite his public show of support, Bush was losing confidence in the drawdown strategy. And Casey had come to believe the president did not understand the war.

"He's never been the head of a country before. He's going to have to learn," Bush said of new Iraqi Prime Minister Nouri al-Maliki in 2006. "And I'm going to have to engage with him personally to help him learn."

"I've decided to replace Rumsfeld," President Bush told Vice President Dick Cheney in early November 2006. "Well, Mr. President," said Cheney, "I disagree, but obviously it's your call."

The bipartisan Iraq Study Group, headed by Republican James A. Baker III and Democrat Lee Hamilton, interviewed every key policy maker on Iraq, including the president, and traveled to Baghdad to meet with U.S. military commanders and Iraqi leaders. The first line of the group's report, released in December 2006, stated, "The situation in Iraq is grave and deteriorating."

In the fall of 2006, General Peter Pace convened a secret internal review with some of the rising stars from every branch of the military. Nicknamed the Council of Colonels, they reported regularly to the Joint Chiefs. But their findings never were presented to the secretary of defense or President Bush.

(Left) Colonel Tom Greenwood worked on Bush's National Security Council staff during 2003–04. As part of the Council of Colonels, he was chosen to deliver the group's bleak conclusion to the Joint Chiefs: *"We are not winning, so we are losing."*

(Right) Colonel H. R. McMaster, the author of *Dereliction of Duty*, which exposed the weaknesses of the Joint Chiefs during the Vietnam War, found success as a ground commander in Iraq. His counterinsurgency tactics in Tall Afar became a model for protecting the population. A member of the Council of Colonels, he later became an adviser to General David Petraeus.

Donald H. Rumsfeld, who had served as Bush's defense secretary from the beginning, wanted to hasten the handoff of responsibility to the Iraqis. "We have to take our hand off the bicycle seat," he said time and again. He vowed to resign if the Republicans lost either the House or the Senate in the 2006 election. The day after the election, Bush announced Rumsfeld's resignation and named Robert Gates as his replacement.

A former CIA director and deputy national security adviser, Robert Gates had worked for five presidents. President Bush asked him to return to public service and take Rumsfeld's place. "Life may be hard" as defense secretary, he told Gates, "but this is a chance to make history."

Hadley had unparalleled admiration for the president and called him a visionary. "He defies the conventional wisdom by his boldness," he said of Bush. "He has a greatness in him."

Secretary of State Condoleezza Rice was skeptical of adding more U.S. troops in Iraq. "If we do it and it doesn't work, it'll be the last bullet. The last card," she told the president. "If you play 30,000 American forces, put out 30,000 American forces and things don't change, what do you do then?"

The Iraq Study Group recommended a drawdown of all U.S. combat forces by early 2008. But group member Chuck Robb (far left) had threatened not to sign the report unless it included an option for a short-term "surge" of American forces, the approach the president eventually adopted.

"The government is unable to govern," CIA Director Michael Hayden told the Iraq Study Group about the political situation in Iraq. "We have spent a lot of energy and treasure creating a government that is balanced, and it cannot function . . . the inability of the government to govern seems irreversible."

J. D. Crouch (top left), Hadley's deputy, headed up the administration's formal Iraq strategy review. He believed the president had one chance to get it right. "There will not be another bite at this apple," Crouch told the group. Meghan O'Sullivan (top right), the deputy national security adviser for Iraq and Afghanistan, was among the first administration insiders to realize in spring 2006 that the strategy wasn't working. When Bush asked her about life in Baghdad, she said, "It's hell, Mr. President."

As counselor to Rice, Philip Zelikow (bottom left) wrote in 2005 that Iraq was a "failed state." He proposed a new strategy of "stepping back," a middle course between adding forces and withdrawing. A career foreign service officer and Rice's senior adviser on Iraq, David Satterfield (bottom right) thought adding more U.S. forces would fail to quell the violence in the long run. He also worried that the president's rhetoric was too triumphant.

"I'm willing to commit tens of thousands of additional forces," President Bush told Maliki privately in Amman, Jordan, on November 30, 2006. "You've lost control of your capital. You're losing control of your country."

"We don't have a plan to defeat the insurgency," retired Army General Jack Keane told the president in late 2006. A mentor to General Petraeus, Keane was a strong advocate for a troop surge. He traveled to Iraq often and reported back to Vice President Cheney.

Bush and Cheney met with the Joint Chiefs at the Pentagon on December 13, 2006. The chiefs made clear that they opposed a troop surge. It could break the military. The president had all but made up his mind, yet he decided to hear them out. "They may have thought I was leaning, and I probably was," he said later. "But the door wasn't shut."

General Peter Schoomaker, the Army chief of staff, worried that the Army was being stretched too thin and told the president that a surge of five brigades would not work without extending Army tours. "These kids just see deployments to Iraq or Afghanistan for the indefinite future," he told Bush. "I don't think you have time to surge."

On February 10, 2007, General David Petraeus relieved Casey as the top U.S. commander in Baghdad. Casey still wanted to turn responsibility over to the Iraqis as soon as possible. "It is going against everything that we've been working on for the last two and a half years," he said of the new strategy.

24

On March 29, 2007, President Bush met privately with Nancy Pelosi, the new Democratic speaker of the House. "Mr. President," she said, "we owe it to the public to try to reach some consensus." Bush replied, "My views are well known. I've made myself clear."

25

26

On April 19, 2007, Senate Majority Leader Harry Reid (left) said the Iraq War "is lost." Bush later said of the comment, "I'm not shocked by anything in Washington anymore. This war has created a lot of really harsh emotion, out of which comes a lot of harsh rhetoric. One of my failures has been to change the tone in Washington."

Senator Carl Levin (right), the chairman of the Armed Services Committee, acted as a sounding board for Defense Secretary Gates, who wanted to know how reappointment of General Pace as JCS chairman would be received in the Senate. "It's going to be a battle royal," Levin said. Gates soon told Pace he would have to retire.

General David Petraeus, the Iraq commander, agreed to give Congress regular updates on the war. His first, on September 10, 2007, was in the words of one commentator, "the most important testimony of any general in 40 years." Sitting at attention for hours was so painful, Petraeus gobbled Motrin tablets during breaks. He reported progress but tried to avoid overstatement.

As the new Central Commander, Admiral William J. Fallon questioned Petraeus's constant requests for more manpower in Iraq. "This is nuts," he told Joint Chiefs Chairman Peter Pace. "Nobody's doing strategic thinking. . . . Now I understand why we are where we are. We ought to be shot for this."

Radical Shia cleric Moqtada al-Sadr and his Mahdi Army were a powerful force in Iraq. When he ordered the group to suspend attacks in 2007, it helped reduce the violence. In 2008, he announced the creation of a new paramilitary unit to attack U.S. forces, but some officials thought his influence was declining as the Iraqi government became more assertive.

Mowaffak al-Rubaie, the national security adviser to Prime Minister Maliki, frequently met with administration officials in Washington. On May 9, 2007, as violence kept rising in Iraq, Stephen Hadley told Rubaie, "We have to dramatize progress. We need a dramatic event."

In the spring of 2008, Defense Secretary Robert Gates announced that General Raymond Odierno would succeed Petraeus as the U.S. commander in Iraq, while Petraeus would take over as Central Commander. Retired General Jack Keane said the appointments would lock in the current strategy. "Let's assume we have a Democratic administration and they want to pull this thing out quickly, and now they have to deal with General Petraeus and General Odierno," he told Gates. "There will be a price to be paid to override them."

Republican presidential nominee John McCain and Democratic nominee Barack Obama greet each other on Capitol Hill in 2007. One of them will inherit the presidency and the Iraq War on January 20, 2009.

"We've got to pull this together now," Hadley said. "We've got to do it under the radar screen because the electoral season is so hot, but we've got to pull this together now and start to give the president some options."

They needed to cross-fertilize, she agreed, though she wasn't necessarily ready to begin listing options.

Hadley said he would put Meghan O'Sullivan in charge along with several of her most trusted assistants from the NSC staff, and Rice said she would add her Iraq coordinator Satterfield to the group. No one from the military or intelligence communities was asked to participate in the White House review—most notably Casey, the man Bush had publicly declared he trusted on strategy.

On the Sunday, October 15, television talk shows, two prominent Republicans—Senator John Warner of Virginia, the chairman of the Senate Armed Services Committee, and Chuck Hagel of Nebraska—said that U.S. policy would have to change if the Iraqis did not restore some kind of order. Warner said the administration should wait no longer than two to three months to change direction.

At 7:40 the next morning, President Bush spoke with Prime Minister Maliki by secure telephone, according to a SECRET summary of the conversation.

The president stressed that the prime minister should not pay attention to the political rhetoric in the American press in the run-up to the November election because he himself did not. Know that you have my confidence, he said.

I am confident of your support, Maliki replied, but public comments by some in and out of the administration were playing poorly in Iraq, harming his government. He had heard rumors that the United States was giving him a two-month ultimatum to stop the violence. Also, he said, discussions about the partitioning of Iraq were emboldening the terrorists and extremists. A book titled *The End of Iraq* by Peter W. Galbraith, an expert with two decades of experience on Iraq, claimed that partition was inevitable. Maliki said he hoped the president would make a public statement that there was no two-month ultimatum and that he supported Maliki and had no intention of recommending that Iraq be broken up.

A committee to find proposals to end the militia problem had been set up, the prime minister said. We need "to prepare the law enforcement agencies to confront militias and terrorism."

Bush reiterated his support for Maliki and promised that he would not let Iraq be torn apart. Don't let rumors and criticism consume you, the president counseled, but rather lead in the face of them. In the United States, Bush said, he did that all the time. He said it was important for Maliki to make a commitment before the end of Ramadan to resolve the political issues by a definite date in the future—the kind of deadline that he himself almost religiously avoided. Nonetheless, such a deadline, Bush claimed, would help stem the political rumors. The president also asked Maliki to take a personal interest in the investigation into the murder of Vice President Tariq al-Hashimi's brother, a Sunni. It would help demonstrate that he was the prime minister for all Iraqis, not just the Shia.

I'm fully committed to doing this, Maliki replied.

Bush expressed concern about Baghdad. Bring your political and security efforts into alignment, he said, in order to quiet down the capital. Tough decisions had to be made for this purpose, he said. Many innocent Iraqis were relying on Maliki to do this.

Maliki launched into a long response, claiming he would not hesitate to make sure the situation was brought under control. "There are still problems in Baghdad," he said, "but there are efforts, planning and political initiatives under way for achieving national reconciliation, and we will see the result. We are determined to combat terrorism and isolate the militia. There will be an agreement with Zal and Casey regarding the reform of the Ministry of Interior. My message is that we need to end [sectarian] activities. We will try all options, but in the end we are prepared to use force."

The president and the prime minister agreed to speak every two weeks.

18

Meghan O'Sullivan was increasingly fixated on the approach to Iraq. Though she never really bought into the idea of accelerating a transfer to the Iraqis, in her view it was at least an acceptable strategy in 2005. But by mid-2006, she believed, it was indefensible. It flew in the face of the facts. If there was one abiding lesson from her years of work in war and conflicts—writing her doctorate on the Sri Lankan civil war and working on the Northern Ireland peace process— it was that only a neutral party could resolve the enmity and contain sectarian violence. The U.S. military was the only neutral force in Iraq. Hadley seemed to agree but was moving too slowly.

In October, that began to change.

"I want to start an informal internal review," Hadley told the president, after he summarized the work of Pace's and Rice's groups. A small group of NSC staff and Rice's coordinator, Satterfield, would operate under the radar. They could decide later to formalize it.

"Do it," the president said.

Bush recalled telling Hadley, "Steve, let's take a look and see where we are." The president told me, "Let's just cut to the chase here. Hadley drove a lot of this. Why? Because I trust he and his team a lot."

On October 17, Hadley summoned O'Sullivan to his office. He asked her to start the review quietly. The military and the intelligence agencies wouldn't be involved. "I don't want to assume we know the answer," he cautioned. Do a thorough, bottom-to-top review. "We've got one more shot to get this right. I want to go back, and I want to do it in a systematic way. I want to look at our assumptions. What were our assumptions? What our assumptions should be?"

The NSC needed to take the lead on a new way forward. O'Sullivan and her group should assess everything—"candid, no kidding." He wanted her to examine a few questions in particular: What are the strategic impediments to our policy? How come it isn't working? What's in the way of success? Does the strategy need changing? What resources might be needed if they did change the strategy?

Only a handful of her staffers and Satterfield from the State Department could be included, Hadley said.

Rice similarly encouraged Satterfield to think about radical change. The current strategy was failing. "This cannot succeed, this will not succeed," she said, "and no amount of fine-tuning around the edges is going to fix it."

On October 21, O'Sullivan gathered the small group in her third-floor office in the Eisenhower Executive Office Building, next to the White House, for their first meeting.

Satterfield wanted to consider all options—even the extreme, dramatic ones—from a significant drawdown of forces to a significant addition of forces. "Let's think as if everything were possible," he said. Personally, he dismissed the notion of adding more U.S. forces. That would be, he argued, a final throwing of the dice, exposing more American soldiers to harm with possibly little to show for it. In addition, he felt certain that Maliki would make it impossible for more U.S. forces to operate in an effective way. But they had to include it as an option.

The group listed the problems: lack of a political center; ethnic and sectarian agendas; individual Iraqi politicians pursuing their own ambitions; an inadequate military strategy to halt the violence; the impossibility of proceeding on a political track as the chaos spread; a Baghdad that was changing shape before their eyes due to sectarian divisions; and Iran as a looming strategic threat that the United States could not deal with adequately because of its preoccupation with Iraq. The United States had become Iran's biggest strategic asset.

"Let's list all our assumptions that our strategy is based on," and then see what has changed, O'Sullivan said.

Peter Feaver, 44, a Duke University political science professor, Navy Reserve officer and special assistant to Hadley, was assigned to work on the secret strategy review. He was glad to see them asking about basics, listing not only assumptions but asking: What are the problems? What don't we know? Is it a problem of military capacity or a problem of the will of the Iraqis and the Americans? In addition, they wanted to prepare the president to ask tough questions of the military. Feaver was struck by how pessimistic Satterfield seemed about the prospects. Satterfield's pessimism matched O'Sullivan's and his own.

The question of adding more troops was on the table. But many questions accompanied that option. How many? When? How many were even available? What would they do that might make a difference?

Satterfield was skeptical that adding more force could quell sectarian violence or impact Iraq's dysfunctional leadership. But any serious discussion of the idea had to include a military voice.

"Guys, we can only go so far," Satterfield said at one point. "We can't make judgments about military force capabilities, about readiness capabilities. I don't even think George [Casey] necessarily knows those things. It's the chiefs, J-3 and J-5"—the divisions in charge of operations, and plans and policy, respectively—who could say "what exists out there. You need a military input."

They were conducting a strategy review of an ongoing war without anyone in uniform in the room. And while the Council of Colonels was meeting separately, as long as Rumsfeld was in charge, the two groups could not merge.

On Thursday, October 19, in Baghdad, Army Major General William B. Caldwell IV, Casey's chief spokesman, issued a grim verdict about Operation Together Forward, the 12-week-old U.S.-Iraqi military campaign to stem sectarian and insurgent attacks in the capital city. It had failed to reduce the violence, which had continued to rise in large part due to counterattacks in the targeted areas, Caldwell said. Already 74 American troops had died in October, with the month barely half over.

Operation Together Forward "has not met our overall expectations of sustaining a reduction in the levels of violence," Caldwell said. "We find the insurgent elements, the extremists, are in fact punching back hard. They're trying to get back into those areas" where Iraqi and U.S. forces have targeted them, he said. "We're constantly going back in and doing clearing operations." The violence, he added, "is indeed disheartening."

The news made instant headlines back in the States, fodder for the congressional elections, and increased the outcry for the president to change course.

A few days later, Rumsfeld sent a snowflake to Casey:

"Make sure you let Gen. Caldwell know that he is doing a darn good job, and not to worry about the press comments on that last briefing. He is doing very well and we appreciate it. Thanks."

On October 23, the Council of Colonels held its third session with the Joint Chiefs in the tank.

"We have some dark days ahead before we can mobilize the support to do what needs to be done," Chairman Pace said, neglecting to indicate exactly what that was. "Our country does not think we are at war." Contradicting what the president had said during his 9/11 anniversary address, the chairman said, "We may be safe, but we are not safer."

The colonels had reviewed most of the public and classified documents outlining Bush's national security strategy for Iraq, including the November 30, 2005, "National Strategy for Victory in Iraq." It was maddeningly vague, with statements such as "No war has ever been won on a timetable and neither will this one" and "Our mission in Iraq is to win the war. Our troops will return home when the mission is complete."

"We have this strategic boilerplate in documents and public statements that masks our real interests," General Schoomaker protested. "How do we measure progress against boilerplate?"

There were no meaningful responses, but General Moseley expressed the need for regional allies. "We can't do this alone."

"Israel and Iran are two problems that we can agree are problems," Schoomaker said. "We need to deal with them." They should at least be agenda items, he added, not simply the "big elephants in the room."

But the elephants remained uncommented upon.

"How do we sustain the good trends and correct the bad trends?" Pace asked, referring to Iraq. "Some say things we are doing now are making the problem worse." He added, "We need a sanity check."

The colonels showed a slide of the goals that the administration hoped to achieve in Iraq, taken from the "National Strategy for Victory in Iraq."

"I am underwhelmed here," Schoomaker said. "Look at these words! Civil rights is not achievable in Iraq probably in my lifetime. Domestic order is not achievable." He looked at the rest of the list. "In fact I would argue we cannot realistically achieve the last three bullets on this slide." They were an Iraq that could sustain itself, defend itself, and be a partner in the global war on terror. He summarized, "We have not figured out how Iraq fits into the overall strategic context of our nation." Schoomaker did not let up. What was the big picture? What was the national interest? "We are accepting the proposition that Iraq's and America's survival are one and the same. I am not so sure."

That same afternoon at the White House, press secretary Tony Snow was asked by a reporter at the daily briefing, "The president met with Secretary Rumsfeld today and General Pace. Tomorrow, General Casey and Ambassador Khalilzad have a news conference in Baghdad. Is something afoot?"

"No," Snow replied. "What's afoot is simply trying to keep people apprised of what's been going on in Iraq and how we intend to proceed. But there's nothing dramatically new going on. The problem we have a lot of times when we talk about this is that there are constantly adjustments being made, so in that sense there are new things going on. But are there dramatic shifts in policy? The answer is no."

•   •   •

As promised, Khalilzad and Casey held a rare joint news conference in Baghdad, as Casey said, "to explain our strategy and plans for success in Iraq."

Khalilzad spoke first, insisting that "success in Iraq is possible and can be achieved on a realistic timetable." He neither defined success nor offered how long a realistic timetable might be. But he said that a plan for transferring security responsibilities to the Iraqis would be ready before the end of the year.

Casey spoke next. "I'm sure for the folks back in the United States trying to look at this, it looks very confusing and very hard to understand. I'm not sure I can cut through all that, but let me try." He described the Samarra mosque bombing in February and the sectarian violence that had unfolded in its wake. He talked about the militias and death squads, and the destabilizing involvement of Syria and Iran.

"Now, what I just described is a fundamental change from how we saw the threat and the general situation here last year," Casey said. "So people are rightfully asking, 'How are you changing? What are you doing differently?'" He offered only the administration line that they had "continuously adapted" tactics to "stay ahead of the enemy."

Later, Casey said the Baghdad security plan "continues to have a dampening effect on sectarian violence" and the coalition and Iraqis were working to further reduce violence in the capital. "The additional U.S. brigades that we've kept here have had a decisive effect. And the Iraqi security forces are having a significant impact as well." It was a direct contradiction of General Caldwell's assessment only days earlier.

Casey added that they were about 75 percent through the process of building the Iraqi forces and that he believed such progress "can put Iraq in a very good place in 12 months."

Asked about troop levels in Baghdad, the commanding general talked about the goals of holding certain areas and improving basic services for the population.

"Now, do we need more troops to do that? Maybe," Casey said. "And as I've said all along, if we do, I will ask for the troops I need, both coalition and Iraqis."

A moment later, he added, "I still very strongly believe that we need to continue to reduce our forces as the Iraqis continue to improve, because we need to get out of their way."

On Wednesday, October 25, at 10:31 A.M., the president walked into the East Room of the White House for a long press conference.

"The outcome will determine the destiny of millions across the world," the president said about Iraq in his opening remarks. "Defeating the terrorists and extremists is the challenge of our time and the calling of this generation." He praised the work of the Baker-Hamilton study group, noting that its members were "taking a fresh look at the situation in Iraq and will make recommendations to help achieve our goals. I welcome all these efforts. My administration will carefully consider any proposal that will help us achieve victory.

"I know many Americans are not satisfied with the situation in Iraq. I'm not satisfied either. And that is why we're taking new steps to help secure Baghdad and constantly adjusting our tactics."

Bush concealed the fact that he and key members of his war cabinet had undertaken sweeping strategic reviews, asking fundamental questions about the current approach to the war.

The first question at a presidential press conference traditionally goes to the senior wire service reporter. That meant Terence Hunt of the Associated Press was up.

"Do you think we're winning and why?" Hunt asked.

The president said he was confident that the United States would succeed. The Iraqis wanted to succeed. But it was a hard struggle, a different kind of war. He went on for nearly 500 words, ducking the question.

"Are we winning?" Hunt persisted.

"Absolutely, we're winning," the president finally said. "We're winning."

About the same time the president declared that the United States was winning the war, Iraq Study Group member Bob Gates was reviewing some memos and notes from his fellow group members. They had completed their interviews and research and were planning to meet in three weeks to begin writing their report and formulating their recommendations.

Included in the material was a memo from months earlier from Bill Perry that had said the group should ask U.S. commanders in Iraq if they needed more troops. Gates liked the idea of more troops. Even though Generals Casey and Chiarelli had told the group that they opposed additional U.S. forces, Gates feared they might be parroting Rumsfeld's company line. Though General Chiarelli, the ground commander, had been vehement in his opposition to more troops, he had acknowledged that there were not enough troops to hold the areas they had cleared.

If one thing was clear to Gates, the former CIA man, it was that the Iraqi security forces could not be counted on, especially to hold disputed areas in violent Baghdad. Clearly, they needed enough competent forces, meaning U.S. troops, to help quell the violence in the capital city so that the political system might begin to work.

Gates sent an e-mail to Baker and Hamilton recommending a surge of 30,000 to 40,000 troops. The presence of these additional U.S. troops should be tied to performance of the Iraqis, he said. The better they did, the longer the U.S. forces would stay.

On October 29, Hadley, O'Sullivan and Hadley's special assistant Peter Feaver left for an on-the-ground survey in Iraq.

The next day, Rice summoned her top advisers to a meeting in her small inner office at the State Department. She closed the doors behind them—a rare precaution. She began by asking for their latest takes on Iraq.

"There is minimal chance of success on our current strategy," said David Satterfield.

Jim Jeffrey worried aloud if Iraq was edging toward "near-genocidal" levels of violence.

Rice asked if it were possible to scale back the goals. Suppose, she said, that the U.S. objective was simply to try to enforce a balance of power inside Iraq, to stabilize the existing and merging divisions of political power. Suppose they concentrated on the oil-revenue-sharing law and fighting al Qaeda, as well as limiting population exodus and ethnic cleansing? The United States could enforce the rules but not try to be a "leviathan." How might they look after the most important matters while limiting U.S. exposure?

"You could look at a lot of different options," Jeffrey said, including reduced force levels depending on how the mission was redefined.

Subdued, almost mournful, Rice said they had to play power politics. The United States had to be able to live to fight another day.

19

Rice found herself "wandering," as she put it, in search of what they were going to do next. Was there some way to redefine what they needed to achieve? Had they put too much stock in the ability of the Maliki government to survive? Was the Iraqi government just a collection of self-interested power brokers? Were the Iraqis going to be able to come together as a national government?

The Bush administration couldn't afford to watch the violence continue to spiral out of control. "Suppose the Iraqis declared martial law in Baghdad?" Rice proposed to the president and to Hadley. But the Iraqis had always fallen short, and martial law would be a big step. Would it be unenforceable?

Rice raised the possibility of restructuring. Had they put too much on the shoulders of the Iraqi government? Were the various factions irreconcilable? Perhaps the president needed to face the sectarianism and accept it as part of the nature of Iraq. Would the United States be better off saying to the Kurds in the north, "We'll put forces in Kurdistan"? And then find some group of Sunnis and make a deal with them to protect the center of the country? And then come to some arrangement with the Shia leaders in the south? Would that stop the violence? Would that help maintain order?

Rice talked to Hadley about this other, secret option.

He said they had to consider it. Maybe reconciliation would not work. "Is reconciliation a fool's errand?" he had been asking.

Rice talked to the president about the Iraqis. "Look," she said, "if they're going to play a power game rather than the national unity game, should we play the power game?"

The president was not opposed to the idea. "Sure would be nice if this got better," Bush said, seemingly open to any option that would improve the situation.

As they explored that notion, they decided that maybe it really was about a lack of capability rather than will on the part of the Iraqis.

At every meeting now, Rice was arguing, "This is not about Maliki. This is Maliki and Talabani and Hashimi and al-Mahdi. Don't let them walk away from this and make it Maliki's problem."

In a practical sense, if the United States tried to make deals with the different factions, it might lead to the partitioning of Iraq. It could mean the end of a national democracy, Bush's much enunciated goal.

Rice kept returning to the power broker option because it reflected the conditions on the ground—a so-called unity government was proving incapable of governing or reducing the violence.

In moments of brutal reality, Rice felt they needed to preserve the democratic institutions in Iraq but no longer rely on them. They would have to cut deals with anyone necessary in order to stabilize the country.

But even if deal making were the right way to go, it would be seen by many as a retreat. And a retreat could turn into a military rout. Leaders in the Shia majority might decide, "These guys are bugging out, so what the hell? Why shouldn't I just make a name for myself by being the guy that liberates Iraq from the Americans?" That might lead to pictures of helicopters evacuating the last Americans from the Green Zone. And nobody in the administration wanted to entertain that thought.

Satterfield drafted a SECRET/NODIS memo to Rice, dated October 31. In an unusually long paper, he sketched out possible courses of action and listed assumptions and conclusions.

Among the assumptions: The nature of the conflict had changed over time, moving from a Saddamist, al Qaeda, insurgency terror campaign to sectarian violence. The situation was profoundly different from expectations in 2002 and 2003. Another assumption: Iraqi security forces were unable to decrease significantly the levels of sectarian violence. The Baghdad security plans had revealed "serious flaws" in the transition strategy and in the will and ability of the Iraqi security forces to hold territory.

Another assumption: the political process to date had made little impact on the violence, and most state institutions were minimally functional without U.S. direction and support. None of the historic indicators of success or reconciliation—amnesty, cease-fire arrangements, a truth-and-reconciliation commission to ferret out past wrongdoing—were present in Iraq.

Maliki may seek to be a national leader, Satterfield wrote, but his actions and failures to act increasingly reflected a Shia sectarian identity. He also worried about the coalition's ability to counter al Qaeda influence in the western Euphrates River valley, to protect Sunnis in Anbar from al Qaeda domination and from Shia attacks in Baghdad and other mixed areas. His most worrying conclusion was that America and its allies were becoming "increasingly irrelevant" to key Iraqi political constituencies.

Satterfield also felt that the United States had become preoccupied and fixated on Iraq, unnecessarily so, to the detriment of its strategic interests. And the president had only made that worse by talking about Iraq as if all America's hopes rested upon the outcome.

Satterfield concluded that continuing the present strategy of pursuing a national unity government with functional institutions "offered only a small and diminishing chance of success over the next two years of establishing a stable democratic Iraqi state."

There had to be a change in strategy that protected both the Shia and Sunni communities "from bloodshed and full-blown civil conflict, preserved the structures of national governance until such time as further progress on a truly national basis was possible, and allowed the U.S. to pursue key U.S. interests compatible with the majority Iraqi interests."

The president has to be able to argue that the United States is adapting its strategy and its posture in Iraq to deal with changing circumstances, Satterfield wrote. He emphasized that Bush must also explain that a new strategy would both permit and require that the United States progressively and significantly reduce forces in Iraq. "So you are drawing down, but you are not leaving" was how Satterfield put it. The goal would remain a peaceful, stable Iraq, but the United States' priority must be its own interests well beyond Iraq.

Satterfield added a final and important caveat: "We should understand that it is possible that our approach to the Iraqi political leadership may not be accepted. Iraq's Shia leaders may prefer to continue their campaign for power and resources unimpeded by the presence of U.S. forces; all justified by the fight against 'Sunni terror.' Iraq's Sunnis may be so distrustful of the Shia and us, and in Anbar so intimidated by al Qaeda, to be effectively unable to support our efforts or to do much more as an organized community than simply inflict harm on the Shia. And even if our approach were accepted, our forces would be taking on a challenge that has been and maybe remains beyond our ability to achieve—breaking the back of al-Qaeda in Iraq, and even with the support of Shia leaders, truly turning back the tide of Shia sectarian violence and separatism."

Satterfield was stating simply that there were no guarantees. Any strategy, no matter how good on paper, might falter in the field. Satterfield, after all, had his own Iraq experience. He had seen security plan after security plan fail. He had lost confidence that the United States was capable of putting a plan into place that would *not* fail.

Satterfield, Rice and others began a quiet effort to persuade President Bush to tone down his lofty rhetoric about the stakes in Iraq.

They felt the myopic focus on Iraq, the way the president had made it the end-all, be-all test of American strength or weakness, the prism through which all success or failure was defined, harmed U.S. interests and its standing in the world. The United States could no longer allow itself to be dominated by Iraq—it wasn't a national survival war, after all, but a war of choice.

The president, however, continued to fuel that perception. "The outcome will determine the destiny of millions across the world," Bush had said days earlier in the Rose Garden. It had made members of his administration squirm.

But as it became more clear that the president would eventually have to give a speech laying out a new strategy, Satterfield suggested, why not pull back the lens? Turn everything on its head. People expected the president to give a speech about Iraq, Iraq, Iraq. Instead, he might open such a speech with words to the effect of "I want to talk to you tonight about issues beyond Iraq, to which Iraq is critical, but which have a transcendent and long-term impact on U.S. interests. Let's look at the world; let's look at the region."

In other words, Bush could argue the value of proceeding with certain core goals in Iraq, but without attempting to defend them in the context of success in Iraq, victory in Iraq. Instead, he might address Iran and its nuclear program, speak about the Israeli-Palestinian peace process, talk about ties to friends and allies.

Yes, Iraq was important, the president could say, but there were a hell of a lot of other interests in the region and beyond that were absolutely critical.

Satterfield's ideas never got much traction. They stayed buried and forgotten in his State Department computer.

After nearly two weeks of meetings, Meghan O'Sullivan gathered the findings of her informal review group and drafted a lengthy SECRET memo for the war cabinet members. She called it "The Way Forward: Four Organizing Constructs."

The United States had four basic options for how to proceed in Iraq, each with its own set of benefits and risks. She took each in turn:

1. *Adjust at the margins.* This option would mean staying with the current approach, avoiding a large influx of new resources and focusing on transitioning security responsibilities to the Iraqis as quickly as possible. Doing this would assume that the current strategy was sound

and sufficiently resourced, and that a major change would risk abandoning past gains.

2. *Target our efforts.* This approach would "remove coalition forces from the line of fire." American forces would focus on al Qaeda in Iraq and leave Iraqis to deal with sectarian violence. O'Sullivan noted that al Qaeda posed a threat to America's national security, whereas sectarian violence was directed inward. And yet, she wrote, the United States did have "a moral and humanitarian interest in limiting mass violence or expulsions." She believed this option would limit American exposure to sectarian violence and was more likely to have the most bipartisan support, at least initially.

3. *Double down.* The concept here was to "significantly increase coalition political and military efforts in Iraq to win the 'Battle of Baghdad' and put the unity government on a sure footing." She said that in considering this option, U.S. leaders must believe that the "present trajectory in Iraq is more likely to lead to failure than success," that "an infusion of resources is likely to yield positive results to warrant the costs and risks associated with doing so," and that "the American public will support one last push for victory in Iraq."

Among the key features of the plan would be an infusion of up to 30,000 U.S. troops to protect the borders, clear and hold neighborhoods, speed up reconstruction, and target al Qaeda and death squads. To pull this off, she wrote, the president would have to "put America on a war footing," expanding the size of the armed forces, changing rotation times and deploying more civilians to help with the effort.

The advantages O'Sullivan saw to doubling down were that it would match U.S. resources to Bush's rhetoric, provide maximum leverage for America to influence Iraqi and regional behavior, and that it had the "highest likelihood of securing success as we have defined it." But there were risks. Among them: Few Iraqis had asked for more U.S. forces. Maliki had not yet proven himself a reliable, nonsectarian partner. More forces could "exacerbate the problem of Iraqi dependency in the short term. . . . American casualties may rise, at least in the short term" and "securing bipartisan support would be very difficult and would likely not endure without quick and visible progress."

Doubling down could break the all-volunteer military. The cycle of violence could return after U.S. forces ramped down, "leaving no lasting gains." And most of all, if this strategy failed, little support would remain for a long-term U.S. commitment. In essence, the war would be lost.

4. *Bet on Maliki.* This option would enhance the political and security resources of Iraqi leaders so that they could dampen the violence and build toward reconciliation. Whereas doubling down would invest more resources across the board, this strategy would focus more resources exclusively on Maliki and his government. But to do so, O'Sullivan wrote, Maliki would have to convince the United States that he shared the vision of a nonsectarian, united and federal Iraq and that he could bring together "moderates across the political spectrum."

This option would "dramatically but quietly" increase the quantity and reach of the embedding/training program. The upside was that Iraqis would be more visibly in the lead and feel more empowered. The risks were that Maliki might prove too sectarian or the government too dysfunctional to overcome its divisions.

O'Sullivan had concluded that the "double down" option represented the best, if riskiest, path ahead. But she didn't take sides in the memo. The president would decide.

Satterfield was less than impressed with O'Sullivan's memo on the four constructs. It represented what he called the "Meghan-ization" of the process—taking a vast, complex issue and attempting to reduce it to the perfect PowerPoint presentation, a jumble of strategic assumptions and impediments, key features, advantages and disadvantages and risks that, if phrased just right, might unravel the Iraq knot. O'Sullivan, he thought, seemed to favor continual fine-tuning. Satterfield thought they needed a policy that was sustainable and practical. He had spent a lot of time on Capitol Hill, and it was clear to him that the administration was on shaky ground with members of both parties, not to mention with the American public. Whatever strategy they settled on, it had to make sense. And it had to have some chance of success.

"Don't talk about winning!" one key Republican leader implored Hadley. It sounded arrogant, triumphant and overconfident. "Stop talking about success!" another said.

Hoping to accommodate the administration's Republican allies, Hadley told the White House speechwriters, "Let's tone this down." Out would come "victory," out would come "win," out would come "success" when referring to Iraq.

But the president wouldn't hear of it. "We don't talk about victory here," he said when he saw one draft. "I want to say 'victory.' I want to say 'win.' I want to say 'success.'"

The words went back in.

Some leading Republicans, even Bush's friends, argued that the American public was tuning out the president. "The American people don't believe that we're going to win," one Republican told him, "or that there is victory. Or at least they don't believe in winning and victory the way they seemed to be defined in '03 and '04. So, Mr. President, they think by your continuing on about winning and victory, they think you're out of touch."

"I'm not out of touch," Bush replied. "I know how difficult it is. I talk about how difficult it is. But I've got to make it clear for our troops, for Maliki, for the Iraqi people, that I am committed to winning and to victory. I understand that for some people back here, they don't like to hear it. And they think it's sort of out of touch. But I've got other audiences I have to address."

20

From the vice president's suite in the West Wing, Cheney let the O'Sullivan strategy review go forward. He was making no attempt to lead it or curtail it, and no one from his office was attending her meetings. He knew that Rumsfeld had told the president he would resign as defense secretary if the Republicans lost either the House or Senate. Beyond that, Cheney did not know the president's plans.

From the beginning, Cheney had been a steamroller in pushing war with Iraq as the only way to deal with Saddam Hussein. But Cheney never had quite the overwhelming influence his reputation suggested. As *Washington Post* reporters Barton Gellman and Jo Becker wrote in their Pulitzer Prize–winning 2007 series on the vice president, "Cheney is not, by nearly every inside account, the shadow president of popular lore." Stephen F. Hayes, the author of *Cheney: The Untold Story of America's Most Powerful and Controversial Vice President*, a biography written with Cheney's extensive cooperation, agreed that everything Cheney does is either directed or approved by the president.

By the fall of 2006, the influence of Cheney and Rumsfeld was eroding. The two had the longest-lasting friendship in the Bush administration, dating back 37 years to 1969, when Rumsfeld gave Cheney his first government job in the Nixon administration. Five years later, when Rumsfeld was the White House chief of staff in the Ford White House, he selected Cheney as his chief deputy. When Rumsfeld became Ford's defense secretary the next year, Cheney was elevated to White House chief of staff at the age of 34. He had a calm, reassuring manner and seemed old even in his youth.

Cheney later served 10 years as the congressman from Wyoming, his home state, rising to become the number two House Republican leader. In 1989, he became secretary of defense for the first President Bush. Cheney had strongly recommended Rumsfeld in 2000 to become George W. Bush's secretary of defense. Since then, Cheney and Rumsfeld had operated as a kind of iron wall on defense and war policy that no one could get around. At every turn, Cheney praised and defended Rumsfeld, publicly and privately and personally to the president. He was Rumsfeld's biggest fan and made no secret of it. As vice president, Cheney technically outranked the secretary of defense. But Rumsfeld was like the older brother.

Cheney advised the president in private, separately from the rest of the Bush team. The president liked it that way. When I asked Bush about Cheney, he said, "I meet with him once a week, and we have private conversations. . . . He doesn't talk about it, and neither do I." Neither apparently realized how this private channel hindered the full airing of views and alternatives within the National Security Council. No one could challenge Cheney because no one knew exactly what he said to Bush. And intentionally or unintentionally, the president's decisions carried the implied blessing of the vice president.

Cheney liked to half joke that he was the only person in the West Wing who could not be fired because his name had been on the ballot in 2000 and 2004. But he knew that a vice president could be cut off by the president, excluded from meetings and policy debate.

Cheney calibrated his public words and actions so that he was seen as an extension and an echo of Bush. He served as the president's messenger. In 2004, when the Abu Ghraib prisoner abuse scandal was exposed, Rumsfeld twice submitted a resignation letter. The president dispatched Cheney to the Pentagon to talk to his old mentor. Sitting in the secretary of defense's office, which he had occupied from 1989 to 1993, Cheney made the case for staying.

We're not going to accept your resignation, Cheney said. Abu Ghraib was a problem, but it wasn't appropriate for Rumsfeld to shoulder the entire burden. You shouldn't lose your job because of a handful of out-of-control soldiers, he said. You are too valuable.

It took an hour, but Rumsfeld agreed to stay. "Look, if I ever get to be a liability here," he told Cheney, "I'm out of here. The president needs to know I'm prepared to move on."

Bush later told me that he had realized for quite some time that he needed "new personnel, including the secretary of defense, as well as the commander on the ground. Secretary Rumsfeld was also sending signals: 'New eyes, new ears.' I remember he said that at one point in time. And Don Rumsfeld is a professional. And Don Rumsfeld is a friend of mine. He is a person that has been around a long time. And as you begin to think new, it's more than just new strategy. It's new personnel."

Rumsfeld had told Bush, "Mr. President, maybe you need fresh eyes on the target."

"I was beginning to smell the problem politically at home," Bush recalled. "The politics of the moment, obviously, wasn't driving me, because of the strategic implications of this. On the other hand, I also know that the president's got to work hard to give people a sense of hope in the mission . . . Part of making sure the change of strategy became a change in people's minds was to also change some of the players, some of the personnel."

Bush realized that replacing Rumsfeld would be a delicate matter. After all, a major election was looming. And it was imperative to have a secretary of defense and maintain the chain of command during a war. He didn't believe he could send signals that he wanted to replace Rumsfeld without a replacement standing by.

How did you decide you needed to get a new secretary of defense? I asked him.

"It was evolutionary," Bush said. "When I decided on a new strategy, I knew that in order to make the strategy work, for people to understand that it was new, there had to be new implementers of the strategy."

"It'd be good to put that phrase" in the book, Hadley said to me.

"Steve would like you to use the word 'evolutionary,'" Bush said, laughing. "Just remember this. Once you make up your mind you need a new strategy, in order to convince others that the strategy is in fact new—people that really aren't aware of the military terminology—new people to implement the new strategy is an exclamation point on new strategy."

Bush said that Rumsfeld had realized this, and he insisted there had been no angry interchanges. He clearly had wanted as quiet and soft a landing for Rumsfeld as possible. "Don Rumsfeld is one of the true professionals who understands Washington about as well as anybody, that you serve at the pleasure of the president, and there's nothing personal."

The president said Rumsfeld didn't even have to say he would resign. "All the people who work for me, I have their resignation letter anytime I want . . . I'm the kind of person that if I lose confidence, and need to, I will ask them to move on."

In early November, the president told Rice that he had decided to replace Rumsfeld and was going to talk to Bob Gates about the job. Gates, 63, a 26-year veteran of the CIA, had been a key member of the first Bush's national security team, serving as deputy national security adviser under Brent Scowcroft and later as CIA director.

Rice was relieved and said she thought Gates was terrific. When she had served on the NSC staff from 1989 to 1991, Gates had run the deputies committee brilliantly. Somewhat playfully, she reminded the president that Gates, a Ph.D. in Russian and Soviet history, had been a hard-liner at the end of the Cold War, knowing that that would enhance Bush's view of him. The biggest problem would be getting Gates to accept, she said. For the last four years, Gates had been president of Texas A&M University and he had told her that when he left Texas, he and his wife, Becky, were heading back to Washington state, which they loved, as quickly as they could. Mr. President, Rice said, the only way to get him may be to appeal to his patriotism.

•   •   •

How did you pick Gates as the new defense secretary? I asked the president later.

Bush said that a friend he had gone to college with, whom he declined to identify, had first made the suggestion. According to the president, his friend said, "You know, have you ever thought about Gates being the secretary of defense? He's an impressive guy."

The friend had met Gates at Texas A&M. "So, I said, 'That's interesting,'" the president recalled. "And thought about it, and then called Hadley. And the reason why it was interesting is that Bob Gates had done an amazing job at Texas A&M, managing a big institution, which also happens to have, interestingly enough, a military component. Secondly, he understands Washington, D.C. Thirdly, he'd be a fresh set of eyes to look at the problem. And fourthly, curiously enough, he was on the Baker-Hamilton study group."

I asked Bush if he had consulted his father on the decision, as Gates had been his father's CIA director and deputy national security adviser.

"I don't think I needed to because I've heard my dad talk about Gates a lot in the past," he said. "Admires him a lot. Oh, look. This whole A&M thing. Dad is involved with Texas A&M." The elder Bush's presidential library and museum were on the A&M campus, and he "loved having Gates at Texas A&M," Bush said. "And was effusive about Gates's leadership at Texas A&M. No, I didn't need to talk to him."

Gates would be a good choice, Hadley agreed. They had known each other for 32 years, dating back to the last days of the Nixon administration, when they had been junior staffers on the NSC.

In 2005, the White House had tried to recruit Gates to become the first director of national intelligence. He had met with the president's senior staff at the White House, had a string of discussions with them and exchanged letters about the extent of the authority he would have. But they never brought President Bush into the conversations to close the deal. When Gates declined the job, Hadley seemed surprised and a little upset. Gates privately joked back at Texas A&M that the White

House could have taken a lessen from a car dealer, because they had let him "off the lot without a sale, without having it in their pocket."

Gates was convinced that he had burned whatever bridges he might have with the administration. "I will never get any other call from these people," Gates had told his wife, Becky. "I'm safe."

And yet now, in late October 2006, the White House had come calling again. Hadley reached Gates at home.

"Would you consider becoming secretary of defense?" Hadley asked.

This time, Gates asked no questions. He didn't hem and haw. He had always wanted to lead State or Defense. And with kids dying in two wars, he wondered how he could he say no.

"Yes," he told Hadley, he'd be interested.

It was a short conversation, and after he hung up he sat slightly stunned. My wife is going to kill me, he thought. They had always vowed to return to their home in Washington state as soon as possible.

"Gates is interested," Hadley reported to Bush.

"Follow up on it," the president said.

A couple days later Josh Bolten, the White House chief of staff, called to make sure Gates was really serious. He was. "We need to get you together with the president," Bolten said, and they agreed that Gates would have a private dinner with the president on Sunday, November 12. But Bolten called back to say the president wanted to do it sooner, and the meeting was moved to November 5 at the Crawford ranch.

Gates consulted with only one person about the job—former President George H. W. Bush. Gates had worked for him, and they belonged to one of the most exclusive clubs in the U.S. government—former CIA directors. After he explained Hadley's call, Gates said, "You can't tell a soul. But do you think I should do this?"

The former president said he didn't want Gates to leave Texas A&M. But at the same time, he said, "This would be a great thing for you to do."

•   •   •

In the National Military Command Center in the Pentagon, the Council of Colonels was aggressively chipping away at the Iraq riddle, pulling 12-hour workdays, usually heading home long into the evening darkness. Greenwood drove back to his house in Arlington. Mansoor headed north to the spare bedroom in Silver Spring. McMaster took the Metro subway to a hotel in downtown Washington.

The colonels eventually pieced together slides to present to the chiefs. One dealt with "understanding the operating environment." Among the bullet points: There was a layered, hydra-headed insurgency; sectarian violence remained on the rise in the form of ethnic cleansing; Sunnis often regarded the Iraqi army as a Shia militia; and the Iraqi government was plagued by corruption, ineptitude and sectarian bias.

The presentation included a hard look at the strategy of the various enemies. Their goals, the colonels had concluded, were to expel coalition forces, weaken the fledgling Iraqi government, prevent political reconciliation, attack symbolic targets in order to incite sectarian violence, and make ordinary Iraqis feel perpetually insecure.

As their next tank meeting with the Joint Chiefs approached, the colonels drew up a list of "trends and impediments" in Iraq. While some members of the group saw more hope than others, the overall sense was that the United States was facing a quandary. They agreed that Greenwood would brief the group's solemn findings to the chiefs. Some of his peers seemed nervous for him. "They're going to skewer you," one told him.

"They wanted the truth," Greenwood replied.

The time allotted for the Monday, November 3, session in the tank was shorter than usual. Greenwood knew he would have to speak fast.

The chiefs sat silently as he pulled up a slide on the screen behind him: "Six major trends." Each was negative.

1. Our current strategy is not working.
2. The government of Iraq is unable to produce tangible and credible results in the eyes of the Iraqi people.
3. Iraqi security forces remain weak and ineffective.
4. Ethnic and sectarian conflict is increasing.

5. The rule of law is lacking.

6. Economic progress is lacking.

Greenwood moved quickly on to the three major impediments to progress the colonels had identified. They were direct and harsh.

First, he said, until we acknowledge that we are in the middle of a complex insurgency and a low-level civil war, our nation will not come to grips with the true character and nature of the conflict. This was necessary, Greenwood said, to promote and facilitate an honest discourse.

Second, we have a short-war mentality and a short-war strategy that are ill matched to the long war that we are in.

And finally, after three years of sacrifice the United States is running out of time. As the invading foreign power, the burden is on us to win or at least show credible progress in Iraq.

Because this is not happening at a rate that is convincing to the Iraqi people, the American people or the international community, Greenwood said, "Our group thinks we are losing in Iraq today."

He had typed a final phrase in capital letters across the bottom of the last slide:

"WE ARE NOT WINNING, SO WE ARE LOSING"

The chiefs looked on in silence. None of them suggested anything different.

Chairman Pace had an unusual sullen look on his face, almost crestfallen, as if to say, "How could I have not realized this?"

On Sunday, November 5, Bush welcomed Gates to his ranch in Crawford, Texas, for a one-on-one meeting. Gates arrived quietly and met the president in his private study adjacent to the main house, where a crowd of guests had gathered to celebrate Laura Bush's 60th birthday.

Gates had met the president only in passing during the first Bush administration and he had once had his picture taken with Governor Bush at the Texas Capitol.

He was an obvious and yet surprising choice for defense secretary. With nearly three decades of experience in the CIA and on the National

Security Council staff, he was very much a government man. But he also had an independent and irreverent streak.

In his 1996 memoir, *From the Shadows*, written when it seemed his days in public life were over, he wrote, "I would ultimately work in the White House for four presidents, and I saw it all. . . . Intrigue. Back-stabbing. Ruthless ambition. Constant conflict. Informers. Leakers. Spies. . . . Egos as big as the surrounding monuments. Battles between Titans. Cabinet officers behaving like children. High-level temper tantrums."

One of Gates's closest associates was Brent Scowcroft, who had served as national security adviser to the first President Bush from 1989 to 1993. Gates had been Scowcroft's deputy for two of those years, and together they oversaw a pragmatic, nonideological foreign policy. To invite Gates into the inner circle now was a nod to that old school of foreign policy, practiced by the president's father and by Scowcroft, a fierce critic of the Iraq War. Theirs was a more rigorous, cautious style in which war had been the last resort.

"He worked in, you know, Dad's administration, but I didn't know him that well," the president later told me. "Anyway, we sat down and just visited. And I like to, you know, talk to people about their background and just get a sense for who they are as a person . . . when you ask them questions about their families, how they react to the questions."

He said that he told Gates, "We're in the middle of a war, and I need your leadership. What we have been doing is not working. We're going to change our strategy. I need a new face. Would you be interested?"

Gates said he was interested.

"We've got to make some changes in our strategy," the president said of Iraq. "We've got to change our approach."

Gates agreed. But he told the president he had several concerns beyond Iraq. First, the Army was too small for the missions being required of it. Second, he felt they had pulled a bait-and-switch on the National Guard; many of its members had signed up as part of the strategic reserve for national emergencies, but it had been transformed into an operational force with regular deployments. Third, the Pentagon was buying equipment suited to the Cold War, when what the U.S. military needed was equipment for the kind of antiterrorism and counterinsurgency conflicts it was facing now.

"After a little more discussion," Bush recalled, "I said, 'Fine. I'm offering you the job.'"

Gates accepted on the spot. "I think he was intrigued by the opportunity," Bush said.

The president asked Gates what he thought about the idea of a surge in forces to Iraq. Gates told him that he could support an increase, though he believed it should be tied to Iraqi performance.

"He said he thought that would be a good idea," Bush recalled. "So what I'm beginning to get is a man who is competent, who has a track record, knows Washington, recognizes we need a new strategy . . . because at this point in time, in November, I'm beginning to think about not fewer troops, but more troops. And, interestingly enough, the man I'm talking to in Crawford feels the same way."

Bush said he told Gates that day in Crawford, "Life may be hard" as defense secretary, "but this is a chance to make history."

In the Pentagon the next week, the 16 colonels and Navy captains continued to grapple with Iraq. They debated a list of possible strategic options, which Colonel Greenwood would later brief to the chiefs. Among them:

1. *Go Big/Full Court Press*. A large increase in troops, perhaps several hundred thousand, in order to "overmatch" the enemy and break the cycle of sectarian and insurgent violence. Colonel McMaster was an outspoken advocate of the option, though many colonels rejected the idea on the grounds that there were not enough available U.S. forces and that the Iraqi forces were not effective enough.

2. *Go Long/Extended Presence*. Commit to keeping a sizable number of troops for years, perhaps even a decade, in order to create a stable and competent Iraqi army. Colonel Mansoor and a few others strongly backed this option.

3. *Go Home.* A swift withdrawal of U.S. troops. Though a few colonels leaned toward this option, most agreed it could leave Iraq in a full-blown civil war.

4. *Enclave Strategy.* Walling off and separating certain areas to control comings and goings and to maintain peace.

5. *Partitioning.* Splitting up the country into distinct regions based on ethnic/sectarian identity.

6. *Gradual Withdrawal.*

7. *Combinations of the Above Strategies.*

"With 10 Iraqi divisions and 15 U.S.-coalition brigades," said General Schoomaker, the Army chief, "it is hard for me to imagine that we don't have enough troops."

"Can we shopping-cart the options?" Pace asked, suggesting that they pick parts from several of them.

But there wasn't a lot of enthusiasm for that, considering that the current strategy seemed to have been cobbled together in much the same way.

On November 6, the day before the election, Rumsfeld sent a SECRET memo to the White House. "In my view it is time for a major adjustment," he said, stating what had become almost a consensus within the administration. "Iraq is not working well enough or fast enough." He listed some possible options: "an accelerated draw-down"; a withdrawal of U.S. forces from vulnerable positions and patrols; or providing money to key political and religious leaders, as Saddam had done. He added, "Announce that whatever new approach the U.S. decides on, the U.S. is doing so on a trial basis. This will give us the ability to readjust and move to another course, if necessary, and therefore not 'lose.'"

Rumsfeld wrote that the "less attractive options" included continuing on the current path, moving "a large fraction of all U.S. forces into Baghdad to attempt to control it," increasing U.S. forces "substantially," or finally setting a "firm withdrawal date." He was all over the map.

That same day Bush asked Cheney to stay behind after an Oval Office meeting. They walked down the little hallway to the president's private dining room.

"I've decided to replace Rumsfeld," the president said.

With whom? Cheney asked, knowing that Bush wouldn't make such a move without a replacement lined up.

"It's going to be Bob Gates," Bush said. He wanted Cheney to know, but the vice president was not to talk about it or say anything to anybody.

"Well, Mr. President," Cheney said. "I disagree, but obviously it's your call."

Cheney was disappointed. Rumsfeld certainly was carrying a lot of baggage, he thought, but hell, so was he. But he could tell the president's decision was final.

Cheney knew the president's style. He would call Rumsfeld "a good guy," a "friend" and a "professional" with vast experience who worked tirelessly. Bush wouldn't want anyone to "dis"—disrespect—Rumsfeld or portray him as the villain. They would dress up the matter carefully, giving the secretary a dignified send-off at the Pentagon with as much pomp and ceremony as could be mustered. Cheney would be able to declare publicly that Rumsfeld had been "the finest secretary of defense this nation has ever had." It would be another soft landing. The focus on Rumsfeld's accomplishment would also spare the president. There would be no assigning blame or speaking of failure.

On Tuesday, November 7, the Democrats won the midterm congressional elections, taking control of the House and Senate. The next afternoon, the president dropped his bomb: Rumsfeld was out, and Gates was taking his place.

Republicans in Congress, who had just lost their long-held leadership positions, were furious. "I wanted to throw the breakfast dishes through the TV," said Representative Peter Hoekstra, the Michigan Republican who lost the chairmanship of the House Intelligence Committee. Like many Republicans, although they would not say so publicly, he felt that if Bush had fired the unpopular Rumsfeld weeks before, it would have helped Republicans in tight races. Some Republican stalwarts began looking for a way to jump ship on Bush's Iraq policy, though it was unclear where or to whom they might jump.

When I asked the president two years later, he said he had thought his party would retain control of the Senate in the midterm elections. But he did not attribute the losses to the Iraq War alone. Rather, he said, the rash of Republican scandals had played as big a role. "I considered it as much a vote on people not being honest. Some of our members were being indicted. Some of our members went to jail. Some of our members resigned from the House for a variety of reasons.

"And I'm out there campaigning in safe seats."

On November 8, Hadley reported on his firsthand look at Iraq. In a five-page SECRET memo, which later leaked to the press, Hadley wrote, "The reality on the streets of Baghdad suggests Maliki is either ignorant of what is going on, misrepresenting his intentions, or that his capabilities are not yet sufficient to turn his good intentions into action." One course of action Hadley recommended was "Ask Secretary of Defense and General Casey to make a recommendation about whether more forces are needed in Baghdad."

The colonels met again with the chiefs on Thursday, November 9, a session designed to prep Pace for a White House meeting the next day with Bush, to discuss what Pace described as "an unscripted way ahead" in Iraq. Rumsfeld and Hadley were expected to present memos. Pace said he was inclined to show some of the colonels' strategic options. But he tossed out several, including Go Home. Everyone knew the president wouldn't consider anything that suggested losing, or cutting and running.

•   •   •

On the morning of Friday, November 10, Bush called Cheney, Rice, Rumsfeld, Hadley, Pace, then–Director of National Intelligence John Negroponte and Hadley's deputy, J. D. Crouch, into the Oval Office. They were to begin a formal review of Iraq strategy, the president said.

Pointing to Crouch, Bush said, "J. D., you'll head it." To facilitate this and give the matter proper urgency, each of those present was to nominate a senior representative to the review group. The representatives would be expected to devote themselves full-time to the assignment, and Crouch would have meetings daily, including weekends. The president wanted a report within 16 days.

In Baghdad that day, November 10, Casey attended an event for the Marine Corps's 231st birthday, an annual ritual that the Marines treat with great seriousness. From 5 to 6 P.M., he prepared for a secure videoconference with President Bush and the NSC. It would be his first discussion with Bush since election day and Rumsfeld's dismissal.

At 6:15 P.M. Baghdad time—10:15 A.M. in Washington, as the Veterans Day holiday weekend was beginning—Casey and Khalilzad appeared on the secure video. Bush was in the Roosevelt Room with his national security team.

The general and the ambassador gave their now routine updates.

In more than two years dealing with Bush, Casey had never experienced anything like it. The president was irritated, distant and unmistakably cold. He had always been upbeat, warm and friendly. But on this day, he was icy and almost rude.

"Wow," Casey said to Khalilzad after the conference, "that was something. I wonder what's going to come out of this?" Whatever it might be, it was obvious to both that their lives were going to change dramatically.

The next day, Saturday, November 11, Hadley and Rice met with their Iraq team leaders—Crouch, O'Sullivan, Zelikow and Satterfield—to lay out the questions they wanted to examine: Are the Shia pursuing a hegemonic agenda? Can the United States really influence Iraqi leaders to make decisions in the interest of Iraq, or are they bound to carry out sectarian agendas? What is the relationship between security and political reconciliation? What is the relationship between U.S. force levels and security?

The State Department group—Rice, Zelikow and Satterfield—wanted to see if there were some way to make the point that the Iraq War was not the sole dominating issue in American foreign policy. They proposed that the review address the following: How would we define core U.S. interests? Should we refocus on more modest efforts?

A final question: If Iraqis don't have the capability to handle the security situation themselves, can we create a bridge to a more sustainable situation over time?

Hadley dispatched a SECRET memo early the next week. "The president authorizes an Iraq review to draw upon work already underway in order to . . . describe the current situation . . . outline the strategic assumptions upon which the effort in Iraq should now rest . . . define America's core objectives and interests."

After months of secretly studying the problems with the Iraq strategy, the search for possible solutions was at last officially under way. The first meeting was set for 5 P.M. the next Wednesday, November 15.

21

Just after 8 A.M. on November 13, 2006, the members of the Baker-Hamilton Iraq Study Group sat in leather chairs around the dark wooden conference table in the windowless Roosevelt Room, across from the Oval Office.

Bush arrived, accompanied by Cheney, Hadley and chief of staff Josh Bolten. After a few pleasantries, the president began. "Iraq is part of an ideological struggle," he said, speaking without notes. "If you don't think this is an ideological struggle, then my comments are wasted."

The president cited foreign leaders who still agreed with him about Iraq, including Pakistan's President Pervez Musharraf, Afghanistan's President Hamid Karzai and King Abdullah of Saudi Arabia. They all support the U.S. presence in Iraq, Bush said.

"Al Qaeda is still there. It is active," Bush said. "In our judgment, they are the ones responsible. They are fomenting sectarian violence . . . With al Qaeda, our job is to find them and kill them." Bush added Baathists to his list of troublemakers. He said that the Shia were protecting their majority by fighting off the Sunnis.

The president then turned to Maliki. In June, when he had first met with the study group, he had radiated optimism about Maliki. "The prime minister is committed to a unified Iraq," he said now. "He knows he has to reach out to the Sunnis."

The challenge, he said, was to strike a delicate balance between Iraqi authority and the American presence.

"We ought to do everything we can to strengthen Maliki," Bush said. "We've got to help and sustain him. We need to strengthen Maliki, not undermine him."

The president said the prime minister had grown angry about military strikes in Shia neighborhoods. He had expressed frustration with Ambassador Khalilzad. He took it personally when Khalilzad gave the impression that the United States was dictating to him.

"I understand these frustrations," the president said, adding that on the whole, they were a good sign. "We are holding the Iraqi government to too high a standard, one that our own government can't meet," Bush said. "It is an impossible timetable for a democracy to meet these goals. I would pull our troops out if we could not achieve these goals."

He added, "It is very possible that our goals can be achieved . . . I am running this war." Commanders simply had to tell him what they needed, he said.

"There is deep concern on the international front that the Americans will leave," Bush continued. "The dynamic in the region is that the Sunnis see the Iranians as the problem, the Israelis less so."

Concerning Iran, the president stated, "We can't put ourselves where we trade off help on Iraq for Iran's nuclear weapon. History will condemn us."

The president opened the floor to questions.

"What is victory?" Lee Hamilton asked.

"The word that captures what we want to achieve is victory," Bush replied. "We want an ally in the war on terror, a government that can govern, sustain and defend itself."

Hamilton thought that this was awfully vague and that the president hadn't really figured it out. But he did not follow up.

Baker asked, "How do we get the Maliki government to do the things we know they need to do?"

Bush said he had told the prime minister that he must make tough decisions on de-Baathification reform and on an oil-revenue-sharing law. "I'm not making excuses," Bush said, then quickly corrected himself. "I guess I am making excuses for the guy."

"What happens if there are inflexible benchmarks—perform or else?" Baker asked.

"There's a temptation to say, 'You must do this or else,'" Bush said. "We are concerned this will be viewed as an imposition. And Maliki is more likely to respond if he is with us."

Vernon Jordan said that when his mother asked him to clean out the garage, he always knew what she meant. But when the president spoke of victory, what exactly did he mean? In Iraq, Jordan said, "What does 'finish the job' mean?"

"The people want to know why we are in Iraq," Bush replied. He avoided Jordan's question and turned to what defeat would mean—a safe haven for al Qaeda, loss of American influence, the lost confidence of Saudi Arabia and Jordan, greater Shia influence in the region. The Iranians would "laugh at us" and Israeli-Palestinian talks would disappear from the table.

"The consequences of defeat would be a disaster for future generations," the president said. "You won't know the moment when you achieve victory. Victory is when the government is functioning, when there is an oil law, when the army is capable of stability. That is a signal of progress. An end to violence, an end to sectarian violence—that won't happen."

Leon Panetta was struck that the president never defined what it meant to win, nor what the United States was ultimately after.

Bill Perry asked about sending up to 100,000 additional troops. We could do it for a short time, Bush replied, noting that General Casey didn't think anywhere near that number was necessary.

Is a draft necessary? Perry asked.

"Absolutely not."

What about increasing the size of the armed forces?

"Well, we're considering that."

Sandra Day O'Connor said that Maliki was very weak. How could the United States help strengthen him?

"We can strengthen him by giving him more authority over his security forces," Bush replied.

"How much patience do we have?" Hamilton asked. "The fact remains Prime Minister Maliki has not taken the hard steps. How long can we go down this road at the cost of $2 billion a week, losing men every day?"

"Maliki actually is taking steps," Bush replied. "He is working to isolate Shia militias from al-Sadr, trying to get al-Sadr to help. We have lots of intelligence on Maliki going after death squads, and it is not fair to say that he is a catalyst for sectarian violence. He gets a bum rap."

When the United States goes after Shia militias, the president said, "We notify the prime minister. We have well-meaning plans, but the military is heavy-handed. Maliki has to deal with his people saying, 'What the hell are you doing in our neighborhood?'"

Ed Meese asked about reconstruction.

"We've pretty well run our string on reconstruction," Bush acknowledged. "Congress won't spend any more. That's why we want the international community to come forward." No one needed to point out that the international community had pretty much left Iraq in the hands of the Americans.

Bush said that Saudi king Abdullah's attitude had shifted dramatically. He no longer was focused on Maliki but rather viewed success in Iraq as a buffer against Iran.

"It's tough to sustain these policies without progress on the ground," Panetta said. He asked about the hold and build strategy and the Baghdad security plan: "How are we doing?"

"Baghdad is a mixed bag," Bush replied. He said he often got asked if the soldiers were sitting ducks at the neighborhood outposts, or whether they were fighting. "They are fighting," he assured them, adding with pride, "We killed or captured 1,700 just in the month of October."

Seventeen hundred of what, he didn't specify.

"I am as frustrated as the American people," Bush continued. "Death trumps success. When you are building schools or opening hospitals, that's success. Mosul, success. Tall Afar, that's pretty good, but now it's being challenged. We can build schools every day and that won't be reported as success.

"If I didn't think it was worth it, we would leave. We need to win an ideological victory. I am not making excuses, but we cannot improve in the short term. This is worth it because of the consequences. . . . Your report can make a significant contribution here, if you deal with the tendencies toward isolationism in the country. There is an attitude in the country—'Let's get out. Let's protect our trade. Let's keep immigrants out.' We need to deal with the psychology of engagement in international affairs and position this country so it remains a leader. If we count on Europe or anyone else to lead, they will not lead. The United States has to take the lead on all these tough issues, or it just won't happen."

Chuck Robb, the early advocate of adding more troops, asked if the president was prepared to do something very dramatic in the short term in Baghdad.

Bush mentioned a short-term bridging mechanism—a clear reference to a surge. If Gates, the designated new secretary of defense, and the commanders recommended it, he said, he'd be inclined to accept it.

I later asked the president about his comment to the group about a "short-term bridging mechanism."

"I don't know what that means," he said.

Hadley chimed in. "You're talking about, and you say this, 'Look, we want to get to the point where the Iraqis can take responsibility for security.'"

"Right," Bush said.

"Which is what we had been doing under Casey and Rumsfeld," Hadley answered. "But you're saying, 'They don't have the capacity to get there right now.'"

"Yeah, that's right," Bush said.

"We need something to bridge to the point where they take responsibility," Hadley said. "And that's the surge."

"Okay," Bush said.

At the November 13 meeting, Robb pointed out that the president had offered a strong defense of Maliki.

"Is Maliki the right man?" Bush asked. "Casey says yes."

Robb asked whether Maliki had set internal benchmarks.

He's talked about it, Bush said, but he hasn't really set any.

"We by God need to lean hard on 'em!" Baker interjected, referring to Maliki and other Iraqi leaders. Baker was given to spontaneous outbursts during the course of the study group's interviews.

Americans are not united, Hamilton said. The country is moving away from this war. He wasn't sure whether the country could sustain a foreign policy without unity of effort.

Bush at first offered no response, but he later returned to the question. "Most Americans don't want to leave," he said. "Most Americans want to support a plan that is working. . . . We can succeed. It won't be pretty. We need the help from fresh eyes outside the government. We will be in Iraq for the duration of my presidency.

"Those running in 2008 don't want to deal with this. That is a chance for us." He seemed to be suggesting that the study group and he might work something out. "This is a big damn deal," he said. "Our idea is to make the American people know we're working for victory. . . . If I say we're looking for something short of victory, I am out of here tomorrow."

Bill Perry later recalled in an interview that Bush was both passionate and overbearing. "He was not seeking advice from us," he said. "He was telling us what his view of the war was. The president held forth on his views on how important the war was, and how it was tough, how we stay together. It was a Churchillian kind of a thing. . . . There's going to be blood, sweat and tears and all that. It was that sort of a moment. It is quite clear that he had this image of a great global struggle, and he was presiding over it, and Iraq was just one element of that, and that the people who were wavering on Iraq did not see the big picture the way he saw it.

"To my mind even as he was saying it," Perry said, "I thought he was comparing himself to Churchill. This is not the way we think of Bush in his public statements. It really was an eloquent Bush. He was wrong, I thought, but eloquent."

When I spoke to the president later, I told him that Bill Perry had called his statement to the Iraq Study Group "Churchillian."

"That's kind of him," Bush said. "That makes me feel good when somebody says something nice like that."

After the president left the Roosevelt Room, the members of the Iraq Study Group remained in their seats for a secure videoconference with General Casey in Baghdad.

Bush's ice-cold reception after the election had been a jarring confirmation for Casey that the commander in chief was on his final tuneout with the current strategy, and with him.

"It's not about us. It's about the Iraqis," Casey told the group.

"Enduring strategic success will only be achieved by Iraqis," he explained. "And if it happens, it will take longer than we want. The government of Iraq and their leaders must make tough decisions and they're not likely to do it on our timeline. We're relying on a government that lacks capabilities. The government is relying on Shiite militias."

The real problem, Casey said, was the sectarian violence by Sunni and Shia extremists, but "the Iraqi government just wants to focus on al Qaeda and the Baathists."

Casey wanted a drawdown unequivocally. "We have to reduce our footprint to a level that is acceptable to the Iraqis. We are two thirds of the way through a three-step process to transfer security responsibility by the end of 2007."

He said the United States had enough troops in Iraq and sufficient resources. If he'd seen a possibility to achieve goals by having more troops, he would have asked for them.

"Here are the problems with more troops," Casey said. "It's an Iraqi problem. The more coalition forces we put in, the longer it will take the Iraqis to achieve the objectives that they need to and to take responsibility.

"More troops can have a temporary effect in a highly local area, but it will delay the long-term resolution that needs to happen."

Perry asked about troop levels.

"More U.S. troops will have a temporary, local effect," Casey repeated. "There will never be enough troops in Baghdad to stop them from killing each other. More U.S. troops can help briefly, but the city is huge . . . Baghdad is a troop sump."

That last line hung in the air. The idea that the commanding general thought of the primary battlefield much like a swamp soaking up American soldiers was jarring.

The Iraqis have a higher threshold for violence than we do, Casey continued. "They are not troubled by the level of violence."

Casey was asked about the effectiveness of the U.S. troops in Baghdad.

"They're having a dampening effect on violence," he said. "They hold it in check. If they weren't there, there would be a more significant bloodbath. Maliki has not demonstrated the political will to deal with the militias."

"Is it too late?" Panetta asked. "Are the Shia playing for time?"

"I ask myself that question every day," Casey responded. "You see the Shia hand moving things around Baghdad all the time. I just don't know."

After the video teleconference with Casey, CIA Director General Michael Hayden joined the study group in the Roosevelt Room at 10:15 A.M.

A small, balding four-star Air Force general, Hayden, 61, had headed the CIA for just five and a half months. He had 36 years' experience in the intelligence world and had made his mark as director of the National Security Agency from 1999 to 2005. The largest of the U.S. spy agencies, the NSA intercepts worldwide communications, including those of suspected terrorists in the United States communicating abroad under the controversial Terrorist Surveillance Program ordered by President Bush after 9/11. But Hayden, a skilled briefer, had weathered that storm after secretly presenting the details of the program to the Senate, which confirmed him by a vote of 78 to 15.

Before his testimony to the Iraq Study Group, Hayden had spoken with Secretary Rice. Their friendship dated back 20 years, to when they had worked together during 1986–87 on the Joint Staff in windowless rooms across from each other in the Pentagon, she on an academic fellowship and he a lieutenant colonel. They had served together on the NSC staff of Bush senior. Rice believed Hayden was one of the smartest people she'd met, with a cool, dispassionate style. She had told him he could do a great service with his assessment to the study group. "This is the time to be pretty blunt about what is going on," she said.

"Our leaving Iraq would make the situation worse," Hayden now told the group. "Our staying in Iraq might not make it better. Our current approach without modification will not make it better.

"It's a legitimate question whether strengthening the Iraqi security forces helps or hurts, when they are viewed as a predatory element. Strengthening the Iraqi security forces is not unalloyed good. Without qualification, this judgment applies to the police. The army is uneven. Uneven, in this case, is good."

He added later, "We and the Iraqi government do not agree on who the enemy is. For all the senior leaders of the Iraqi government, Baathists are the source of evil. There is a Baathist behind every bush . . . Their view is to get rid of the Baathists, and the militias will go away."

Hayden's comments agreed precisely with what the study group had seen and heard on the ground during their short visit to Iraq. Hayden said the violence could be traced to several sources—the insurgency, sectarian fighting, criminality and anarchy, and then al Qaeda.

The study group found it interesting that Hayden put al Qaeda last as a cause of violence in Iraq. It was almost always the first cause that the president mentioned.

When asked about regional influence, Hayden responded, "If Iraq were on the dark side of the moon, it would be as bad as it is today," meaning that the country's problems would exist even if it weren't in the turbulent Middle East.

Baker asked about Syria. Hayden said there was "a running gun battle" in the intelligence community on what to do about Syria.

On problems of national unity, he said, "The Iraqi identity is muted. The Sunni or Shia identity is foremost."

Hayden, who had access to the TOP SECRET intercepts and human sources focusing on the Iraqi government, reserved his harshest view for Maliki and the leadership in Baghdad. "The government is unable to govern," he said flatly. "We have spent a lot of energy and treasure creating a government that is balanced, and it cannot function.

"The inability of the government to govern seems irreversible. We have placed all our energies in creating a center, and the center cannot accomplish anything. The levers of power are not connected to anything." He said Ambassador Khalilzad ran from ministry to ministry talking to people, trying to get services running. But nothing ever happened. Nothing changed. "The violence is incredibly disorganized," he added. "There is strife over neighborhoods, strife over bridges."

Hayden seemed to be shaken by the growing intensity and prevalence of the violence. An avid marathon runner, he offered an analogy. In every marathon, he said, there's a point where you know you can make it to the finish line, where you know you'll be okay. There had been no such point in this war. "I cannot point to any milestone or checkpoint where we can turn this thing around," he said.

Hamilton sat still. It was the most pessimistic—and credible— assessment he had heard.

But Hayden was not finished. "A government that can govern, sustain and defend itself is not achievable in the short term." These were, verbatim, the president's articulated goals. "There is merit in recalibrating our effort to help the regions within Iraq," Hayden said. U.S. efforts might have to be redirected to the sectarian regions of Iraq, not just the central government of Maliki.

He mentioned Bosnia as an example. "In Bosnia, the parties fought themselves to exhaustion," he said, suggesting that perhaps the same scenario might have to play out in Iraq.

Perry repeated what Casey had told to the group earlier that morning—"We cannot succeed without national reconciliation." He asked Hayden for his take.

"Given the level of uncontrolled violence," Hayden said, "the most we can do is to contain its excesses and preserve the possibility of reconciliation in the future."

The study group members had heard plenty of bleak assessments about Iraq, but the CIA chief's was among the most disturbing. For some, it marked a pivotal moment.

Next up was Khalilzad, the U.S. ambassador to Iraq, who offered a more muted assessment.

"Powerful forces are not helping the achievement of a common vision," the ambassador said. "Reconciliation is necessary."

Former Secretary of State Lawrence Eagleburger, who had replaced Gates on the study group after the president had nominated him as the new defense secretary, asked, "Does Maliki believe we are prepared to carry out threats if he does not perform?"

"There is a sense in Iraq that we are more interested in progress in Iraq than they are," the ambassador said. "We need to change that psychology."

Panetta asked, "Maliki said he wants more control over security forces. Isn't that an invitation to attack Sunnis?"

"For this reason," Khalilzad said, again avoiding answering directly, "it is imperative that they conclude the national reconciliation process."

And on it went, leaving most of them shaking their heads.

22

At 1 P.M., Secretary Rice sat down with the study group. "We need to establish a course that is sustainable," she began. "We're in a different phase now with the democratic government. It's good that Iraqis want responsibility. The United States may need to be more tolerant about letting them make the next moves.

"It may be time for us to pull back a little."

A "pullback" sounded encouraging to many members.

Overall, Rice said, there was a realignment taking place in the Middle East. "There are extremists within the Arab world, and then there are more moderate Arabs. Many of the Arabs see Iran now as a more dangerous problem than Israel." Syria is widely viewed as destabilizing, she said.

"Can we flip Syria?" asked Perry, meaning get it to help with Iraq.

"The Saudis don't talk to them," Rice replied. "So why would we go around our allies, the Saudis, who after all are much more important to the peace process?"

That response agitated Baker. "These Arab governments fight each other all the time," he said. "The real question is who is going to lead?"

The former secretary of state and the current one quarreled for a moment, with Rice acknowledging that diplomatic outreach to solve the Israeli-Palestinian problem might be worthwhile. But she had reservations about establishing relations with Syria and Iran.

"I am concerned that Syria is too high a price," she said. "For the Arabs, the rise of Iran is the threat. The Iran factor today is different than it was 15 years ago"—a pointed reference to Baker's tenure as secretary of state—"so I have to challenge the notion that Iran could be an ally in this process."

Her position did not sit well with Baker and several others. Nearly everyone else had told the study group that active diplomacy with Syria and Iran was vital to stabilizing Iraq and the Middle East.

Panetta asked about the growing sectarian divisions in Iraq.

"In Iraq, there is an existential fear of others," Rice explained. "These are people who want to be united, but they don't want to be left in the room with each other."

No one challenged that contradiction.

Each element saw the United States as a good luck charm, a "talisman," against the other, Rice said. "For the Shia, we help assure that they preserve their majority role. For the Sunnis, they want us to stay in order to defend them against repression and massacre." That role for the United States, she said hopefully, "allows us to step back and think about how to work toward unity without getting bogged down in the day-to-day responsibility for how Iraqis interact with each other.

"They may do a lot of things that we don't like. We don't want to impose things. We need to give them confidence. Maybe we smother them too much."

O'Connor asked about the grim CIA assessment they had received that morning from CIA Director Michael Hayden.

"We are aware of the dark assessment," Rice answered. "It is not without hope."

Hamilton asked how the Iraqi leaders could be pressured more effectively. Hayden had been adamant about the Iraqi government's inability to govern. Time was running out.

Rice said she had been blunt with Maliki, telling the prime minister, "Pretty soon, you'll all be swinging from lampposts if you don't hang together."

Concerning the Iraqi police, Rice said, "You've got police that are abusive," and referred, as she had to the president, to the "Bull Connor problem."

"Are you persuaded Maliki is a national leader?" Hamilton asked as the meeting wound down.

"I am persuaded he is a national leader," Rice answered, "but I'm not sure that he understands what that means."

Hamilton launched into an impassioned lecture. "We have a government that cannot govern or that has not governed in Iraq," he said. "We're counting on them to do difficult things. How do you get them to move?" The longtime congressman slid off his glasses for emphasis. "We're spending $2 billion per week. We're losing men every day. The American people have soured on this war." A country should be united in war, and this one wasn't. "There is not unity of effort between the Congress and the president. There is not agreement on what to do in Iraq."

Rice sat quietly and gave no response. Hamilton had no idea just how much disagreement there was within the administration.

Rumsfeld and Pace arrived at 2 P.M. in the Roosevelt Room. Though Bush had announced five days earlier that Rumsfeld was leaving the Defense Department, he would remain secretary until Gates was confirmed.

"There are certain bureaucratic and legislative changes that you could recommend that would be helpful," Rumsfeld told the group. Sounding calm and sedate, he suggested the budget process in the U.S. Congress was too slow to get security assistance to the Iraqis. There were too many restrictions on U.S. efforts to train the Iraqi police. Civilians in the U.S. government had little willingness to serve abroad in a war zone. His Defense Department had more than three times as many civilians working in Iraqi ministries than all the other U.S. government departments.

Hamilton and several others found it mind-boggling that given the critical problems, Rumsfeld would single out these sideline issues.

"The military cannot lose the battle of Iraq," Rumsfeld declared.

"But we cannot win without nonmilitary capabilities within the government."

Pace then took his turn. "There are a lot of fixes that you need in Iraq," the general said, "security, economic and governance. The U.S. military can kill people all day long, but we need other capabilities in Iraq. The U.S. government needs to get younger, more energetic people to go to Iraq."

Is training the Iraqi army the highest priority? Hamilton asked.

"Yes," Rumsfeld interjected, "training is the highest priority. That's where we're beginning to put the money, the time and the effort." It had been nearly two and a half years since the *Newsweek* cover story called Lieutenant General David Petraeus, then the man charged with training the Iraqis, "the only exit plan the United States has."

"What about the surge to Baghdad?" Hamilton asked. "Can we do it?"

"We can surge to Baghdad from the current level of 15 brigades," Pace replied, adding that to sustain a surge beyond July of 2007 would require extending Guard and Reserve tours.

"The more you look like an occupier in Iraq, the more you create a dependency among the Iraqis," Rumsfeld said. "We need to be pushing responsibility onto the Iraqis."

Panetta asked about Operations Together Forward I and II.

"Fundamentally, we still have a problem because Sunnis and Shia are still killing each other," Pace said. But then he added with unusual candor, "You could have a soldier on every corner, but Sunnis and Shia would still be killing each other. It will take Iraqi leadership to stop this killing. We can keep the lid on it, but they will continue to kill each other without reconciliation."

Perry asked about Anbar province. Are the tribal leaders living up to their promise to pursue al Qaeda? And are we supporting them through Special Operations?

"The tribal leaders have been delivering," Pace said. "Most of the fighting is now being done by the tribes. The Marines are backing them up. Special Operations are going very well in tribal areas, using intelligence from the tribal leaders."

"Have we talked to the Iraqis about bases?" Baker asked.

"We don't talk about it at all," Rumsfeld said. "We do need the capability to give them a sense of security. The U.S. military is not looking for more places to put bases. But the president of the United States would not want to forgo that possibility."

Hamilton asked, "Do you need a base?"

Rumsfeld didn't reply.

Panetta asked if it were possible to have fewer brigades on the ground and maintain better trainers.

"That is a concept that would depend on developing Iraqi capability," Rumsfeld said. We should reduce our forces based on conditions on the ground. We should say something along the lines of "We will remove X amount of forces from X provinces when you achieve these X benchmarks . . ."

He insisted that the United States must put pressure on the Iraqis and instill in them a level of responsibility. "We essentially have to say to the Iraqis, 'Don't you want our forces to leave?' and make it their initiative to make progress so that U.S. forces leave. We have to give reassurances to the Iraqis that this is their country, and we have to give reassurances to the American people that we are leaving."

"What should we say about failure in our report?" Baker asked.

"You have to be clear that there would be dire consequences," Rumsfeld replied. "And that has to be part of the thinking here. We have to get that into their thinking. We have to get across these dire consequences to the Iraqis too. There has to be a timetable for progress." And then with great passion Rumsfeld delivered one of his favorite lines, one he had delivered to the president and the war cabinet many times: "We have to take our hand off the bicycle seat."

"What is the period of time here?" asked Vernon Jordan.

"To the Iraqis, it's a period of years," Rumsfeld said. "The American people clearly don't want to stay as long. The American people's timetable is not as long as the Iraqis."

The next day, November 14, the study group held a secure videoconference with British Prime Minister Tony Blair. It was Blair who had requested the interview, apparently aware that his views were in line with those of a majority of the study group members.

Blair had recently sent his top foreign policy adviser, Sir Nigel Sheinwald, to Syria to see if there was a way to pry open the diplomatic doors. Sheinwald had not succeeded, but Blair remained a strong advocate of talking with the Syrians.

Baker asked Blair if he thought another big international conference on the Middle East and the Israeli-Palestinian issues would be helpful—much like the 1991 Madrid Conference that Baker had engineered when he had been secretary of state.

"That would be great," Blair said. "The sooner people think we are determined to move in this area, the better. We need a big, visible expression of our determination."

Hamilton went so far as to ask Blair about his expectations for the Iraq Study Group's report and recommendations.

"We need well-respected, serious people, moving in a consensual way, with a plan for inside Iraq and a plan for the region," Blair said. "This is a bold, strategic opportunity. . . . It is the optimal moment for this report."

At 2:30 that afternoon, in a cozy fourth-floor conference room inside the Woodrow Wilson International Center for Scholars, which Hamilton headed, the members of the Iraq Study Group gathered for a much anticipated session with former President Bill Clinton.

Clinton showed up as usual, all charisma and fanfare. He was dressed in a sharp suit and tailed by an entourage so large that there weren't enough seats in the small meeting space. On the short walk from the elevator to the conference room, the incurable campaigner stopped in every office to shake hands.

The study group had just finished talking with senior members of the Clinton foreign policy team—National Security Adviser Sandy Berger, U.N. Ambassador Richard Holbrooke, and Secretaries of State Warren Christopher and Madeleine Albright. As they were leaving, Clinton invited them to stick around for his interview—the old White House and State Department team reunited.

"There are no good options," Clinton said in his opening statement. "If you're going to change course, there are three things you can do. You can go up 100,000 troops. You can hang around and get bled to death. Or you can redeploy [home]. What else are you going to do? Those are your choices.

"We don't control the situation now. We will have even less control once we draw down. . . . They are not tired of killing each other."

Clinton urged the study group to be frank about the downsides of every option. Be clear that there's no easy solution, he advised. "This cannot be solved in the near term within Iraq. This cannot be solved within the four corners of Iraq," he said. "We have to be better than lucky."

Clinton then went on a lengthy tangent about Afghanistan. "If you don't act in Iraq, the chances of losing Afghanistan are greater and more calamitous for the United States than the loss of Iraq," he said. "The Taliban is making inroads. Our ally, Pakistan, is part of the problem. More troops for Afghanistan is absolutely essential. We cannot address Afghanistan unless we leave Iraq."

He reminded them that the United Nations and the world supported America in Afghanistan. That's not the case in Iraq, he said.

It was a typical Clinton performance, drifting from one topic to the next. At one point, the former president took out an unlit cigar and twirled it in his fingers as he began to talk about diplomacy.

Clinton suggested initiating talks with Iran without any preconditions. "We have to have some trusted adviser and start to talk to Iran," he said. "If you might fight somebody someday, you sure ought to talk to them."

He turned to the Arab-Israeli peace process. "Bush hasn't asked [Israeli Prime Minister Ehud] Olmert to do anything," Clinton said. That was a mistake. "In the first four years of this administration, three times as many Israelis and Palestinians have died as during my administration.

"Whenever we fool with it, less people die and it reduces the animosity toward America. . . . We may fail on one or all these fronts and still be better off than we are now."

Clinton made a strong pitch for engaging the Syrians in the peace process: "Go to the Syrians and ask them, 'Do you really think this relationship with Iraq works for you?'" The war in Iraq was weakening America in the eyes of the world. "Iranian and North Korean foreign policy is to stick it up America's ass because we're tied down in Iraq," he said.

Robb asked him how to convince President Bush to buy into a new approach.

"President Bush deeply believes that Iraq was the right thing to do, and he cannot abandon that belief," Clinton replied. What you must say to President Bush is that "history may still vindicate the decision to invade Iraq. . . . They may fight it out for two, three, four or seven years before they grow weary and reach a settlement.

"But history may still vindicate the decision to go to war. So let them fight it out. You cannot stop them from killing each other."

Clinton said he had just returned from Vietnam. Look at that country today. Look at the economy. It's better off than it was before the war. Thirty years from now, some American president might go to Iraq and find a place that's far better off than it is today. Bush has to think in that broad context. "The president believes what he did is right, and that history will vindicate his decision on Saddam."

Clinton displayed a heartfelt empathy for Bush, defending the sincerity of his successor. Right or wrong, Clinton said, Bush doesn't make his decisions based on politics. He believes in this. As president, "ninety percent, maybe 98 percent, of your decision making is not politics, no matter how stupid that may seem to you," he said.

Clinton was in favor of a troop withdrawal from Iraq, but he was against setting deadlines. "You lose leverage with a deadline," he said. He'd prefer pulling people out without advance warning. His preference would be to take some troops out right away to send them to Afghanistan. "You've got to write your report in such a way that what you advocate will make the country stronger and that we can still come out of this right.

"The American people are against" this war. "They think it was a mistake. But they are 50–50 about what to do. Americans hate to lose, but they also hate to pour good money after bad. We're on a psychological razor's edge. When you write the report, you have to show how America can come out stronger at the end." He paused. "Americans have to feel like they're on the right side of history."

"Mr. President," Baker said, "you came closer than anyone to a deal with Syria."

He also agreed with Clinton on the need for continued diplomacy on the Palestinian issue.

"It doesn't help Israel when we just sit and wait for the next arms order," the former president said. Leon Panetta thought it sounded almost as if Baker had worked under Clinton.

Hamilton asked Clinton about the consequences of failure in Iraq, as well as the consequences of our current policy.

"It's important to announce that we're pursuing a different course," Clinton said, something Bush had been reluctant to do as the war deteriorated. He said America had alienated much of the world. "We pay a price when everyone hates us."

Panetta asked: How would you get Maliki to move on national reconciliation?

"I would just spend lots and lots of time with him and with them [Iraqi leaders] . . . I would spend a hell of a lot more time with him. Massive amounts of time." That, of course, was Clinton's style, not Bush's.

Clinton returned to the necessity that Bush implement the study group's findings. "If the president announces a change in course, he will get more time—if you can convince him to change. Nixon was reelected easily. More people were killed [in Vietnam] after Nixon was elected."

He added, "The president may feel this is good for him."

"He wants us to give him a chance to change policy," Baker said.

"The president and the country want you to give the country a way forward," Clinton said. "The costs are very adverse for staying where we are. It's costing us a lot of lives and money."

Clinton's hour had stretched to an hour and a half, and no one seemed eager for it to end, especially Clinton. Even the Republicans were impressed.

Vernon Jordan posed a last question. Would you talk to Bush after the report comes out?

"I'll do it if it helps," Clinton said. "We may differ. But we have a responsibility when we differ to be respectful and to be precise. . . . There's not a Democrat alive that doesn't want things to go better in Iraq."

23

At 5 P.M. on Wednesday, November 15, J. D. Crouch assembled his strategy review team for an introductory, organizational one-hour meeting. The group of about a dozen gathered in Room 208—known as the Cordell Hull Room—of the Eisenhower Executive Office Building across from the White House.

Crouch, O'Sullivan and her top Iraq staff represented the NSC. Bill Luti, the senior defense director on the NSC staff who had authored the feasibility study of a surge the previous month, also attended.

For State, Rice had appointed Zelikow and Satterfield. Rumsfeld had designated Steve Cambone, a longtime aide and the current under-secretary for Pentagon intelligence, and Peter Rodman, an assistant secretary of defense. Pace sent two lieutenant generals—Doug Lute, the head of operations for the Joint Staff, and John Sattler, the Joint Staff's head of plans and policy. David Gordon, vice chairman of the National Intelligence Council, represented the director of national intelligence (DNI).

John Hannah, Cheney's national security adviser, represented the vice president's office. He made it clear that anything he asked, said or wrote would reflect only his personal views and not necessarily those of Cheney, who, as they all knew, offered his views directly to the president.

Crouch handed out binders that included O'Sullivan's long paper

on the four constructs, or options: adjust at the margins; target our effort; double down; bet on Maliki. A cover sheet noted that the four
were not mutually exclusive. They could mix and match as they saw fit.

The group would get down to business the next day.

On Thursday, November 16, General Casey gave an update to Rumsfeld by secure video teleconference. He had no role in Crouch's strategy review and had become so out of the loop, it seemed as if he were
speaking from another planet. Casey had learned that Rumsfeld was
leaving just before Bush announced it the week before. Considering
that they shared the same basic view of the war, he was sorry to see the
secretary go.

"Bottom line up front," he told Rumsfeld. "We are in a position in
the campaign where accelerating and completing the transition of security responsibility to capable Iraqi security forces is both strategically appropriate and feasible.

"Enduring strategic success will be achieved by the Iraqis." His
SECRET briefing paper had read, "It will take longer than we want."
But Casey edited out the last three words.

"We are two-thirds of the way through a three-step process to bring
the Iraqis to the point where they can credibly assume responsibility
by the end of 2007 with some lower level of support from us." That
was a year away. He listed four possible options: "acceleration of the
transition to Iraqi control; reinforcement; status quo"; and the almost
forbidden notion of a "fixed withdrawal schedule."

About this time, General Abizaid passed word to Casey that the White
House was thinking about a surge of more U.S. brigades to Iraq. The
question immediately arose: What would Casey do with more
brigades? Neither he nor Abizaid wanted them, but they agreed that
Casey had better ask his subordinates.

Casey and Lieutenant General Pete Chiarelli, the corps commander
for all U.S. forces in Iraq, met with the new Baghdad commander,
Major General Joseph F. Fil Jr.

"We have to secure Baghdad," Casey said. "We have to do that now. We have to. We've tried twice." He was referring to the two summer operations, Together Forward I and II, which had failed. "It hasn't worked. Third time's got to be the charm, man, or we're in big shit." Casey turned to Fil. "Take a blank sheet of paper. Tell us what the hell we need to do to help you guys secure Baghdad."

Fil, a boyish-looking combat veteran with 30 years in the Army, came back with a request for two more brigades—about 7,000 more troops. That way, he said, he could put a battalion of 600 to 1,000 with a larger Iraqi brigade in each of Baghdad's 10 districts. Casey wasn't surprised. Fil was new to his position, and it was natural that he would be inclined to rely on his own forces rather than on the Iraqis. Even though he didn't want to bring one more soldier than necessary into the Baghdad troop sump, Casey decided to go along with Fil and began the formal process of an RFF—Request for Forces.

Rice kept in close contact with Zelikow and Satterfield as they worked the White House strategy review. They told her that the "double down" option for more forces seemed to have little backing, except with the NSC staff. "What are more forces going to do?" Rice asked. "Are they just going to get into a civil conflict? Are we going to put our people between Iraqis fighting old problems and then have the Iraqis pull the rug out from under them?"

Zelikow and Satterfield had been working on a memo outlining what they felt was a realistic view. They hoped the White House strategy review would offer a change that would be seen as an outreach to Congress, accommodate the Baker-Hamilton study group and even give Democrats some cover for compromise.

They wanted to get their say in early, so the final version of their 12-page SECRET paper was circulated Friday, November 17. Crouch, O'Sullivan and the others read it with great interest, knowing it would reflect the views of Rice, still probably the person closest to the president.

"The original objectives of America's invasion of Iraq have been substantially accomplished," the memo began. "The key choices about the future of the country must now be made by Iraqis." Zelikow and Satterfield advocated "a more traditional state-to-state relationship" that is "more arm's length." The Green Zone, where U.S. and Iraqi government officials were holed up, has "limited relevance and reach" elsewhere in Iraq.

"Foreign troops are wearing out their welcome," they wrote. "Most Iraqis resent the U.S. presence," which is "rapidly becoming either an irritant or irrelevant."

In boldface, they added, "We may actually recover leverage and achieve greater success by stepping back, picking our spots and being willing to withhold aid."

If the Iraqi leaders continue to support sectarian violence and "organized campaigns of mass killings or mass expulsions, we would announce and execute a withdrawal of all U.S. forces from Iraq, along with our civilian support for the Iraqi government. We believe the credible threat of such an action would be effective." As part of an incentive, they suggested, "The United States would offer to protect Prime Minister Maliki's government against the Baathist coup he fears."

O'Sullivan thought it sounded like a proposal for "a graceful defeat," representing the State Department view that the United States had very little ability to impact the narrative in Iraq, and that the goals had to be much more modest. After all the treasure committed and lives lost over three and a half years, she argued it was simply unacceptable not to try everything possible to achieve success.

Bill Luti, who had drafted a concept for a surge, was equally appalled by the State paper. It was a recipe for defeat and a dishonorable exit, in his view.

Satterfield disagreed with any suggestion that the State paper was defeatist or timid. He thought the paper offered the clearest outline of realistic options and consequences.

Zelikow's argument was "We actually kind of need to get out of the center of their politics and force them to take the responsibility of having to sort these things out for themselves." Take the Iraqi army, for instance. The United States was essentially running it—had become the general staff, the logisticians, providers of everything from intelligence to food.

"What are our no-shit, bottom-line objectives and interests in Iraq?" Satterfield asked. He repeated his view that U.S. national security interests had suffered because of the "myopic focus on Iraq, defining everything that is happening in the world by Iraq." Iraq had become the lens through which they were seeing everything, he said, "and increasingly, the United States is being judged as a success or a failure—strategically dominant or weak—because of Iraq." He said they needed to "draw back the lens" and see the entire world.

During the earlier, less formal review, Meghan O'Sullivan's group had discussed what could be done if the sectarian violence reached genocidal levels, what Rice called "a Srebrenica-style massacre," resembling the wave of ethnic cleansing in the Bosnian city of Srebrenica, which fell to the Serbs in 1995 during the Clinton administration. An estimated 8,000 men and boys were slaughtered, scores of women and girls raped, and tens of thousands forced to flee.

Violence was bad in Iraq, but it did not yet include mass executions by the thousands.

"How do you protect civilian populations against a Srebrenica-style massacre," Crouch asked, "while you're standing back and standing down forces?"

Satterfield thought it was a valid question. They could send stern political messages to the Iraqi leaders or threaten to pull out.

"Guys," Crouch told Zelikow and Satterfield, "your argument really is a weak one here."

The pair mustered every conceivable argument against a surge, or a "double down" option. It simply wouldn't work, they said. America didn't have the resources. "We don't think this is right," Satterfield said.

The Defense Department team and the two generals from the Joint Staff also opposed the surge. "There's got to be a political process here," said General Lute. "And you guys keep saying that the application of forces will create space for political process. Well, I don't see the linkage."

Finally, Hadley showed up. "You have got to give the president the option of a surge in forces," he told the group. "You present him everything else you're talking about, but I'm telling you, you have got to give him that option of a surge in forces. He will want to see it, and he'll want to know what it means. You all can take your positions for or against or in between, but you have to present him that as an option."

Hadley didn't say that Bush had already decided. But they all knew that when Hadley spoke emphatically, he was a pure transmission belt for Bush's views.

With Rumsfeld a lame duck and Gates yet to be confirmed as his successor, there was a vacuum at Defense. Hadley rushed to fill it.

He told General Pace that the president wanted a surge option. Pace, ever dutiful, had the Joint Staff conduct an analysis: What was the maximum amount of troops available? The answer came back that the Army could provide five additional brigades temporarily. That was it.

On November 18, the Defense Department representatives, led by Steve Cambone, presented a six-page SECRET strategy paper to Crouch's review group. It was material recycled from Rumsfeld, Abizaid and Casey. "Accelerate the transition to self-reliance," the paper said. "Transition security responsibilities to the government of Iraq in 2007." The only new idea was a proposal to triple the number of teams working on the transition.

The others could see the hands of the Defense representatives had been tied by Rumsfeld, even though he was on his way out.

The SECRET paper from the two Joint Staff generals was five pages long and contained some sharp language and pessimism. "If we do not adjust our strategy," they wrote, "the result could be the fragmentation of Iraq, escalating sectarian violence, a strengthening insurgency and a destructive civil war that could spill over into neighboring countries."

In the near term, they listed the standard goals of an Iraq that could maintain order and the rule of law, defend itself and prevent terrorists from establishing safe havens. "In the long term," they wrote, they envisioned an Iraq "that evolves into a free and unified federal republic that is representative of all Iraqi citizens. The U.S. will fail strategically if we fail to fulfill our strategic guarantees for Iraq." The generals felt that by invading Iraq, the United States had both strategic and moral obligations to leave the people of Iraq with a working democracy.

But they adopted a line straight from the Council of Colonels: "We are losing in Iraq because we are not winning."

Satterfield agreed. "There is no tie," he said. "A tie is losing."

The two generals also wrote, "Time is not on our side, because the American public does not see progress. Time is also running out in Iraq." And yet their memo ended with a surprise, a bureaucratic O. Henry short story. Rather than a bold new proposal to turn the tide of the war, the generals focused on the transfer of "responsibility for governance and security to Iraqis." They wrote, "The United States military will shift from a U.S.-led counterinsurgency effort to training and partnering efforts."

It was the Casey strategy: "Leave to win."

The generals were well aware that the administration's actions were limited because public support for the war had plummeted.

O'Sullivan disagreed. She believed that even when the president decided on a new strategy, it didn't have to be the final answer. They would be able to look at the strategy again down the road. In short, they always had more time.

"No," Crouch retorted. "We have a shot in this administration— just one—at this now. There will not be another bite at this apple." He said the decision the president was about to make was the strategy that the administration would take into the 2008 presidential elections and through the end of the Bush presidency on January 20, 2009.

Satterfield was with him. "There is no other bite," he said. That is what most troubled him about the idea of a surge. "You've got to get this right this time. If we blow it, what we will have done is we will have precipitated a political process for the last thing any of us want, which is a precipitous withdrawal. We do not want by our own actions to create a circumstance that we are desperately trying to avoid."

David Gordon, the representative from the intelligence community, presented a TOP SECRET paper that examined four approaches.

"Strengthen National Governance" was the first. Based on the British precedent in Northern Ireland and Malaysia, "more than 500,000 U.S. and Iraqi soldiers would be needed to secure all of Iraq, with 100,000 to 120,000 in Baghdad," his paper said. But that was perhaps too high, he acknowledged, adding that "U.S. stability operations in Mosul and Tall Afar suggest a lower number of U.S. and capable, nonpartisan Iraqi troops, between 207,000 and 263,000, might be enough." That did not include 80,000 to 90,000 support troops, according to the paper. That meant there were 15 U.S. combat brigades currently in Iraq, perhaps some 60,000 troops. It depended on how they determined "capable, nonpartisan Iraqi troops," and no one had a good answer. By any measure, the number fell far short.

Gordon's intelligence paper was not optimistic about the formation of a strong national government, saying that even with reforms such as "robust guarantees of resources sharing" of oil revenue with all sects and regions, "the national government will be fragile."

The second approach was partitioning the country, and the paper said that would probably only make things worse. A third approach of backing the Shia would likely result in "a large increase in violence," he wrote.

Gordon was the only one to address seriously a withdrawal of U.S. troops, the fourth approach in the paper. "Most analysts judge the immediate results of a rapid U.S. withdrawal would be largely negative: Further escalation of communal civil war, strengthening of al Qaeda in Iraq and terrorists, severe damage to U.S. prestige and destabilization of the region."

In summary, the paper concluded, "No approach stands out as clearly preferable to the others, and all entail significant risks and dangers to the United States."

The others generally found the paper interesting but unhelpful. After the intelligence blunder about weapons of mass destruction in Iraq—the supposed "slam dunk" case—the intelligence agencies had become increasingly cautious and tended to hedge more and more, making their analytic work less and less useful.

At one point during the review, intelligence analysts provided Zelikow with a report about the serious sectarian divides within the Iraqi army. It showed that the Shia dominated to the point that no one could seriously call it a nonsectarian army.

"Let's circulate this to all the other people here in the review," Zelikow said to Crouch.

No, it couldn't be circulated, Crouch replied.

"You're saying I can't give this to Condi?" Zelikow asked. That was too preposterous, so Zelikow appealed to John Negroponte, the director of national intelligence. He ruled that it wasn't finished intelligence, had not been approved by the intelligence community formally, and could not be further circulated.

So Zelikow summarized it in the brief report he wrote for Rice after each strategy review meeting.

The Defense and JCS representatives several times argued that the State Department had to provide more personnel to the Iraq War. Zelikow noted that the State Department was a small operation compared to the Pentagon. He checked and reported back that there were about 6,500 foreign service officers. The American military had more musicians than that.

John Hannah, Cheney's man, wrote a paper that he insisted reflected only his views, which said that the strategy of reconciliation called for a large investment in talking to the Sunni insurgents, and in so doing the United States had paid a big price with the majority Shia, who had become more distrustful. This investment in trying to bring the Sunnis in and cater to them had not really worked. Essentially, Hannah said, let's stop forcing the Sunnis down the Shia's throats. Let's not be so scared of saying the Shia are the majority and that they have won.

Because the Shia and the Kurds made up 80 percent of the population, Hannah's paper was quickly dubbed "The 80 percent solution."

Despite Hannah's disclaimer, Cheney basically agreed with the paper. The Shia were the majority, and they had won the election. Too many people in the Middle East looked down on the Shia, especially the Sunni Saudis. He didn't want it to look as if the United States was in any way undermining the legitimately elected government in Iraq.

· · ·

At the end of many intense days, the discussions and papers had yielded no consensus. Crouch, nonetheless, said he was going to put it all together for the briefing Bush wanted after Thanksgiving. He would control the pen, which meant he and Hadley would decide what to report to the president.

24

Tom Ricks, a well-sourced Pentagon reporter for *The Washington Post*, published a front-page story on Monday, November 20, about the Council of Colonels and its "closely guarded" review, and he attempted to parse out its recommendations on Iraq.

Pace met with the colonels that day to thank them for their good work so far. Someone on the council has a big mouth, he said. The leak had really hurt their efforts to stay underneath the radar. "We, the chiefs, want you, the colonels, to tell us what you really think," he said.

Then he dropped a bomb. "General Casey has been asked by the SecDef and White House for his view on a surge. Would it be a good idea? If so, what would you do with five more brigades?"

That caught many of the chiefs and colonels off guard. Of the options they had debated and presented, that was not among them. Where had this come from? Was it a serious option? Was it already a done deal?

Pace said he had another White House meeting in two days and he wanted as much input as possible. "I want to be able to give the president a recommendation on what is doable," he said. Though Sunday—six days from then—marked the president's deadline, he did not expect any decisions from the White House. "Only flavors and vectors," he said. "I am willing to take forward other options."

"How fast must we make this happen?" Mullen asked, referring to a surge.

By late spring or early summer, Pace replied.

Lieutenant General Sattler, the head of the directorate of strategic plans and policy who was participating in the J. D. Crouch review at the White House, summarized for them other positions currently circulating. The State Department is arguing that reconciliation is not possible, he said. Cheney's office is leaning toward taking sides with the Shia—"that is, backing a winner." The Defense Department continues to support the current strategy and "believes there is a 'ray of hope.'"

The chiefs began editing and tweaking the slides developed by the colonels, taking a much more status quo emphasis; a conservative, less disparaging approach, softening the criticisms, emphasizing any sliver of optimism. Some of the colonels wondered why their presentation had to be watered down for the president. But the chiefs prevailed.

As the chiefs sorted through the language and the slide presentation, Schoomaker again let go with a burst of frustration.

"If you listen to the discussion here, it is obvious," he said. "We have run out of time. . . . Our strategic thinking has been reduced to recommending the fastest option, not necessarily the best option."

Some colonels felt the group's work was falling on deaf ears. A few also suspected that Pace wasn't representing their views very forcefully, if at all, at the White House.

The chairman was told that he had some frustrated colonels on his hands. He called the group together the next day, November 21. "What's wrong?" he asked. "I want to hear your concerns."

The colonels vented, but cautiously.

"You've given me some great things to think about," Pace said. "Let's meet tomorrow morning."

The next day, November 22, a secure video screen beamed General Casey from Baghdad to the tank, where the chiefs and colonels had gathered. They were to discuss a possible surge.

"Additional coalition forces will have a temporary, local effect," Casey warned, repeating his mantra. "Is the tactical gain worth possibly unhinging progress with the government of Iraq to assume responsibility for their own security?

"There is a struggle for division of power between Iraqis. The longer we take to give them responsibility for their own security, the less incentive the government of Iraq has."

Despite his reluctance to surge, Casey offered four suggestions if it were to happen:

1. "Thicken the belts" around Baghdad, meaning put more troops in the areas surrounding the city, where intelligence showed al Qaeda had moved.

2. Pass control of Baghdad to Iraqis during the first 90 days of 2007.

3. Put troops in Diyala or Anbar to tamp down the sectarian violence.

4. Use additional forces to secure the borders and protect infrastructure.

As a precondition to sending more troops, Casey said he would first want a commitment from Maliki to expedite reconciliation.

If the president were to approve the surge during the next 30 days, Pace said, five additional U.S. combat brigades could be in Iraq by April 2007, some 20,000 to 30,000, depending on the number of support troops. That would grow the force from 15 to 20 brigades. After six months, the number would drop back to 15 brigades due to normal rotations.

It'd be "a lot of pain to do this, but if it sustains support in the region and at home, it might be worth doing. But I am not convinced," Pace said. "I recognize that John [Abizaid] and you, George, are not recommending this at this time."

The number of divisions in the Iraqi army was growing, Casey said, "So progress is being made." If everything proceeded as planned, all provinces should be under "full national control" of the Iraqi government by the end of 2007.

"I am concerned about our lack of capacity to deal with any other threats in the world," Schoomaker said. "Building forces takes time. Investing all our eggs in Iraq is a big risk."

"We need to have contingency forces available," Admiral Edmund Giambastiani, the 58-year-old JCS vice chairman, added, "and to maintain a strategic reserve."

It was the type of abstract discussion that raised McMaster's blood pressure. "You can't manage your way through a war," he had confided to others privately. "You got to fight the war, man! Your enemy's fighting the war. Drives me fucking crazy." It seemed to him the chiefs and Casey were more worried about threats that *might* come rather than the very real war raging right in front of them.

"Now to your paper," Casey said at one point, referring to the recommendations that the colonels had compiled. "If H. R. wrote it," he said, referring to McMaster, "I would only give it a C-plus."

Chuckles around the room.

"Seriously, let me start with your assumptions," he said. "You are assuming away the tough problems."

The colonels' JCS paper had made three assumptions—that reconciliation between Shia and Sunni would occur in the near future, that the U.S. and Iraqi governments have the same interests, and that U.S. government agencies would work together.

"What you guys have listed as assumptions, I consider major tasks," Casey said. "If we achieve the three assumptions you have in your paper, we will be on our way to winning in Iraq. But the problem is, what strategy will get us there?"

McMaster spoke up. "You have to assume those things will work," he said, gently rebuffing Casey. If those things didn't happen, there was no ball game and no point in continuing.

"Your end state is incomplete," Casey told the group. The government of Iraq "will need our security guarantees even after fighting stops. . . . They will need our assistance in building institutional capacity and self-reliance for years to come. I would include language about the current conflict being as much about division of political and economic power as it is sectarian violence," he said, repeating his long-held conclusion: "The fundamental strategic assumption: Success will be achieved by the Iraqis."

It was clear that a majority of those in the room, among them the most powerful military leaders in the country, had little stomach for sending more troops to Iraq, even as it became clearer that the president intended to do exactly that.

On November 26, the Sunday after Thanksgiving, the president called a meeting for 5 P.M. in the White House residence for a presentation on the J. D. Crouch strategy review. The gathering was to be held in the White House Solarium, a rooftop room with glass bays on three sides. Calvin Coolidge's wife had called a smaller, earlier version of the room the Sky Parlor. President Nixon had called it the California Room. It had been Ronald Reagan's favorite White House room, and he had used it often during his recovery from his bullet wound in the 1981 assassination attempt. The Clintons had used it for private political and policy meetings when they wanted to limit access to top advisers.

In all her years as national security adviser and secretary of state, Rice had never been in the Solarium. The plan was to make this meeting different—a new place on a late Sunday afternoon following a big holiday. She took a seat next to Treasury Secretary Hank Paulson, the former head of Goldman Sachs, the legendary New York investment bank. Paulson, 60, a former All-East lineman at Dartmouth, where he'd also been Phi Beta Kappa, had made a fortune at Goldman. Though he had been treasury secretary for only five months, he was invited to the meeting to offer an outside perspective.

Rumsfeld, serving out his last days as defense secretary, took a seat. His successor, Gates, had not been confirmed but attended, hovering over the proceedings like a ghost, saying almost nothing.

Crouch had finished the final version of his 14-page briefing at 9 P.M. the Friday before. Summarizing a lot of familiar material about the importance of Iraq and the absence of a "silver-bullet solution," Crouch got to the present situation.

"Situation in Baghdad has not meaningfully improved," he said. "The government of Iraq has been slow . . . Iraqi police in Baghdad are largely ineffective or worse . . . Iraqi army is better prepared but still fragile . . . Force levels overall in Baghdad are inadequate to stabilize a city of its size."

Despite his positive comments, Maliki was unable or unwilling to act, Crouch said. The Sunnis and Shia were all "hedging." He pronounced the grimmest line of all, that the "enemy has the initiative." He then presented a chart of nine key assumptions, illustrating what they had been optimistic about in the past versus the current reality. "Iraqi leaders are advancing sectarian agendas" was one. Another, an understatement: "The tolerance of the American people for efforts in Iraq is waning."

Summarizing what he called the "Emerging Consensus," Crouch said the ultimate goal was still to "accelerate the transfer of security responsibility to Iraqis." It was the Rumsfeld-Casey concept. He added, however, that they should "consider a significant surge in U.S. forces."

A free-flowing discussion followed, with Rice arguing that there was too much focus on Iraq and that it was possible to create leverage by stepping back. Hadley made it clear that he recommended a surge of forces. The president didn't say much.

"You're not getting a clear picture of what's going on on the ground," Rice finally said. She had said it before to the principals but never this directly in front of the president. With Rumsfeld virtually out of the picture, she let loose. "The briefings from the military are a bunch of maps that nobody can read—statistics that don't relate to anything." With such a blurred and incomplete picture, she said, it was hard to judge the truth. She turned to the president. "I don't know how anybody's going to tell you whether or not more troops are going to help when you don't know what's going on on the ground.

"Is this government so sectarian that it can't function?" she asked. "I don't know. And it makes me really uncomfortable. And if we're going to do anything, we better make sure that you've got that one tied down."

"We have to do something about the violence," Hadley insisted. When was the violence going to come down? He had been pressing this point for months. He was still carrying around the chart of escalating violence in his "GWB" file. As he often said, "I'll believe we got it right in Iraq when that chart starts going down." Because, as Crouch had pointed out, the Iraqi police were "ineffective or worse" and the army was "fragile," Hadley said the best chance to get violence down was "with American forces."

"What if we can't do anything about the violence with more American forces?" Rice asked. What specifically would be the mission of those extra forces? How would it be different from the 150,000 U.S. troops already there? Her worst nightmare was that they would send another 20,000 or 30,000—the five brigades they were talking about—to do the same thing the others had been doing, with the same results.

Rice understood that the idea was population security, sending the U.S. troops out with Iraqi police and army to neighborhood outposts. "But who was going to be responsible for population security?" she asked pointedly. If the Iraqis can't do it, and particularly if they themselves are undermining population security through sectarianism, how in the world are you going to use American forces to do it?

In his briefing, Crouch had argued against the idea that American forces could stay out of the sectarian violence and step in only to prevent genocide. It would be unsustainable politically in the United States, he said, to have a policy where all you're trying to do is stop major humanitarian suffering—mass killings and displacement. More important, he said, it's unsustainable with our forces on the ground. You cannot ask U.S. military personnel to stand by and remain detached as Iraqis are slaughtered in sectarian violence. You simply cannot ask U.S. forces to look the other way.

Bush said they must not lose sight of national reconciliation, and to underscore his point he added, "The U.S. forces will come home if we can't achieve it."

The question arose whether more obvious U.S. support of the Shia and Kurds might ease the pressure on them so they would be more amenable to reconciling with the Sunnis. But the intelligence indicated that the Maliki government still showed signs of backing a sectarian agenda. In addition, it was pretty clear that the Sunnis did not want to reconcile.

The president said the problem was the extremists on both sides. The United States had to fight them and do it in a balanced way, not tilting one way or the other. At the same time, he indicated, they had to support the Maliki government and help the Shia majority succeed.

They returned to Rice's question, which had been one of Hadley's major inquiries during his grilling of Casey and Khalilzad four months earlier: Who could really be responsible for quelling sectarian violence? Who should have that mission? Could the United States take it on?

General Pace made it clear that from a military point of view, the dangers were so great that the task would be virtually impossible. The U.S. military might not have the ability to pull it off.

Also, it would put the U.S. Army between the Shia and Sunnis, Rice said, clearly an untenable position.

She said she felt strongly that they had to be much clearer about what the American interests were, because they were losing sight of that. One was to preserve democratic institutions in Iraq so they could be of use in the future. Is it in America's interest, she asked, to try to achieve population security in Iraq? If you are going to pursue it, you'd better succeed. Because if you don't succeed—if you take on that mission and don't succeed—you won't be able to go back and secure those other interests. She looked toward the president. "Instead," she said, "you'll be run out of the country."

"I've come into this with no background whatsoever," Treasury Secretary Paulson said. "But I don't understand what it is we're actually talking about here when we talk about putting more American forces in. What is it we're actually talking about? I don't know what it is you're trying to do."

It had been 1,348 days since the invasion of Iraq and six months since the president had privately agreed with his top advisers that they needed a strategy review. But no one had an answer for the treasury secretary's simple question.

The strategy had lost its way, Rice thought. Everything was spiraling downward so badly that the answer to Paulson's question was simply another question: Could they reestablish some kind of minimum security and live to fight another day? In other words, could they survive?

Bush said he would take input from everyone over the next three weeks and that he anticipated announcing a new direction by mid-December.

Crouch left the meeting feeling down. Though it wasn't clear whose arguments had won out, he had the impression that the Iraqis might soon be left with the responsibility for their own security, a job he didn't think they were ready to handle.

The next day, Monday, November 27, Pace met with the chiefs and the Council of Colonels in the tank to brief them on his meeting at the White House. "I walked out happy because I got my views on the table," he said, making it clear that this was not always the case.

"Did Hadley have a new perspective after his trip to Iraq?" Marine Commandant General James T. Conway asked, referring to his recent visit.

Yes, he came back convinced that security is the number one issue, Pace replied, and unless we can find a way to protect the Iraqi people, all the other political and economic objectives remain elusive.

"Since 2003, violence has gone up and never once has security been adequate," Admiral Giambastiani noted. Everyone knew he was right.

Pace said that Rice had made it clear she wanted more security before the State Department would get serious about the Provincial Reconstruction Teams—the small civil-military groups that worked on reconstruction—for Anbar province.

"Was there any sense of urgency displayed at the White House?" Schoomaker asked impatiently and sarcastically.

"There was a clear sense of urgency with the president," Pace answered. "He is leaning into announcing a new phase in the war that will help us achieve our original end state . . . by April 1, 2007, we would have five more brigades in Iraq."

Schoomaker was dismayed. Suppose that didn't work, he asked, "What is our fallback plan?"

"A 1 January decision should allow us to get five brigades in place by mid-April at the latest," Pace answered. There was no fallback.

"Are people engaged on this," Schoomaker asked almost defiantly, "or is this politics?"

"They are engaged," Pace replied. That's why the administration was contemplating the ways a surge might help. But if the progress is still lacking "after we surge five brigades," Pace said, "then you are forced to conscription, which no one wants to talk about." So this was the last desperate effort, and if it didn't work, they might have to return to the draft. To mention a draft was to invite the ghosts of Vietnam into the tank.

"Folks keep talking about the readiness of U.S. forces. Ready to do what?" Schoomaker growled, launching into a long monologue. "We need to look at our strategic depth for handling other threats. How do we get bigger? And how do we make what we have today more ready? This is not just about Iraq!"

Their jobs were to make the U.S. military ready for the unexpected crisis which would someday come. We have to figure out how to accelerate our overall global readiness and capacity, Schoomaker said. "I sometimes feel like it is hope against hope. I feel like Nero did when Rome was burning. It just worries the hell out of me."

Several colonels wanted to stand up and applaud. It worried them too. Others disagreed, feeling it was more important to fight the current war. But they all maintained their poker faces.

"Look, no one is whistling Dixie here," Pace said. "Serious folks are giving this a dispassionate and balanced look." He insisted, "The president and the White House understand the resource constraints."

It was not clear that anyone believed what the chairman was saying or whether he believed it. What was clear was that there was lots of "whistling Dixie."

"I want to be sure we are using time to the best advantage," Schoomaker said. "We can't recover lost time. I fear we will be caught flat-footed, the president and Rumsfeld will make a decision and we won't be able to execute."

"We need to position ourselves properly for the decision likely to come," Pace said.

As chief of staff of the Army, Schoomaker was responsible for recruiting, equipping and training. He worried about the long-term strength and future of the Army. He wanted to recruit a larger overall force. "If there is a spike in violence in Iraq, Afghanistan, Lebanon, North Korea, we don't want to be caught flat-footed." He told Pace, "I know your meeting was not about this."

"The sense of urgency is over Iraq, but not over the other issues," Pace said. "Now, I want to be able to tell him [Bush] what is possible with a bigger Army and Marine Corps. What does it buy the nation?"

Admiral Mullen was worried. "We need to do the worst-case, not best-case planning here," he said. "We might want to hold some reserves out for other threats—say, eight brigades for Iran."

Schoomaker knew they didn't have eight extra brigades.

Mullen said that they would break the all-volunteer force with extended and repeated deployments. "We will continue to hollow out the force. . . . Bottom line: You decrease the deployments or make the force bigger. This is a small price to pay for sustainable security."

"I agree we need larger ground forces," Air Force chief Moseley said. "We are using Marines as a second land army."

Pace returned to five months earlier, when Casey had decided not to reduce the force in Iraq by two brigades, as he had planned. "Let me tell you, my world changed in July when I realized we were not going to off-ramp," Pace said.

Along the wall, Colonel Greenwood was startled. All the talk about drawing down was empty. They didn't have a strategy. When they had a plan for a drawdown but did the opposite, there was no one in the system to blow the whistle.

Pace asked for a wrap-up summary.

Mullen said he was worried that combining a JCS paper with one from the civilians in Rumsfeld's office would result in their "best military advice being watered down."

Pace knew what Bush wanted. "I am more interested in how a surge will work," the chairman said.

"I am still searching for the grand strategy here," Mullen said. No one seemed to disagree, including Pace. Mullen continued, "How does a five-brigade surge over the next few months fit into the larger picture? We have so many other issues and challenges—Afghanistan, Pakistan, North Korea and places we are not even thinking about today."

For several days during the last week of November, the members of the Iraq Study Group met to hammer out the final details of their report.

Lee Hamilton thought the Democrats favored what he called "a responsible exit" from Iraq, and Bill Perry had drawn up a timetable for withdrawal. The Perry draft recommendation said, "By the first quarter of 2008"—barely a year away—"all combat brigades not necessary for force protection should be out of Iraq."

"I can't accept that," Baker said. He did not want a rigid timetable. He knew that President Bush was adamantly opposed to anything that would tie his hands.

Perry wondered what was so awful about a timetable. Businesses and armies live by them. They make for good planning. "Look," he said in his gentle voice, "I'm not willing to sign a report that papers over it."

"Well," Baker replied in his steely Texas drawl, "maybe we'll have to go with the report without you signing it."

Perry knew it wasn't a bluff.

"We can work this out," insisted Hamilton. He wanted a target date for withdrawal.

Panetta noted that General Casey himself had suggested the first quarter of 2008 as a goal.

Baker would not accept a hard-and-fast timetable. He knew that Bush would dismiss it out of hand and argue that wars can't be fought on timetables.

Baker and Perry went off alone to hash out their differences.

Any recommendation had to be tentative to give the president some flexibility, Baker insisted. The "should" in Perry's draft had to be ditched. "Suppose it said, 'could,'" he proposed.

"Okay," Perry said. It wasn't a legal document, after all, and the "could" was acceptable to get the issue out in the public. So the final language read, "By the first quarter of 2008, subject to unexpected developments in the security situation on the ground, all combat brigades not necessary for force protection *could* be out of Iraq."

Meese, the former attorney general to Reagan, had served 32 years in the U.S. Army Reserve. He felt that qualified him as much as anyone to make military judgments, and he was convinced that there had not been enough troops in Iraq from the beginning.

It was a mistake that President Reagan would not have made, he said later. "He would have had many more troops there. And the reason I say that is, the first time he put troops in combat in any large way was Grenada." Meese recounted how Reagan had made the decision. "He had said to [Army General] Jack Vessey, the chairman of the Joint Chiefs, 'General, figure out how many troops you're going to need for this operation, and then double that number. There'll be less casualties on both sides.'"

Meese and Chuck Robb wanted to make sure that the report included a "surge" option of more troops. So Meese sat down with Bill Perry to see if there was some way to work out a compromise.

Meese wanted the report to say something like "We could, however, support a short-term redeployment or surge of American combat forces to stabilize Baghdad."

That was okay, Perry said, but he wanted two qualifiers. First, a surge could also "speed up the training and equipping mission," which he believed was the ultimate goal so that everything could be turned over to the Iraqis.

Meese said okay. They could add that.

But given that General Casey and his deputy, Lieutenant General Chiarelli, had said unequivocally that they did not need or want more U.S. forces, Perry said that the study group had to say it could support a surge only "if the U.S. commander in Iraq determines that such steps would be effective."

Meese agreed to the language, and the two returned to the others, saying they had settled on a solution.

Perry was relieved. His grandson, a lance corporal in the Marine Corps, had by then served two tours in Iraq—gung ho the first time around, less enthusiastic on the second. "God, we worried about him," Perry said later. Because the generals had been so opposed to more force and had assured the study group—and Perry personally—that they did not want a surge, Perry convinced himself that its inclusion in the study group report would have no effect. Given Bush's public and private assurances that he looked to General Casey for advice, Perry felt confident that a surge was not going to happen.

25

President Bush flew to Amman, Jordan, for a November 30 meeting with Maliki. General Casey also came, and the ice appeared to melt for the moment. "Hey, George," Bush said warmly. "How you doing?"

Casey gave the president a couple of one-liners about what to expect from Maliki. In conjunction with Casey, Maliki had developed a Baghdad security plan. It called for accelerating the transition to Iraqi control by the end of 2007. The plan divided Baghdad into 10 districts with an Iraqi brigade in every district. Iraqi police and some U.S. and coalition forces would aid them. It included the imposition of military law on Baghdad to keep the Shia militias and the mostly Shia police force from operating by themselves in Sunni areas.

Casey told Bush that the big message to deliver to Maliki was "We've got to have reconciliation if this is going to work. Mechanically, all this can work, but if the government can't cause the factions to reconcile, you'll risk unhinging the whole thing."

Maliki was facing another problem. Moqtada al-Sadr was threatening to pull his loyalists out of the government if Maliki attended the meeting with Bush. But the prime minister had decided to come anyway.

After presenting a plan that would put control in Iraqi hands by the end of 2007, Maliki said he wanted his Iraqi forces to have a free hand in Baghdad. U.S. forces could be around Baghdad, but not necessarily in the city. "This is our first attempt at independence. We developed this ourselves," the prime minister said.

But he added, "I had your people look at it because I wanted to know if it's realistic. We need to take responsibility for this." They all knew the extreme level of violence. "If violence remains in the capital at that level, we can't make any progress on anything," Maliki acknowledged. He seemed uncertain and asked for another review of his plan. "Now I need your people to go over this and tell me if it's possible. Already I know that they're saying I may not have enough forces. I think I do."

"He was proud of his plan. He's chomping at the bit," Bush recalled to me. "It's like, 'I want to lead! They need to see me in the lead.' I view that as positive. Because I'm pushing him on this thing. Also, I think I'm wise enough to be able to do it in a way that doesn't sound paternalistic. In other words, we're partners. This is a period of time when people have gone to Baghdad and said, 'Get rid of Maliki!'"

Bush offered me his view of how to manage a fellow head of state such as Maliki. "One of the things you've got to understand is, I'm trying to set the conditions so that bold leadership is possible, and that if he thinks that I'm one of these people that says, 'If you don't do it exactly the way I want you to do it, you're going to be removed from office,' he's going to [reject that]. You can't be a bold leader if somebody's getting ready to knock the ground from underneath you." At the same time, Bush told me, "I'm absolutely tough with him. I work hard to have personal relationships with people, and oftentimes, it opens up a lot of criticism. But you have got to be in a position, if you're the American president, to be able to say to a variety of leaders, 'Here's what I think.' And you have to be in a position where they say, 'I'm willing to listen.' And so, this was a realistic discussion with Maliki. But I have spent a lot of time with Maliki, both on the phone, SVTS [secure videoconference] eventually and also in person. I've worked hard to get in a position where we can relate human being to human being, and where I try to understand his frustrations and concerns, but also in a place where I am capable of getting him to listen to me."

In Amman, Maliki's proposed plan was dead on arrival. Bush

had listened, but he had a different idea. "We can't be in a situation like we got into last summer, where your army would go to do something, and then they'd get a phone call saying, 'Oh, you can't go after that person.'"

Bush then asked to meet privately with Maliki. Only their translators stayed. Rice and Hadley were banished to the hallway, where they pulled up chairs alongside Maliki's aides. One of them started in about all the problems Maliki was having with the Sunnis.

"No," Rice said, "there is also a Shia problem, and you must recognize that. Look, we've got reports—people going into villages, killing all the men and sending the women into exile. Are you telling me that's not true?"

None of Maliki's aides challenged her.

In their private meeting, Bush was direct with Maliki. "I'm willing to commit tens of thousands of additional forces," he said. He would surge U.S. forces if necessary. "You've lost control of your capital," he told the prime minister.

"That's right," Maliki confided. "And I've got to do something about it. I can't have this happen."

"You're losing control of your country," Bush continued. "Now, we are willing to help, but we will not do that—because it won't work— unless I have certain assurances from you. They are: There will be no further interference in the conduct of military operations. There will be no political intervention in your generals' decisions."

Bush then went through a list of additional requirements. There could be no areas that were off limits and no more "don't touch" lists of Shia leaders or Shia militia who were free to do as they pleased. "No matter who the perpetrators of violence may be, we—your forces and ours—will go after them. And that includes the JAM and the Sadrists"—meaning the Mahdi Army and its political wing. "We are going to take on elements of any group engaged in violence. If they don't engage in violence, they don't get hurt.

"And," Bush continued, "I have to have your assurance that you are committed to a political reconciliation process, because that has to be moving on as well."

Yes, Maliki said. He was.

Later, Bush told me about Maliki in Amman, "He's a man who is in many ways overwhelmed by the moment. And he's getting his feet on the ground. And I've spent a lot of time talking to him. But he has always assured me that he is going to take on the extremists. I remember distinctly telling him, 'A Shia murderer is just as guilty as a Sunni murderer. And in order for you to be viewed as a just and fair leader, you have to deal with both equally.'"

But that wasn't happening at the time. Sunni and Shia extremists were running wild in Baghdad. "Out of self-preservation, people begin to pick sides," Bush recalled. "Not, you know, political sides, but they begin to pick the side of the closest strongman or the most reliable strong person or the most active gang to hide behind."

It was not clear that day in Amman that Maliki had understood how seriously Bush was considering a surge. And Casey, left on the sidelines, had no idea that the president had so bluntly told Maliki how willing he was to send more U.S. troops.

Casey left the Amman meeting believing that the president and Maliki had agreed with Maliki's Baghdad security plan.

In a joint press conference at the Four Seasons Hotel in Amman afterward, Maliki said that he and Bush were "very clear together about the importance of accelerating the transfer of the security responsibility." And in a joint statement, the two leaders said only that they had "discussed accelerating the transfer," not that they had agreed on it, but no one apparently picked up the difference.

In the statement, they agreed that they would take steps to "track down and bring to justice those responsible for the cowardly attacks last week in Sadr City." The week before, a barrage of car bombs, mortars and missiles had killed more than 200 people in the massive Shia slum.

Afterward, Bush told Rice that he thought Maliki had gotten it. Maliki had pledged to save Baghdad. That was the bargain. And he added, "He said the right things. I heard the right things. And now we'll see."

From Amman, Rice went on to the Dead Sea in Jordan for a meeting of the foreign ministers of the Gulf states, the Gulf Cooperation Council

(GCC), including the foreign ministers of Saudi Arabia and Egypt. The gathering of predominantly Sunni Muslim states was called "Forum for the Future."

About this time, reporter David Sanger of *The New York Times* published two detailed, front-page stories on what the Baker-Hamilton Iraq Study Group was going to recommend. The first was headlined "Panel to Weigh Overture by U.S. to Iran and Syria." The second, headlined "Iraq Panel to Recommend Pullback of Combat Troops," ran the day Rice arrived at the GCC forum.

When Rice sat down with the foreign ministers, she expected the usual complaints about peace between Palestine and Israel or the conflicts in Lebanon.

Instead, it was all about Iraq. One by one, the foreign ministers said they felt convinced the United States was about to fold and leave Iraq. In turn, they would then have to make their own deals with the Sunnis in Iraq and with one another. Their big fear was what they called a Shia Crescent—a half-moon-shaped swath of large Shia populations running from Iran, through Iraq and into Lebanon, Syria and Jordan, among other countries—that would threaten the Sunnis of the region.

Rice received an earful. "America is going to give up," one foreign minister told her. Bush was going to redeploy and talk to Iran and Syria. They went so far as to say that they were worried that the president was going to make a separate peace with Iran. That would be like Nixon going to China or Reagan going to the Soviet Union. Such an outreach would upset the regional balance of power.

"You don't need to be thinking about pulling your forces down," said one of the foreign ministers, "you need to think about doubling your forces."

After returning to Washington, Rice went to talk to Bush. They both knew the regional allies had split personalities. As she once put it, "On the one hand, the countries of the region don't want us to be aggressive and bellicose, and on the other they want us to be aggressive and bellicose." Because of the chaos and uncertainty in Iraq, she told the president, others in the region now worried that the United States wasn't going to be aggressive enough. They were terrified about a pull-back or an exit.

"I came out of that meeting convinced," she said bluntly, "that not only did they believe that we were about to fold in Iraq, but that that was going to be the end of American power in the Middle East."

"Are you saying to me that we can't win it?" the president asked.

Rice said she believed that the 60-plus years of American influence in the Gulf, dating back to President Franklin Roosevelt, were very much at risk. The stakes were that high. "If you don't show strength and resolve," she said, "then they're going to have to cut their own deals." There was no better way to persuade Bush than to urge him to show strength and resolve.

More than ever, they had to find a way to turn things around, Rice continued. What was clear from the meeting, she said, was that "The very act of increasing American forces would have a salutary effect, whether or not it achieved population security. The fact that the president of the United States, against all odds, against all voices, would in effect double down, would have a hugely important effect on the region." Rice herself was not yet in favor of adding more U.S. forces, but the benefit of sending a needed message to the regional allies was now clear.

"Can we win this?" the president asked again.

"I can tell you," Rice said, "we're not winning it now."

On December 5, former President George H. W. Bush broke down in tears as he was speaking to the Florida House of Representatives. His son, Florida Governor Jeb Bush, was leaving office after serving two terms. Referring to Jeb's loss in his first governor's race years earlier, the former president said, "He didn't whine about it. He didn't complain." He went on, "A true measure of a man is how you handle victory, and also defeat." The 82-year-old Bush choked up, began to sob and pulled out a handkerchief to dab at his tears. The rare emotional display by a former president made the national television news.

Peggy Noonan, Bush senior's former chief speechwriter and close friend, wrote a column about it in *The Wall Street Journal*, saying, "No one who knows George H. W. Bush thinks that moment was only about Jeb." It was more likely about "another son." She noted that "growing older can leave you more exposed to the force of whatever it is you're feeling. Defenses erode like a fence worn by time.

"Think of what a loaded moment in history it was for Bush the elder," she wrote, noting that the bipartisan Iraq Study Group report would be out the following day. "Surely" Jim Baker, Bush senior's oldest adviser, had called to say the report "would not, could not, offer a way out of a national calamity." Bush senior had to know "his son George had (with the best of intentions!) been wrong in the great decision of his presidency—stop at Afghanistan or move on to Iraq?—and was now suffering a defeat made clear by the report.

"And the younger President Bush, what of his inner world? . . . The president presents himself each day in his chesty way, with what seems a jarring peppiness. . . . Unlike anguished wartime presidents of old, he seems resolutely un-anguished. Think of the shattered Lincoln. . . . Or anguished Lyndon B. Johnson." Was it "serenity or a confidence born of cluelessness? You decide. Where you stand on the war will likely determine your answer. But I'll tell you, I wonder about it and do not understand it, either what it is or what it means. I'd ask someone in the White House," she wrote, but they were still stuck on the talking point that the president was sustained "by his knowledge of the ultimate rightness of his course."

It was a true cry from the heart from one of the old Bush senior hands—one that Jim Baker no doubt felt but could not make publicly. Noonan wrote of the current President Bush: "If he suffers, they might tell us; it would make him seem more normal, which is always a heartening thing to see in a president. But maybe there is no suffering. Maybe he outsources suffering. Maybe he leaves it to his father."

26

Bob Gates headed to the Senate on Tuesday, December 5, for his confirmation hearing.

"Mr. Gates," asked Senator Carl Levin, the Michigan Democrat who would soon take over as chairman of the Armed Services Committee, "do you believe that we are currently winning in Iraq?"

"No, sir," Gates said, realizing he was going out on a limb.

Soon, it was John McCain's turn. "Do you agree," he asked, "that at the time of the invasion, we didn't have sufficient troops to control the country, in hindsight?"

"I suspect, in hindsight," Gates said, "some of the folks in the administration probably would not make the same decisions that they made. And I think one of those is that there clearly were insufficient troops in Iraq after the initial invasion to establish control over the country."

When I later asked the president whether he should have sent more troops earlier, he said only that history would have to judge and that "I haven't spent a lot of time analyzing whether more troops in 2003" would have changed the situation.

In the confirmation hearing, McCain pointed out that while the situation continued to deteriorate, Abizaid and Casey kept insisting that there were a sufficient number of troops. How could that be?

"Senator," Gates replied, "I was a part of the Iraq Study Group . . . I would tell you that when we were in Iraq that we inquired of the commanders whether they had enough troops and whether a significant increase might be necessary. And I would say that the answer we received was that they thought they had adequate troops . . . the response that we received in Baghdad was that they had enough troops."

Later, Senator Hillary Clinton, on the verge of announcing her presidential bid, asked Gates, "Can you tell us when and how you came to the conclusion that you expressed in your testimony, that we were not winning—a conclusion different from the president's?"

"I think that, frankly, if the president thought that the current tactics and strategy that we were employing were successful, he wouldn't be looking for fresh eyes and looking for new approaches and new tactics in our situation in Iraq," Gates said. "I suppose that I came to that conclusion during my service on the Iraq Study Group, which was really the first time I'd had the opportunity to look at some of these circumstances in detail."

"We have this conundrum," Clinton continued. "We have a president and a vice president who will ultimately decide—as the president is fond of saying, he is the decider—about the direction to pursue going forward in Iraq. And it is quite frustrating to many of us to see the mistakes that have been made—some of which you have enumerated—and to wonder whether there is any change that will be pursued by the president. Do you have an opinion as to how and when the process will occur that might lead to some changes in options and strategies?"

"My sense, Senator Clinton," said Gates, "is that that this process is going to proceed with considerable urgency."

Their report complete after eight months of work, the Iraq Study Group members met privately with President Bush just after sunrise on Wednesday, December 6, in the Cabinet Room of the White House.

Baker and Hamilton summarized the unanimous report, subtitled "The Way Forward—A New Approach," which urged a drawdown of troops with the goal of having all combat brigades not necessary for protecting a smaller U.S. contingent out of Iraq by the first quarter of

2008. In addition, the group recommended a diplomatic initiative, including talks with Iran and Syria.

"Mr. President," Panetta said, "you've got the work of five Democrats and five Republicans who've tried to come to a consensus here, and it's really important to look at these recommendations. I don't know of any president that can conduct a war with a divided nation. This gives you at least the opportunity to try to begin to repair the divisions that have taken place and try to unify the country."

Bush nodded but didn't say anything.

When Chuck Robb had a chance to speak, he noted that the report said, "We could, however, support a short-term redeployment or surge of American combat forces to stabilize Baghdad."

After all the members had spoken, reporters and photographers were ushered into the Cabinet Room at 7:58 A.M.

"I just received the Iraq Study Group report, prepared by a distinguished panel of our fellow citizens," the president said. "We will take every proposal seriously." He noted that he probably would not agree with all of its 79 recommendations. "It, nevertheless, is an opportunity to come together and to work together on this important issue. The country, in my judgment, is tired of pure political bickering that happens in Washington, and they understand that on this important issue of war and peace, it is best for our country to work together.

"This report will give us all an opportunity to find common ground, for the good of the country—not for the good of the Republican Party or the Democrat Party, but for the good of the country." It was perhaps the strongest bipartisan statement Bush had made since the invasion of Iraq. He was effusive in his praise of the study group members. "You could be doing a lot of other things. You could have had a lot more simple life than to allow your government to call you back into service, but you did allow us to call you back into service, and you've made a vital contribution to the country. . . . We applaud your work."

He's going to accept our ideas, Perry thought.

As Bush was leaving the Cabinet Room, Robb again urged that he consider the provision supporting a "surge." A smile stretched across Bush's face, and he promised that he indeed would.

Bush said later that he understood that it was Robb who had first voiced the concept of the surge months earlier. Robb, he recalled, "was very encouraging, and during the meetings, he would say—he's a kind guy—'Hang in there, Mr. President.' He was the kind of person that was hoping we'd succeed."

The news media treated the release of the Iraq Study Group report as if it might mark a turning point in the war. "Iraq Panel Proposes a Major Strategy Shift," *The Washington Post* said. "Panel Urges Basic Shift in U.S. Policy in Iraq," read the headline in *The New York Times*.

"This was such a sobering report!" said Tim Russert, NBC News Washington bureau chief. "Powerful, passionate, bipartisan, unanimous—I think it's not only a wake-up call for the Bush White House, but I think for the whole country."

"There's almost a biblical thing about wise elderly people," added Representative Frank Wolf, the Virginia Republican whose idea it had been to create the study group. "They can speak truth."

Hadley realized that the president was going to go with the surge. It was the only option that seemed to offer a bold change. Talk of an exit seemed absurd to Bush. The Iraq Study Group's ability to turn the tide in any other direction was neutralized because the members unanimously agreed that they could support a "short-term redeployment or surge of American combat forces." So Hadley continued his deliberate strategy to bend the Iraqi and U.S. governments to Bush's will. But there were obstacles.

First, Maliki wasn't on board. His most recent position, at his November 30 meeting with the president in Amman, Jordan, had been "I don't need your forces. We can do it ourselves. We should do it ourselves."

A second obstacle was the military. With Rumsfeld finally out, they would have to make sure Gates continued to support a surge. But Casey remained opposed. He and Abizaid would have to be replaced. The Joint Chiefs and their Council of Colonels were a problem, but Hadley knew he could sway General Pace by making it clear to the chairman what the commander in chief wanted.

A third obstacle, a formidable one, was Rice. In Hadley's view, she had fallen under the spell of her advisers, Zelikow and Satterfield, and their idea of stepping back. Both he and the president would have to work hard to get her to drop her resistance.

On December 7, Pace came to the White House for a private meeting with Hadley. Gates had been confirmed by the Senate the day before by a vote of 95 to 2 but would not be sworn in for about ten days so he could attend a graduation ceremony at Texas A&M before resigning as university president. Hadley was acting as the de facto secretary of defense.

"We have a strategy to win," Pace said defensively. "Most of the military actions we need to execute this strategy to win are already going on. They've come from our review. And they will look different to the American people."

He knew that the president wanted something different and visible. "But a lot of them are already going on in things that George Casey is already doing," he said. "They just haven't gotten the visibility, and they haven't been part of an integrated whole." For example, they are going to transition more of the provinces to Iraqi control, he said. Casey has been identifying U.S. brigades already in Iraq that could be moved to Baghdad for "an internal surge." All of this "has been approved by George [Casey] up through the chain and approved at the top. On the military side, we need to factor in what the Iraqis must do and what we need to do to support them if they're going to succeed."

More than three and a half years into the war, the chairman of the Joint Chiefs felt he needed to tell the president's national security adviser that he was not a naysayer.

"We are in it to win. We are not in it for a draw," he said, apparently still stung by President Bush's earlier statements that he didn't want the military playing for a tie. Pace said that much of this would depend on the Iraqi political leaders, adding, "Absent Iraqi leaders prepared to step up and do hard things, we can't succeed."

About the proposed surge, Pace said, "It's a military mission. It's got to have an impact. It can succeed. It'll have to be time-limited," meaning they could supply more troops for only a year or so. "It can't go on forever.

"If we can do something in Baghdad, it will have a good impact for both countries. But it must be accompanied by political and security steps. People need to step up. If we do it all together, we have a chance to succeed. And we also need to look at the surge requirement to support the Maliki assault on the Mahdi Army. Five brigades need to move forward. Some are going to have to be kept more than a year in theater."

The Army rotation policy was a one-year tour followed by a year at home. That policy would have to be changed. Soldiers would have to serve longer tours, and in addition, some brigades would not get a full year at home. "We can't have the active force take the full weight," Pace said. The Reserves would have to do more. "All 34 National Guard brigades have been mobilized. They're supposed to be home for five years before they go back. We may have to break that compact." He said it would take four months to get five more brigades there. "We don't have five equipment sets for five brigades lying around. So they will have to bring the equipment along and some of the equipment now is showing the toll of these deployments. Some of the equipment's broken."

"How'd it go?" Bush asked Hadley after the meeting with Pace.

"Mr. President, it went pretty well," Hadley said. "They're working the problem."

Bush and Hadley had managed—quite artfully, they thought—to circumvent the normal chain of command and get the idea of a five-brigade surge on the table. After all, for all practical purposes, they didn't have a secretary of defense. Rumsfeld was on his way out, and Gates hadn't yet arrived.

O'Sullivan was in her element, churning out memos, PowerPoints, charts and options. One SECRET document, circulated to the principals on December 7, showed what Hadley considered an emerging consensus. It still said the goal was "accelerating the transfer of security responsibility to Iraqis"—the old Casey goal—but that the United States would have to help the Iraqis quell sectarian violence.

Another five-page SECRET document, "Iraq, the United States and Sectarian Violence," said the agreed-upon facts included a statement that "the Iraqi security forces do not yet have the capability to handle the mission of quelling Iraq's sectarian violence" and if it were turned over to them, even with increased U.S. forces embedded with the Iraqis, the mission "is likely to fail."

Through a maze of "bullish assumptions" and "bearish assumptions" and risk analysis, the issue got down to two propositions. Proposition one was that the United States needed to help Iraqis quell the sectarian violence. Proposition two was that "the United States should limit its interventions to stop sectarian violence only when the violence threatens to reach Srebrenica-type proportions or greater."

At the NSC meeting December 8, Rice argued in favor of the second, more limited "proposition two," saying that they should intervene only in extreme cases of sectarian violence. "The Iraqis have to have responsibility. The U.S. should minimize its role in punishing sectarian violence."

"We need to mitigate the risk so this doesn't become a gamble," the president said.

"Iraq needs to be responsible," Rice went on. "Get them to the point where our role is diminishing."

"Well, it needs to be a slow-motion lateral," Bush said, "as opposed to a fast lateral. Look, the Iraqis need to be responsible. We all agree with that. But the issue is, responsible under what time frame?"

General Pace said that the military could not accept option two—intervening only in major genocidal actions. They couldn't sit and watch from the outside as sectarian violence raged. From a practical point of view, how would they know what constituted major violence during the middle of a combat situation? Where do you draw that line? We don't work that way, he said. That's not how our folks operate.

"We now know that the way forward is up to the Iraqis," the president said. "The issue is, how fast can they take responsibility?"

"It'll be summer before we could expect them to do this," General Casey said from Baghdad via the secure video.

Summer? Rice thought. That was seven or eight months down the road. There wouldn't be any Baghdad left by then.

Bush said they needed some kind of "bridge" to get the Iraqi army to the point where they could take over. "What do we need for them to commit? Is there a forcing mechanism? If they don't commit, there won't be success. So how do we get them in?"

From Baghdad, Khalilzad said, "They understand they need to commit. The issue is JAM"—the violence-prone Madhi Army—"They know they have to confront JAM, but they haven't finally decided."

"Waiting till the summer is a cop-out," Bush said, firmly and quickly making a decision that had been batted about by the principals for hours beforehand. "Look, we can sit with Maliki. We can develop a plan so this whole thing can happen sooner. We can't wait till the summer. Do we dare go after the JAM with force?" he asked.

No one answered. Going after JAM, a militia with potentially as many as 70,000 members, would be a monumental undertaking and put the United States squarely in the middle of the sectarian warfare.

The intelligence indicated that Maliki increasingly realized that the Mahdi Army could ultimately undo him.

"How do we give him the responsibility," the president asked, "which we all say he has to have, without failing?"

Hadley thought the president's line of questioning was on the mark.

Others seemed to agree that going after JAM would have to be an Iraqi decision but that U.S. forces could help.

"So what do we do in the interim?" the president asked. "What does he lack?"

Some suggested that Maliki lacked the political will because he had enough military force to deal with JAM with U.S. support.

"We can force it, but there are high risks," Bush said. "One guy can determine the way forward." It was an acknowledgment that Maliki's actions were critical to the situation. "We need to have, in a reasonable time, a plan for taking on the militias before my speech"—his plan to unveil a new strategy in a nationally televised speech. "We need to give the ball to the Iraqis, but on a scheduled timetable. We're committed on going after al Qaeda and the Saddamists. We're committed to protecting them against Iran and Syria on the border. The issue is sectarian violence and the militias."

Overall, Bush said, the stakes were too high to "gamble" that the Iraqis would be able to handle the responsibilities of curbing sectarian violence on their own. If they failed, the Iraqi armed forces could fracture, and the Maliki government could collapse. While the United States would not unilaterally take on the mission of ending sectarian violence, he said he had decided on proposition one. America would help the Iraqis do so until they could do it on their own.

In a later interview, Bush told me he saw his options in stark terms: "One was kind of pull out of Baghdad and if it burnt down, so be it, so long as it doesn't spread. And the other was, get in there and get after it and make it work.

"And I obviously chose the latter."

27

The NSC gathered at 7 A.M. on Saturday, December 9, with Casey and Khalilzad on secure video.

The general and the ambassador were scheduled to meet with Maliki the next day. They said they anticipated he would ask for additional Iraqi forces and more help from U.S. Special Forces. In addition, they said Maliki believed he was winning over Iraqi moderates.

"Isn't it part of the deal for Maliki to go after Sadr?" the president asked. "He needs to go after him and say he's going after him."

No, Casey and Khalilzad said. Maliki would say he was going after militias and those who break the law. He wouldn't single out Sadr, who still had ministers in the government and had been in a dialogue with Maliki at one point. Sadr and his Mahdi Army were too powerful. But Maliki would go after JAM under the pretext of going after the militias. This, in turn, would allow the United States to go after JAM and the militias.

"How does this all differ from where we are now?" Bush asked.

"The difference," Casey said, "is we're going to do it. We're going to have an operational plan. We're going to have a timeline for doing it." Maliki would "declare on the 18th of December that by a specific date, if the militia don't stop carrying weapons, stop the violence against civilians and accept the DDR"—disarmament, demobilization and reintegration—"then there will be a joint operation in January that we are planning now."

After the previous day's NSC meeting, Bush and Hadley had talked about some downsides of helping with sectarian violence. So the president asked, "What if JAM won't fight? What if they adopt the Hezbollah model of protesting the government? We don't want our troops in riot control. That's for the Iraqis. And if they go to ground"—into hiding—"it has to be a most wanted list of people to track down. How do you fight a ragtag group that goes to ground?"

"We will restore Iraqi control of Sadr City," Casey said. "It'll be clear when people are standing outside the law. If you see weapons, you can pick people up. Sadr City is now a safe haven."

Hadley said that would be a big test for Maliki. If he went into the Mahdi Army's stronghold of Sadr City and targeted fellow Shia, it would demonstrate some nonsectarian bona fides.

"Well, if we go into Sadr City," Bush asked, "who goes in? How? Do we have enough forces to go in? Whose forces? Who stays behind after we go in? We're not going to sit there. Who stays behind? Us? Iraqis? What's the concept here?"

"We would work on him to set the political conditions," Casey told him. "Then we would go through the areas with significant JAM presence first. We'd reposition Iraqi and coalition forces from within Iraq. We would preposition two brigades in Kuwait if the action spreads outside Baghdad. We don't need to see a repetition of April and August of '04." That was when the United States had gone after the JAM, touching off violence throughout Iraq.

"Who holds after we go in?" Bush asked, zeroing back on Sadr City. "Iraqi forces? Is it the police? Is it the army?"

He was told a mix of Iraqi army, Iraqi national police and some local Iraqi police.

"It has to be successful," Bush said. "To the extent that we rely on police, that's a problem. Should we add more Iraqi army? Should we fold the national police into the army?"

"We need to be realistic," the president went on. "We need to have a realistic time frame and a criteria to judge Maliki's intentions. Once we go down this road, if there's not 100 percent effort toward achieving the goal, we're going to need to be prepared to do something dramatically different."

A voice from outside the usual group spoke up. "Look, Mr. President, I agree," said Treasury Secretary Paulson. He was there at Hadley's request. "How much time do we have, and how many bites at the apple do we have? Do we need to develop more radical options and have them ready?" He mentioned Rice's option, in which the military would intervene only if violence reached genocidal levels. He suggested that the president not wait too long. "Make a judgment about Maliki. But my experience is people don't change much."

Hadley knew that the president's view was somewhat different, particularly concerning Maliki. He believed he had helped Maliki change and grow in his job.

And now Bush sprang to the Iraqi prime minister's defense. "Maliki's right when he says he doesn't have enough tools to do the job," he said. "We need to take that excuse away from him. We need to give him the right tools. But I will be making the decisions, and the goal is radical action to achieve victory."

For Hadley, that was the headline. But Rice thought otherwise. "It's not just Maliki that's involved here," she cautioned. "Remember, it's not just one man. But we should be challenging the entire moderate establishment: 'Unless you are willing to go after the extremes, we will leave you to fight each other, and we'll go after al Qaeda and secure the borders and you guys can all fight it out. So if you're willing to do it and step up, we'll help. But if you don't, we'll protect our interests.'" Those interests, she said, included preventing Iraq from entirely falling apart and continuing the American campaign against al Qaeda.

Someone mentioned the sensitive intelligence reports, which showed the Iraq security forces were not up to the task of taking on the sectarian violence. Were they expecting the Iraqis to take on too much?

The president said that Maliki, with some legitimacy, had often complained to him about the Iraqi army's equipment. Quoting the prime minister, the president said, "You run around in APCs [armored personnel carriers] and tanks. We run around in pickup trucks." Maliki also had complained that the bad guys had rocket-propelled grenade launchers, while his army had only AK-47s.

"How can an army instill fear when it looks like the militias they're fighting?" Bush asked. "So we have to tell Maliki that we will give his army a lot of equipment." For more than three years of war, the basic strategy had been to turn over security responsibilities to the Iraqis. But the U.S. military was still not providing the best equipment, and enough of it, for a simple reason—a basic lack of trust.

The military officers said they would look into their ability to provide more equipment. The Iraqis, it was noted, did have Humvees and armored vehicles in addition to their pickup trucks.

"Iraq should pour all its resources into Baghdad," the president said. He had been told that 33 Iraqi battalions in nine quiet provinces could be moved. "Why not move them to Baghdad?" he asked.

"We're doing that," Casey told him.

"Will Maliki have the best available Iraqi forces in Sadr City?" Bush asked.

"They have divisions, one each in the south and west, that are more capable than the ones in Sadr City now," Casey acknowledged. "But they're otherwise engaged in some pretty important stuff."

"How many Iraqi brigades will be involved?" the president asked.

Some 50,000 to 60,000 Iraqi security forces were involved in Baghdad, Casey said. That was three times the number of U.S. troops in the capital.

Bush was surprised. "What portion of the army are the most capable Iraqi forces?" he asked. "Do we need more American troops if Maliki agrees to do this?"

That, of course, was the primary question, but no one offered a direct answer. Casey instead said they were considering martial law.

The president, meanwhile, was focused on the number of troops. "We need to understand if we can have more troops in both Anbar and Baghdad," the president said. "It's the other shoe."

Hadley realized that Bush wanted more troops in both places and was trying to show where he was going.

But the discussion returned to Sadr City, and it was noted that many Shia viewed the JAM as protectors.

The NSC seemed to agree that there was going to be a battle for Baghdad one way or another. Once begun, it would have to go to the finish. Bush said he agreed with the suggestion that they would need additional air and naval power in the region to deter Iran, given Iran's support for and connections to the JAM and other Shia extremists.

Referring to Gates and Pace, he added, "Bob and Pete need to think seriously about this. But what does it mean? If something happened, if Iran calls our bluff, how will we respond? Once Bob is sworn in, Pete, Bob and John"—Abizaid—"need to come in and brief me on this."

"We need a strong message to Iran to stop fooling around," said Cheney.

The conversation returned to Maliki. "We need a deft touch to get Maliki to the position where he succeeds," the president said. "It doesn't mean cramming it down Maliki's throat. We want him to succeed, and we need to help him to get there."

Rice repeated her frequent warning to the Iraqis, that they needed to hang together or they would hang separately from lampposts.

"We need something to deter Iran and Syria," said Cheney, "and that's important not just for Iraq but for the region and for Lebanon, too."

Early the next Monday, Bush met with the NSC for a report on recent conversations with Maliki. The prime minister had agreed to a joint, immediate operation in Baghdad against all purveyors of violence, Casey and Khalilzad reported, even though U.S. planning called for the operation to begin the next month, in January.

"Maliki needs to announce to his people and to our people that he's going against all who act outside the law, that he's asked the coalition for help," the president said. "And Maliki then needs to announce the plan that you're going to help him develop in a speech to the nation." Maliki's speech should be a day or two before Bush's speech.

"Iraqi forces would need to be in the lead. What does that mean? Do the Iraqis have the forces?" Bush asked.

"We want the Iraqis to take ownership," Casey told him. "They have the command and control. They have enough forces. But the issue is reliability. We're working through it. And the result may mean that they have to lean more on coalition forces."

"How will we ensure Maliki will see it through?" the president asked.

It was suggested they start with the plan that Maliki had submitted in Amman.

"If the politics get hot, will the Iraqi leadership stick to it?" asked the president.

Casey and Khalilzad reported that there were conflicting pressures. The Iraqi government wanted to do it. But they were going to want to minimize the political cost. So Maliki would say it needed to be his plan, his troops, as much as possible against all elements, not just JAM. And when they briefed the plan, they would have to run through the contingencies with Maliki.

"We can't have him back out once he sees the plan," Bush said, "especially if it isn't until a couple days before my speech. If he needs more help, will he accept more coalition forces?"

Several said they believed Maliki would accept more coalition forces, but no one had yet discussed the specific number with him.

"Maliki needs to be bold and aggressive," the president said. "He needs to tell his country that they need to end the violence and that he needs our help to do it."

Discussion again turned to Maliki and the requirement that he hold his government together. A military effort alone would not be enough. Then someone—it is unclear who from the notes of the meeting—added optimistically, "We'll see a gradual diminution of violence over time with some spikes . . . may be a month or two before people see things as different."

"We need to buy time," the president said, "so the moderate coalition can emerge and the police can function. We need to bridge and buy time for the government so that violence does not get out of hand and prevent the government from taking steps it needs to take. We need to try to tamp down the extremist cleansing so the government can function. Does that mean we need more U.S. forces?"

The discussion turned to what resources Maliki possessed. The reports indicated that 40 percent of the local police were suspect as to their loyalty, an astoundingly high number. It was clear that Maliki didn't have enough force.

"Maliki should take credit, getting the U.S. to put in the forces that are needed for success," Bush said.

They discussed the importance of getting religious leaders to call for calm.

"What about martial law as a way to achieve a psychological impact?" Bush asked.

"We need a security plan, an economic plan and a political plan," Rice said.

"Once we get Maliki on board, and once we start this plan, we can't stop it," the president said. "Keep me posted on how the conversations with Maliki are going. Raise the martial law with him."

Discussion turned to which moderates in Iraq might support Maliki and the importance of making Baghdad the main priority.

But what about Anbar province? The local U.S. commander there was submitting plans for new troops. Would more troops help there?

J. D. Crouch, Hadley's deputy, had visited Anbar during a trip to Iraq earlier in the fall and gotten a strong sense from the soldiers and officers on the ground that more troops would help solidify the gains that had been made there. "They basically said, 'Look, Anbar is a big place, but it's really not a big place,'" he recalled. "'Because if you control the river and you control the road, that's all of Anbar. The rest is dust.'" They told him there wasn't enough force to hold the river and the road, and in sections the insurgents could move freely. He said they had told him that a little more U.S. force, coupled with the local uprising against al Qaeda, might make a big difference. Crouch saw it as an opportunity.

"Don't be timid about asking for more troops," the president finally said, and he adjourned the meeting.

General Jack Keane had been working for several days with Frederick W. Kagan, a former professor of military history at West Point and expert on ground warfare who was a scholar at the American Enterprise Institute, a conservative Washington think tank. Kagan, 36, heavyset and mild-mannered, did not fit the model of a hawkish, detail-oriented military planner. For years he had been publishing articles calling for more force in Iraq, and for months he had been working full-time with an Iraq planning group he had assembled at the think tank. Retired senior and midlevel military officers and several currently on active duty had joined his group. Kagan hoped his freelance effort would raise the level of discourse and get some attention in conservative circles.

Kagan was appalled by the conclusions of the Baker-Hamilton Iraq Study Group. "The default function of politicians is to come to consensus. The problem is that the consensus strategies in war almost never work," said Kagan, a 19th-century military warfare expert. "A reason why Napoleon did so well against people for so long is because they were having councils of war, and he was just doing stuff, and he wasn't compromising."

Kagan was a good friend of Colonel H. R. McMaster, who had thanked him in print for his help with *Dereliction of Duty*. The two had taught together at West Point, and Kagan was impressed with the work McMaster had done to stabilize Tall Afar, calling it a model of counterinsurgency. Kagan and his team figured out which Army units could be sent as part of a surge. It came to at least five brigades. They were preparing charts, tables and maps detailing how counterinsurgency could work in Baghdad. One map divided Baghdad into 75 different districts and showed the sectarian or mixed affiliation of each. They planned to issue a 45-page report the next month, after a crash weekend work session starting December 9.

Keane went to the AEI offices that weekend for detailed briefings on the plan. He'd spent years as a member of Rumsfeld's Defense Policy Board, getting TOP SECRET briefings and traveling to Iraq. But he was stunned by the depth of the material the AEI group had compiled.

"Where the hell did you get all of that?" he asked Kagan and his experts, figuring the active duty officers had brought much of it from the Pentagon. "Don't bullshit me, guys. Where'd you get that stuff?"

They insisted it all had come from the Internet and other open sources. They showed him some examples, much of which matched up with the classified material he'd seen. In any case, it was impressive work. Keane left convinced that it carefully and systematically answered the question of how additional U.S. troops could be used to protect the Iraqi population.

28

On Monday, December 11, Hadley had arranged for five outside experts, including Jack Keane, to come to the Oval Office and share their views on the military strategy in Iraq with the president, Cheney and himself. Each had several minutes to make his pitch.

Eliot Cohen, a member of the Defense Policy Board and director of the strategic studies program at the School of Advanced International Studies at Johns Hopkins University, said there had been no accountability for failure. "Everybody's just a great guy," he said. "You know what? It's true. They're all great guys." But the war could not be about how likable the generals were. "It has to do with how effective they are." Neither the status quo nor the timetables for withdrawal were going to work, Cohen said. It was a clear repudiation of Casey's plan.

"Hey, big guy," Bush said to Keane. "You're looking pretty good."

"I finally got a life," Keane replied.

"Well," the president joked, "I got to get a life, too."

Keane had brought notes for his presentation. "I believe we're in a crisis and that time is running out," he said. "All the recommendations that are being made in and around town—and also by the Iraq Study Group—none of these actually solve the crisis. They actually permit, in many cases, the crisis to get worse. The crisis is that the level of violence has increased to such a high level that the Iraqi government is being pushed toward a cliff, in terms of being fractured, and then that would lead to civil war inside the country. And we wouldn't have to debate it—whether it's a civil war or not. It would be obvious."

This crisis "has brought to light that security is the single most important issue in Iraq." Keane noted the steady increase in violence, each year "outrageously" higher than the last. "And it demonstrated to us clearly that our political strategy in Iraq—the rush to get a representative democracy—has failed to stem the violence. And the military strategy of training Iraqis and transitioning to them has failed."

The result, he said: "We don't have a plan to defeat the insurgency."

A quizzical look crossed the president's face, but he didn't say anything.

Keane said that this was a "short-war strategy"—establish democracy and train the Iraqis, all with the intent of getting out. "We need a comprehensive shift in strategy. It would not just be a surge in the numbers of troops that would make a difference, but what we would do with them is really the difference. So for the first time, we would secure the population, which is the proven way to defeat an insurgency that we have never, ever done before, except in Tall Afar. And the place to start, with the main effort, is in Baghdad, where we would secure the population 24/7." He explained that that would entail living among the Iraqi population instead of returning to big bases after patrols and operations. It would take about five brigades in Baghdad, more than doubling the U.S. combat power there, and another two battalions in Anbar province, he said.

"To use a military term," Keane said, "there is such a thing as key terrain." He said they should direct their attention toward Baghdad's Sunni/Shia mixed neighborhoods on both sides of the river, home to about 1.8 million people. "The military operation would focus there . . . it's where most of the violence is."

This plan would "show the Sunnis and the Shia that we intend to protect them both, that we are not choosing sides." He ambitiously predicted that the Sunni insurgents, al Qaeda terrorists and Shia death squads would all be removed. "Once we've cleared that force out, then a combined U.S. and Iraqi force would stay in the neighborhoods 24/7."

Keane recommended a two-tier economic reconstruction package—first to get basic services to the people and then "an enhanced quality-

of-life package, but it would be based on their willingness to cooperate." He said they should not risk a major confrontation with Shia militias in Sadr City. An all-out military operation in Sadr City could
potentially unite the fragmented Shia militia of up to 70,000. "We
should not be distracted by Sadr City," he said.

Finally, Keane said, "Don't let people tell you that this is going to
break the back of the Army and the Marine Corps, because it will not.
These forces are available. We can extend tours." The opportunity to
win, he said, would give a boost to the military. Morale, motivation and
dedication would rise. There have been many lessons in the nearly four
years since the invasion, he said. "One of the most significant things
that we have learned is that security is a necessary precondition for political and economic progress."

Agreeing with Eliot Cohen, Keane said, "If you're going to put new
generals in, then hold them accountable for their performance. And
tell them you're holding them accountable and you expect them to be
successful."

Retired Army General Barry McCaffrey went next. "I don't believe
we need to escalate forces," he said. "We need to increase the advisory
program, put our money on the Iraqi security forces. We shouldn't be
stepping in the middle of a civil war."

Wayne Downing, another retired Army general, said he was opposed to increasing forces and proposed a dramatic focus on Special
Forces. He had headed the Special Operations Command during the
1990s. A determined concentration of Special Operations Forces in
Iraq could turn the Iraqi army around, he said.

Stephen Biddle, a senior fellow of the Council on Foreign Relations,
said he basically thought that adding force was the only option that offered a chance to turn things around.

After the meeting, John Hannah, Cheney's national security adviser, called Keane. He complimented him on his presentation and
asked him to come brief Cheney in detail. Later, Keane and Kagan gave
the vice president and Hannah the extended version of Kagan's briefing, which went on for hours. The patron and chief defender of Rumsfeld, Cheney had largely stayed out of the strategy review, which clearly
was aimed at changing Rumsfeld's approach to the war. The AEI plan

was the first detailed presentation Cheney had seen of how a surge of additional forces might work, and the plan seemed all the more credible because it had been conceived of by a respected former West Point professor and had the backing of the former vice chief of staff of the Army.

At 10:30 that morning, the president went to the State Department to meet with members of the Provincial Reconstruction Teams, units of American civilians in Iraq helping to rebuild the country.

"I want to know how to win," Bush told the group.

Several of Rice's senior aides who were present were surprised. "God, what is he talking about?" one wondered. Considering the war was such a mess, was the president out of touch? The State Department view was that the United States needed to take a step back. Nonetheless, Jim Soriano, a longtime foreign service officer and the leader of a team in Anbar province, came up on the secure video link to brief Bush.

"You know, Mr. President," Soriano said, "I can't tell you exactly what it is, but something's going on out here in Anbar. Things are starting to turn." He talked about how local citizens were starting to come to the Americans with their problems and how al Qaeda's brutal intimidation tactics were making the terrorist network more and more unpopular. "I don't want to say anything's changed," Soriano repeated, "but things are starting to turn."

It was the first time Rice had heard that Anbar might be really changing. She walked the president back downstairs after the meeting.

"That was great," Bush told her. "Those people are really something." He seemed energized by the flicker of good news and one field officer's optimism.

Later that day, the president called Hadley and said he would postpone his decision and the planned speech to the nation about a new strategy. He wanted to wait for Gates to be sworn in, visit Iraq and come back with a recommendation. There was no way to take such a significant step without the direct involvement of the new secretary of defense.

The next day, Tuesday, December 12, the NSC returned to the Roosevelt Room at 9 A.M.

From Baghdad, General Casey repeated that enduring strategic success would be achieved by the Iraqis and would require political reconciliation. On the proposed "surge operation," he stuck to his view that additional forces would have "a temporary, local effect in reducing sectarian violence where they are committed." He wrote in green pen on his copy of the SECRET brief that they faced "prolonged, tough choices." Though a surge might provide "breathing space for a committed government," a surge "could be seen as a step backward" from putting Iraqi security forces in the lead. It also would result in additional casualties and might be perceived as targeting the Shia.

"I'm going to delay the speech until early January, ease up on the throttle," the president said. "We're going to empower Maliki to go into Sadr City right off. Is that the right priority? Would it be better to start with mixed neighborhoods? Especially if we want to surge, it may be a better way to get security in Baghdad than doing the hardest thing first." He didn't want the operation to look anti-Shia or anti-Sadr. It should be anticriminal and antiextremist.

"We never intended to go immediately into Sadr City," Casey said. "We need to feel Maliki out on this, but we need to strengthen the presence in the city peacefully and leverage the political elements in Sadr City first."

"We have to do something different," Bush said. "We have to demonstrate that we're doing something fundamentally different." And he reminded his general, "We've got to win." He posed the question: "Okay, what can you do that's fundamentally different?"

Casey said they could increase the number of troops. That would be different. But again, he was not recommending it.

"What else can you do?" the president asked.

Put in more money and perhaps increase the Provincial Reconstruction Teams made up of State Department officials and other civilians, Casey said. "But that's not going to be fundamentally different."

It was clear to Casey that the president had tuned him out. From his mind-set to his body language, Bush had changed in the month since the midterm elections. More to the point, Casey realized that he had lost a basic, necessary ingredient for a commanding general in wartime. He had lost the confidence of the president, a stunning and devastating realization.

At another point, Bush addressed General Abizaid. "Yeah, I know," the president said, "you're going to tell me you're against the surge."

Yes, Abizaid said, and presented his argument that they needed to get out of Iraq in order to win. But the president was not listening to Abizaid anymore, either.

"The U.S. presence helps to keep a lid on," Bush said toward the end of the session. "It buys time for the Maliki government and the Iraqi security forces. It gets the situation to a more manageable level in Baghdad." Troops added under a "bridge" or "surge" would "also help here at home, since for many the measure of success is reduction in violence. And it'll help Maliki to get control of the situation. A heavier presence will buy time for his government."

Someone said that the rest of Iraq wasn't as tenuous as Baghdad.

"But it's the capital city that looks chaotic," the president said. "And when your capital city looks chaotic, it's hard to sustain your position, whether at home or abroad." In closing, he said, "The speech won't be tomorrow. But let's use the time to work with Maliki."

General Abizaid was scheduled to leave his post as CentCom commander in about three months, March 2007, and Casey was planning to leave sometime in the months after that, later in the spring or summer.

"You're going to be leaving" sooner than scheduled, Abizaid warned Casey.

That night, December 12, Rice and Gates had dinner at the Watergate Hotel. It had been a decade and a half since they had worked together at the NSC for Bush senior.

"Bob," she said, "this doesn't work the way it did when we were here. It doesn't work that the president gets options from the Pentagon. What he gets is a fable, a story about what's going on," overconfident briefings that skirted the real problems. "They don't come in and let him deep-dive into what's really happening on the ground. And that's what he's hungry to do." The result, she said, was that "He doesn't have answers about how to fix this." And frankly, she said, the basic questions had not been answered for her. What was to be done? If they added force, what was the mission? What would two, five, even 10 brigades do that was different?

Gates said he'd be taking stock, talking to lots of people. And as soon as he was sworn in, his first priority would be to get to Iraq to see for himself.

Gates, who seemed a little shocked to find himself defense secretary, said he was already thinking about new generals who knew counterinsurgency. He planned to empower them.

Rice and Gates agreed that, as the heads of the two key departments, they had to level with each other, support each other, be totally honest and try to help turn the NSC into a functioning war council.

Bush and Hadley were more convinced than ever that they needed a surge. "How can we get a process that will cause the military to come to these conclusions?" Hadley asked. He was pushing for the kind of consensus that would allow him to say, "Mr. President, we're all on the same page. Some people less, but we're all on the same boat, heading the same direction."

General Pace was facing every JCS chairman's nightmare—a potential revolt of the other chiefs. The heads of the four services were increasingly frustrated. Their work with the Council of Colonels was being marginalized, and now, they suspected, their opinions were being ignored by the White House.

"Why isn't this getting any traction over there, Pete?" General Schoomaker, the Army chief, asked at one tank meeting. Was the president being briefed?

"I can only get part of it before him," Pace said, "and I'm not getting any feedback."

How much was the president seeing?

"It's really hard to get this before him," Pace said.

In several tank meetings, Admiral Michael Mullen, chief of naval operations for nearly 18 months, voiced concern that the politicians were going to find a way to place the blame for Iraq on the military. "They're orchestrating this to dump in our laps," Mullen said. The generals would wind up responsible for all the problems, and the military would take the fall. Mullen raised the point so many times that Schoomaker thought the Navy leader sounded "almost paranoid."

Schoomaker was outraged when he saw news coverage that Jack Keane, the former vice chief of the Army, had been to the White House to brief the president on the new Iraq strategy proposed by the American Enterprise Institute.

"When does AEI start trumping the Joint Chiefs of Staff on this stuff?" Schoomaker asked at a chiefs meeting.

Pace, normally given to concealing his opinions, let down the veil slightly and gave a little sigh. But he didn't answer.

"Do you realize how serious this is?" Schoomaker asked. He thought Pace was too much of a gentleman to be effective in a business where forcefulness and a willingness to get in people's faces were survival skills. "They weren't listening to what Pete [Pace] was saying," Schoomaker said later in private. "Or Pete wasn't carrying the mail, or he was carrying it incompletely." Under the law, the chairman was the principal military adviser to the president. But the service chiefs, also advisers, could take the extraordinary step of communicating their views to the president themselves.

The chiefs' frustration level got so high that Pace told Bush, "You need to sit down with them, Mr. President, and hear from them directly."

Hadley saw this as an opportunity. He arranged for Bush and Cheney to go to the tank on December 13. The president would come armed with what Hadley called "sweeteners"—more budget money and a promise to increase the size of the active duty Army and Marine Corps. It also was a symbolic visit, important to the chiefs because the president would be on their territory. Rumsfeld had rarely met with them in the tank in recent years, but now he and Gates were in attendance.

The president, Cheney and Hadley took the short ride across the Potomac River in the presidential limousine. The vice president suggested orchestrating a series of questions that would make it clear that the U.S. military wasn't on top of the security situation in Iraq and that the Iraqis were even less on top of it. None of the chiefs could disagree with that.

"Mr. President, if you'd like," Cheney said, "I'd be happy to ask probing questions at the outset."

"Sure," Bush said, "Go right ahead."

As they gathered in the tank, Cheney asked the chiefs: Do we want to bet the farm by dumping it all on the Iraqis now, particularly in Baghdad? And do we want to make that big bet without knowing that the Maliki government can be nonsectarian and function?

The chiefs suggested that the president test the Iraqis. Make them prove they can reconcile, and only then make the bet of adding more force.

Cheney recognized the argument. It was one the Democrats, as well as Rumsfeld and Casey, had been making: Force the Iraqis to step up. But he felt they weren't yet capable.

Cheney could see that the president was not about to move off course. He knew where he wanted to go.

"You can't ask them to reconcile in this security situation," the president said. "Don't we have to make our bet to get the security situation in hand before, in some sense, it's fair to put them to the test?"

As they went around the table, the chiefs made three points: The Iraqis would have to execute a security plan in a nonsectarian way; Maliki needed an Iraqi army commander who would have unfettered authority to go anywhere, even Sadr City, where Maliki was blocking operations; and there could be no more safe havens for al Qaeda.

"All right," the president said. He would get those commitments from Maliki.

Several concerns were raised about Maliki himself. Even if he wasn't controlled by Iran, was he too close to the Iranians?

The president said he was totally behind Maliki.

"Mr. President," Schoomaker began, turning to the real issue—a proposed surge of five brigades. "You know that five brigades is really 15." Schoomaker was in charge of generating the force for the Army. To send five additional brigades to Iraq, they would need to accelerate the deployment of those five. Another five would have to take their place in line, and if the surge were to be sustained, it would take yet another five. This could not be done without calling up more National Guard and Reserves units or extending the 12-month tours in Iraq. The Army, he said, had hoped to go the other direction and cut tours to nine months. Just to level with you, Mr. President, Schoomaker said, the force is not available without a radical change to the Army's 12-month rotation policy or to how it utilizes the Reserves. Besides, he asked, would a surge really bring violence down? Would it transform the situation? If not, he asked, why do it? "I don't think that you have the time to surge and generate enough forces for this thing to continue to go," Schoomaker said.

"Pete, I'm the president," Bush said. "And I've got the time."

"Fine, Mr. President," Schoomaker said. "You're the president."

Several of the chiefs noted that the five brigades were effectively the strategic reserve of the United States military, the forces on hand in case of flare-ups elsewhere in the world. There was no telling what new crisis might occur that would require sizable ground forces. It had happened before. Surprise was a way of international life. Should the strategic reserve of the United States be committed, leaving the last superpower unprepared for a big crisis? The president had always made the point that it was a dangerous world. Did he want to leave the United States in the position of not being able to deal with the next manifestation of that danger?

The president disagreed, saying, "I'm not worried about a North Korean invasion of South Korea at this point. That's a potential hypothetical, might someday happen. We've got a war on our hands and we've got to win the war we've got."

But would the rest of the government step up, the chiefs asked. They worried that the civilians wouldn't do their part.

The president said he would ensure that they would and that the

State Department's Provincial Reconstruction Teams would be expanded.

Bush turned again to Schoomaker. "Pete, you don't agree with me, do you?"

"No, I don't agree with you," Schoomaker said. "I just don't see it. I just don't. But I know right now that it's going to be 15 brigades. And how we're going to get those 15 brigades, I don't know. This is going to require more than we can generate. You're stressing the force, Mr. President, and these kids just see deployments to Iraq or Afghanistan for the indefinite future."

"We have to send a signal," Bush said, promising to make requests to Congress to expand both the Army and the Marine Corps.

Gates had said nothing during the meeting.

Bush and the chiefs met with reporters at 2:45 P.M. They revealed no details of their discussion, though the president said, "The enemy has also suffered. Offensive operations by Iraqi and coalition forces against terrorists and insurgents and death squad leaders have yielded positive results." If no one else would give the body count, he would. "In the months of October, November and the first week of December, we have killed or captured nearly 5,900 of the enemy." He said he had been on a secure videoconference with General Casey the previous day, discussing all that was being done "to defeat these enemies."

Of course, Casey had also presented his arguments against the surge. In the face of what should have been a serious analysis of strategy, the president's insistence on publicly reporting the 5,900 "killed or captured"—a useless statistic—was additional proof for Casey that the president did not understand the war.

Schoomaker never shook his fear that a surge would be a ticking time bomb for Army policy. He and the other chiefs left unsatisfied, but at least they had had their say. Rejected advice was not grounds for a revolt.

"The chiefs and I had reservations," Pace later reported to Hadley. "They have been addressed in the new strategy, and I am now comfortable with the new strategy."

Hadley was delighted.

Cheney thought it had been quite effective. Bush hadn't summoned the chiefs to the Oval Office, sat them down, chewed them out and said, "I'm damn unhappy. This isn't working. I want a change. I want a new strategy." Instead, he had heard them out and then made clear that he was going to do what he wanted to do.

"The tank meeting was a very important meeting," Bush told me later in an interview. "In my own mind, I'm sure I didn't want to walk in with my mind made up and not give these military leaders the benefit of a discussion about a big decision." He said that if he were just pretending to be open-minded, "you get sniffed out. And there'd be nothing worse than the president getting ready to make a decision relative to the military and these commanders, these Joint Chiefs and all the other people in the room who are watching like a hawk, not think that I was genuinely interested. And so I might have been leaning, but my mind was open enough to be able to absorb their advice. And so it could be that I made that decision right after that."

I told him that, based on my reporting, some of the chiefs thought he had already decided, that they had sniffed him out.

"I am trying to get them to be in a position where they fire back on an idea," the president said, noting the chiefs had felt free to express themselves. "They may have thought I was leaning, and I probably was. But the door wasn't shut."

Still, Bush fully understood the power of his office.

"Generally," the president said, "when the commander in chief walks in and says, 'Done deal,' they say, 'Yes sir, Mr. President.'"

29

On December 15, Bush and Maliki talked by secure video. The president asked the prime minister to approve additional U.S. forces. "View our coalition troops as troops that can help you do the hard work until yours are ready to go," Bush said. "Use our troops to generate calm in Baghdad."

Maliki mentioned he was speaking at a national reconciliation conference the next day and he would announce his approval publicly. When the translated text of Maliki's speech arrived the next day, there was no mention of approval.

The president was furious. Intelligence reporting indicated that Maliki had lost confidence in U.S. troops—they had not solved the violence problem. Maliki was saying: Why would I want more of the ineffective forces that will cause me only more problems?

Rice remained deeply skeptical of a surge, but she couldn't ignore the admonition of the foreign ministers of Saudi Arabia, Egypt and the Gulf states. The administration could not even appear to be pulling back from Iraq. For her, that killed the carefully drafted idea of stepping back, what she called the "Zelikow option."

In a subsequent meeting of the NSC, Rice was in a challenging mood. "Mr. President," she said, "I know you're going to get tired of hearing me say this, but I don't believe that the circumstances will permit a success based either just on a continuation of the status quo or just a surge in forces. You can surge all the forces you want, but [suppose] the Iraqis don't do what they're supposed to do?" She said Maliki's Shia government had to be willing to take on their own people—the Shia militias. "How are you going to make American forces deal with sectarian violence if the Iraqis won't?"

"I want to make clear what I see as the options here," Bush said finally. "We can hold steady. None of you say it is working. We can redeploy for failure"—he looked over at Rice—"that's your option, Condi." Or, he added, "We can surge for success."

"That's not what I'm saying," Rice replied, realizing that she had set Bush off. "But what are you going to surge them for, is what I'm saying. It is also possible to surge for failure if we don't know what the additional troops are going to do." It was one of the most direct challenges Rice had ever made to the president, and she persisted. She said the Ministry of Interior was still practically overseeing death squads and a hundred bodies a day were still showing up in Baghdad. "We have got to determine whether or not this is a case of will" or a case of "capability" on the part of the Iraqis, she said. "If it's capability, then 20,000 American soldiers will make a difference. If it's will, they won't."

Rice refused to back down from her question about what more U.S. forces would do. "Tell me how that's supposed to improve security? And if they go in and just train more Iraqis in the way we have been training them, where half of them don't show up, that's actually not going to improve security."

Casey felt strongly they could never bring the levels of sectarian violence down in Baghdad—no matter how many U.S. forces were put in—unless the Iraqis embraced political reconciliation. Otherwise, Baghdad was indeed a "troop sump."

He didn't think much of the pressure from Bush to get the Iraqis to sign off on a surge of U.S. forces. Instead, he was spending a lot of time trying to get Maliki to stop interfering with the military and start permitting operations against the Shia militias.

"We have an opportunity now to accelerate the transition of the security to the Iraqis," Casey said during his next briefing to Bush. That was what they had agreed to two weeks earlier on November 30 in Amman. There was still no question in Casey's mind that sending in more American troops would have only a temporary, local impact. He agreed that two brigades should be added because General Fil had said he needed them, but otherwise they needed to continue with the strategy they had. Of course, without political progress on reconciliation between the Shia and Sunnis, the transition to Iraqi-led security would not happen and the Iraqi security forces would likely collapse.

On December 19, his first full day in office, Gates asked Lieutenant General David Petraeus to come to Washington from Fort Leavenworth, Kansas, where he was overseeing the writing of the military's new counterinsurgency manual. Petraeus was on everyone's list to take Casey's place as Iraq commander.

Petraeus does not fill the stereotype of an Army general. Given the nickname "Peaches" as a youth because of his lack of facial hair and because people had trouble pronouncing his name, he was no roaring George Patton. But he had successfully led the 101st Airborne Division, the Screaming Eagles, in the initial Iraq invasion of 2003, and posed an intellectually tantalizing question to Rick Atkinson, a *Washington Post* reporter, who had embedded with the division: "Tell me how this ends."

It was a question no one had come close to answering. Though the 101st had seen more than 60 of its soldiers killed, it had initially brought some semblance of order to Mosul in northern Iraq. In 2004–05, Petraeus had spearheaded the Multi-National Security Transition Command—Iraq—MNSTC-I, nicknamed "Minsticky"—a newly created command responsible for training, equipping and mentoring Iraq's security forces and infrastructure. Tens of thousands of new Iraqi soldiers had been trained during his tenure, though the effort had produced mixed results.

Now he sat in Gates's new office.

"I'm going to Iraq," Gates said. He was leaving later that day. "What is it I should look for?"

"Is the strategy working?" Petraeus said. "Is this approach working?" In the eight months since he had told the Iraq Study Group, which then had included Gates, that he thought the strategy was correct, Petraeus had become increasingly doubtful due to the ever-increasing levels of violence.

"There is an enormous conceptual issue here," he said. "Is the priority security of the people," which he had emphasized in his new counterinsurgency manual, "or is it transition to Iraqi security forces?"

"Are there enough troops?" Gates asked.

"I just can't conceive that there are," Petraeus answered. "But I'm not on the ground. I haven't done the troop-to-task analysis." He would have to systematically study the mission and carefully ascertain the number of troops required to complete it.

He knew the level of violence in Iraq had become overwhelming to the U.S. military. How could anyone expect the Iraqi military to do better?

Early Wednesday, December 20, Colonel Tom Greenwood, serving his last few days on the Council of Colonels, walked to the end of his driveway and picked up *The Washington Post.*

"U.S. Not Winning War in Iraq, Bush Says for 1st Time," read the front-page headline. Well, thought Greenwood, maybe the colonels' message was making some headway with the chiefs: "WE ARE NOT WINNING, SO WE ARE LOSING." He read on. Bush was quoted as saying, "I think an interesting construct that General Pace uses is, 'We're not winning, we're not losing.'"

It was enough to make Greenwood's head hurt. Pace or Bush—or perhaps both—had turned the colonels' line on its head. "Losing" had somehow become "not losing." What the hell did Bush's remark mean? It was Orwellian.

In notes written later, Greenwood said, "We never met with the SecDef. We never met with the president. And I never got the feeling from General Pace that much of what we generated ever saw the light of day in his world. Just who was Meghan O'Sullivan????" After returning to his assignment as director of the Marine Corps Command and Staff College in Quantico, Virginia, Greenwood put together a PowerPoint briefing on the colonels' work. On the slide labeled "What Did I Learn?," he wrote:

"WAR . . . IT SHOULD STILL BE THE LAST RESORT!!!"

"Take care of George," the president had said to his new secretary of defense, adding, "I don't want Casey dumped on."

After Gates's first day as secretary, he and General Pace flew to Iraq. One day after lunch, Gates asked to see Abizaid and Casey privately.

He told them that he and the president were considering Casey for promotion to become Army chief of staff, the nominal head of the Army and a member of the Joint Chiefs. It was the initial promotion given General William Westmoreland when he left Vietnam in 1968—a kind of soft landing.

"I'd be honored to do that," Casey told Gates, "and if I did it, if you ask me to do it, I'd like 60 days between this job to kind of recharge my batteries." He had already held the command in Iraq for almost 30 months.

Who should replace you? Gates asked.

Dave Petraeus, Casey said. Petraeus's two tours in Iraq and his time as head of the Combined Arms Center, rewriting the military's counterinsurgency manual, had given him plenty of time to ponder what the hell they were doing in Iraq. If anyone would be able to look at this a little differently, Casey said, it would be Petraeus.

At Gates's first press conference outdoors in Iraq, a firefight erupted in the background. "Holy shit," the new secretary said sarcastically to his aides, "This is a lot of fun."

He knew that the United States was in serious trouble in Iraq. He had concluded that it was important America not fail because the regional consequences would be too severe. But he could see that stability was going to take longer than Congress or the American people anticipated. Gates made it his personal goal to get Iraq in a better place so that it would not become the overriding issue in the 2008 presidential campaign. He didn't want the next president to be forced into making commitments during the campaign that would lead to failure.

Jack Keane forwarded a copy of the American Enterprise Institute plan to Lieutenant General Ray Odierno, another longtime Army friend, who was Casey's new deputy in Iraq and the corps commander in charge of tactical ground operations.

"We don't need as many forces in Anbar," Odierno said in a call to Keane, "because Anbar's starting to turn around." But the proposal for five more brigades for Baghdad was in the right direction. His boss, Casey, had approved a plan for only two brigades for Baghdad, but there had been discussion of having three more in line waiting to be called if needed. One could be added each month.

"God, Ray," Keane said, "that's a broken strategy. Every time we need more forces, we're going to make another announcement of a brigade moving into Iraq?" Dribbling the decision out that way would be political suicide, he said. The president had to make a one time announcement of all five brigades.

"My problem's Casey," Odierno said. "I can't get this through him, and he's still here. I can't get any more out of this guy."

"Let me see if I can work it on my end," Keane said.

On December 22, Keane went to see Hadley at the White House.

"We may not need all these brigades," Hadley said. "There's a lot of pressure on us about this."

"Steve," Keane said, "you can't shop this around like it's an amendment to a health care bill or something. You've got a military requirement. We've defined the requirement. The ground tactical commander in there, Ray Odierno, agrees with that requirement." The problem was Casey. "There's some constipation in this process with Casey, I'll admit to that," Keane said. "But you can't trade these things off for political expediency, because this is a military problem here. And our problem here for the last three years is, we've never had enough forces. Now we're trying to get enough forces and do it right."

"We'll just sequence them in there based on need," Hadley said.

"Militarily, it makes no sense," Keane said. "They have to come in one at a time anyway because of when they are ready. Think about what it means politically to you. We've got two brigades on the ground fighting, and the commander says we need more troops. We move another brigade to Kuwait and on into the theater"—into Iraq. "You're going to do this three times, with *The Washington Post* sitting right on the fence line watching everything that you do, listening to everything?" Each time the request went out for another brigade, there would have to be an explanation, Keane said. The explanation would inevitably be: Well, we don't have enough troops. And the questions would be predictable: So you underestimated and lowballed again? Things aren't going right? "They're going to pounce on you. You want three more bites of this political problem of escalating forces? Why would you do that? Militarily, it doesn't make any sense. But certainly, politically it doesn't either."

Hadley said he saw the argument but added, "We can probably get this done in about six months, so some time around the summer, we can make an announcement that we're going to start to pull back."

"Steve, listen to me," Keane said, alarmed. "We'll just be getting there by the summer. It'll take all the way through the rest of '07 and well into '08 to have the kind of cause and effect of what we're doing. Protecting the people, which means changing attitudes, changing behavior, forcing the Sunnis to see they can't win and seeking reconciliation, convincing the Shia that they don't have to fight the Sunnis anymore—this'll take time. We won't really have an answer until '08. That's the reality of it."

Hadley wasn't sure. "We have to depend on what comes out of the Pentagon," he said.

"Like you've been dependent on it for the last three-plus years, that's what you're saying?"

They agreed to stay in touch.

Several days later, a two-star general who worked in the operations directorate (J-3) of the Joint Staff called Keane.

"We've got Casey's plan in here," the general said. "It's two and two."

"What do you mean?" Keane asked. "Two brigades of Army and two battalions of Marines?" That would amount to about 7,000 Army soldiers and 4,000 Marines.

"Yes," the J-3 general said.

"What's your view of that?"

"Our collective view on the staff here is that this is failing. It'll be just Together Forward III." That was about as damning a comparison as could be made because the first two Together Forward operations had failed completely and Casey's command had publicly acknowledged the failure.

"God, that is just awful!" Keane said.

"We're taking it to Pace," the general said.

"You've got to tell Pace it just can't succeed, just like you told me," Keane said. This was the moment to step up and speak truth to power—a very difficult task considering the head of the J-3, Lieutenant General Doug Lute, opposed the surge.

The two-star general called Keane back to report. "We took it to Pace. We said, 'It's two and two. This plan won't work.'"

So what did Pace say? Keane asked.

The general reported Pace's words as follows: "I don't want to know that. I don't want to hear it won't work. I want you to tell me how to sell this at Crawford." The president was meeting with the NSC at his ranch on December 28.

"Holy shit," Keane said. He had always considered Pace a sycophant, but this, in his opinion, was letting down the people wearing the uniform and fighting in combat. He concluded that it would be futile to call Pace, who clearly did not want to contradict Abizaid and Casey, even though they were going to be replaced. Such a challenge to the ground commanders would be inside the danger zone for a chairman. The senior military leader, the chairman was only an adviser and not technically in the chain of command. Keane figured that Pace was making the safe move, in effect hiding behind Abizaid and Casey's recommendation. "He takes refuge among them," Keane said, "and uses them as protection for himself."

Keane made another call, this one to John Hannah, Cheney's national security adviser. Hannah and the vice president were headed to the Crawford meeting.

"It's two and two," Keane told Hannah. "It's wholly inadequate. It cannot be executed militarily. If that's the case, we should not do it because we're raising the risk of more violence." It was another Together Forward, an operation destined to fail. "It would put more troops at risk without the capacity to bring down the level of violence."

Keane spoke with Hadley again and told him the president or the vice president should ask a single question of Pace: Is this a decisive force? "Now, the answer to that is a resounding no, and he will know it's a resounding no. He'll probably tell you, he'll stammer over it and say, 'General Abizaid and General Casey—this is their recommendation.'" If you press him, Keane said, he'll say something like "Well, I have not asked that question of them. I'm assuming they think it is, or they wouldn't have given us the recommendation." Keane said that the president had to demand an answer about whether the recommendation was a "decisive force." If the answer was no, he said, the president would have to overrule his military advisers.

Meanwhile, Hadley had another backchannel contact. His Iraq deputy, O'Sullivan, kept in regular contact with General Petraeus. The two had first met in Iraq more than three years earlier, in 2003, when she was working for Jerry Bremer and he was the commander of the 101st Airborne Division. They had stayed in touch, frequently e-mailing and phoning each other, sharing an occasional meal.

During one lunch, Petraeus had persuaded O'Sullivan to speak at a counterinsurgency conference with lots of "big wheels" in attendance. "Meghan, there's nobody from the White House at this conference," he told her. "This is huge." O'Sullivan went to the conference with Petraeus and gave an impromptu set of remarks.

Another time, Petraeus contacted O'Sullivan and invited her to the first Iraqi Ranger School graduation at Fort Benning, Georgia. "I want you to come down and see this," he said. They flew down together, and Petraeus delivered a speech to the graduates.

Petraeus thought the world of O'Sullivan and had great respect for her academic thinking and her abilities as a manager. They shared a common problem: trying to find a successful counterinsurgency plan.

Petraeus told O'Sullivan he believed counterinsurgency tactics could be applied effectively in Iraq. Typically, 20 counterinsurgents per 1,000 residents—or about 2 percent of the population—is considered the minimum required for effective counterinsurgency, he had written in the Army's updated *Counterinsurgency Field Manual.* "However, as with any fixed ratio, such calculations remain very dependent upon the situation." U.S. forces alone could not match such a ratio in Iraq—that would mean a minimum of about 120,000 security forces just to control the 6 million residents of Baghdad—but he did believe the mission could be accomplished with additional help from Iraqi security forces and private contractors.

O'Sullivan ran Casey's proposal of two extra brigades by Petraeus. "Can you change your strategy with one or two brigades?" she asked.

"No," he said.

"How many troops, how many brigades, do you need to do this?" she asked.

"I want all the force you can give me," he said.

O'Sullivan passed the word to Hadley and Crouch that she had talked to Petraeus. "It's my understanding that we can't change the strategy with only one or two brigades," she said. "We're going to make the same mistake. Now we're going to get the mission right, but we're not going to resource it appropriately. And it's going to fail."

Bush confirmed to me that he'd been told of Petraeus's conclusions. And he obviously already had Petraeus in mind as his new Iraq commander. "If you're thinking about changing the strategy to 'clear, hold and build' and you've recognized that there's not enough to hold," the president recalled, "and if you're the new commander coming in, it makes eminent sense to say, 'Give me all you've got.'"

The president later told me, "The military, I can remember well, said, 'Okay, fine. More troops. Two brigades.' And I turned to Steve and said, 'Steve, from your analysis, what do you think?' He, being the cautious and thorough man he is, went back, checked, came back to me and said, 'Mr. President, I would recommend that you consider five. Not two.' And I said, 'Why?' He said, 'Because it is the considered judgment of people who I trust and you trust, that we need five in order to be able to clear, hold and build.'"

Those trusted people, of course, came largely through back channels: Ray Odierno telling Petraeus he needed five brigades, Petraeus telling Meghan O'Sullivan he wanted all the force he could get, and Jack Keane telling Hadley and Cheney that a minimum of five brigades were necessary.

Hadley maintained that the number "comes out of my discussions with Pete Pace."

"Okay, I don't know this," Bush said, interrupting. "I'm not in these meetings, you'll be happy to hear, because I got other things to do."

Despite Hadley's characterization, Pace had told the Joint Chiefs weeks earlier that it was actually the White House that had come asking what could be done with five extra brigades.

After Gates returned from Iraq, he spoke with Petraeus again about the level of forces that might be required. How would the general go about figuring that out?

Once the mission was established, Petraeus said, a commander would have to establish what specific tasks had to be accomplished and determine how many troops would be needed. If those resources weren't available, the commander had an obligation to say, "This is the risk that is incurred by not having that level of resources." And at a certain point, the risk might be so great that the commander would say, "The mission cannot be accomplished." Then you would have to change either the tasks or the mission.

Petraeus said it was important to have an open conversation about military requirements, to welcome transparency. "We have committed the nation," he said. "And if the nation is not going to provide the commander on the ground with what he asks for, then everyone needs to know." The requests, of course, had to be reasonable. "I can't ask for something that doesn't exist. Look, I can take no for an answer. But then, other people have to know that the answer has been no."

"You need to tell me what you need and not worry about the politics here in Washington," Gates said. "Let me handle that. I'll work that part of the problem. And this building [the Pentagon], as part of the problem. You focus on what you need to do in Iraq, and I'll take care of the rest."

Aware of the Rumsfeld legacy of discouraging dissent, Gates added, "I expect your candor. I expect you to tell me exactly what you think, and in very plain terms. I want to hear what you have to say."

30

On Wednesday, December 27, Pace briefed the chiefs and colonels in the tank about his trip to Baghdad.

"We are looking at a two-plus-two plan now," the chairman said, referring to two brigades to Baghdad and two battalions to Anbar province. "The thought process is that a fundamental change is required. We need to show 'clear, hold and build' can work."

Pace was heading to Crawford the next day to deliver his recommendation. He gave a homework assignment to the colonels: "How do we describe the surge inside and outside of the U.S. government?"

At 4 P.M. that day, Rice arrived in Crawford to have a private dinner with the president and his wife, Laura. The rest of the national security team was coming down the next morning. Before dinner, Bush and Rice sat on a bench in front of the president's ranch house.

She said she could tell that he had come, in his own mind, to the belief that he had to do a surge. "I think you've got to do this," she said. "You're going to, aren't you?"

"Are you now for it?" the president asked.

"Well," she said. "I've never been against more forces." She simply wanted to know what their mission would be.

"Are you telling me that you're now for it?"

"I think you probably have to do it," she replied. "But this is going to be one of the most consequential decisions of all time. You are probably, because of the things that you've chosen to do, one of the four or five most consequential presidents—maybe in our history, certainly of the last 100 years, but maybe in our history. And you have to think about how you're going to do this and hold the country together. Because consequential presidents can't be divisive."

"I have to do the right thing," he said.

"Yeah, I know that," she said. "But what we've got to do is, we've got to find a way to bring as many people as we can along." The surge was not going to be popular. The country and Congress were expecting a drawdown. So it was going to be important how he explained it. She told him that he couldn't say, "I've made this decision, and to hell with all of you who disagree." That simply wouldn't work. It would have to be "This was hard. And people have good reason to be concerned. This has been harder than we ever thought, and we've done a lot of things wrong, but we cannot lose in Iraq. And I don't think Americans want to lose in Iraq."

He would have to be conciliatory, she said. He would have to acknowledge that those who disagreed with him had valid arguments. He indicated that he agreed.

"What if it doesn't work?" she asked. "What do we do then?"

Bush didn't answer.

Such an addition of forces, she said, depends heavily on Maliki. Did the president have a feel for whether Maliki was really up to this?

Bush said he would talk to Maliki again.

There is a very specific set of things, Rice said, that we could ask him to do that would be measurable and visible. She returned to what plan B might be. "If we do it and it doesn't work," she said, "it'll be the last bullet. The last card." This is our ace, she said. She figured the total surge would be about 30,000, when support troops were included. "If you play 30,000 American forces, put out 30,000 American forces and things don't change, what do you do then?" If the violence doesn't come down, she said, and the fabric of the society doesn't stop tearing, then what would be the argument for the continuation of the war in Iraq?

Bush didn't answer, and they headed inside for dinner.

"I'm not sure I bought the last card concept," Bush told me later. "First of all, to me the last card would be to pull out and hope for the best. Hope the thing, you know, fizzled out, the enflamed sectarianism just petered out on its own energy as opposed to exploding inside the capital and we sat there and watched it happen. To me, that's the last card."

"Does the president ever have a last card?" I asked.

"That's a really interesting question," Bush replied. He paused for a few seconds. "No. There's always another card."

At about five the next morning, the rest of the national security team flew to Texas for the 9:30 A.M. NSC meeting.

General Pace said he had been consulting the Army's counterinsurgency expert, Dave Petraeus, as well as Ray Odierno, Casey's deputy and the tactical ground commander in Iraq. They wanted the maximum force available. Casey's recommendation was still two additional brigades to Baghdad and two Marine battalions to Anbar province.

"Do we have an accomplishable mission here?" Bush asked. "What's the test of success, of accomplishing the mission?"

They seemed to agree that the test was the level of violence. The chart in Hadley's "GWB" file that month was showing still more than 1,200 weekly attacks in Iraq.

"We have to have the right measure of violence," the president said.

"The goal is that the Iraqis are able to establish control over their capital," Rice said. She was still worried that the Iraqis might not step up and U.S. troops would be held responsible. "The measure is not that America has to get the violence down. Iraqis need to get the violence down. They need to do it."

Several others suggested that the measure was still political reconciliation. Only true reconciliation would lower violence.

Then the president had a surprise. He said the surge could not be a onetime action. Otherwise, there was "a risk that they'll wait us out."

Having follow-up forces to the first five-brigade surge would require many more brigades in the pipeline, even more than General Schoomaker had said would be required. Nonetheless, he wanted

Gates to begin to identify follow-on units so that the surge could be sustained.

Sustaining the surge would be impossible without a larger Army.

"Will Maliki give the Iraqis and the U.S. forces freedom of action?" the president asked. Would a new Iraqi commander in Baghdad have the freedom "to go after death squads and into all the neighborhoods?"

Hadley wrote a note to himself: "We need to confirm with Maliki and have Maliki say this in a speech."

The discussion turned to new personnel. The president, Gates and Hadley wanted Petraeus. Casey would be promoted to Army chief of staff. Khalilzad would be promoted to U.N. ambassador. Soft landings for both. Abizaid would retire and be replaced early the next year.

Finally, at the end of a long, meandering meeting, the president said, "I'm going to talk to Maliki" in a few days, "and before I finally decide on the Baghdad plan, there are some questions Maliki will need to answer. And I'm willing to provide an increased commitment, but I need to know if Maliki is committed and willing to perform. It needs to be a strong military presence that's going to take over security without political interference. And it's going to look different to both Iraqis and Americans. . . . And Maliki needs to make clear he wants coalition forces and help."

Bush also said that he was not going to commit to a timetable on how long the surge would last. But he was going to send more brigades.

"Yes, sir," General Pace said. "Yes, sir."

Rice realized that Bush was aware that he had decided on too few troops for the initial invasion and occupation and was determined not to come up short again.

Just after Christmas, Casey returned to the United States and was with his wife in Phoenix when he got an e-mail from one of his contacts.

"Hey, you need to know that the White House is throwing you under the bus," it read.

A couple days later, Abizaid gave Casey a warning. "Look," he said over the phone, "the surge is coming. Get out of the way."

•   •   •

General Pace told Gates that Petraeus was the unanimous first choice of the Joint Chiefs as the next Iraq commander. Gates passed along the recommendation to the president but said some people in the Army had voiced concern that Petraeus was too outspoken and welcoming of media attention.

Bush, however, found that appealing. Casey and Abizaid had been too reticent and reluctant to engage the press. The president saw Petraeus's willingness to speak out as positive, and he approved the appointment.

Gates also faced another immediate personnel problem. Who would replace General Abizaid at Central Command? Who had enough experience and seniority to be Petraeus's boss? Gates and Pace examined the candidates, and Admiral William J. "Fox" Fallon, the current combatant commander in the Pacific whom Keane had recommended, rose to the top of the list.

Fallon, 61, was a blustery, hard-charging career naval aviator. Aside from Pace, he was the most experienced four-star in the U.S. military. He had flown combat missions in Vietnam, commanded an aircraft carrier wing in the 1991 Gulf War and a Navy battle group during Bosnia. He had played the role of viceroy in the Pacific skillfully, hopping from one Asian capital to the next, meeting with top political and military leaders and preserving American interests.

Fallon embodied the *Top Gun* swagger and self-confidence of the "brown shoe" Navy, so called because aviators often wore khakis and brown shoes. Prior to the Pacific Command, he had had two other four-star posts—first as vice chief of naval operations and then as Atlantic Fleet commander.

Fallon was on leave from the Pacific at his family getaway in Big Sky, Montana, when Pace called. Gates wants to see you, Pace said. How fast can you get to Washington?

Fallon was soon back at the Pentagon.

I'd like you to take CentCom, Gates said. "I need you to do this. You're the best guy in uniform for the job."

Why me? Fallon asked. Central Command was overseeing two

ground wars, Iraq and Afghanistan, and the post had always gone to an Army or Marine general.

Gates said he wanted someone with experience, and Fallon had a reputation for speaking his mind. "And you know," the secretary said, *"they've* made the decision to put General Petraeus on the ground in Iraq." By *they,* he implied the White House. Petraeus was a done deal. Gates liked that Fallon was very senior because he didn't want someone who would be overwhelmed by Petraeus.

On top of that, everyone knew the administration was reviewing the Iraq strategy, and a new course would be announced soon—a decision Fallon would not participate in.

Let me think about it, Fallon said. It was a big deal, not just for him but for his wife, Mary. Over nearly four decades, she'd stuck with him through tours in Vietnam, the Gulf War and other assignments around the world, from Hawaii to Saudi Arabia.

Fallon went to dinner with his three adult daughters, all of whom lived in the Washington area. They unanimously told him to reject the offer. Too much had been or was about to be decided without his input. But they said they knew he would wind up accepting. After consulting with Mary, he did just that.

He had two main reasons, he told her. First, over the years he had traveled a great deal in the Middle East and knew lots of the foreign leaders and other players there. "The problem isn't going to be solved unless it is worked two ways: inside the country and outside," he said. "And the regional commander's job, of course, is outside." Second, as Pacific commander, he had sent thousands of troops from his command to Iraq and Afghanistan. "For two years I've been feeding people into this problem, and so I'm going to say no? The kids can go, but I can't?"

Fallon told Gates he would take the job.

On Tuesday, January 2, 2007, Petraeus was driving in Los Angeles, on his way to the assisted living home where his 90-year-old father lived, when his cell phone rang.

"I just want to confirm that you are willing" to take over in Iraq, Gates said. "I'd like you to take it. Are you willing to do that?"

Petraeus had been all but certain that the job offer was coming. He briefly wondered whether he should insist on one condition: that Gates ask Jack Keane, the mentor who had helped save his life, to come back from retirement to be Abizaid's replacement at Central Command. Petraeus believed Keane deserved to be chairman of the Joint Chiefs, but that job was taken. Petraeus wavered on whether he could or should impose conditions and in the end decided against such a request.

So there on a cell phone on a Los Angeles freeway, two days into the new year, the 54-year-old general accepted history's invitation. He knew he was taking on the responsibility of a lifetime as the commanding general in a major war that most of his country had lost faith in.

Pace called Petraeus to ask how many brigades he might need.

"Sir, I've got to call Ray," Petraeus said, referring to Casey's deputy, Ray Odierno. "Is it okay for me to call Ray?"

"Yeah, of course," Pace said.

The number of brigades was a decision Petraeus was going to have to live with, and it would be made before he took over in Iraq.

Petraeus phoned Odierno on a secure line.

"We need all five," Odierno said. "We've got to flow them all."

"Okay, great, I've got it," Petraeus said.

On an earlier visit to Iraq, Senator John McCain had also learned that Odierno wanted five more brigades, even though Casey did not.

McCain, who believed a significant surge was in order, was upset with Casey. When General Pace learned of his frustration, he called Casey in Baghdad.

"McCain is saying that you're being a toad in the road and blocking all these policies," Pace said.

"That's bullshit," Casey replied. Yes, he was opposed to the surge of five brigades, as were most commanders on the ground. But he insisted that he was trying to posture Petraeus for success.

After Pace's call, Casey spoke to Odierno.

"Hey, Ray, where the heck would McCain be getting this impression?"

"Well, it wasn't from me, because I haven't talked to anybody," Odierno said, adding, "But Petraeus did call me to talk about some things."

Casey saw that Odierno was sheepish. The incoming commander was not supposed to start poking around, talking to the outgoing commander's subordinates. It was a violation of Army protocol. Casey immediately directed his executive officer to get in touch with Petraeus's executive officer: "Call," he said, and "make sure to knock this shit off."

But he decided he'd also better deliver the message himself. So he called Petraeus.

"Look," Casey said, "we've got a transition plan set up here for you. I'm personally working on it myself. We're going to make sure you get the information that you need. But you can't be calling the subordinate commanders."

"Yeah, I know," Petraeus replied.

"Hang on there, guy," Casey said. "You'll come in here soon enough. But Ray's working on my directions right now."

"I am in a really awkward position here," Petraeus said. "I'm being asked my views. And I'm the one who's going to have to execute what is eventually decided, so I really need to talk to the operational level commander on the ground"—Odierno—"who I know has made a recommendation, and talk through the rationale that he has for that." Petraeus also said he would need additional information. "Could I start getting some briefings and things like that?"

Casey said no.

Petraeus spoke with General Pace again.

"Sir, I believe you should announce and make plans to flow all five," he said. "If you don't do that, then what's going to happen is every time you have to ask for an additional brigade, it's an admission that you haven't succeeded with what you said you'd succeed with in the beginning. By the way, Ray Odierno's told me he's asked for five. If that's what he requires, then announce all five."

On January 4, 2007, word of the Fallon and Petraeus appointments leaked. Fallon, who had been a four-star for six years, called his new subordinate, who would soon become the newest four-star in the Army. They exchanged congratulations and voiced high expectations for working together.

Petraeus soon sent over his new counterinsurgency manual, which Fallon read cover to cover. Interesting, Fallon thought, but definitely OBE—overtaken by events. He considered it an update of counterinsurgency practices in Southeast Asia. Iraq was very different, in his view, with its sectarian strife and religious overtones. But that would be Petraeus's business as the commander in Iraq.

Fallon later insisted that he had shared his view directly with Petraeus, who with equal insistence said that Fallon had never conveyed such conclusions to him.

Also on January 4, Bush spoke with Prime Minister Maliki by secure video.

"I want to talk to the prime minister one-on-one," Bush said. He kicked everyone out of the rooms on both sides, except the translators. He made it clear to Maliki that he needed an unequivocal, public welcome for at least two additional U.S. brigades, and that this time there could be no hedging. He wanted a promise, and if the promise was made, Maliki had to deliver.

That same Thursday, the new Congress was sworn in, and Nancy Pelosi, 66, took the oath as the first female speaker of the House. She

now sat two heartbeats from the presidency, behind only Vice President Dick Cheney, which made her the highest-ranking woman in the
history of the U.S. government.

For nearly 20 years, Pelosi had represented a heavily Democratic
district that encompassed much of San Francisco. She had waited until
1987, after raising five children, to run for office.

Pelosi believed the American people had sent a message by electing
the Democratic majority. They wanted an end to the war, a war she herself had called a "grotesque mistake" and an "epic catastrophe." She
felt her first priority was to bring it to a close.

"The election of 2006 was a call to change," Pelosi said in the House
chamber after she was sworn in. "Not merely to change the control of
Congress, but for a new direction for our country. Nowhere were the
American people more clear about the need for a new direction than in
the war in Iraq. The American people rejected an open-ended obligation to a war without end."

31

On January 6, 2007, Maliki said in a speech in Baghdad, "The army must be a model for everyone . . . and it must not side with any political or sectarian group." The Iraqi army would carry out a new Baghdad security plan, he said, adding, "The multinational forces will extend support and backing for our armed forces." Maliki then made one of his strongest nonsectarian declarations to date, saying, "The Baghdad security plan will deny all outlaws a safe haven, irrespective of their sectarian or political affiliation."

Bush and Hadley felt it was enough of an opening for the president to announce a surge of whatever number of U.S. forces he chose. Drafts of Bush's upcoming address were undergoing revision after revision. Pace again consulted Petraeus, who wanted the president to make clear that the primary mission of U.S. forces had changed from training Iraqis to population security. Petraeus also wanted Bush to commit the maximum number of brigades.

Bush wanted to give the new commander what he wanted and finally decided on the maximum available of five brigades. In addition, he would send 4,000 more Marines to Anbar province. That, he said, would send a stronger message of his commitment to the Iraqi people, al Qaeda, insurgents, extremists and friends in the region.

Senator McCain had been advocating more troops for years. But he had always had a strained relationship with the Bush White House. I recall running into McCain in the West Wing lobby three months before the 9/11 terrorist attacks. He told me he was disturbed that the White House had said that a recent dinner he had with the president had been "awkward." He thought the dinner had been quite friendly. With his arms at his sides and his fists clenched tightly, he looked around the room. "Everything is fucking spin," he said.

As the White House was grappling with what to do in Iraq, McCain had written the president a letter saying that no new strategy "will be successful without an increase in the number of forces." McCain had proposed "surging five additional brigades into Baghdad."

Hadley called McCain several times, trying to seal his support. McCain wanted details. Hadley told him he would be happy with the president's decision.

On Wednesday, January 10, about 2 P.M., only hours before Bush's evening speech, McCain was asked on MSNBC if he would support the president.

"I can't comment until I find out the exact details," he said. "I've been assured in conversations with the president's national security adviser and others that I will be satisfied."

Hadley tracked down McCain. "If you don't support it, John, nobody will," Hadley said. He reported that the president had decided that all five brigades would go; none would be kept on a string. "You've got to decide, because this is the surge we're going to get."

McCain said he would support the president.

Several hours before the president was to present his new strategy on national television, Hadley held a conference call with members of the Iraq Study Group.

The president's decisions were pretty much "Baker-Hamilton plus a surge," Hadley said, adding that they should all be pleased because the president had embraced many of the 79 recommendations.

"Steve," Leon Panetta said, "there are three principal recommendations we made." The first had been an international push for more diplomacy, including Iran and Syria.

Hadley said they were doing a lot of the international diplomacy, but they just couldn't do Iran and Syria.

The second was holding Iraqis to benchmarks and threatening them with reducing forces if they didn't meet certain milestones and reforms.

"We can't put deadlines," Hadley said.

The third was making the transition from a combat to a support role, with an eye toward completing that by the first quarter of 2008.

Hadley said that the president would emphasize transition, "but we don't want to set any time frames for that."

"Well, Steve," Panetta said, "that's kind of the heart and soul of what our recommendations were all about."

"But you have to look at all of your recommendations," Hadley said, "and they really have been very helpful."

The president seemed tense, almost rigid, as he began his 20-minute address to the nation at 9:01 P.M. from the White House Library.

"The situation in Iraq is unacceptable to the American people—and it is unacceptable to me," Bush said. "Where mistakes have been made, the responsibility rests with me."

He said it was "clear that we need to change our strategy." The Iraqi security forces would make a new push to secure Baghdad, he said, but it would require help from the United States. The president said he had committed 20,000 additional American troops. Five brigades would go to Baghdad; another 4,000 Marines would head to Anbar province.

Bush also pledged to expand the Army and Marine Corps.

"Victory will not look like the ones our fathers and grandfathers achieved," the president said. But "we can, and we will, prevail."

The backlash came swiftly, from both Democrats and some Republicans. Minutes after the president finished speaking, MSNBC flashed to Senator Barack Obama in the Capitol.

"I am not persuaded that 20,000 additional troops in Iraq is going to solve the sectarian violence there," Obama said. "In fact, I think it will do the reverse. I think it takes pressure off the Iraqis to arrive at the sort of political accommodation that every observer believes is the ultimate solution to the problems we face there.

"So I am going to actively oppose the president's proposal. I don't doubt his sincerity when he says that he thinks this is the best approach. But I think he is wrong."

Republican Senator George Voinovich of Ohio said, "I've gone along with the president on this, and I bought into his dream. And at this stage of the game, I just don't think it's going to happen." Republican Senator and Vietnam veteran Chuck Hagel of Nebraska called the plan "the most dangerous foreign policy blunder in this country since Vietnam, if it's carried out."

Rice thought it had been a textbook way of reaching a decision, even though she had opposed it and it had taken longer than half a year. Zelikow deemed the final decision a gamble. Instead of approaching Iraq as a problem of uncertainty, requiring a diversified strategy or portfolio—military, diplomatic and economic—the president had acted more like a stock picker hoping for a big payoff on a single stock.

David Satterfield did not agree with the final decision of investing the United States deeper and deeper into Iraq. He remained troubled by the way Hadley had forced a consensus where none had existed—taking conflicting positions, plucking out the most unrecognizable common ground, and cobbling together an accord over a strategy he had quietly advocated all along. He was disappointed that Rice had gone along in spite of her reservations. He agreed with a colleague's assessment that "She believes wholly in a thing until she decides to believe in something else."

Hadley was more satisfied. He had figured out where the president wanted to go and had brought everyone around to that view. Bush had not adopted the stepping back suggested by Rice and her colleagues. He had rejected the pessimism of the CIA and various versions of a drawdown favored by Rumsfeld, Casey, the chiefs, the Iraq Study Group and most Democrats. Forcing consensus was an art form, Hadley believed, and he had worked it. "Could we have done this earlier?" he asked himself. Given the many obstacles, he didn't see how.

Neither did the president. "Prior to the Samarra bombing," he later told me, "it looked like the strategy was working. It was the Samarra bombing, the lack of government, and the not enough holding after the clearing that caused the whole situation to change quite dramatically. And we respond to what's happening on the ground."

But the record shows that meaningful change could have come sooner if the president had insisted on moving when he first realized that the strategy "was not working," that "what was happening on the ground was unacceptable," and if the specter of the fall elections hadn't made them proceed so secretly.

In the end, one lesson remained, a lesson played out again and again throughout the history of American government: Of all the forceful personalities pacing the halls of power, of all the obdurate cabinet officers, wily deputies and steely-eyed generals in or out of uniform, of all the voices in the chorus of Congress clamoring to make themselves heard, one person mattered most.

The president was in control. And like most of his predecessors, he had worked his will.

I asked him if he could locate exactly when he had made up his mind.

"I can't. I can't," he said. "It is incremental, but there is a moment. . . . For me, I often believe that sometimes the answer gets easier with the more study, the more discussion, the more kind of pushing things back. These guys will tell you that I'm the kind of person that . . . I'm a Socratic Method person. Like, they'll be sitting around thinking they're here to talk about something and I'll provoke their thoughts on this issue, just to see where they are. And I wish I could tell you the moment. But there had to be a moment. Maybe Steve knows it."

According to Hadley, that moment had come when the president called him in mid-December 2006 and said, "I'm getting comfortable with my decision, but I don't want to give a speech yet. I want to give Gates a chance to get out there, take a look at it and have input."

I asked Bush if he had prayed about his decision.

"Sure," the president said. "It's very personal."

You understand why I'm asking, I said.

"No. Why?"

"There are a lot of people who don't understand prayer."

"Well, then they're going to have to consult with a religious expert."

You ever talk to your pastor about this?

"No."

Did you consult with your wife?

"She knows I was thinking about it. We're close." He laughed. "I don't think I did."

What about John McCain?

"I'm confident he said, 'You need to put more troops in.' I've got a relationship with him where he will, 'I'm here to tell you . . .' and he tells me. And he was very useful. I knew there weren't going to be a lot of people cheering for it in Washington on both sides of the aisle. But if you want somebody out there punching and if you want somebody out there saying this is the right thing to do, there's nobody better than John McCain. He's got a lot of credibility."

"Do you wish you'd listened to him earlier?" I asked. "Because from '03 he was pounding publicly, 'Send in two more divisions. We need more troops.'"

Bush replied, "I seriously considered everything he said. And ultimately the president, you know, relies upon the considered advice of his military on a matter such as this."

"I'm still going to ask it. Do you wish, as you look back on it? Here was the man who now wants to succeed you essentially on this issue, for years advocating . . . And he's knowledgeable, in touch with the military."

"Yeah, he is knowledgeable."

"Do you wish you'd listened to him?"

"The question really is," Bush replied, "should you have put more troops in earlier? Whether it's listening to McCain or listening to anybody else. And history is just going to have to judge."

Did he ever consider full mobilization, given his own pronouncements that the stakes in Iraq were so high?

"No. I did not," he said, "because maintaining an active military presence in a long ideological struggle is going to require a firm commitment by those who wear the uniform, and the only way to guarantee that firm commitment is through the volunteer service. And secondly, I remember the unbelievable angst that gripped America when kids were being drafted into a military in which they did not want to serve" during Vietnam.

Instead of full mobilization, which would almost certainly include a draft, he said, his approach was to "increase the volunteer Army and make darn sure that the benefits of serving are real, tangible and are competitive with other lines of work that people could have. And take care of the families."

Bush maintained that he understood how hard the war was on the country, the soldiers and their families. "I fully understand how painful war can be. I understand how hard it is for a congressman to go to the funeral of a soldier in his district. I understand how hard it is for the community to put ribbons up for a young, heroic kid that died. Look, war is very difficult for a country to accept, particularly long, drawnout war."

Bush said he understood that he faced a giant decision that fall and winter of 2006.

"I thought about this decision all the time. . . . This was a very, for me, a very all-consuming decision. Now, this is a period of time where I've got, I don't know how many, holiday receptions. I mean, it'd be interesting for you to know. We probably shook hands with 9,000 people when they came through."

He added, "I'm not a brooder, but I am a contemplative person. And I thought a lot about this. Actually, there were times probably when I just had some downtime and people would walk in here and they could see my mind was . . . I'm sure they saw it was kind of off somewhere else. And what I'm doing is, I'm hashing through all the different data points that I've been given, all the different consequences.

"At least from my perspective, the hardest part of making a big decision is the run-up to the decision. But once you make up your mind, it's a liberating moment."

For at least seven months during 2006, President Bush had known that the existing strategy in Iraq was not working. No matter how he tried to dress it up with positive language and sugarcoat it to the American public, he was losing the war. But somehow he had set no deadlines, demanded no hurry, avoided any direct confrontation with Secretary of Defense Rumsfeld, General Pace or General Casey about the need for change.

The fear of a "hothouse" news story that would expose the administration's secret deliberations before the 2006 congressional elections delayed a serious strategy review. U.S. military planners were not brought directly into the review until after the election. Rumsfeld had made his resignation contingent on a political event rather than on the war itself—he would resign if the Republicans lost control of either the House or the Senate.

The president delegated the responsibility for finding a new strategy to Steve Hadley, his national security adviser, according to my reporting and to the president's own words. The national security adviser is an appointed staff position in the White House that requires no Senate confirmation. The president can choose anyone to fill it, and he had chosen Hadley.

"If what you're trying to do is get inside my head," Bush said to me, "which I presume you might be trying to do, which is fine, I don't mind that. . . ."

He kept hammering home the point about Hadley's key role. "See," he said, "you've got to understand Steve. I'm telling you, he drove a lot of this, you want to get it right in the book."

We discussed how many of his key staffers on Iraq—Rice, Gates and Hadley—had worked together in previous Republican administrations. I joked that I might someday write a book about people who never leave Washington, like Hadley.

"No," the president said, "it ought to be 'The Life and Times of Stephen J. Hadley, Great American Patriot.'"

"It'll be a book that has two covers and no pages," Hadley quipped.

"Hard worker," the president said. "Clear thinker. Organized mind."

"And likes to be Mr. Invisible," I said.

"Does he ever," the president said. "When you've got a complex problem to describe on major national security issues, unleash Hadley." The president smiled and suggested a title for my book. "That ought to be the book: 'Unleash Hadley.'"

Bush had done exactly that. The commander in chief had handed off a war he was losing to his national security adviser.

BOOK TWO

BOOK TWO

32

The morning after his speech announcing the surge, the president went to Fort Benning, Georgia, to address military personnel and their families. His decision had been opposed by General Casey and General Abizaid, his military commanders on the ground. General Pace and the Joint Chiefs had suggested a smaller increase, if any at all. And General Schoomaker, the Army chief, had made it clear that the five brigades didn't really exist under the Army's current policy of 12-month rotations. Gates had been largely a bystander in the process, though the execution would now fall to him. But on this morning, the president delivered his own version of history.

"The commanders on the ground in Iraq, people who I listen to—by the way, that's what you want your commander in chief to do. You don't want decisions being made based upon politics or focus groups or political polls. You want your military decisions being made by military experts. And they analyzed the plan, and they said to me and to the Iraqi government, 'This won't work unless we help them. There needs to be a bigger presence.'"

Bush explained, "And so our commanders looked at the plan and said, 'Mr. President, it's not going to work until—unless we support—provide more troops.'"

• • •

No matter how he looked at it, Casey kept coming to the conclusion that the surge was more a political maneuver than a military one.

"I've always felt that the surge was more to build domestic support than it was for success on the ground in Iraq," he later said privately. "It bought the president some time. How much time it bought in Iraq, I don't know."

Even so, Casey thought building domestic support was legitimate, because without it, the war effort could never succeed. The question was whether the president had bought himself enough time to turn the tide of the war or had merely postponed a day of reckoning.

On January 23, Lieutenant General David Petraeus sat before the Senate Armed Services Committee for his confirmation hearing. Susan Collins, the independent-minded Maine Republican, said, "I have read a very interesting article that you wrote on counterinsurgency that was published a year ago in the *Military Review*. And you offered 14 observations based on your previous tours of duty.

"And as I look at those observations—observations that I think are insightful and that I agree with—I conclude that they don't—that they are not consistent with the new strategy that we're about to embark on. Your first observation—you quote T. E. Lawrence in August of 1917, and you say, 'Do not try to do too much with your own hands.' And you talk about the need for the Iraqis to step up to the plate. I worry that the strategy that we're about to pursue in this country relieves pressure on the Iraqis to do what must be done . . . and that we're making the mistake that you caution against."

"What you described really has been truly an intellectual tension, frankly, about the mission in Iraq all along," Petraeus replied. "You do have in the back of your mind always the wisdom of Lawrence of Arabia about not trying to do too much with your own hands, and we used to say, 'What we want to do is we want to help the Iraqis get up on their feet. We want to sort of be near them. We want to back up.' But there are times when they start to wobble, and the question is: When do you move back in and provide assistance? And in the wake of the bombing of the Samarra mosque and the violence that escalated throughout the latter part of 2006, I think we have arrived at a point where, in fact, we do need to help them a bit more in providing security in particular."

Nearly four years after the initial invasion, Petraeus would be starting over in Iraq.

Three days later, on January 26, the Senate unanimously confirmed Petraeus by a vote of 81 to 0. Bush met that morning with Gates, Hadley, Pace and Petraeus in the Oval Office.

"I'd like to talk with my commander," Bush said after a while. When they were alone, the president briefly reviewed his decision to surge the forces, what he called a "double down."

"Mr. President," Petraeus said, "this is not double down." The entire U.S. government and the entire U.S. military needed to be involved. "This is all in."

On January 30, 2007, the Senate Armed Services Committee held Fallon's confirmation hearing.

"What's your degree of confidence," asked Senator John McCain, "that the Iraqi government and military are up to the task that we are now embarking on in this new strategy?"

Fallon said his initial assessment was that some good Iraqi troops existed and some needed a lot of work. Some Iraqi leaders were effective, others weren't. The important task, he said, was to make an honest assessment of what was realistic and practical.

"And maybe we ought to redefine the goals here a bit," Fallon added, "and do something that's more realistic in terms of getting some progress."

Afterward, Fallon had a private moment with McCain. I hear you're not really behind President Bush's surge plan, McCain said.

"There *is* no plan," said Fallon. "It's just an allocation of additional resources. We'll have to see the plan when Petraeus gets out there."

•   •   •

On Saturday, February 10, 2007, Petraeus relieved Casey in a formal ceremony at Camp Victory, not far from Baghdad International Airport, in an opulent main hall of marble columns and crystal chandeliers inside one of Saddam Hussein's former palaces. He declared the situation he'd inherited "hard" but "not hopeless."

The two generals also met privately for a couple of hours. Casey stood before a map of Iraq and described the current situation in each province. "You know I've asked for two brigades," Casey said. "I don't support the rest. But I've set them up for you if you need to bring them in.

"We have these brigades on a string," Casey said. "One of them will be here next week, the first one. The second one's approved by Maliki. The rest are not, but they're programmed to come into Kuwait one a month, and you work that with him.

"What we're seeing here is a major shift in strategy from them doing it to us doing it. Whatever you do, whatever you decide, just be clear about it, because it's a major change."

Casey was stepping down to become Army chief of staff, technically a promotion. It would put him in the business of recruiting, training and equipping the force, but no longer in the chain of command. A proud man, he said with a measure of sadness, "It is going against everything that we've been working on for the last two and a half years."

Petraeus had been in charge of training the Iraqis when the transition strategy had been developed, and he had supported it. This change, Casey said, must be conveyed clearly to both U.S. troops and Iraqis.

"Everybody you bring in here is going to stay for the full duration of his tour," Casey warned. "You just need to understand that." They had deluded themselves into believing that some troops could be sent home early. But that never happened. "Anybody you get in here, there's so much to do, ultimately becomes indispensable," Casey said. It's what he meant when he called Baghdad a troop sump.

Both men remembered former Secretary of State Colin Powell's warning to President Bush six months before the invasion of Iraq. "You are going to be the proud owner of 25 million people," Powell had told

Bush. Privately, Powell and his deputy and closest friend, Richard Armitage, referred to this as the Pottery Barn rule: You break it, you own it.

That first day, with the enormity of the task at hand and the pressure to succeed back home, Petraeus felt the weight of the world was on him. But he told his closest advisers, "Take the rearview mirror off the bus. Let's focus forward. We are where we are. You may be frustrated with it. I'm frustrated with it, candidly. It can make you angry. But now let's figure out, how do you make it better?"

He told his staff he wanted to implement his new approach at once. Right off the bat, he instituted an interim joint campaign plan, making clear that the mission was to protect the population and do it by living among the people.

"The biggest of the big ideas is secure the population and serve the population," he told his staff. "That's a hugely significant, big idea. To secure the population you must live with it, partner in everything you do." They were to move out and establish joint security stations, combat outposts, patrol bases and checkpoints around Baghdad.

He sent a short letter to everyone in his command. He had pondered each word. In it, he used the word "security" three times. "We will conduct a pivotal campaign to improve security for the Iraqi people," he said. Of those who opposed the new Iraq, he said, "We must strike them relentlessly. We and our Iraqi partners must set the terms of the struggle, not our enemies." The goal was to buy time for the Iraqis to save their country. "To do that, many of us will live and fight alongside of them."

"We're going out with the troops," Petraeus told his staff. "We're going on some patrols and we're going to do it in Baghdad." He went to a map and selected neighborhoods that he remembered from when he had headed the training of the Iraqi security forces, and about which he had now heard horror stories. "Let's go here and here."

The first was Ghazaliya, the neighborhood Meghan O'Sullivan

watched closely from the White House. Petraeus remembered it as a vibrant, upper-middle-class neighborhood. Their patrol also took them through Amiriya, a Sunni enclave in western Baghdad, and Dora, another Sunni neighborhood. He walked the neighborhoods for hours, and what he saw hit him like cold water. They were ghost towns. He had never seen anything quite like it.

"This is where we're starting," Petraeus ordered. The first joint security station to protect the Iraqi population would go into Ghazaliya. They called it "pushing cement," literally isolating each day's battlefield with concrete barriers to encircle and protect the population. Al Qaeda or the insurgents could attack, but they would no longer be able to get vehicles carrying explosives or rocket-propelled grenade launchers into the protected sections of the capital.

He realized that Ghazaliya and Dora were the two canaries in the Baghdad mine shaft. Until they could be brought back to life, perhaps even sing a little bit, the new mission would go nowhere. He had ended the first day of his command feeling the weight of the world on his shoulders. Now the second day ended with the weight of two worlds. He remembered the Roman dramatist Seneca the Younger's adage that "Luck is when preparation meets opportunity." He felt prepared, and this was the opportunity. Would that equal luck?

On the next secure video with the president, Rice and Gates, he reported that the neighborhoods he had visited were "ghost towns."

"You have to recognize," Petraeus said, "this is going to get harder before it gets easier."

On Monday, February 19, 2007—a chilly, breezy Presidents Day—Bush visited Mount Vernon, George Washington's sprawling estate on the banks of the Potomac River, 16 miles south of Washington.

"With the advantage of hindsight, it is easy to take George Washington's successes for granted," he said. But "America's path to freedom was long, and it was hard, and the outcome was never really certain." Washington's Continental Army "stood on the brink of disaster many times," but "his will was unbreakable."

He kept portraits of Washington and Lincoln in the Oval Office and repeatedly compared himself to some of his predecessors, noting that history often judged them more kindly than did contemporary accounts.

Rice had been present when Bush pointed out certain paintings to White House visitors. "George Washington, you know, they're still writing books about number one," he said. "I'm not going to worry about what they're saying about 43." Or he would mention how Lincoln, whom Bush called the greatest president, had persevered during the Civil War despite the massive casualties, the many battlefield losses, and persistent doubts that the war could be won.

Harry Truman was another Bush favorite.

"President Truman made clear that the Cold War was an ideological struggle between tyranny and freedom," Bush had told the graduating class at West Point the previous year. "By the actions he took, the institutions he built, the alliances he forged, and the doctrines he set down, President Truman laid the foundation for America's victory in the Cold War. . . . Today, at the start of a new century, we are again engaged in a war unlike any our nation has fought before. And like Americans in Truman's day, we are laying the foundations for victory. . . . We have made clear that the war on terror is an ideological struggle between tyranny and freedom."

Within days of his arrival, Petraeus invited Jack Keane, his mentor and the retired Army vice chief of staff, to spend nearly two weeks in Iraq. Keane spent four days in Baghdad, a day in Anbar province, another in Diyala province. He met with Khalilzad and the embassy staff. He coached commands at the brigade, battalion, company and even platoon level.

On March 6, Keane briefed Vice President Cheney on his trip, establishing a secret backchannel line of communication—Petraeus to Keane to Cheney to Bush—around the chain of command.

"There are early signs of success, but the operation is just beginning," Keane reported. "We cannot predict success." But he said Petraeus had reenergized the mission. "He's given them a hope that we can do it."

Keane said he had attended a meeting between Petraeus and former Iraqi Prime Minister Allawi. Since losing to Maliki, Allawi had not been helping the new prime minister. Allawi wanted to be prime minister again. "This government isn't going away," Petraeus told him. "Stop sitting on the fence hoping it will. Get behind what we're doing here. Get in the game."

Keane said Petraeus had won permission from Maliki to go after the Shia militias. Maliki wanted to take control over his Iraqi forces for the first time, and Petraeus had let him, but "we call most of the shots," Keane said, and Iraqi tactical commanders "in just about all cases default to ours."

"We must be cautiously optimistic, not triumphant. We have always underestimated this enemy," Keane said. It would take 12 to 18 months to realize the full effect of the surge and the new population security strategy. Any notion of judging the results in six months "is an absurdity," he told the vice president.

"The embassy is unsatisfactory," Keane added. As far as he was concerned, it might as well be in Singapore or Paris, given its commitment to the war.

"You need to guard against having success in the summer and then beginning to withdraw by the end of the year," Keane said. "It's a recipe for disaster in '08. What's happened is, we'll just start to slip back gradually to '06 levels of violence." Everyone needed to be on the same page, he said, "CentCom, the DOD, JCS, Department of State, interagency effort, NSC."

He said Secretary Gates and others in the Pentagon weren't on the same page with Petraeus.

"What do you mean?" Cheney asked.

Look at Gates's recent comments that he wanted to pull back by the end of the year, Keane responded. Gates had said during a recent Senate Armed Services Committee hearing that if the plan to quiet Baghdad succeeded and the Iraqis began to step up, that he hoped "to begin drawing down our troops later this year."

"That is an indication to me that he really hasn't embraced this policy," Keane said, "because from the military perspective, you've got to go into '08 to cement this thing. We're two brigades into the surge.

Why would a secretary be already giving ground on something unless he doesn't necessarily agree with it?"

As far as Cheney was concerned, Keane was outstanding—an experienced soldier who maintained great Pentagon contacts, had no ax to grind, and had been a mentor to Petraeus. There was nothing esoteric about Keane. He was all meat and potatoes, blunt and to the point. His reports proved accurate, and he didn't inflate expectations or waste Cheney's time.

Later, Cheney's deputy, John Hannah, informed Keane that the vice president had passed along his report to the president.

In Iraq, Petraeus had another "big idea."

He asked his staff: Who's the enemy? They were fighting al Qaeda, insurgents and extremists, both Shia and Sunni. But some were reconcilable, while others would have to be captured, killed or driven out. The question was how to identify them. It required the meticulous shifting of intelligence to pinpoint exactly who could be won over and who could not—the reconcilables and the irreconcilables.

He had his analysts draw diagrams and charts. Al Qaeda was clearly irreconcilable. But what about the 1920 Revolutionary Brigades, a Sunni insurgent group named after an uprising against the British in the wake of World War I? What about the various elements of Moqtada al-Sadr's Mahdi Army? Who could be broken away? Individuals? Groups?

"This is where you have to be immersed," Petraeus told his staff. He also brought in Derek Harvey, the DIA intelligence analyst, who would report directly to him.

33

That spring, Admiral Fallon attended a White House meeting on Iran.

"I think we need to do something to get engaged with these guys," Fallon said. Iraq shared a 900-mile border with Iran, and he needed guidance and a strategy for dealing with the Iranians.

"Well," Bush said, "these are assholes."

Fallon was stunned. Declaring them "assholes" was not a strategy. Lots of words and ideas were thrown around at the meeting, especially about the Iranian leaders. They were bad, evil, out of touch with their people. But no one offered a real approach. No one wanted to touch diplomatic engagement.

I later asked the president about this, and he insisted that he had been clear about the Iran policy. "Our strategy was to try to first convince them to give up their nuclear weapons ambitions, which means verifiably suspending their enrichment program," he told me. "And if they were willing to do so, they could come to the table. We'd be there with our other partners. Secondly, is to push them back where they're trying to promote their brand of government, one with the creation of a Palestinian state, two helping the young democracy in Lebanon, and three, succeeding in Iraq. And I was pretty clear about what our strategy was all along and our objectives."

Fallon tried to work the problem with others in the White House and Pentagon. But every time he tried to raise the issue, tried to argue that they couldn't solve Iraq without involving its neighbors like Iran, the reaction was negative.

"Don't go there," he was told.

"Bullshit. We're going to go there," he told some of Hadley's and Gates's deputies. "Because I can't do my job unless we get engaged with these guys."

The same went for the Syrians. He explained that when he went to see the other leaders in the Middle East, each had a variation on the same theme: "You started this goddamn war, and you had no idea what the hell you were getting into, and look what you've done, and look at the mess we're in now, and what are you going to do about this problem?"

There was lots of private hand-wringing about Fallon. Even Gates got involved.

"If they want to spend all their time worrying about me," Fallon told Gates, "and what I'm saying and what I'm doing, as opposed to trying to figure out where this country [the United States] ought to be, then I guess I'm the wrong guy for this job. Somebody probably made a big error when they decided to sign me up."

Petraeus traveled to every region of Iraq. He sought input from generals and privates. He walked the streets. He toured the neighborhoods where residents had been forced out and took stock of how much had changed for the worse. E-mail by e-mail, phone call by phone call, he also assembled his own team to come to Iraq and study the situation in depth.

He tapped Colonel H. R. McMaster, the bulldog architect of the Tall Afar campaign, to lead the effort. The assignment was to round up the sharpest military and civilian minds to appraise the current coalition strategy and determine how best to change it. It would become known as the Joint Strategic Assessment Team, or JSAT.

By early March, Petraeus and McMaster had assembled a team of nearly two dozen people, including economists, counterinsurgency experts, Iraq scholars, military officers and diplomats. Petraeus knew that many of them were critical of the effort in Iraq. That was fine by him. He could bear people saying that the emperor had no clothes, as long as they helped find a solution.

The group gathered in the North Ballroom of a former palace in the Green Zone. At the center of the ballroom, a table sagged under the weight of a stack of paper several feet tall. The documents—mostly classified—dealt with every aspect of the war. The reading list included current campaign plans, character assessments of Iraqi politicians and statistics on violence, government services and institutional capacity. The JSAT members dove into the mountain of reading. They split into small teams. One team headed into the Kurdish territories and Ninewa province. Others headed to Kirkuk, Tikrit and Baquba and west to Anbar. A group went south to Basra and neighboring provinces. Another toured Baghdad. Other members of the JSAT exploited their many Iraqi contacts to try to gather as much information as possible.

Back in the North Ballroom, the group members briefed one another. The Iraqi government was in worse disarray than they had expected. Levels of violence remained alarmingly high. The U.S. strategy that Casey had pursued until his last day—to train the Iraqis and withdraw as soon as possible—had made the security situation more tenuous.

At present, the JSAT determined, the United States was "rushing toward failure."

After weeks of 14- to 20-hour workdays, the JSAT concluded that the conflict boiled down to a struggle for power and survival. The question was one that Hadley had asked months earlier: Is seeking reconciliation a fool's errand?

The JSAT recommended that coalition officials demand transparency from the Iraqi ministries and insist that they spend their budgets, something they hadn't done in 2006. It also recommended what some called the "lamppost strategy." Basically, that meant the Americans should take corrupt and incompetent Iraqi officials and publicly rebuke them, making it clear they were being removed from office because of their sectarian tendencies and setting an example that such behavior wouldn't be tolerated.

Militarily, the main thrust was to deliver population security on a local level by expanding "joint security stations," fortified outposts manned by Iraqi army, police and U.S. forces. "There's no commuting to the fight," Petraeus and officers under him were fond of saying.

There also was a focus on setting the proper conditions for economic reconstruction and revitalization, drawing Moqtada al-Sadr into substantive negotiations, identifying and eliminating irreconcilable enemies, and working toward accommodation both locally and nationally. The paper ran more than 100 pages. It would become Petraeus's new campaign plan and the best hope for salvaging some measure of success in Iraq.

Admiral Fallon took over from Abizaid at Central Command on March 16. "We're going to start immediately," Fallon said to his staff that afternoon. One of his first questions was: What's our mission? He read the mission statement and nearly gagged. It was too tactical. He said Central Command was supposed to be a strategic command thinking big thoughts, engaging the world from the Middle East to the Horn of Africa. "We need to rewrite the mission statement. You can't have a dozen priorities," he said. "That tells me that we're doing everything and nothing."

He broke the senior staff into small groups to think and debate for an hour. When he called them back, he said, "Now let's see if we can articulate what it is everybody said." It was pretty obvious. "Two houses are burning. And they're burning very brightly." Iraq and Afghanistan would be the priorities.

"How many people are down here?" Fallon asked, inquiring about the size of the CentCom staff.

One of his deputies reported that it was precisely 3,415.

"You've got to be shitting me," Fallon replied. "Give me a breakdown of where they are. How many people are on my personal security detachment?"

Several answers came back: 53, 49, 60-some.

"Okay, let's take the lesser number," he said. "Forty-nine people are on my personal security detachment. For what?"

That's how it's been, he was told.

"Show me the breakdown of these people," Fallon ordered. "What they're doing, where they came from."

Several dozen were reservists mobilized to protect the commander.

"We have a war going on in two places," Fallon said, "and you've got three dozen guys mobilized for how many years now to guard me? This is bullshit. I had one guy in the Pacific. Get rid of them. Now."

You will be going to war zones, staff members told him. You'll need protection.

"If I go to Iraq, Petraeus better be protecting me," he said. In Afghanistan, his commanders would do the same. Let's trim it to 12, he said.

But the security detail had to cover his deputy, his wife and his house, staff members replied.

His quarters at MacDill Air Force Base in Tampa sat on a small compound with a fence surrounding it and a manned guard shack behind it—inside an already heavily guarded base at the tip of a peninsula.

"He goes now," Fallon said of the guard. "Get him out of here. Gone."

He saw that two big black SUVs were parked at his headquarters, blocking the front walk. "What the hell are these?" he asked. That was part of his security. He would be driven a half mile from his office to his quarters. "They go too, right now. Get rid of them. Get me a goddamn sedan I can actually sit down in."

Did he want an armored sedan?

"No."

Fallon believed he was witnessing the legacy of the draft that had been in effect when he entered the service in 1967. To the Army, labor was free. People were available on demand, and the military had not changed its ways of using forces carelessly and ineffectively, as though there were an unlimited supply.

Speaker Nancy Pelosi felt confident that the Democrats, with their new majorities in both the House and the Senate, would be able to force a drawdown of U.S. forces in Iraq. She saw the surge as the president's attempt to disrupt the antiwar movement and the efforts of the Democrats. Pelosi knew that since 2004, Bush had ordered at least four troop increases, each of 20,000 or more, mostly for additional security during Iraqi elections. One such increase had stretched from May to October 2006, when the violence had escalated nearly out of control. So why was this surge different? She took the question directly to the president in the early days of her speakership.

"Mr. President," she said. "We've had surges." She briefly cited the others. "What makes you think this one is going to work?"

"Because I told them it had to," Bush answered.

"Well, Mr. President," she said, "why didn't you tell them before?"

Pelosi later told her closest staff members, "I'm very, very worried about the state of mind of a person who has decided to stay in a war without the public support." In early 2007, polls showed that two thirds of Americans didn't think the war was going well, while only 30 percent thought it was.

On Thursday, March 29, 2007, Bush and Pelosi were to speak at a ceremony under the U.S. Capitol Rotunda to honor the Tuskegee Airmen of World War II. Before the event, the president and the House speaker had a private moment in Pelosi's office.

"Mr. President," she said, "we owe it to the public to try to reach some consensus." She was convinced that the public wanted Congress and the president to come together on a solution, and she was willing to support legislation that would not require a troop drawdown, merely set it as a goal.

"My views are well known," Bush replied. "I've made myself clear."

"My views are well known too," Pelosi said. "But that's not the point. The point is we owe it to the public to try to find some common ground."

Bush wasn't interested.

The president later told me in an interview that he did not remember Pelosi's suggestion that they find common ground after his surge decision. "It created a lot of turmoil in the Congress," he said. "A lot of people on both sides of the aisle were hoping that I would pull troops out rather than put more troops in. And once you commit to more troops in, then the common ground, as far as I was concerned, would be to fund the troops going in and make sure they had what it meant to succeed."

Fallon had taken his first trip to Iraq as Central Commander, and afterward, Keane called Petraeus to see how their first meeting had gone.

"It was okay," Petraeus said halfheartedly.

"Aw, shit," Keane said. "Come on. What happened?"

"I know you like this guy," Petraeus said, "but I'll tell you what, sir, he was on transmit here an awful lot." It reminded him of a public address system on a Navy ship, where the captain comes on and says, "Now hear this; now hear this." Fallon had plenty to say—what was wrong in Iraq, how to fix it—but "he has no experience," Petraeus said.

Keane had hoped that Fallon would watch Petraeus's back in Washington. Every wartime commander needed an advocate to work the executive branch, the Congress and the media. But instead of a protector, it looked as if Petraeus might have another problem.

On Friday, April 6, 2007, Gates held a small farewell luncheon in his office for General Schoomaker, who was retiring as Army chief of staff. Schoomaker had volunteered to leave several months early so that General Casey could take his place. Under Army rules, unless a four-star position was available, Casey would have reverted to a lesser rank, an unacceptable demotion for an Iraq commander the president had lavished praise on for 30 months. Gates invited some of the former Army chiefs, including retired General Gordon Sullivan and retired General Eric Shinseki, who had caused a stir in 2003 when he said publicly that there weren't enough U.S. troops in Iraq.

Gates asked Schoomaker, who had been brought out of retirement by Rumsfeld and Cheney to take over as Army chief in 2003, if he wanted to say something.

"I'm very proud of what we have done in the Army," he said. By his calculation, Pentagon projections had shown eight times during his tenure that the troops in Iraq would be drawn down, but each time the number had stayed relatively steady. He was proud that the Army had fulfilled its obligations despite the repeated failed assumptions.

"But let me tell you," he continued, "I really am very disappointed about my experience in the Washington community. I've got to tell you that this town, as far as I'm concerned, is full of midgets." There was a lot of tactical thinking to solve political problems, he said, but not enough long-range strategic thinking. The main problem was that too many people in Washington never really understood the warrior's heart, never knew deep down inside what it meant never to quit, to be in a position where you would die rather than quit. Too many thought a fight was what happened on the Senate floor or in the White House. The real fights were the struggles for physical survival.

The former chiefs seemed a bit surprised by his speech, but at the end of the table, Gates smiled and nodded.

Casey relieved Schoomaker four days later, and on his first day on the job, he was invited to a briefing in Gates's office. The 12-month Army tours in Iraq and Afghanistan were to be extended to 15 months. Without the extension, five active duty Army brigades would have to deploy without a full year at home. It was the only way to surge forces, as the president had announced.

Lieutenant General Pete Chiarelli, now the senior military assistant to the secretary, had also warned Gates that something was going to have to be done to extend the Iraq tours.

"If we're going to maintain 20 brigades in Iraq through the end of the summer, there are five brigades that we are going to—between now and July—have to extend," he said. "Now, we can do this the way we've done it before and we can dribble out the extensions. And you're going to have bad news every single month for five frickin' months" as the extensions are announced.

Or it could be done all at once by announcing universal tours of 15 months. Chiarelli said that soldiers in Iraq understood the situation and that the secretary would be better off acknowledging it and announcing the extensions to provide some measure of predictability.

"Every kid over there knows this," Chiarelli said. "They understand the math and they think you're an asshole for not doing it."

Gates and General Pace had quickly approved the recommendation and said they were going to the White House to get the president's approval. Casey was surprised at the hurry. The Army's rotation policy fell very much under the Army chief's responsibility. If it hadn't been his first day on the job, he might have said, "Wait a minute, there's no need to rush this out." But there had been leaks to the news media about the new policy, and Gates had decided to go ahead and announce it.

At 3 P.M. the next day, Gates and Pace appeared in the Pentagon press briefing room. "All the units that are there," in Iraq and Afghanistan, Gates said, "and all the units that will deploy are now extended—will be extended to 15 months."

Schoomaker was caught off guard by the announcement, which came a day after his retirement. He had not been consulted. And the problem he had outlined to the president four months earlier, about the lack of forces to undertake the surge, had been addressed without anyone consulting either the incoming or outgoing Army chief of staff.

"It didn't take them long," he told his wife.

What Fallon called the "big food fight" with Petraeus developed throughout the spring of 2007.

Fallon began getting RFFs, Requests for Forces, from Petraeus that he and his staff were to examine and forward to the secretary of defense, who had to approve every deployment order. There were complaints from Petraeus's staff that various units in Iraq were smaller than in the past. "There's a reason they're smaller," Fallon said. "They're supposed to be more effective."

Fallon also raged at his own staff as they shuffled the requests. "You guys," he said. "You're wasting my time trying to have me decide—a four-star—whether or not to have five guys or 15 guys here. This is nuts!" They asked him constantly to approve or disapprove specific requests. "Stop, stop, stop!" he finally said. "Bring me all of the requests that you're dealing with."

Fallon examined the list of RFFs. "Two thousand here. Ten there. Fifteen hundred here. Fifty here. Sixty there," he said, reading them aloud. "This is lunacy. We're going to stop rubber-stamping this shit."

Fallon was determined to challenge the merit of every personnel request and not send any more than necessary to the war zone. Each time Petraeus asked for more people, Fallon protested. "Look at all these extra people," he said once. "What are they doing? I have a study in my pocket that John Abizaid had commissioned that said there's 20,000 excess people on the ground in Iraq right now."

Petraeus thought the number was 5,000 at most, and those were in the logistics and supply areas.

Fallon decided to say no several times, and Petraeus protested. He would accept a no, but he wanted everyone to be aware that requests, no matter how small, were being denied.

"Sir," Petraeus said. "We need to be very clear with each other. If you want to say no to me, say no. But then tell the secretary of defense, the president, and tell the American people that the commander has asked for something and not received it."

"Pete," Fallon told General Pace, "this is nuts, one of the reasons we're so AFU"—all fucked up. "We have all these people with all this experience and brainpower, and they're supposed to be making operational decisions. And what are they spending their time on? Detailing people. Flesh peddling. Look at all these RFFs."

As best Fallon could tell, it was consuming a thousand hours in Baghdad, his headquarters in Tampa and in Washington. "Nobody's doing strategic thinking," he said. "They're all tying their shoes. Now I understand why we are where we are. We ought to be shot for this."

34

It was a hair-raising time for the administration, as Republican support continued to fade rapidly and few allies remained steadfast. But none was more vocal than John McCain. In early April 2007, Petraeus had led McCain, the 70-year-old Republican presidential contender, through the Shorja market in Baghdad. Attack helicopters overhead and more than 100 soldiers in armored Humvees provided security for McCain and three U.S. congressmen. At a press conference following his hour-long tour, McCain said that the American public was not receiving "a full picture" of the improvements in security. "Things are getting better in Iraq, and I am pleased with the progress that has been made."

Later, McCain was widely criticized for making such a judgment after touring a market fortified with blast walls and cement barriers, surrounded by a virtual cocoon of American security. One U.S. military official told *The Washington Post* that McCain's diagnosis of Baghdad security was "a bit of hyperbole."

Condi Rice appreciated McCain's positive comments. She invited him for a private visit at the State Department at 8:30 A.M., on April 12. McCain seemed tense when he arrived. Rice had expected him to reiterate his optimism, but after some pleasantries, he let loose.

"We may be about to lose the second war in my lifetime," said the man who had been held and tortured for five years as a prisoner of war in Vietnam. The senator launched into a full-throated critique of the State Department's role in Iraq. You guys aren't fully in this, he said. You don't act like we're really at war. The civilian side is not doing its part. Rice listened calmly. His criticisms echoed a lot of State Department bashing.

"That's not true, John," Rice finally said. She led him through the institutional changes that had been made, including a revamped personnel system that ensured high-quality people were sent to Baghdad, as well as the transformation of the Provisional Reconstruction Teams (PRTs), which she said were now doing their fair share in Iraq. Rice also praised the new ambassador, Ryan Crocker. He and his embassy staff are the A team, she insisted.

After 20 minutes, they walked out of Rice's office for a photo opportunity and a brief exchange with reporters.

Asked about a suicide bombing that day in the cafeteria of the Iraqi parliament building in Baghdad's Green Zone, Rice said, "There will be good days and bad days."

"What does this say about security overall in Iraq and the surge," a reporter asked, "and how that is working?"

Attacks by the terrorists were expected, she replied.

"Hang on a second," McCain said. "We're just getting the third of the five brigades over to Baghdad." Spectacular attacks were designed to "erode the American public's will." But there was a larger picture, he said. "We are achieving some small successes already in the strategy being employed by General Petraeus and General Odierno."

McCain did not mention his private fear that the United States was on the brink of losing.

At a press conference with several Democratic senators on Thursday, April 19, Senate Majority Leader Harry Reid said he believed that "this war is lost and that the surge is not accomplishing anything, as indicated by the extreme violence in Iraq yesterday."

Reid also drew a parallel between Bush and former President Lyndon Johnson, who 40 years earlier had deployed additional troops in Vietnam after 24,000 U.S. troops had already been killed.

"Johnson did not want a war loss on his watch, and so he surged in Vietnam," Reid said. "After the surge was over, we added 34,000 to the 24,000 who died in Vietnam."

Reid's statement was met with widespread criticism from friends and opponents alike.

Privately, Carl Levin, the Michigan Democrat and Senate Armed Services chairman, lit into his colleague. He said he disagreed with both Reid's message and the way he had presented it. It was an awful, demoralizing message to send to the troops. Reid later told colleagues that Levin had "chewed his ass."

"Could I have couched my words more carefully? Maybe," Reid later wrote in his memoir, *The Good Fight*. "But I said it, and I meant it, and I am not apologizing for it."

The president was furious but didn't say anything publicly. I later asked him, "Were you shocked when you heard that?"

"I'm not shocked by anything in Washington anymore," Bush said. "This war has created a lot of really harsh emotion, out of which comes a lot of harsh rhetoric. One of my failures has been to change the tone in Washington. It's the failure of others as well . . . but the rhetoric has sometimes gotten totally out of control. And my concern is not me. I mean, I'm used to it. And I fully understand if you're the person that is making these decisions, then you're going to be subject to a lot of serious criticism, and I accept that. I am concerned about people who are risking their lives for an effort that will have incredibly important long-term consequences to the United States of America, to the security.

"We got kids that hear the call and are volunteering to go into combat because they believe in the cause. And when they hear contradictory signals coming out of Washington, you just got to wonder what that says to them. The other thing is, remember, we're dealing with a pretty fragile mind-set in Iraq at this point in time. I've always felt like it's very important for the Iraqis to understand that the United States is a reliable partner."

By spring, with Iraq in worse shape than ever, the Bush administration faced increasing pressure from its Middle Eastern allies. Saudi Arabia, one of the United States' largest oil suppliers and its most reliable Arab ally, went public. In March, King Abdullah, the 82-year-old monarch, issued a stinging rebuke of the large U.S. troop presence in Iraq, calling it an "illegitimate foreign occupation." In late April, Rice dispatched David Satterfield to meet with the king.

Saudi Arabia and the United States had fought the 1991 Gulf War together, ousting Saddam from his occupation of Kuwait. In 1994, the Saudis had proposed to President Clinton a joint U.S.-Saudi covert operation to overthrow Saddam. In 2002, the year before the Iraq invasion, the Saudis were suggesting the two countries spend $1 billion to remove Saddam covertly. After the 2003 invasion, Saudi Arabia, a predominantly Sunni Muslim country, envisioned an Iraq ruled by a Sunni strongman less aggressive than Saddam and more willing to cater to Saudi interests. Instead, a Saudi nightmare had come true, with a Shia-led government in Iraq and the increased influence of Shia Iran.

Satterfield understood the Saudi king's unease. His country was haunted by the prospect of a "crescent" of largely Shia states to the north, from Iran through Iraq to Syria. Iran was supplying lethal weaponry to insurgents in Iraq and dispatching members of its Quds Force, the Iranian Revolutionary Guard. The Americans were aware of this and had said so publicly. The United States had tried to combat Iranian involvement within Iraq's borders, but it had done little or nothing inside Iran. So the Iranians sat taunting America, demonstrating that they had the upper hand. The Saudis, like other Gulf states, feared that the United States not only would quit Iraq but would abandon the region.

Satterfield had a tough and uncomfortable meeting with Abdullah on Sunday, April 22. The United States has handed Iraq to Iran on a golden platter, the king said. "You have allowed the Persians, the Safavids"—the Shia rulers of Persia in the 16th and 17th centuries—"to take over Iraq."

Satterfield attempted to counter. Iraq could be a strong independent state.

"I warned you about this," the king said. "I warned the president, the vice president, but your ears were blocked. I have no interest in discussing this further."

Satterfield understood that the king couldn't imagine that a Shia state could be independent of Iran. For the king, a Shia nationalist leader who would work against Iran simply could not exist.

"We're here," Satterfield said, trying to reassure him. "We have been here for 50 years plus. We're not going anywhere. Not only is the president committed in Iraq, I assure you we're committed to the region. That is why we are launching a package of steps." Giant arms sales packages for the Gulf states, for the Egyptians and even for the Israelis were in the works. "These all signal we're here. We're not going anywhere."

The king made clear that the topic of a Shia-run Iraq not allied with Iran was impossible and not worth discussing. It could not exist. The meeting was over.

Satterfield wrote a memo to Rice. She passed it along to the president, who dispatched Cheney to talk to King Abdullah. Cheney was a hero in Saudi Arabia. In 1990, when Saddam Hussein had invaded Kuwait and threatened Saudi Arabia, the first President Bush had sent Cheney, his defense secretary, to promise that the United States would protect Saudi Arabia—Operation Desert Shield. Bush senior and Cheney had led the coalition, which prominently included Saudi Arabia, in the successful 1991 Gulf War.

When Cheney arrived in Saudi Arabia, King Abdullah asked about the president's father, also a hero in the kingdom. During a four-hour meeting that included dinner on May 12, the vice president tried to explain the younger Bush's Iraq policy. But he moved the Saudis precisely zero. With all due respect, Abdullah said, I'm not going to talk about this anymore.

"I'd like to send a couple of guys out," Fallon told Petraeus that spring. "I'd like them to be flies on the wall. I want them to learn as much as they can. I want them to be as familiar as possible with everything that's going on so we can try to figure out where I need to be in this thing."

"Fine, sir," Petraeus said.

Fallon's team was headed by Rear Admiral James A. Winnefeld Jr., who previously had served as Fallon's executive assistant. Fallon thought Winnefeld was about the smartest person in the military and able to cut through the fog to the core of any problem.

Winnefeld hung around for several weeks, but Petraeus found him clandestine and secretive. Petraeus respected Winnefeld personally, but he had never served in Iraq and seemed to have been given only a brief amount of time to survey the situation. Petraeus didn't think Winnefeld was qualified to construct a new strategy or fully assess the war on the ground.

By the end of his review, Winnefeld had concluded that there were too many U.S. military personnel in Iraq and too many Requests for Forces.

"We are going to ask for what we require until we no longer require it," Petraeus told the rear admiral. He had been sent there to win a war. "If somebody wants to tell us to take [forces] out, they'll have to tell us to take [them] out. But they're going to have to tell the whole world that they told us to. This is the way it works. If it's a big issue, the American public needs to know."

Winnefeld reported back to Fallon, "If you think for a minute that these guys are going to volunteer to accelerate anything or to shed anybody, forget it. It's not going to happen. It'll have to be directed from above."

On Wednesday, April 25, the House narrowly passed a $124 billion war spending bill that would require American troops to begin withdrawing from Iraq by October 1. The vote was 218 to 208.

"Last fall, the American people voted for a new direction in Iraq," Speaker Pelosi said. "They made it clear that our troops must be given all they need to do their jobs, but that our troops must be brought home responsibly, safely and soon."

A day later, the Senate approved the bill. Bush vetoed it.

Pelosi could continue to muster votes in the House for other troop withdrawal legislation, but Senate rules required 60 votes to stop a filibuster on nonspending bills, and Senate Democrats, who had only a one-vote majority, never came close to getting that many votes.

Later, at another meeting, Pelosi again reminded the president that the public opposed the war. "They've lost faith and confidence in the conduct of the war." This time she wasn't expecting an answer, and she didn't get one.

"There's something wrong there," she told her staff. A devout, practicing Catholic, she insisted that she prayed for the president. "I say this with great personal, almost affection for him and respect for the office he holds. I respect the office maybe more than he does . . . he has just decided that he's going to have a tantrum anytime anyone doesn't agree with him . . . to just be completely, completely, completely obstinate. Something is wrong. It's not right." She said historians would forever ponder Bush's behavior and try to answer this question: How could a president of the United States hijack the good intentions and fears of the American people?

The lack of progress three months into the surge wasn't sitting well with many Republicans. Representative Peter Hoekstra of Michigan, who had lost his chairmanship of the House Intelligence Committee when the Democrats gained a majority in the fall, was particularly worried. An earnest hard-liner known for doing his homework, Hoekstra had made half a dozen trips to Iraq. He thought the larger war on terror was not getting sufficient attention. He had been offended during the fall at a White House meeting when one of his colleagues had complained to Bush that the president had not asked for any sacrifice from the American public. "That's nothing more than a code word for raising taxes," Bush had replied. So Hoekstra had spoken privately with Representative John Boehner, the House Republican leader.

"The president is about to lose all Republicans on the Intelligence Committee," he had said. The nine Republicans who knew the most about the dire situation in Iraq had been about to jump ship on the surge decision. Soon, all nine were invited to the White House for a private meeting with Bush. Many voiced deep concerns about the surge. Where did it come from? What was it about?

Bush listened and gave stock answers about the need to win. Hoekstra had already concluded that the war was a mistake. And he felt the president wasn't really listening to the questions or opinions of members of his own party.

Some questions were about Osama bin Laden. Why did it seem the United States had let up on the search?

Bush insisted that the hunt was continuing, and Hadley assured them that all the issues on their list were getting attention. The hour-and-a-half meeting didn't assuage the Republicans' doubts, but it kept them from staging an open revolt.

Fallon was haunted by the 1975 decision by Congress to cut off all funding for the Vietnam War. Like many others, including President Gerald Ford, he felt that the funding cut forced too early an American exit. Fallon now feared "that we're going to flush the toilet, as we managed to do in the '70s in Vietnam, where we actually, tactically, had ourselves in great shape and then we cut the legs out from under the thing by Congress" pulling the plug. "We don't want to be in a position where we've now thrown away three or four years' worth of hard work and we're now walking out." He wanted to find "a position where the American people and the Congress feel that we are exercising due diligence." He wanted to buy time to find a reasonable outcome.

Fallon felt he needed to assess the political climate in Washington. It would have a significant impact on what he could do in the region and specifically in Iraq. He had to find out what was politically tolerable. He knew he had to deal with Congress, and he believed he had a good enough rapport with both Republicans and Democrats that he could get a pretty good sense of where they stood. It didn't take him long to figure out the story on Capitol Hill: Political support for the war had all but vanished.

Just before 3 P.M. on Wednesday, May 9, 2007, a 60-year-old Iraqi physician with glasses, a salt-and-pepper beard and a passing resemblance to movie director Steven Spielberg entered the West Wing of the White House to visit Steve Hadley. Mowaffak al-Rubaie, Iraq's national security adviser, was eager to meet with his American counterpart. He was not happy that the meeting had been expanded to include the Iraqi ambassador to Washington and the deputy prime minister, Barham Salih. He asked an aide, "Find out whether these people invited themselves. How did they get in my meeting?"

They had been invited by Hadley. Meghan O'Sullivan also sat in.

"What are we going to do, the U.S. and Iraq, in the next nine to 12 months, to put Iraq in the best possible position to avoid having to do a precipitous withdrawal of troops?" Hadley asked them. "What steps do we have to take so that it doesn't appear that the coalition is backing down and so it doesn't appear that Iraq is going to be left high and dry?

"We need concrete steps. We don't want to prematurely terminate the coalition or cause a precipitous withdrawal. The key, as seen from the United States, for success is a reduction in sectarian violence. I know we have to buy space and time for the completion of the Iraqi security force—building of its capabilities. Iraq has to continue to be in the lead and successful so that it builds a case for its real sovereignty." Though Iraq technically had been sovereign since June 2004, Hadley was making a point that was known by all. With nearly 170,000 U.S. troops now in the country, Iraq was far from "real sovereignty."

Turning to Shia-Sunni relations, Hadley said they had to "buy the space for political reconciliation."

Salih observed, "We do not have the political framework. It's not in place to be successful. We lack Sunni buy-in." There was no national figure who could unify the country. "We have no Mandela.

"The bad guys are forcing the agenda." To Salih, that meant the Sunni insurgents and al Qaeda terrorists. "What we have is a proxy war," he said. It was a battle between al Qaeda and the United States on Iraqi soil.

"We have a lot of common ground," Hadley said, "and a lot of work to do. It's late in the game, but the security situation has changed, and we have to take that into account." He was referring to the escalating violence. Turning to Rubaie, who had visited with members of the U.S. Congress, he said, "It's good that you went to Congress. You see how volatile the situation is. You see what a push we're getting to the left on Iraq."

Rubaie agreed.

"No one wants to go to zero," Hadley said, meaning zero U.S. troops in Iraq. "The consequences of failure are unthinkable. But if we don't manage the near term, it'll happen." He said they had to work on five issues—budget, constitution, oil, de-Baathification, reconciliation. Iraq's own national budget was a giant problem because about 25 to 30 percent was left unspent, while the United States poured billions into the war. On the Iraqi constitution, he said, "We thought the constitutional process would yield a grand bargain. And now we're trying to patch it up with moss. The patches don't add up to enough." It was a discouraging assessment on all fronts. There was a melancholy tone to his next question: "How can we move ahead?"

No one answered.

"We have to dramatize progress," Hadley said. "We need a dramatic event. I don't know what it is." He looked over at Salih and Rubaie. "You'll have to tell me what it is."

The Iraqis offered no ideas.

"Meghan, what have I left out?" Hadley asked.

"You've got to have a dramatic something," O'Sullivan said. "Something with drama."

"There is no single magic wand," Rubaie said. He was sure that by the fall there would be progress on the budget and the oil law and that a date would be set for provincial elections. But Maliki himself did not have the power to do these things. "You," Rubaie said, looking at the Americans, "have to twist arms" at all levels of the Iraqi government.

"The biggest challenge is time," Salih said. "They"—al Qaeda and other extremists—"can wait us out." He also said that there was a misunderstanding. Al Qaeda and JAM—Sadr's Mahdi Army—were not seen as extreme by many Iraqis.

All the focus on bringing the former Baathists into the government had created problems, he said. "We've managed to turn the Baathists into victims."

"In the long run," Hadley said, "we have to redeploy our forces to strategic bases." Neither the promise of protecting the population nor the surge itself could last indefinitely. "This may mean recalling U.S. troops to the forward operating bases." He said of the governing process, "You do have to bring all of the enemies into the cabinet. You have to come up with a formula." He returned to the theme that made his desperation evident: "But you have to have some visible progress."

Rubaie said that they needed to add amnesty to the list of key issues, meaning insurgents and other anti-government terrorists had to be offered an opportunity to avoid penalty or prison. "This plays to the hard core. But it's probably going to be necessary. If you grant amnesty, with all its disadvantages, they don't have a leg to stand on." It would rob them of their excuses for violent opposition. "You have to take a risk of amnesty. You even have to consider unconditional, general amnesty."

Hadley was very uncomfortable with that. "The problem is, if you let the bad guys out, they'll kill again," he said.

"I'm not for blanket amnesty," Barham Salih said.

Rather than attempt to referee, Hadley said, "Okay, Meghan, what did we forget?"

"The only thing I'd like to say is, I'd like to emphasize, underscore, the need for drama." She had advocated for the surge and was disappointed that it had not yet shown results.

As if to demonstrate how far expectations had fallen, they agreed how great it was that Maliki had visited Ramadi, once the violent heart of the insurgency and now a mostly peaceful city. Yes, Maliki ought to do more such visits, they chimed in. Someone suggested the prime minister visit al-Qaim, in far western Anbar province.

"Yes," Hadley said, "get the prime minister out to al-Qaim. It would be huge."

Rubaie asked for a private minute with Hadley. When they were alone, he said he had a bombshell. He had spent three hours several days earlier in Cairo with the head of Egyptian intelligence, Omar Suleiman. Egypt was involved in a covert action to try to change the Iraqi government by overthrowing Maliki, Rubaie said.

"Well," Hadley said, "I take this seriously."

The Egyptians were later warned to stay out of Iraqi internal politics.

•   •   •

On May 14, 2007, a daily SECRET noon summary on Iraq was sent to the president:

"Iraq small arms fire attack killed two U.S. soldiers and wounded four U.S. soldiers . . .

"Sniper fire killed one U.S. Marine in Fallujah . . .

"IED attack killed one U.S. soldier and wounded two U.S. soldiers in Baghdad.

"Furthermore, RPG [Rocket Propelled Grenade] and IED attack killed one U.S. soldier and wounded four U.S. soldiers in Baghdad.

"Finally, small arms fire attack killed one Danish soldier and wounded six Danish soldiers in Basra."

The summary said that an al-Qaeda group called "Islamic State in Iraq" had issued a demand about three U.S. soldiers who were missing: "Your soldiers are in our grip. If you want the safety of your soldiers, then do not search for them."

The TOP SECRET/SCI Iraq update that evening told the president that 4,000 U.S. troops were searching for the missing men. And his casualty chart read:

"Killed in action: 2,755.

"Wounded in action: 25,389."

35

In May, Keane went to Iraq for another 11 days on the ground. On May 25, he reported to Cheney.

"There's a significant shift in momentum," he said. He had spent most of his time in the neighborhoods of Baghdad. "Casualties will rise as we continue to go into areas we have not been in the past. IEDs still represent 75 percent of the instruments used against us." The advanced IEDs, the explosively formed projectiles—or EFPs—supplied by the Iranians could pierce all U.S. armored vehicles and were capable of killing everyone inside. "The IEDs have gone down in terms of their use, but they're getting more lethal."

"We need to buy time back here," Keane insisted. "The operations must go into '08 to have any chance of success."

Keane told Cheney that the U.S. troops in Iraq were idealistic. When the president had changed the mission, changed the strategy, changed the leaders and asked them to take on more risk, they had responded. The troops were committed, and their morale remained high. "They like being on the offense, and they believe they've been given a winning hand," he said, but recent leaks and statements "pull the rug out from underneath. This is very frustrating."

Cheney said that Petraeus and Odierno had just talked to the president about it. "Petraeus just did a SVTS [secure video] with the president and said that he and Ray were just scratching their heads

wondering what is going on." He said that the president had told them
that he was fully committed.

Overall, Keane said, the Sunni insurgency was considerably weaker.
"Popular support is eroding. The AQI [al Qaeda in Iraq] relationships
are fractured. The Sunnis are expressing a willingness to join the ISF
[Iraqi security forces] in a political process. This is very significant.
And negotiations are promising, but we must be wary of a fight-
bargain-subvert strategy" on the part of the Sunnis. "The key military
enemy is AQI. Its capability to undermine political support in Iraq and
in the United States is real. They are weaker. They have lost their safe
haven in Anbar."

U.S. commanders, he said, "are very much aware that they have the
initiative with the al Qaeda, and they are focusing a significant, coordi-
nated effort to go after them."

The bad news was that JAM, though not monolithic, "enjoys unimpeded access to Iranian support in southern Iraq and Sadr City."

On the political side, he said, "Maliki is beginning to move away
from Sadr, which is a significant sign. We should make an all-out effort
to discredit Sadr, because he's clearly emerged as our number one political enemy in Iraq."

Keane said that the CIA station chief in Baghdad had told him about
a TOP SECRET covert operation that could be undertaken to stop foreign fighters from coming in through Syria. The full effects of the surge
would not be felt until the end of July because the last of the five additional brigades would not arrive until June. "Every area of operation
since last February that I visited, 90 days previous, especially in Baghdad, shows improvement," he said.

"There is a Shia or JAM problem in east Baghdad, and there's a safe
haven in Sadr City. The commander's aware of it, and as they get all the
forces in, in June, they're going to work against it. There are belea-
guered Sunni enclaves that are hosting al Qaeda, still." He named six
areas—East Rasheed, Dora, Ghazaliya, Mansour, Amiriya, and Adel.

"There's a very difficult and complex fight against al Qaeda and the
JAM in Diyala province. We probably could use some more troops on
the ground," but instead the commanders were going to take troops
that had been providing force protection at U.S. bases.

"The sectarian behavior that still exists inside the Iraqi government undermines the government's legitimacy." At times in the past, U.S. officers partnered with Iraqis involved in sectarian activity would look the other way. "General Petraeus has changed that policy," he said, taking a shot at Casey. "That was a holdover from the previous leadership.

"The Maliki government is under extraordinary pressure. His intentions remain unclear. He's subject to bad information and malign influences," Keane said, but Petraeus had more leverage than any American commander before him. "We're occupying their capital city with our forces in a way that we have never done before."

Petraeus had publicly promised to return to Washington in September to report to Congress. Keane thought that was a problem, considering the expectations. "In a sense, it's become a timetable in itself to make an up-or-down" evaluation of the surge. It was supposed to be only a progress report. By September, security would in all likelihood be much improved, but "we probably will not have met everyone's political benchmarks. And the danger is: Should that political uncertainty trump the very real progress that has been made? In my judgment, it should not.

"This is doable," Keane insisted. "We can succeed. We have to be given the time to succeed."

A week earlier, the president had forced Congress to fund the war for three more months with no timelines for withdrawal attached. But he hadn't quelled the discontent within his own party.

On May 26, Senate Minority Leader Mitch McConnell of Kentucky kept up the drumbeat of Republican dissatisfaction with Iraq. "The handwriting is on the wall," he said, "that we are going in a different direction in the fall, and I expect the president to lead it. I think he himself has certainly indicated he's not happy with where we are."

Key Republicans said they expected a new strategy the coming fall after Petraeus reported to Congress.

"I'm not going to dime that guy," the president later told me, declining to elaborate on what McConnell had said privately. "There was a lot of members that were sending signals, some directly to me. So I don't want to speak about a single guy. But I was getting word from all the senior team that were getting pinged by members that were saying, 'Petraeus better pull out,' 'We'd better do this,' 'We'd better do that.' 'Progress can only be made if fewer troops are there,' was kind of the attitude.

"I understand the politics of war, and I will listen to these allies and friends. But for me, the overriding concern is to succeed in Iraq. These political concerns are short-term compared to the long-term consequences of failure. And I would, from my perspective, I am more than willing to sacrifice short-term popularity to do what is absolutely right, so that in the long term, people will say, 'Now I understand why he made the decision he made.'"

Cheney arranged for Keane to come to the White House on May 31. He joined the president, vice president and Hadley for lunch in the small dining room just off the Oval Office.

Keane reiterated much of what he had told Cheney but expanded on it. He said U.S. casualties were up, but that was because it was a true counteroffensive, similar to the Battle of Inchon in the Korean War and the Normandy invasion during World War II. If the Normandy counteroffensive had been damned because of high casualties, he said, "We would have folded up and gone back on the ships and gone home."

The strategy was working, Keane said. "The issue is time." He didn't want to lecture or sermonize, "but at the risk of doing this, there's something I do have to say to you. This military that we have in Iraq may be the most idealistic force we've put on a battlefield since the Revolutionary War."

"Maybe include the Civil War," the president said.

"That's possible," Keane said. "But the American people have soured on the effort and are no longer supporting the war." Similarly, Congress. "But nonetheless, every single day, they go out there and are willing to risk everything that they care about in life."

The New York Times had published a front-page story that weekend headlined "White House Said to Debate '08 Cut in Troops by 50%." It reported that Rice and Gates allegedly were proponents of the cuts, which would leave only 100,000 U.S. troops in Iraq by the next year. Such stories were "undermining" and "corrosive," Keane said.

Officers in the military, he said, even senior officers, didn't understand the nuances of Washington. "They don't separate the commander in chief, the president of the United States, from the White House. They assume if it came out of the White House, the president's involved in the process."

"Petraeus said something like that to me when he started out our last VTC," Bush interjected. "He said, 'Mr. President, to be quite frank about it, Ray Odierno and I were wondering what's going on?' I told David, he's got my 100 percent support, as well as the administration's."

"The good news," Keane continued, "is that Maliki is moving away from Sadr. And that Maliki has never turned down a Petraeus request to kill or capture a Shia militia leader. That is absolutely astounding." Maliki had approved about 50 such requests.

"We must stick with Maliki," Keane said. "As weak as he is, and as weak as his coalition is, given the time that we have available back here in our own country, I don't believe we have time for the government to be changed out." Maliki was under extraordinary pressure. "He reacts to the last cell phone call that he gets." Petraeus had told him how Maliki gets bombarded by the Shia, then the Sunnis, and then each night by the Americans. They all want something different from him.

Bush said that he believed Maliki had grown in the job.

"Ambassador Crocker is very well received by everybody," Keane added.

"Yeah, Crocker's a great guy," the president said.

"And he's well thought of. And he's got a wonderful reputation," Keane said.

"He and Petraeus have just a great relationship," he added.

"Maliki doesn't like Petraeus much," Bush said.

"No, of course, he doesn't," Keane said. "George Casey's strategy was to turn over to the Iraqis and let them do it. Therefore he was giving them the lead and letting them drive all the issues and being somewhat passive. Enter Petraeus. He is putting demands on Maliki. Every time he walks in his office, it's about something Petraeus wants from Maliki." Keane said that Crocker needed some help. "None of his new people have arrived."

"They're going to be due in there in summer," Hadley said.

That was because the State Department still had a policy of not transferring its people during the school year, Keane explained. He noted that the military moved people when the military needed them, period.

Keane said it was unfortunate that Congress had insisted that Petraeus come back in September and give a public report. Requiring an American field commander to return to Washington and brief was setting a bad precedent. The field commander should report only up the chain of command, he said.

"I had nothing to do with that," Bush said.

Congress had passed a law requiring that Petraeus testify.

On June 6, 2007, I spent three hours in New York City with Bill Perry, the former Clinton defense secretary who had been very active in the Iraq Study Group. Perry, like most of the study group members, recognized that Bush had dismissed their main recommendations by adopting the surge. He was particularly dumbfounded because both General Casey and General Chiarelli had told him that adding forces would not be effective.

"Let me make a forecast," said Perry, normally a cautious man. "In October, there's going to be a major change in the way the war is conducted. The reason I say that is because when Dave Petraeus testified to the Congress at his confirmation hearing, he told them he would come back in September and give them a report. Dave's an honest guy, so he'll give an honest report. My own forecast is that the so-called surge is not going to be successful. So his report is going to lay out a continuing disaster and he'll say it honestly . . . then I think the president's going to lose about a third of the Republicans in the Congress, who up until now have been holding their noses and supporting him. At that point, the dynamics will change altogether." Congress would then have the votes to override any Bush veto, Perry said. "The legislature will gain control, and the ones who are in control are going to want to end the war."

Petraeus's forces were beginning to flip tribes in Anbar regularly, signing up leaders who had grown frustrated with al Qaeda violence and intrusions. It was an effort that had started in late 2005 with Marines in the al-Qaim area in the farthest reaches of Anbar, near the Syrian border. Slowly and steadily, the movement had spread along the Euphrates River valley to Ramadi, where tribal sheiks were now sending hundreds of local young men to join the Iraqi police force.

But what about Baghdad? Petraeus had heard that a former Iraqi Special Operations Forces captain and leader of a Sunni insurgent group called the Baghdad Patriots wanted to sign with the United States against al Qaeda. Abu Abed, also known as Saif, brought with him a force of somewhere between 40 and 100 experienced fighters.

Abed's sudden unemployment when the Iraqi army was abolished in 2003, like so many others, left him feeling disrespected and disdainful of the Americans. Since then, however, al Qaeda had taken over the Amiriya neighborhood, a Sunni enclave. They had blown up Abed's house and killed his brothers, and now they were coming after him. Amiriya was so violent that U.S. and coalition forces couldn't enter the area in Humvees. An M1 tank and a Bradley armored personnel carrier had been blown up in the neighborhood.

The first notice American forces had of Abed's change of heart was a cell phone call on May 29 from a local imam, who informed the U.S. battalion commander in the area that the militia intended to take its neighborhood back from al Qaeda. News of the Baghdad Patriots' request—they wanted the Americans to provide weapons and stay out of the way—rocketed up the chain of command.

Petraeus, out jogging with some young officers, was joined by a U.S. Army major who worked in Amiriya. A dozen soldiers from his battalion had already been killed that month. The major told Petraeus that the overture from Abed was significant, though there were considerable risks to helping him and his men. Prime Minister Maliki wouldn't be happy to see the Americans stand up a Sunni militia. And several officers wondered if the Americans were making a deal with the devil. After all, Abed was a former insurgent who undoubtedly had killed U.S. soldiers.

"We've got to support him," Petraeus ordered after the run. "Drive him on our Bradleys. Get ammunition from the Iraqi army and give it to him."

Within 24 hours, the neighborhood began to quiet. The Iraqi fighters knew the area, and they began leading the Americans to arms caches, al Qaeda hideouts and IEDs. While some in the battalion held on to their deep reservations, most saw the arrangement and the subsequent reduction in violence as a sign of progress.

Privately, Petraeus saw it as a potential turning point in the capital. The key to drawing down U.S. forces was to get the Iraqis to protect their own population so Petraeus's troops wouldn't have the job.

Gates approached a handful of senators, including the new chairman of the Armed Services Committee, Carl Levin, to inquire about the prospects of getting Pace confirmed for another two-year term as chairman of the Joint Chiefs.

"What do you think?" Gates asked.

"It's going to be a battle royal up here on Iraq," Levin replied.

Gates asked Levin to "sound out" colleagues.

Levin felt it mostly boiled down to accountability. Congress had held no one at the highest levels accountable for failed policies. He knew there was no way Pace could get through a confirmation hearing without it becoming a venting session.

"Well, can you see whether or not others feel that way?" Gates asked.

Levin, who had served in the Senate since 1979 and had voted against the war in 2002, approached half a dozen of his Democratic colleagues and some Republicans. They all told him it would involve a real fight to get Pace confirmed. A few said, "Hell, no."

For starters, Pace had played a role in shaping a strategy that had not worked. But worse, there was a feeling among the senators—

reinforced by various military officers—that Pace had not been outspoken, that he wasn't the kind of guy who would stand up to the administration and say things were on the wrong track. Retired General
James Jones, for example, the Marine commandant from 1999 to 2003,
had said Pace was too docile in dealing with Rumsfeld and had likened
him to "the parrot on the secretary's shoulder."

It'll be a bloody battle, Levin warned Gates. A confirmation hearing
would focus on all the failures in Iraq and Pace's role in them. He
didn't see how Pace could get confirmed. Gates decided not to take the
chance.

On Friday, June 8, Gates announced that General Pace would step
down as chairman of the Joint Chiefs in September. He said he wanted
to spare Pace the rancorous congressional hearings. "I think that the
events of the last several months have simply created an environment
in which I think there would be a confirmation process that would not
be in the best interests of the country," Gates told reporters at the Pentagon. "I am disappointed that circumstances make this kind of a decision necessary."

Despite Gates's effort to sugarcoat his decision, Pace was being
fired. He would retire after just two years in the post, the shortest
tenure of any chairman in more than four decades. Along with the si-
multaneous retirement of Admiral Edmund Giambastiani, the JCS vice
chairman, it meant that the top Washington generals linked to Rumsfeld's tenure were all but gone.

In June, Hadley sent O'Sullivan to Iraq. She saw panic everywhere.
The additional brigades and the new strategy were in place, and yet
violence was skyrocketing, with attacks reaching more than 1,550 a
week, about 220 a day—a new record. And on top of that, the politics remained stagnant. Reconciliation was nowhere in sight. But as
unbelievable as it might seem, she found Baghdad preferable to
Washington.

36

On June 13, about 9 A.M., insurgents launched a second attack on the al-Askari Mosque in Samarra, one of the holiest sites in Shia Islam. The bombing destroyed the mosque's two ten-story minarets. The first attack, 16 months earlier, had been the trigger that set off massive sectarian violence. In Baghdad, Petraeus and the American military intelligence officials held their breath.

Prime Minister Maliki was furious.

"How could this happen?" he asked Petraeus in an accusatory tone. "With all the coalition forces there, with all the Iraqi forces there, you and the coalition must have let this happen. How can these people get in?"

"There were plenty of forces present," Petraeus answered. "Something else is involved. What I suggest, Mr. Prime Minister, is I will give you a helicopter and my personal assistant. Go there. Go yourself. Have a look. Go talk to the commanders and see what happened."

Petraeus's assistant was a skillful translator and civilian contractor named Sadi Othman, who had attended a Mennonite college in Kansas and once worked as a driver in New York City. Known to everyone simply as Sadi, he was a towering man and former basketball player whom Petraeus referred to as "the Michael Jordan of Jordan," his native country. Sadi had begun working for Petraeus as a translator in Mosul after the invasion of Iraq in 2003. When Petraeus returned as the commanding general, he made Sadi one of his senior advisers. He answered Petraeus's cell phone in Iraq, and as far as most Iraqis were concerned, Sadi was Petraeus.

Maliki and Sadi flew to Samarra and were received by the local Iraqi commanders.

"Every time I ask you about Samarra," Maliki began yelling at the national police commander on the scene, "you say it's perfectly okay, there's nothing to worry about. How can this happen? You're an idiot! You're incompetent! You have all these protective guards" around the mosque.

Maliki then ordered a curfew shutting everything down—no walking, no driving. Later, it became clear that the bombing had been an inside job by members of the Iraqi police.

The next day, June 14, Maliki, Petraeus and Crocker met at about 12:45 P.M.

"We really understand two things about the terrorists now," Maliki said. "The first is that they target essential services because these have a direct impact on the people, and the people then have a direct impact on the government. It shows the government to be ineffective in stopping the attacks and restoring essential services." He specifically mentioned interruptions of oil and electricity. "The second thing we know is they'll target holy sites in order to generate sectarian violence between the groups."

Ignoring this recital of the obvious, Ambassador Crocker told him, "I applaud the orders you've given as a consequence of yesterday's events. I think you did exactly the right thing. The importance of these statements in your orders is that you're placing the blame squarely on al Qaeda and are demonstrating that this is an attack against all elements of Iraq—the Sunnis, the Shia and the Kurds, as well. This is very important that it is seen as an al Qaeda attack on Iraq, not on any particular sect."

"Yes," Petraeus said, "I strongly agree. You did all the right things. And things are calm now, but we can't count on this calm."

"That's why we have this extended curfew," Maliki said. "And we also postponed the exams," referring to secondary school exams.

"Your trip yesterday was very important," Petraeus said. "You demonstrated leadership."

"We have closed off the entire scene."

"How quickly can this be rebuilt?" Petraeus asked. "Can construction start right away, with or without the U.N.?" He was referring to the plan to rebuild the mosque from the bombing 16 months earlier.

"Yes," the prime minister replied, "in fact yesterday we were about to sign the papers, UNESCO and the Turkish company that won the award, to begin the reconstruction." UNESCO was the branch of the United Nations collaborating on Iraq reconstruction projects. Maliki said President Bush had called him the previous day "to say that the U.S. would provide any support necessary for the reconstruction."

"It would be a powerful signal to the public," Crocker said, "to sign the contract in the next couple of days, with lots of media. The world would be pleased."

"Well," Maliki answered, "it's up to UNESCO."

Petraeus and Crocker recognized the typical Iraqi political response. Instead of reaching over and strangling Maliki as they seemed to want to do, Petraeus said, "There's a saying that you're really good if you can turn adversity into opportunity, and you can in this case."

"Right now the people of Samarra are intimidated," Maliki said, adding confidently, "But when they see the Iraqi security forces there, I am sure they'll openly support them."

U.S. intelligence showed, however, that the Iraqi police forces were highly sectarian, and some still carried pictures of Saddam. But neither challenged Maliki's assertion.

"Keep this quiet for two days," Petraeus said, "but we're about to start a major national, nationwide attack against al Qaeda sanctuaries." He promised that if the U.S. had any intelligence from the operations, he would share it with the prime minister. Crocker said that Kurdish leader Massoud Barzani had agreed to compromise on the Iraqi law to share oil revenues with the provinces, an important piece of legislation. "And the next step is to introduce it to the parliament," Crocker said.

Maliki was nodding yes. "Not only do we have this agreement," he said, "but we also have the framework agreement on the de-Baathification law."

Petraeus pounced on the public relations opportunity. He knew that Hadley and others in the administration were searching for a dramatic event. He suggested that Maliki capitalize on the agreement to rebuild the Samarra mosque and the news of a compromise on the oil law. "In another day," he said, "you have all the Sunday talk shows. So why don't you orchestrate a media campaign on these favorable events to show you in a good light?" He added, "Let me help generate the talk shows."

"There's another bit of good news," Maliki said. "Sadr has suspended his members' participation in the council, and the parliament can then expedite all of this activity." Recently, six government ministers loyal to Sadr had quit in protest at Maliki's refusal to set a timetable for a U.S. troop withdrawal. It had left Maliki free to choose their replacements.

"I'll be on Fox Sunday," Petraeus said, "and I'll emphasize all these points, so that you get from me support on the talk shows. Or at least on Fox."

"Yes," said Ali al-Dabbagh, Maliki's spokesman. "We should participate in the shows."

"We'll line it up," Petraeus said. He pointed to Dabbagh. "You do Al Jazeera."

"And we have more good news," Petraeus said. He made a point of ending meetings with Maliki on a positive note. The repairs on the oil platforms in the Gulf that allow the loading of tankers had just been completed. "We should highlight this too," he said, "the completion of the repairs on the Basra oil terminals." He also had photographs of southwestern Baghdad, an area of focused redevelopment.

The Petraeus philosophy on media coverage was that the reporters would unearth the bad news on their own. If he and Maliki didn't serve up good news, however large or small, it most likely would go unreported.

On *Fox News Sunday* with Chris Wallace on June 17, General Petraeus said, "Yesterday, there was an agreement with UNESCO and the government of Iraq to rebuild that Samarra mosque." Wallace showed little interest, asking instead about the levels of violence and the absence of an oil law. Petraeus said all the problems in Iraq were not "going to be resolved in a year or even two years. . . . Historically, counterinsurgency operations have gone at least nine or 10 years." But, he insisted, "there is good prospect for progress in the months ahead."

Ultimately, the contract to rebuild the Samarra mosque was signed, but agreements on de-Baathification reform and an oil law stalled.

On June 28, Rice gathered 20 senior State Department officials, the most senior undersecretaries and her closest seventh-floor aides for a two-day private retreat at Airlie Center, a conference facility in the Virginia countryside. After they had discussed various programs to transform diplomacy and foreign assistance, she raised the real question.

"Do you want to talk about Iraq?" she asked.

All indicated that they did. Violence was at a peak, Iraq as much a mess as ever. Already, 3,562 U.S. servicemen and women had died.

Rice urged them to speak openly and honestly. It was as if someone had pushed a button to release pressures and tensions that had accumulated for years.

"The senior people kind of let loose," recalled a participant and a Rice ally within the department. "They were concerned about the strategy. Would it work? Could it work? What is the long-lasting impact of the Iraq War on the U.S. position in the world? In the region? Domestically, the impact on the United States? Rice didn't say much, but it was a very dreary moment because they were all saying, 'We don't know where we're going and we don't know what this is, and we don't know the surge strategy can work.'" Other participants confirmed how pessimistic the discussion of Iraq had been.

Rice, true to form, chose to focus on the sliver of optimism she heard. She later recalled, "Three or four assistant secretaries said, 'Not only can we not lose, we can't be perceived to lose.'" A loss in Iraq would have a devastating impact on American leadership, they had argued. So they had to win. No one was arguing for outright withdrawal.

But a majority left the conference deeply disheartened. The Bush administration's new strategy of sending more U.S. troops to protect the population had shown few signs of working.

On June 29, Bush met with the Republican leaders from the Senate and House.

"Mr. President," said Representative Roy Blunt, the Missouri Republican and the party's number two House leader, "you have no credibility on communicating about Iraq."

"I know," Bush replied.

"The worst thing you could do is talk about Iraq," Blunt said.

"People believe I've been too optimistic for too long," Bush conceded.

Blunt remarked that in four years, the Iraqi people had not taken the opportunity to set up a functioning democracy. "No one in the country has much concern for Jeffersonian democracy."

"I understand people feel that way," Bush replied, "but I disagree." He believed democracy was the only way, and he held high expectations for the surge.

Several times the president asked Petraeus, "Are we taking the fight to the enemy?" or "Are we on offense?" And on a number of occasions, he asked about enemy casualties, saying, "Well, and how many did we kill?"

Petraeus gave him numbers only every few weeks. "Mr. President," he said, "we are not going to kill our way out of Iraq. This is not about exchange ratios" of enemy killed versus U.S. killed. But, he acknowledged, "We have totaled up, and the exchange ratios are enormous." The coalition was killing dozens of enemy fighters for each American loss.

•   •   •

General Casey went for a routine physical inside the sprawling grounds of Walter Reed Army Medical Center in northwest Washington. He spotted retired General Jack Keane standing in line at the radiology desk.

The two generals locked eyes for a moment, then Keane turned away, as if he hadn't recognized Casey.

"Hi Jack, how are you?" Casey said, extending his hand. He had been waiting for a moment like this. "Has the chairman called you yet?"

"No, why?" Keane asked.

"Because we feel—the chiefs feel—that you are way too out in front advocating a policy for which you're not accountable. We're accountable. You're not accountable, Jack. And that's a problem."

Keane said he'd taken action as a member of the secretary of defense's policy board, whose members were supposed to offer their independent advice. All he was trying to do was help Petraeus, he said. He had supported the Rumsfeld-Casey strategy for three years. "And at some point, I no longer could support it. I'm not operating as some kind of Lone Ranger."

"It's not appropriate for a retired general to be so far forward advocating a policy that he is not responsible or accountable for," Casey said again.

"I'll take your counsel," said Keane, but he didn't suggest he would act any differently.

On the Fourth of July, Pelosi invited a group of wounded veterans to watch the celebration from her offices in the Capitol. Her balcony provided a sweeping view of the Mall and the evening fireworks display.

One young Marine officer had no legs, just a torso sitting in a wheelchair.

"Madam Speaker," he said, straining up out of his wheelchair and pointing to where presidents take the oath of office. "I was there at the president's inauguration in '05. And I sang. And I stood there as part of the Naval Academy choir."

He had heard the president give one of the most ambitious inaugural addresses in history. "It is the policy of the United States," Bush had said that day, "to seek and support the growth of democratic movements and institutions in every nation and culture, with the ultimate goal of ending tyranny in our world."

"How are *you*?" Pelosi asked the Marine.

"I've had some very dark days," said the young lieutenant, who'd survived a roadside bomb and was recovering at Walter Reed after numerous surgeries. "I'm trying to come around. I've had very dark months."

Petraeus tried to find a few minutes to read each night before he fell asleep. Little by little, he made his way through *Grant Takes Command,* by Bruce Catton, about General Ulysses S. Grant's campaigns to turn the tide for President Lincoln in the Civil War. Petraeus was particularly struck by how Grant handled setbacks. After the bloody first day of battle at Shiloh, General Sherman found Grant well past midnight, standing alone under a tree in heavy rain.

"Well, Grant," Sherman said, "we had the devil's own day, haven't we?"

"Yes," said Grant, his cigar glowing in the darkness as he gave a quick, hard puff. "Yes. Lick 'em tomorrow, though."

Among Petraeus's inner circle, "lick 'em tomorrow, though" became a rallying cry after many bad days, including one in which 160 Iraqis were killed by car bombs. Petraeus was astounded by the way Grant had taken one pounding after another from General Robert E. Lee, who stubbornly refused to be outflanked. Grant wrote, "I propose to fight it out on this line if it takes all summer." This became another rallying cry.

"You don't think you're Grant?" a friend asked Petraeus.

"No," Petraeus said. He was also reading about General Matthew Ridgway, who had helped turn the tide of the Korean War.

In the spring of 2007, my assistant, Brady Dennis, and I tracked down notes of key interviews conducted by the Baker-Hamilton Iraq Study

Group. Included was CIA Director Michael Hayden's bleak assessment of the Maliki government. Hayden had said that "the inability of the government to govern seems irreversible," adding that he could not "point to any milestone or checkpoint where we can turn this thing around." A majority of the study group members said that Hayden's assessment was the chief reason they began their report with the line "The situation in Iraq is grave and deteriorating."

I took this information to Len Downie, the executive editor of *The Washington Post*. Even months after Hayden's testimony to the group, I said, his dire assessment constituted news and should be published as soon as possible. Downie agreed. Because the material had been gathered on the condition that it was for a book that would come out the next year, Downie and I met with one of the sources and asked that the ground rules be changed. Downie said he felt it would be a "dereliction of duty" on the part of the *Post* if this information were not made public soon. The source initially refused but eventually acknowledged that because Hayden's assessment was the most important and most authoritative the study group had received, it deserved to be published.

I contacted several CIA officials to ask whether Hayden would speak with me about his statements and whether his assessment had changed. Hayden declined, and he called Lee Hamilton, the Democratic co-chairman of the study group, to complain. According to Hamilton, Hayden said, "Woodward knows an awful lot about this testimony. I presented the dark side, and Woodward is going to make it darker."

The *Post* story ran Thursday, July 12, under the headline "CIA Said Instability Seemed 'Irreversible.'"

That same day, the president was asked about the story at a news conference.

"Mike Hayden was in this morning to give me his weekly briefing," Bush said, "and I asked him about that newspaper article from which you quote. His answer was his comments to the Iraq Study Group were a little more nuanced than the quotation you read." According to Bush, Hayden's recollection of his statement to the study group was that in November 2006 "the current strategy in Iraq wasn't working . . . and that we needed a change of direction." The president used what he said were Hayden's recollections to bolster his decision to change the strategy. Then he went further than he ever had in public: "As I told you last November, right about this time, I was part of that group of Americans who didn't approve of what was taking place in Iraq because it looked like all the efforts that we had taken to that point in time were about to fail."

It was as if Bush had been a bystander, just an ordinary American who objected to the course of the war.

37

Keane made another two-week trip to Iraq in July. Petraeus, other military generals and the CIA station chief told him the Sunni insurgency was collapsing. Thousands of former Sunni insurgents were cooperating with the U.S. and other coalition forces. Some 21,000 Sunnis in Anbar province alone had joined up, and Prime Minister Maliki had authorized 18,000 former insurgents to bear arms and be paid. Keane attended a classified conference that Petraeus had with his subordinate commanders. Then the two went off alone.

Petraeus told Keane that what was mostly on his mind was the September testimony to Congress. There was a lot of good news to report, but Petraeus said he was going to be careful not to overstate the successes. That had been a problem in this war from the beginning.

"You have to be factual, credible," Keane advised, "but also be hopeful. Don't be afraid to be hopeful. Try to find a way to be factual, but also to reveal who you are. Because at the end of the day, the congressmen and senators are nuts, but your audience is the American people who are out there watching. Realize it's television and the power of television. When you're talking with them, you've got to establish a relationship with them, and to do that they've got to see a bit of you. They've got to feel you a little bit, you know, who you are. And let them see it."

•　•　•

On Saturday, August 18, Keane gave Cheney a private briefing at the vice president's residence off Massachusetts Avenue in northwest Washington. Former House Speaker Newt Gingrich had advised Keane that when he saw the president or vice president, "Don't leave anything on the table. . . . Get it all out and you'll feel so much better for it."

With Petraeus scheduled to testify the next month, Keane told Cheney, "I don't see any evidence that the administration, the Department of Defense and the Department of State, is really setting up the conditions for this testimony to be successful."

"What do you mean by that?" Cheney asked.

"The secretary of defense has enormous credibility," Keane said. Gates had been on the Iraq Study Group, and he had been unanimously confirmed by the Senate. "He should be willing to support his field commander with key leaders in the Senate and the House prior to the testimony, setting up the conditions." Keane said Petraeus was getting no help from the chairman of the Joint Chiefs, the chiefs themselves, Central Commander Admiral Fallon or Fallon's staff. Genuine support was coming only from the president and vice president. That was important, but the others should pitch in.

Keane had particular trouble with Fallon. "I'm the first guy that raised Fallon's name," he told Cheney, but Fallon was constantly putting pressure on Petraeus. "Making him do all sorts of analyses to get out sooner or have a deeper withdrawal." He referred to the report that Admiral Winnefeld had issued after Fallon had sent him to assess the situation in Iraq. It had undermined Petraeus. "What happened to Fallon, he bought into all the political concerns in Washington . . . I understand that to a certain degree. But as opposed to coming in here and strengthening the Joint Chiefs' resolve, his own resolve was weakened by the views in Washington and the Joint Chiefs. And he took that and turned it against Petraeus."

Since Petraeus had arrived in Iraq, Keane said, "The Joint Chiefs are more concerned about breaking the Army and Marine Corps than winning the war. They don't say it that way," but that's the way it comes across to Petraeus. "The fact that the Army is stressed and strained is sort of expected during war. That's why it exists." If we happen to break it fighting a war we feel we must win, he said, then so be it. That has happened in past wars.

Cheney's trademark silence invited more.

"Secretary Rice," Keane said, "I'll just speak frankly. She goes around the world dealing with foreign policy issues, but where she stands on Iraq, I'm not sure. And I don't think she's willing to damage her reputation at all over this issue." She should be helping Ambassador Ryan Crocker, who was going to appear before Congress with Petraeus.

Keane tried to explain why this lack of support had such an impact on Petraeus. "Normally, a military commander who is succeeding, it obviously means you are producing results, and it obviously means you are helping the chain of command above you. They're very proud of you. It certainly enhances the organization they're responsible for. When you're succeeding, you've always had a very supportive chain of command."

The irony, Keane said, was that Petraeus had obtained a four-star combat command "in a campaign of war, and dealing with something that is clearly in the national interest, and the stakes are very high . . . and at that point he has an unsupportive chain of command for the first time in his career when he has the most critical job he's ever had and ever will have. The impact of that is stunning for him."

Keane said it was not just Petraeus's immediate boss, Admiral Fallon, but also those above Fallon—Pace, who was not leaving until the fall, and Gates—who weren't fully supporting Petraeus. "We should all be on the same page behind them—the Pentagon on the same page, which it's not, and the State Department on the same page, which it's not. It shouldn't just be up to these two men"—Petraeus and Crocker—"to come in here and sort of walk the gangplank by themselves for the administration."

"We can help here," Cheney finally said. "We can help here."

The conversation had gone on for nearly an hour and a half. At one point Lynne Cheney, the vice president's wife, stuck her head in the room and quietly reminded her husband, "Remember, we're supposed to be there in 10, 15 minutes."

Though he had followed Newt Gingrich's advice to lay it on the line, Keane wondered if this time he had not gone too far—laying into the leadership of both Defense and State.

A few days later, during a secure videoconference with Baghdad, the president said he was troubled that they were not doing enough to bolster Petraeus and Crocker. Their testimony was fast approaching, and everyone in the administration, including himself, had to pitch in to make it successful.

Ed Gillespie, a former lobbyist and chairman of the Republican National Committee, took over as Bush's White House counselor and communications director when Dan Bartlett resigned earlier in the summer.

"Where's the flowchart?" Gillespie had asked Bartlett, referring to the plan he hoped the White House had for how Bush would spend his time and deliver his message.

"There isn't one," Bartlett said, laughing.

Gillespie, 46, a genial Irishman who had made millions lobbying, wanted to be more strategic. He pushed for a series of high-profile speeches in which the president would underscore the stakes in Iraq and offer support to Petraeus and Crocker.

On August 22, Bush spoke to the Veterans of Foreign Wars national convention in Kansas City, Missouri, drawing an unusual parallel between Vietnam and Iraq. "One unmistakable legacy of Vietnam is that the price of America's withdrawal was paid by millions of innocent citizens whose agonies would add to our vocabulary new terms like 'boat people,' 're-education camps,' and 'killing fields.'" He said "the question now that comes before us is this: Will today's generation of Americans resist the allure of retreat?" He added, "Unlike in Vietnam, if we withdraw before the job is done, this enemy will follow us home."

Six days later, the president appeared at the American Legion's annual convention in Reno, Nevada. He said that withdrawal from Iraq would leave "a region already known for instability and violence under the shadow of a nuclear holocaust."

On Thursday, August 24, the U.S. intelligence community released some unclassified key judgments in its National Intelligence Estimate on Iraq. The assessment found "measurable but uneven improvements" in security. Though the violence had gone down, it remained "high." On the political front, the agencies said "Iraq's sectarian groups remain unreconciled."

Not included in the public report was its assessment that Maliki had "a less than 50 percent chance of surviving" in office another six to 12 months, according to a senior U.S. intelligence official. In addition, Maliki had "some real health problems" that "indicated he was going downhill," according to that senior official.

As the summer wore on, Petraeus waited for the tide to turn. Every Saturday, the staff distributed the latest chart, graphing the rise or fall in violence. During two weeks at the end of June, the number of attacks plunged by more than 300, then went back up slightly the next week. The figures rose higher the following week, then went into a generally steady march downward throughout August. By summer's end, the high of 1,550 attacks a week had fallen to just under 800—nearly a 50 percent reduction, but still an average of five an hour.

Why had the violence dropped dramatically?

On one level, the surge was beginning to have its intended effect. Doubling the U.S. forces in and around Baghdad from 17,000 to nearly 40,000 had a clear impact, as such a dramatic influx of forces would in any city. The thousands of additional troops, coupled with Petraeus's counterinsurgency game plan, had quelled some of the sectarian and other violence that had defined the past year and a half. About 30 joint security stations had been established around Baghdad by the summer of 2007. Security along the borders with Iran and Syria had improved, and the Iraqi army was performing better.

But the full truth wasn't as simple. At least three other factors were as, or even more, important than the surge.

Beginning in about May 2006, the U.S. military and the U.S. intelligence agencies launched a series of TOP SECRET operations that enabled them to locate, target and kill key individuals in extremist groups such as al Qaeda, the Sunni insurgency and renegade Shia militias, or so-called special groups. The operations, which were either Special Access Programs (SAP) or part of Special Compartmented Information (SCI), incorporated some of the most highly classified techniques and information in the U.S. government.

Senior military officers and officials at the White House have asked me not to publish the details or the code word names associated with these groundbreaking programs. They argue that publication of the names alone might lead to unraveling of state secrets that have been so beneficial in Iraq. Because disclosing the details of such operations could compromise their ongoing use, I have chosen not to include more here. But a number of authoritative sources say these covert activities had a far-reaching effect on the violence and were very possibly the biggest factor in reducing it. Several said that 85 to 90 percent of the successful operations and "actionable intelligence" had come from these new sources, methods and operations. Several others said that figure was exaggerated but acknowledged their significance. Once again, it was American innovation that provided an edge.

Lieutenant General Stanley McChrystal, the commander of the Joint Special Operations Command (JSOC) responsible for hunting al Qaeda in Iraq, employed what he called "collaborative warfare," using every tool available simultaneously, from signals intercepts to human intelligence and other methods, that allowed lightning-quick and sometimes concurrent operations. Derek Harvey, the DIA intelligence expert and adviser to Petraeus, said privately that the operations were so effective that they gave him "orgasms."

When I later asked the president about this, he offered a simple answer: "JSOC is awesome."

A second important factor in the lessening of violence was the Anbar Awakening, in which tens of thousands of Sunnis turned against al Qaeda and signed up with the U.S. forces. Al Qaeda had made a strategic mistake in the province, overplaying its hand. Its members had performed forced marriages with women from local tribes, taken over hospitals, used mosques for beheading operations, mortared playgrounds and executed citizens, leaving headless bodies in the streets with signs that read, "Don't remove this body or the same thing will happen to you." The sheer brutality eroded much of the local support.

Over many months, U.S. forces worked with tribal leaders, who had once fought Americans, to help build local security forces throughout the province.

"We are the ones who saved our country," Sheikh Ahmed Abu Risha, whose slain younger brother first allied himself with U.S. forces and who now serves as president of the Iraqi Awakening Council, told me. "We were able to fight al Qaeda."

The U.S. military also began setting up groups of thousands of what Petraeus called "Concerned Local Citizens" (later known as "Sons of Iraq"), essentially armed neighborhood watch groups that would patrol their communities and provide intelligence to U.S. and Iraqi forces.

A third significant break came on August 29, when Moqtada al-Sadr ordered his powerful Mahdi Army to suspend operations, including attacks against U.S. troops. Petraeus and others knew it was not an act of charity. The order followed a gunfight between the Mahdi Army and Iraqi forces in the holy city of Karbala, during which more than 50 Shia pilgrims gathering for an annual festival had been killed and another 275 wounded. Sadr's order that his army stand down for six months marked an unexpected stroke of good luck, another in a series for the Americans.

During this period some United States intelligence agencies had extensive coverage on Prime Minister Maliki, his staff and others within the Iraqi government. Some officials knowledgeable about the intelligence gathering believe it provided a transparent view into the prime minister's actions.

"We know everything he says," one source said.

A second source said that Maliki and his people suspected, perhaps even knew, about this surveillance and that they were careful about their conversations and also took other countermeasures. In some specific cases, this source said, human sources had given senior U.S. officials a heads-up on positions, plans, maneuvers and secret actions of the prime minister, members of his staff and others in the Iraqi government.

Of the Maliki surveillance, the source said, "You never have absolute transparency . . . you never get inside someone's head. . . . When he's talking, you can never suspect he's not playing you. We had a lot—a lot—of insights, but to say absolute, no. I could never tell you I thought I had absolute insight into what anybody was doing over there."

A third source said the surveillance on Maliki was more than routine.

A fourth source recognized the sensitivity of the issue and then asked, "Would it be better if we didn't?"

Gathering intelligence on known or suspected enemies made perfect sense. But spying on friends and allies, particularly a young democracy the United States had vowed to help, while not unprecedented, raised all kinds of questions. The intelligence agencies love to deliver the inside goods. But several senior officials asked: What was there to gain? And was it worth the risk? It was not clear that it was that useful to President Bush. Just as General Petraeus has said it is not possible for the United States to kill its way to victory in Iraq, it probably was not possible to spy its way to political stability—the ultimate goal.

38

On August 29, 2007, Petraeus's aide and former Australian Army officer David Kilcullen, a well-known counterinsurgency expert, wrote in an online posting, "We have spent the last four years carefully building up and supporting an Iraqi political system based on non-tribal institutions." He noted that the Coalition Provisional Authority, under L. Paul Bremer, had sidelined the tribes in 2003 in order to focus on building a "modern" democratic state in Iraq.

But, he wrote, "We are now seeing the most significant political and security progress in years, via a structure outside the one we have been working so hard to create. Does that invalidate the last four years' efforts? Probably not, as long as we recognize that the vision of a Jeffersonian, 'modern' (in the Western industrial sense) democracy in Iraq, based around entirely secular non-tribal institutions, was always somewhat unrealistic. In the Iraqi polity, tribes' rights may end up playing a similar role to states' rights in some other democracies.

"To be perfectly honest," Kilcullen continued, "the pattern we are seeing runs somewhat counter to what we expected in the 'surge.' . . . The original concept was that we (the coalition and the Iraqi government) would create security, which would in turn create space for a 'grand bargain' at the national level. Instead, we are seeing the exact opposite: a series of local political deals has displaced extremists, resulting in a major improvement in security at the local level, and the national government is jumping on board with the program. Instead of coalition-led top-down reconciliation, this is Iraqi-led, bottom-up, based on civil society rather than national politics. And oddly enough, it seems to be working so far."

In the end, Kilcullen said, no matter what the United States had imagined or hoped for with the surge, it had to accept the solutions that Iraqis themselves had chosen. "Our job," he wrote, "is to support where needed, ensure proper political safeguards and human rights standards are in place, but ultimately to realize that this will play out in ways that may be good or bad, but are fundamentally unpredictable."

Fallon wanted to replace Petraeus as the Iraq commander that fall. Petraeus was under too much pressure. It was his third Iraq tour. He had spent nearly four of the past five years in Iraq, and was carrying the weight of the world on his shoulders, stressed out and not getting enough sleep.

Fallon recalled the pictures of World War II Navy men who lined the walls of his former Pacific Command in Hawaii. Admiral Marc Mitscher was only 59 years old when he returned to the United States after the war. He looked 90 and died seven months later.

Admiral John S. McCain, the Arizona senator's grandfather, was so worn down by the stress of the war in the Pacific that he weighed barely 100 pounds when it ended. He attended the September 2, 1945, Japanese surrender ceremony and died of a heart attack in California four days later.

The toll of the Iraq War was incredible. It was grinding on Petraeus.

Fallon later insisted that he recommended to Gates that he replace Petraeus. Gates told associates that nothing of the kind ever happened.

On Monday morning, September 10, a full-page ad in *The New York Times* greeted Petraeus hours before he was to testify before Congress. The ad had been placed by MoveOn.org, a liberal advocacy group and political action committee.

"GENERAL PETRAEUS OR GENERAL BETRAY US?" it read in

big, bold letters under his picture. "General Petraeus is a military man constantly at war with the facts."

Petraeus found such a personal attack jolting, a sign of how raw and impassioned the widespread aversion to the war had become.

When he checked his e-mails that morning, Petraeus discovered that a woman in his hometown of Cornwall-on-Hudson, New York, had sent him a copy of the Rudyard Kipling poem "If." He read:

> *If you can keep your head when all about you*
> *Are losing theirs and blaming it on you . . .*

As he read on, the lines took on a personal meaning:

> *If you can meet with Triumph and Disaster*
> *And treat those two imposters just the same;*
> *If you can bear to hear the truth you've spoken*
> *Twisted by knaves to make a trap for fools . . .*

Just after noon that day, Petraeus and Crocker arrived in the cavernous hearing room in the Cannon House Office Building, with its gold trim, heavy drapes and massive chandeliers. The crowds of reporters, TV cameras and protesters had arrived hours earlier, filling every inch of the room and giving the event a circuslike atmosphere. Folding chairs had been brought in to accommodate more than 100 House members, each of whom would be given an opportunity to question the general and the ambassador.

David Gergen, a former adviser to five presidents, said on CNN that it was "the most important testimony of any general in 40 years."

About 1:30 P.M., Petraeus began reading his opening statement. He could hear the cameras of the photographers clicking in bursts, like so many muffled machine guns.

Suddenly, he had the strange sensation of looking down on himself as he recited his statement. It was a bizarre what-in-the-world-are-you-doing moment, an out-of-body experience.

As the hearing droned on, he found his seat so low that he had to sit forward, almost at attention, with his hands on the table. His back began to ache. During breaks, he gobbled Motrin pain relievers.

Throughout a long day that stretched into night, Petraeus and Crocker remained calm and measured, answering every conceivable question about the war. Petraeus said there had been enough progress that a Marine Expeditionary Unit deployed as part of the surge would depart that month, followed in December by the redeployment of an Army brigade. Still, he warned about too fast a withdrawal. He likened the task in Iraq to "building the world's largest airplane while in flight, while getting shot at."

"Petraeus Backs Initial Pullout; General Praises Progress, Warns Against 'Rushing to Failure'" read the next day's front-page *Washington Post* headline. The testimony was praised as credible. Petraeus and Crocker had bought the president more time.

That morning, the sixth anniversary of the 9/11 attacks, Petraeus and Crocker were at the Senate for another marathon. Bush invited congressional leaders to the White House to discuss the Petraeus and Crocker testimonies and to hear them out about Iraq. The president was upbeat. His general and his ambassador had performed well.

Sitting next to the president in the Cabinet Room, Senate Majority Leader Harry Reid, the Nevada Democrat who disapproved of the war and of Bush, noticed an expression of bravado on Bush's face. Reid thought it inappropriate on what should have been a somber anniversary.

Bush said that radical Islamic jihadists were using the war as a recruiting tool, though he didn't seem troubled by it. "Of course, al Qaeda needs recruits, because we're *killin'* 'em," he said, giving a slight smile. "We're *killin'* 'em all."

Jack Keane met with the vice president in the West Wing on Thursday, September 13, two days after Petraeus and Crocker had completed their testimony. The general sat in a chair by the vice president's desk and again expressed his concern about the persistent pressure on Petraeus from the Joint Chiefs, Admiral Fallon and their staffs, who graded his work, insisting on studies and reports to justify even the smallest request for additional forces.

Suddenly, Bush walked in with his chief of staff, Josh Bolten. Everyone said hello, and Bolten left.

"You know, Dick, this is a nice office you have here," Bush said, looking around admiringly. He made it sound as if it were his first visit to Cheney's office, only about 100 paces from the Oval Office.

"Well, Mr. President," Cheney said, "this was your father's office," referring to the eight years when Bush's father served as Reagan's vice president from 1981 to 1989.

"Yeah, okay," Bush said, gazing around. "It looks a little different."

The president turned to Keane. "I know you're talking to Dave," Bush said to the former Army vice chief of staff. "I respect the chain of command."

Keane thought this meant that the president felt he couldn't bring in Petraeus directly because Gates and Admiral Fallon would also have to be present.

"I know that the Joint Chiefs and the Pentagon have some concerns," Bush said. "One is about the Army and the Marine Corps and the impact of the war on them. And the second is about other contingencies and the lack of" forces for a strategic response to those contingencies.

"Mr. President," Keane said, "in all due respect, the issue of the contingencies, for the life of me, I don't see how losing the war in Iraq could possibly help us with any of these potential contingencies. And that's what we're risking by not getting it right here." Defeat, or any sign of weakness, would shake relationships with allies, particularly where the ties already were tenuous, he said, and would encourage adventurism by adversaries. "It seems to me we have to win the war first."

Bush nodded.

Keane repeated his worry about the toll the Joint Chiefs, the Cent-Com staff and Fallon were having on Petraeus. "There is very little preparation for somebody who grows up in a military culture to have an unsupportive chain of command above you and still be succeeding. You normally get fired." Petraeus "is under a national spotlight, and clearly the national interest of the United States and its credibility are at stake, and you're at the point of a spear and then that whole shaft is not in support of you." The result, he said, is that Petraeus "starts to look for ways to get rid of this pressure, which means some kind of accommodation." The proof was that Petraeus had already agreed to take out one brigade by December.

The president said he wanted Keane to deliver a personal message to Petraeus from the commander in chief. He laid out his thoughts, said good-bye and left.

Keane went to the large West Wing lobby, sat down among the couches and chairs and wrote down the president's words. Then he called Petraeus and said they had to meet.

That evening, in a nationally televised address, the president delivered an upbeat assessment. He said Petraeus and Crocker had concluded "that conditions in Iraq are improving; that we are seizing the initiative from the enemy; and that the troop surge is working."

He referred to the turnaround that had taken place in Anbar province with the help of local tribes. In Baghdad, he said, "sectarian killings are down, and ordinary life is beginning to return."

The Iraqi government had a long way to go, but the president said the security gains would allow the United States to not replace about 2,200 Marines scheduled to leave Anbar later in September, and to bring home another Army combat brigade by Christmas. He said Petraeus expected to be able to reduce troop levels from 20 combat brigades to 15 by July 2008, meaning that the troops from the surge would be coming home.

"The principle guiding my decisions on troop levels in Iraq is 'return on success,'" Bush explained. "The more successful we are, the more American troops can return home." He said they would not all come home on his watch. "Success," he said, "will require U.S. political, economic and security engagement that extends beyond my presidency. . . .

"Some say the gains we are making in Iraq come too late," Bush said. "They are mistaken. It is never too late to deal a blow to al Qaeda.

It is never too late to advance freedom. And it is never too late to support our troops in a fight they can win."

At a press conference the next day, September 14, Gates mentioned that he hoped to be able to reduce troop levels in Iraq to 100,000 by the end of 2008. It was a more dramatic reduction than either Petraeus or Bush had endorsed. His comments landed on the front page of newspapers around the country the next day, with headlines such as "Gates Seeks Bigger Troop Cut."

Petraeus called Gates's military assistant, Lieutenant General Pete Chiarelli.

"Whoa," he said. "What's up?"

"Oh, don't worry," Chiarelli replied. "He knows. It's okay. He got a little ahead of himself. We'll wind this back down."

The defense secretary later said he saw no way to reduce to 100,000 troops by the time Bush left office. "The process has gone a little slower," he acknowledged publicly. Petraeus had a detailed plan. The Iraqi government and security forces were a work in progress. And he didn't want to rush it, Gates said. "We'll just have to take it a step at a time."

On Saturday, September 15, Keane went to Quarters 12-A at Fort Myer, in Arlington, Virginia, where Petraeus and his wife, Holly, had Army housing while he was stationed in Iraq. Petraeus would soon be heading back to Baghdad.

The two men sat alone, and Keane described his meeting with the president and vice president. He took out the piece of paper on which he had written the president's message to Petraeus and read it aloud:

"I respect the chain of command. I know that the Joint Chiefs and the Pentagon have some concerns. One is about the Army and Marine Corps and the impact of the war on them. And the second is about other contingencies and the lack of strategic response to those contingencies.

"I want Dave to know that I want him to win. That's the mission. He will have as much force as he needs for as long as he needs it.

"When he feels he wants to make further reductions, he should only make those reductions based on the conditions in Iraq that he believes justify those reductions. These two concerns that we are discussing back here in Washington—about contingency operations and the needs of the Army and the Marine Corps—they are not your concerns. They are my concerns.

"I do not want to change the strategy until the strategy has succeeded. I waited over three years for a successful strategy. And I'm not giving up on it prematurely. I am not reducing further unless you are convinced that we should reduce further."

It was a message of total support. No ground commander could ask for more. That Bush had sent it through backchannels, or even at all, revealed the depth and intensity of disagreements between the president and the military establishment in Washington. He hadn't even told Gates or Hadley he had sent it.

Hadley, who at first was confident he would have known about such a message, later confirmed with Bush that it had been sent. When I asked the president about it in 2008, he explained why he sent the message through Keane. "I just want Dave to know that I want to win. And whatever he needs, obviously within capabilities, he'll have. I don't want my commander to think that they're dealing with a president who's so overly concerned about the latest Gallup poll or politics that he is worried about making a decision or recommendation that will make me feel uncomfortable."

After hearing the president's message from Keane, Petraeus said, "I wish he'd tell CentCom and the Pentagon that." These were the people he had to deal with every day, and they had a very different perspective. The concerns of Washington, as always, were visited upon the commander in the field.

"I tried," Keane told him. He hoped the president and Cheney would force Gates, the Joint Chiefs and the Central Command to embrace the same game plan.

Petraeus said his congressional testimony had been an ordeal he had not anticipated. Sitting at attention in a chair that first day for ten and a half hours had been excruciating. Then, the absurdity of only a few breaks and little nourishment. He said he'd been prepared for the policy disagreements, but he'd been taken aback by the assaults on his character. The "General Betray Us" ad had been particularly hard. "Everybody sort of gets used to that," Petraeus said, "because everybody talks about it. But when it's you, when it's your name and your picture that's there, it's definitely an assault on your character." He said he didn't know if he could ever get over it.

Keane said that as vice chief of the Army, he had given testimony half a dozen times a year. But it had never been about his character. "You have to understand how unusual this is, that kind of behavior," he said.

Keane saw that his friend was emotionally devastated. During his televised testimony, he had seemed a little wounded, but that had made the presentation more effective. There had been nothing defensive or triumphant about it.

Though Petraeus had already agreed to return in six months for a public update to Congress, Keane told him, "If you can engineer not coming back, you should do that." That would be hard because his appearance had taken much of the pressure off the Bush administration. "But if you do come back," Keane continued, "given what we know will continue to take place, unless our assumptions are wrong, you'll have even more of a success story to tell, and I think that level of angst against this whole issue of Iraq will be diminished. I can't predict it for sure, but my sense of it is that while it won't be a love-in, I don't think you're going to get this kind of response.

"The real issue for you is that your entire military life, everything prior to this, and everything that comes after this is defined by one issue: Iraq. You've joined a select group of generals, and we haven't had one quite like this since Vietnam. Given the fact that you're succeeding and will continue to succeed, I think you're closer to the World War II generals than you are to the Vietnam ones." Dwight Eisenhower was the obvious model. "What you will do in the remaining months will define you for the rest of your military career and the rest of your life.

"The issue here is making sure that we don't squander the gains that we have made. It's very frustrating that you have to stand up against your chain of command every single day, to have to fight for this, as opposed to being supported by it."

Petraeus said the Army was considering him for new posts after Iraq. Among them: the four-star spot as NATO commander, the Central Command post that Admiral Fallon currently held, or the head of the Training and Doctrine Command (TRADOC), which oversees Army training, development of operational doctrine and procurement of new weapons systems.

"Dave, TRADOC?" Keane said, half scolding. "C'mon. TRADOC is an important command. I'm not disputing that." But "You have to understand who you are now and what's happened to you." He meant what he'd said about Petraeus being more like the World War II generals. "We haven't had a general like you in a long time. You may not realize it, but you have more influence than any other military leader in this country right now. More that the Joint Chiefs, more than the chairman, certainly more than the CentCom commander." Petraeus's ability to shape public opinion was unmatched. "What you have is beyond what any other leader has," including the president. "You've achieved that status because of the transformation you've made in this war. Everybody knows that this couldn't have been done without you. So given that reality, that is a platform that you're standing on, whether you like it or not."

"I hadn't thought about it that way," Petraeus said.

"So," Keane said laughing, "the TRADOC assignment is out of the question. No thoughtful leader will let you be assigned to TRADOC. That's not going to happen." Speaking as a former superior and for the Army, he added, "We've invested in you. If you want to stay in the military, you certainly will be permitted. You can make a case for you not staying, because there's no job after this that will compare to it."

The implied suggestion was politics.

"There's only two positions you should go to," Keane said. "One would be CentCom. The stature that you've achieved would pay us high dividends as leverage and influence in the region. No other military leader could. This region is the center of gravity for international security and strife in the world."

In the 20th century it had been Europe, where two world wars had been fought. But now it was the Middle East. "We will fight other wars here," Keane said.

The other possibility was chairman of the Joint Chiefs, but that depended on how long Petraeus decided to serve. The new chairman, Admiral Mullen, was just starting a two-year term, so the job wouldn't open up again until 2009 at the earliest.

At Central Command headquarters in Tampa, Fallon could feel his influence waning. He sensed that Petraeus had a "jumper cable" to the White House that circumvented him and the normal chain of command. Still, his relationship with Petraeus had improved substantially over the course of the year, and in Fallon's view, they both had arrived at the conclusion that they could be down to four or five brigades in Iraq within two to three years, though neither would say that publicly.

Fallon continued to be outspoken, however. He told Gates, "If you think this is undercutting the effectiveness of our ability to do work here, just tell me and I'll eject myself."

"Keep working," Gates said, hardly a rousing endorsement.

39

Back in Baghdad, Petraeus became increasingly immersed in the smallest details of Iraqi government operations. A top priority was helping the new government make political progress, but he found that that came in fits and starts, one painfully slow inch at a time. It meant that no issue was too small, no problem too mundane. He refereed internal turf battles and argued over issues more suited to a local city council than to a national government.

At one meeting with the senior Iraqi ministers, Petraeus remarked that a huge number of vehicles owned by the Iraqi government before the 2003 invasion were still marked as Iraqi government vehicles, though it wasn't clear who was driving them. "The majority of kidnap operations," he said, "are conducted with government vehicles." In addition, he said many were not obeying orders at the various checkpoints around Baghdad. So how did the government intend to get control of its inventory?

The Iraqi minister of interior proposed that new markings be required and that "we should accept only an authorization signed personally by a minister that the vehicle is legitimate."

Petraeus grimaced. Until recently, the minister of defense had had to sign even the smallest contracts personally and would spend hours signing foot-high stacks of paper.

The minister of defense said he had appointed the deputy ground force commander to head a committee to oversee "the proper marking and control of vehicles." A major security problem had been turned over to a committee.

"The answer to everything is to appoint a committee, and then you have to help the committee," Petraeus complained privately, though he maintained that things did get done over time, however slowly.

During that same meeting with senior officials, Petraeus and the ministers couldn't agree on which phone numbers to use for the new joint security stations throughout Baghdad, which were manned by U.S. troops, Iraqi army and Iraqi police—the heart of Petraeus's population security strategy. As it turned out, some of the stations didn't even have telephone landlines. After much discussion, they settled on some cell phone numbers for the stations.

On another occasion, Petraeus scolded an Iraqi lieutenant general for the lack of junior officers and noncommissioned officers (NCOs) in the Iraqi army. "We all know what the problem is," Petraeus said angrily. "The problem is that you don't have an NCO corps or junior officers who'll hold your soldiers to standards. Everybody knows this. We've been talking about it for months." In the U.S. Army, noncommissioned and junior officers are the heart and soul of an effective unit. "So where's your plan to get the NCOs? We should be talking here about how to fix the problem, not your coming in wasting our time telling us a problem we all already know."

Afterward, Petraeus stopped an American adviser to the Iraqis and said he wanted to ask the Iraqi lieutenant general to lunch. "Tell him that I really think highly of him and I was just trying to help him," he said. "Tell him I'm not attacking him personally."

At one meeting of the Ministerial Committee on National Security (MCNS), which included Maliki and other top officials in the government, the problem at hand was that the acting minister of transportation had failed to pay the bill for six months to Global Strategies Group, a British contractor that supplied security at Baghdad International Airport. The contract, worth $500 million a year, was in danger of lapsing.

"The problem," said Barham Salih, the deputy prime minister, "is that other countries won't bring their planes here without security assurances."

"This is a huge situation," Petraeus said. "It's not only here, but we have to work also on Basra and the seaport at Umm Qasr that are equally important because that's the only seaport in the country. There must be a firm trusted by the international air carriers charged with security." If not, flights would cease in Baghdad, further isolating the country. Iraq's place in the new global economy could suffer a serious, if not irreparable, setback.

The top ministers in Iraq, along with the country's prime minister and the American commanding general, then turned to the issue of scrap metal. Petraeus cited a study that showed Iraq had as much as $16 billion of scrap metal strewn all over the country. It included shipwrecks that were obstructing the port at Umm Qasr. He said that the minister of industry and minerals would require $75 million to begin the project to clean up and reuse the scrap. But he noticed that the $75 million was not there.

Salih confirmed that the money wasn't in the budget. He said they hoped to privatize the scrap metal project. He promised to keep working on it.

At 1 P.M. on October 2, Iraqi National Security Adviser Mowaffak al-Rubaie went to see Rice at the State Department. Though he was keenly aware that Petraeus and Crocker were calling most of the shots in his country, a new "Status of Forces Agreement" that would allow U.S. forces to remain in Iraq needed to be negotiated. "We don't necessarily need to publicize this," Rubaie told her. Prime Minister Maliki wanted to "eliminate the irritants that are apparent violations of Iraqi sovereignty."

"This is really Doug Lute's problem," Rice said, shifting the responsibility to the new Iraq coordinator in the White House, the 1975 West Point graduate Bush had appointed the administration's "war czar" for Iraq and Afghanistan nearly five months earlier. "He will be the team leader for the United States in getting this relationship developed."

"Well, you have to help us," Rubaie said.

Rice said a working group needed to be set up, but at a meeting she'd attended, Bush had told Iraqi President Jalal Talabani, "They don't want this agreement to happen in the middle of the U.S. election's political season. Because then will it not only be difficult to pass in the U.S., but it may be impossible under those circumstances to pass in Iraq."

"We need a stronger central government," Rubaie said. "And this one isn't. It won't be strong unless you, the United States, become much more aggressive with those people who are obstructionists." He meant the Sunnis and their foreign allies such as the Saudis.

"Okay," Rice replied, "Who do we need to push? What do we need to push?"

"Help us with the political bloc leaders" such as Hashimi, the Sunni vice president of Iraq, he said, "so that they know that they cannot simply resort to violence rather than participate in the political process. You take care of the Sunni party, and we'll take care of Moqtada. We'll take care of the Shia."

Rice asked about the administrative boundaries of the provinces, an issue in dispute.

"There is a general paralysis," Rubaie said. "Total stagnation."

"Why?"

"Because all these administrative boundaries are written in blood," Rubaie said. "And no one will agree voluntarily to change them. There'll be a fight about it." He added, "Very simply, only you, the United States, have enough influence to influence the region. We do not. Only you, by a real dialogue, can do something about Syria and Iran. We cannot."

At 3 P.M. that day, General Doug Lute met Rubaie in a small conference room adjacent to the White House Situation Room. Rubaie told him the Iraqis were having real problems buying U.S. weapons. "We would prefer to have the majority of our weapons in the army, at least, to be to U.S. and NATO standards."

"To be perfectly frank with you," Lute said, "what we have is a Cold War system. Deputy Secretary England is in charge of reforming the foreign military sales system to meet the needs in Afghanistan and particularly Iraq," and a team was working on it.

"Well, we have to put this on the fast track," Rubaie said. The system was way too slow.

Lute agreed, but the system had needed reform for years.

"If you have a problem, call direct," Lute said. "Here's a bunch of my cards." He handed Rubaie several of his White House business cards.

On the sensitive issue of Sadr's militias, Rubaie said it was better for the Iraqi security forces to go after them. "Even if we do it dirtier," he said, "even if we make mistakes, even if we take more casualties, let us do it. We're willing to spill more blood."

"Well," Lute said, "I thought the Iraq security forces did most of this, anyway."

"In reality, no," Rubaie said. "The U.S. is moving the security forces there. It's all seen as a U.S. operation, not as an independent Iraqi operation. Let us make mistakes while you're still around."

On October 4, Rubaie went to see Deputy Defense Secretary Gordon England and Eric Edelman, the undersecretary for policy.

Rubaie told them that Maliki and his government would need lots of help to show more progress by April 2008, when Petraeus and Crocker were scheduled to give their next report to Congress.

"If the Congress doesn't see you as progressing," England said, "we don't get the money, we can't help you, and it's over."

"I have a message from the prime minister," Rubaie said. "It's for the secretary"—meaning Gates. "It's about the Iraqi security volunteers, who some people are calling the Sunni militias. In the mixed areas, because the government of Iraq has to be in charge, it has to be the paymaster." But currently, the United States was paying them. "The coalition is persuaded to go for a quick fix, but the government of Iraq has to be in the lead. It has to establish its policy and its processes. And this is an area of enormous friction between us." The Shia-led government didn't like the many arrangements with Sunnis. He continued, "This looks like an act of desperation by the coalition, who is finding any way that it can to generate force so it can leave." He said this "quick fix technique" could succeed only in all-Sunni or all-Shia areas. "Even in Sadr City, there is a 10 percent Sunni population."

"Petraeus and Odierno are certainly aware of this," said Edelman.

"Yes," Rubaie replied. "But realize that the people brought in have to be seen as value added to the Iraqi security forces, not undermining them. . . . It is a first principle of unity of command that one person be in charge."

While he was at it, Rubaie also complained again about the slowness of acquiring U.S. weapons, warning them, "This will slow down your drawdown."

Jack Keane heard through the Pentagon grapevine that Admiral Michael Mullen, the newly appointed chairman of the Joint Chiefs of Staff, had told colleagues that one of his first plans was to "get Keane back in the box." Keane called and arranged an appointment with Mullen.

"This is a difficult session for me," Mullen said, "but I don't want you going to Iraq anymore and helping Petraeus."

"What the hell? What are you talking about?" Keane asked.

"You've diminished the office of the chairman of the Joint Chiefs," Mullen said. It wasn't clear to the American people who was actually in charge of the military.

"C'mon, stop it," Keane said. "The American people don't even know who the hell I am. This is Washington, D.C., stuff. You can't be serious."

"Yeah, I am," Mullen said.

Keane tried to tell him how in late 2006 he had gone to Rumsfeld and Pace with his complaints about the Iraq War strategy. He had wound up meeting with the president on December 11, 2006, because General Pace had recommended him.

"You probably resent the fact that I've been supporting Petraeus and the execution of the policy and tried to insulate him and protect him from some of the stuff that's going on in this town and in this building," Keane said. "I don't make any apologies for that."

Mullen said that he had become acutely aware of the strains on the Army and the Marine Corps. Military families were shouldering the strain, and the military was losing quality officers.

"Mike, all of that's true," Keane said. "But this is true every time we fight a war of any consequence." Wars break armies, and they have to be put back together. That's the price of war. But the price was worth it. "You've not talked one time about winning here, Mike. Not one time, have you mentioned . . . 'I want to win in Iraq.' I mean, do you?"

It was an insulting question to put to a fellow military man.

"Of course, I want to win," Mullen said.

"I assume you do," Keane replied, "but to the degree that you're putting pressure on Petraeus to reduce forces, you're taking far too much risk, and that risk is in losing and not winning."

"Well," Mullen said, "we're just going to disagree."

"You really don't want me to help Petraeus?" Keane asked. "Dave Petraeus, no matter who he wants to talk to over there, no matter what size he is, shape he is, what his views are, given Petraeus's responsibility—he's got the toughest job anybody in uniform has—why wouldn't you let him have that?"

"No," Mullen said, "I don't want to take the chance. I don't want you to do it."

End of meeting.

Afterward, when Keane couldn't get clearance to go to Iraq, he called Petraeus, who told him that he had met with Mullen in Iraq before he had taken over as chairman and that Mullen had told him he didn't want Keane coming again. "I was really surprised," Petraeus said.

Petraeus told Mullen that he could understand how the chairman would not appreciate Keane's involvement. But it wasn't meddling. Keane was providing military advice to the president, the vice president and Petraeus himself. "Perhaps you could consider embracing him and trying to draw on that over time."

"No," Mullen said. It was too soon in his tenure, and he was trying to reestablish the authority of the chairman's office.

Keane called John Hannah in Cheney's office to report what had happened. Shortly afterward, Keane received a call from Army Lieutenant General Skip Sharp, the director of Mullen's Joint Staff.

"We have an unusual request," Sharp said. "We have a request from the White House to provide assurances that General Keane will be able to visit Iraq and assist General Petraeus as he has been doing in the past." Sharp was apparently doing some staff work before passing the request to Admiral Mullen. "This is really bizarre. Do you have any idea why this would be happening?"

"Yeah, of course," Keane said. "I've been told I can't go."

"Who told you that?"

"The chairman." There was a long silence as Sharp realized it was his boss. "Skip, are you there?"

"I'm trying to figure out what the hell is going on here."

Keane later spoke with Lieutenant General Chiarelli, Gates's military assistant.

"The secretary has received some notes," Chiarelli said, so now the secretary and his office are telling everyone, "General Keane, as in the past, as well as in the future, can go into Iraq to assist General Petraeus whenever they want it to happen. We have no problem with any of that."

Vice President Cheney had noticed Admiral Mullen putting the hammer down on Keane. He didn't agree, so he had sent a note and talked to Gates about how important Keane's assistance had been. The president had also requested that Keane be allowed back in Iraq.

40

President Talabani, a main Kurdish leader, had once said, "Iraq is like a bouquet of flowers—many different, but who nonetheless combine into one." Satterfield thought of Iraq more like a tank of "mutually carnivorous fish."

The intelligence and diplomatic reporting continued to show that several of Maliki's top aides were highly sectarian with strong ties to individuals or movements deeply opposed to the U.S. presence in Iraq, such as Iranians and Sadrists.

Foremost among these aides was Bassima al-Jaidri, an intense woman with three graduate degrees whom one senior U.S. intelligence official described as "anti-Western, anti-American, anti-occupation." Jaidri and Prime Minister Maliki had become confidants, according to intelligence and military officials. She had enormous influence and had used her position in Maliki's office to order Iraqi army generals and others in the government to halt operations against Shia militia members.

"Don't arrest that person," Jaidri would order, and the generals would comply. "Halt that operation," she would say, and they would obey. The previous year, she had been instrumental in the widespread cleansing of Sunnis from neighborhoods in Baghdad. The American embassy, the U.S. intelligence agencies and Petraeus's command had spent countless hours trying unsuccessfully to figure out how to get her out of Maliki's office. Their efforts, including one to get her an ambassadorship abroad, failed.

Jaidri continued to wield immense power. At one point in 2007, despite her strong anti-Sunni disposition, Maliki appointed her to head the committee for national reconciliation that was supposed to bring the Shia and Sunnis together. The intelligence analysts could hardly believe it.

Satterfield reported to Rice that Maliki was increasingly losing touch with reality. Sadr and his Mahdi Army had fragmented and were on the run, and Maliki attributed this to his own leadership genius. He also credited his efforts with the Anbar Awakening and the recruitment of the Sunni Concerned Local Citizens, which were fighting al Qaeda and helping reduce violence in key areas. Maliki's misguided narrative went something like this: Iraq is back on its feet. Everything's fine. We've turned the corner.

Whenever Crocker, Petraeus, Satterfield or other Americans tried to push Maliki, he invoked the support he had from Bush. "I have the support of the president," Maliki said once. "I don't have to listen to you."

In Washington, the president and his principals debated what to do. Bush felt he had developed an important personal relationship with Maliki, and he judged that if he had too blunt a conversation with the prime minister, he might push him too far, causing him to retreat and withdraw. Puncturing Maliki's self-esteem could backfire.

Maliki had been living an incredibly stressful life over the last 18 months. Too much push, Bush concluded, and they could wind up with a new government and a new leader. And who might that be? No one knew. How long might it take? No one had any idea. The intelligence analysts said there was no one on the horizon to take Maliki's place. They said his fall could create "total chaos." They would be taking "a leap into the unknown," the president said. No, thank you. The others could push and be blunt with Maliki, but not him. He would stick with the prime minister they had and continue to support and reassure Maliki both publicly and privately.

•   •   •

That winter, Petraeus's evening reading was again about the Civil War. This time it was *April 1865: The Month That Saved America,* by Jay Winik.

Petraeus read about his hero, General Ulysses S. Grant, and his efforts to force Robert E. Lee out of Richmond. "We've got to squeeze them everywhere," Grant declared, a strategy that Petraeus had adopted in Iraq. At one point, Lee was desperately trying to reach a train that was supposed to have food supplies for his starving soldiers. Lee rushed forward, racing on his famous horse, Traveller, and threw open the boxcar doors. He found only ammunition.

General Lee, Petraeus read, made sure not to let his shoulders slump in front of his men. He didn't want them to sense his frustration. Petraeus took comfort in what generals before him had gone through and embraced the importance of leading even in the face of doubt and disappointment. He resolved that his soldiers would never see his shoulders slump.

On Tuesday, December 18, a week before Christmas, Rice flew to Iraq, where she visited a Provincial Reconstruction Team in Kirkuk and then went on to Baghdad. That evening, she had a 25-minute routine meeting with Maliki, Petraeus and Crocker. At about 7:30 P.M., Rice asked the others to leave so she could talk privately with the prime minister.

"You're not succeeding," she told him bluntly, and attempted to list all the management and political problems in his government. The negotiations over new U.N. Security Council resolutions and other matters could not be conducted with only the prime minister and members of his staff. In the future, negotiations would have to include a representative team of Sunnis and Kurds. "You cannot succeed alone," she said.

"There are people in your office who do not serve you or the Iraqi nation well."

"Who are they?" Maliki asked.

"Prime Minister," she said, "I am not going to list their names, but I can tell you, you are not well served by people."

"I've been waiting a long time to have this conversation," Maliki said. "Let me describe how hard it is to be prime minister of Iraq." He was surrounded by enemies, he said. The presidency council, consisting of Talabani, Hashimi and Mahdi, conspired against him and blocked legislation at every turn. He mentioned specific actions and alleged plots—a mixture of suspicion and accurate descriptions of the struggle for power amid sectarian hatreds. The meeting lasted an hour and 15 minutes.

Afterward, Rice was delayed an hour on the next leg of her trip because a suspected IED had to be cleared. She told her advisers that she would have to come back to Baghdad as soon as possible to establish a rhythm of talking directly to Maliki and other leaders—Sunni, Shia and Kurd.

Later that month, Maliki's fears came dangerously close to being fulfilled. The Kurds, along with Sunni leader Hashimi, formed a coalition and drafted a manifesto saying the government was not performing. They hoped to force a vote of no confidence and bring down the Maliki government. Maliki raged, and two of his top advisers, Sadiq al-Rikabi and Sami al-Askeri, urged him to force an open debate. They drafted an in-your-face rebuttal. But Rubaie, the national security adviser, warned, "That'll just make it public, and you'll have a real mess. Deal with this privately."

Maliki eventually sent Rubaie north to meet with Barzani, the Kurdish leader, who finally agreed not to press a manifesto that might precipitate a government collapse.

On January 12, 2008, the president met with Petraeus alone at Camp Arifjan, a U.S. base in Kuwait. He reaffirmed the message that he had sent through Jack Keane—whatever you need, if it's possible, you will get it. If it was not possible, they would find some way to make it so.

"Okay, now let me confirm now," Bush asked, "They said that you want to go to SHAPE," the military designation for Supreme Headquarters Allied Powers Europe.

"Yes, sir," Petraeus said. "I know a lot of the folks in NATO because of this job. They contribute troops. I've been to London a bunch of times." He had been the military assistant to the American commander in Europe. "I was a one-star and a three-star in NATO." NATO was involved in Afghanistan, where he could contribute. "My wife speaks French, German, Italian and everything else." Her father, General William Knowlton, had finished his career as a U.S. representative to NATO.

"Okay, got it," Bush said.

On January 15, 2008, Rice again went to Baghdad and met with the leaders that Maliki had identified as enemies—Talabani, Barzani, Hashimi, Mahdi. She put the problems in legislative terms, focusing on the political, not the sectarian, and defended Maliki to the others. "Don't tell me he is blocking things," Rice said. "You have more votes."

Maliki overestimated the temporary restraint of his enemies and in a public speech in February 2008 announced, "National reconciliation efforts have succeeded in Iraq, and the Iraqis have once again become loving brothers."

In March, Petraeus and Maliki were intensifying plans to launch joint military operations in Basra, the city in southeastern Iraq about 15 miles from the Iranian border. It would be a test of whether Maliki would get serious about imposing central government rule in the hotbed of Iranian influence and Shia extremism. At the end of the month, intelligence showed that Maliki was going to go it alone, even personally oversee the Iraqi army attack on the ground.

"Holy shit!" Ambassador Crocker said. Petraeus couldn't believe it. Maliki and his forces were ill prepared. Everything could be lost in one impulsive gamble. How could they walk him back? Soon Maliki sent official word that he was going ahead. Many officials in the U.S. government were horrified.

Not the president. Maliki was taking a bold step in the face of all rational judgment. Bush believed it was the right cause. "This is a defining moment in the history of a free Iraq," the president said at a press conference. He also passed word to Maliki: Good for you, keep it up, forward to victory.

•   •   •

Moqtada al-Sadr's forces in Sadr City began shelling the Green Zone in March 2008. U.S. officials locked the area down, and 1,000 officials crowded into one of Saddam's hardened masonry structures, where they slept on cots. One rocket hit the doorway of Ambassador Crocker's residence, and a heavy-caliber 240 millimeter shell—more than nine inches in diameter—hit 100 meters away and blew out windows.

Soon, Maliki had Iraqi forces moving into Sadr City. He was countering the allegations of the Sunni Arabs that he was an Iranian puppet or a tool of the Shia militias. He was taking on the most powerful Shia militia of all, the Mahdi Army, the most direct and important Iranian asset on the ground in Iraq.

Satterfield could barely listen to Bush's inflated rhetoric. It was too overstated, too triumphant, too victorious. Bush was feeling renewed confidence because of the lower levels of violence, thanks to Petraeus's and Crocker's work.

From watching the president up close for several years, Satterfield had reached some conclusions. If Bush believed something was right, he believed it would succeed. Its very rightness ensured ultimate success. Democracy and freedom were right. Therefore, they would win out.

Bush, Satterfield observed, tolerated no doubt. His words and actions constantly reminded those around him that he was in charge. He was the decider. As a result, he often made biting jokes or asides to colleagues that Satterfield found deeply wounding and cutting. In one instance, Rice had raised a budget issue at a meeting.

"Now's not the time and place for you to be advocating the interests of your building," Bush had said. "I told you, I don't want to hear about that."

Satterfield found it offensive, though Rice didn't seem too bothered.

The president had little patience for briefings. "Speed it up. This isn't my first rodeo," he would say often to those presenting. It was difficult to brief him because he would interject his own narrative, questions or off-putting jokes. Presentations and discussions rarely unfolded in a logical, comprehensive fashion. Satterfield thought this reflected an insecurity in Bush. The president was a bully.

Satterfield kept making regular trips to Iraq to help in the delicate negotiations on the Status of Forces Agreement that would allow U.S. forces to remain. As he dealt with various Iraqi officials, he was faced with the extent to which the United States had created and propped up a kind of puppet government. With 157,000 troops, more than 180,000 contractors and 1,000 State Department officials in Iraq, the United States was the shadow government. He knew of no parallel in history. If the United States withdrew, the whole house of cards would crumble.

By the spring of 2008, Satterfield found Baghdad more secure than on previous visits. The markets were open. Iraqis and U.S. troops walked through the streets without body armor. But areas were closed off and surrounded by barricades. Nothing about Baghdad's state reflected normal city life. He concluded that a precipitous U.S. withdrawal would ignite a new struggle for power, resources and territory, and the beneficiaries would be al Qaeda and Iran.

When Satterfield pondered the future of Iraq, he was stumped. There was such a mix of good and bad news. Which would win out? What would last? What would survive?

"You cannot credibly speak of an end state," he said. "Where's the endgame? What's the endgame?"

In early March 2008, *Esquire* magazine published a long article by Thomas P. M. Barnett, a former professor at the Naval War College who had traveled with Admiral Fallon to the Middle East. Headlined "The Man Between War and Peace," the provocative 7,500-word article was mostly laudatory but portrayed Fallon as "brazenly challenging" Bush and Cheney on Iran policy.

Fallon was in Baghdad on March 11 when the article was made public. He realized instantly the uproar it would cause. Fallon knew he already was on shaky ground. Days earlier, he had warned Gates that the article was coming. But now he called again.

"I think I need to be gone," Fallon said.

"Okay," Gates said.

The defense secretary could have offered a vote of confidence and backed his commander. If that had happened, Fallon would have stayed. But he had the feeling that Gates wanted him out, and he now had a reason to make it happen.

One of Fallon's aides called Petraeus and said Fallon wanted to meet.

"Okay, I'll come right over."

The aide said it was intensely personal and Fallon wanted to meet in either Petraeus's office or his quarters.

Fallon arrived in Petraeus's quarters just as Gates was appearing live on Fox News.

"I've resigned," Fallon said. He'd held the job only a year.

"You did?" Petraeus said, astonished, as they turned to watch Gates on television.

"I have approved Admiral Fallon's request to retire with reluctance and regret," the defense secretary said. "Admiral Fallon reached this difficult decision entirely on his own. I believe it was the right thing to do even though I do not believe there are, in fact, significant differences between his views and administration policy."

Keane saw an opening. He sent an e-mail to Chiarelli, Gates's military assistant, at 3:27 P.M. on March 12—the day he was arriving in Iraq for another visit.

"Subject: Food for Thought

"Pete, a way ahead after Fox Fallon: Announce Petraeus as replacement but do not assign till fall or early winter . . . Assign Odierno, who will have had six months back in states, to replace Petraeus . . . Believe this provides the strongest team we have to the key vacancies. For what it's worth. Best, JK."

Chiarelli e-mailed back 20 minutes later.

"Sir—do you want me to pass to the SD?" The secretary of defense.

By all means, Keane said.

•   •   •

During that visit to Iraq, Keane talked to Petraeus about the future. Petraeus's next assignment as NATO commander seemed set.

NATO was important, Keane said, but its time had passed. The international center of gravity had moved to the Middle East. "We're going to be here for 50 years minimum, most of the time hopefully preventing wars, and on occasion having to fight one, dealing with radical Islam, our economic interests in the region and trying to achieve stability." We should be thinking strategically from the military perspective about how to support a national strategy for the region. "Where should we have bases? Where should we have prepositioned equipment? Where should we have forward industrial bases? Because it doesn't make any sense to keep sending that stuff home."

This shift would have huge implications for how the U.S. military would be educated and trained, as well as how the Army would deal with other organizations. "We're going to do it anyway because we don't have a choice," Keane said. "So the issue is: Get over it. Come to grips with it." The Army didn't want that. "It wants to end a war and go home. But that's not going to happen."

Petraeus seemed to agree but waxed nostalgically about NATO.

He had to go to CentCom, Keane said. "Dave, you're the only guy, okay?"

"Wouldn't it be nice to have some time with Holly?"

"Just get the region used to your spouse going to the region with you. Start breaking the paradigm. Come on, we've got a secretary of state that runs all around the region, and she's a woman."

Petraeus shrugged.

"Nobody's going to have the kind of authority and credibility and power and influence that you have," Keane kept pushing. "This is coming to you. It's got to come to you. If people do the analysis, who else should have this job but you?"

The phone rang.

"Hey, Pete," Petraeus said into the phone, "what have you got?" It was Chiarelli.

"Three o'clock, okay, I've got it."

"Secretary of defense wants to talk to me at three o'clock," he told Keane.

"You know what this is, don't you?"

"I suspect I know."

"Hopefully, you'll give him the right answer."

While in Iraq, Keane also met with Senator McCain, who was making another tour of the country. "No doubt in my mind that Petraeus has to go to CentCom," he said. The stature that Petraeus had achieved in and outside the United States was off the charts, and the country had not had such a general for many years. The region respected power. If Petraeus was made Central Commander, he would have more authority and gravitas than his predecessors. More important, once he took over the command, the U.S. strategy in the Middle East would be locked in, no matter who won the 2008 presidential race.

For Petraeus's replacement, Keane also saw only one choice: Ray Odierno. He was head and shoulders above anyone else. He was tough and knew all the players. Odierno had just come back from Iraq to be nominated as vice chief of staff of the Army, so they would probably have to wait six months or so to give him time at home. But that would be fine.

McCain seemed to agree and said he would call President Bush.

Not long after Fallon resigned, Admiral Mullen called Petraeus. "I know you're going to Europe," he said, but, "Would you be willing to do the CentCom job?"

"Let me talk to my wife," Petraeus replied.

He raised the possibility with Holly. She had been looking forward to the NATO assignment. But with what she later called "controlled disappointment," she acquiesced. She knew the unpredictability of Army life and often told friends that she never measured for new curtains until she saw the orders.

41

On Thursday, April 3, Keane gave Vice President Cheney a briefing on his trip to Iraq.

"The security improvement, I believe, is a stunning achievement in such a short period of time," Keane said. "It's unprecedented in the annals of counterinsurgency practice."

The bad news was that, due to the inefficiency of the Maliki government, money was very slow reaching the provinces. From a strategic point of view, Keane said, "We cannot lose militarily. It is impossible at this point because the al Qaeda, for all intents and purposes, has been operationally defeated." They still had to be defeated in the north, but the vast majority of the Sunni insurgents were working with the United States.

"We could still lose politically," he said. "We could lose if our leaders in Washington do not want to continue to sustain the gains that have been made and want to pull out precipitously. If that happens, there could be dire consequences, and we could still lose."

One third of the U.S. forces in Baghdad would be coming out by July, and 60 percent of those in Anbar. It was a drastic reduction made possible by the Sons of Iraq, who now numbered 90,000. In addition, the Iraq security forces had grown by 100,000—an imperfect but significant addition.

The big problem was the Diyala River valley in the north, as well as Mosul and the Jazeera desert to its west. However, Keane said, "our forces are inadequate." Petraeus did not want to utilize the pro-American, Sunni Sons of Iraq in that region because of the tensions between the Sunnis and Kurds. "I would discount that and do it anyway," Keane said, "because the program is so positive, and I think it's worth trying." There were lots of retired Iraqi generals up there, all Sunnis, and he thought the CIA should pay them to reduce the level of violence.

"Aren't they getting some of the pension money?" Cheney asked.

"That hasn't kicked in," Keane answered. A pension law had been passed, and some money was being paid out, but it was not enough to make a difference.

Turning to the south of Iraq, Keane said the Basra area was now the most important strategically, but the command had been slow to get involved. It couldn't be left to the Iraqis, which had been the plan, because of the Iranian influence there and the U.S. interest in diminishing it. The British, who had kept their forces in the south for a long time, said the problem was one of politics, not security. "This is a myth," Keane said. Basra was now like "the wild West," and the Basra police chief had told Keane that 80 percent of the police were aligned with some kind of militia. The area was a major security threat.

Brigadier General Qassem Suleimani, the commander of the Iranian Quds Force, an elite arm of the Revolutionary Guard, had been working the area for ten years. "He's smart, he's savvy, and he's ruthless," Keane said. The Iranians have "two Hezbollah-type battalions that are in Basra." Keane said the administration needed a comprehensive strategy to counter and defeat Iranian influence inside Iraq. It needed to involve the other countries in the region that had interests in Iraq. This could not just be left to Petraeus. The local Iraqi general in the Basra area was incompetent, Keane said. He had told the general to his face that his plan to disarm the militias was absurd. Weapons were so accessible in Iraq that anyone who had his taken could get a replacement within hours. Keane said that the Joint Special Operations Command (JSOC), or what he called classified forces, needed to be brought in to kill or capture enemy leaders.

He said drawing down to 15 U.S. brigades by July was risky. They still needed a minimum of 18, but they could not afford to go below 15 anytime in 2008. Keane then repeated his pitch that Petraeus move up to take Central Command and Odierno to the Iraq command.

"Is Ray willing to go?" Cheney asked.

Keane was working on that.

Four days later, on April 7, Gates invited Keane to brief him at the Pentagon. Keane summarized what he had told Cheney: the security improvement was stunning and validated Petraeus's counterinsurgency practices. He said they needed 18 brigades now and that there was no way to go below 15 during 2008. "One or two brigades could be decisive in Iraq," he said, and should not be held back. Fortunately, he said, there were ways to overcome the lack of 18 U.S. brigades by using the Sons of Iraq.

"Having a stable, secure Iraq is achievable," Keane said. "A government that is aligned with the United States—this is now an achievable end for us. We could not have visualized that in 2006, and we could not have visualized that in 2007. Our opponents who disagree with us say that the war costs too much." He recited statistics about how the United States had spent much higher percentages of its gross domestic product on past wars than it was spending in Iraq and Afghanistan. He said they needed an active campaign to counter the arguments of the war critics.

Most important: "Assign Petraeus to CentCom." Delay the assignment until the fall. Make Odierno the new Iraq commander. He said that Odierno, as the corps commander, was the unsung hero of the Iraq strategy. "When he arrived and started taking his responsibility in November [2006], he started to change the strategy and put together plans to do that and immediately ran into an obstacle called General Casey."

Odierno had both intellect and moral courage, Keane said. After Petraeus had taken over in February 2007, he had gone to Iraq and looked at the situation in detail, realizing that Odierno needed eight to 10 surge brigades rather than the five he was getting. Of course, there were no more brigades, so Odierno had improvised.

But most important, Odierno realized the opportunity of the turn-around in Anbar province. According to Keane, Odierno had told his staff, "What's happening in Anbar can happen all around Iraq. We've got to understand how powerful this is." He instructed part of his staff to do nothing but find Sunnis or former insurgents willing to help the U.S. forces. "He can see things clearly that others cannot," Keane said. "He is in a class by himself.

"Let's be frank about what's happening here. We are going to have a new administration. Do we want these policies continued or not? Do we want the best guys in there who were involved in these policies, who were advocates for them? Let's assume we have a Democratic administration and they want to pull this thing out quickly, and now they have to deal with General Petraeus and General Odierno. There will be a price to be paid to override them."

On April 8, Petraeus and Crocker were back before Congress to offer an update. "We haven't turned any corners," Petraeus said. "We haven't seen any lights at the end of the tunnel. The champagne bottle's been pushed to the back of the refrigerator." There had been progress, but it was "fragile and reversible," he said.

But in mid-May, Petraeus sounded a note of hope in an e-mail to a friend back in the United States. He said he was coming closer to answering the question he had posed five years earlier on the windswept desert during the first week of the invasion: "Tell me how this ends."

"Had the lowest level of security incidents last week since Iraq blew up in April 2004," he wrote. "Nothing's easy, but I can, on some days, very vaguely see how this might end."

Gates knew that Petraeus was the natural choice to replace Fallon. No other commander was more familiar wih Iraq, and he had worked closely and effectively with Odierno. Two weeks later, on April 23, Gates called a press conference.

"With the concurrence of the chairman of the Joint Chiefs of Staff, I have recommended and the president has approved and will nominate

General David Petraeus as the new commander of Central Command. We will withdraw the nomination of Lieutenant General Ray Odierno to be the Army vice chief of staff and nominate him to return to Baghdad as the new Multinational Force Iraq commander, replacing General Petraeus."

Gates said Petraeus would likely stay in Iraq through the late summer or fall. Odierno had been home barely two months and needed the break between tours.

"This arrangement probably preserves the likelihood of continued momentum and progress," Gates said. Asked by a reporter whether the move marked a "stay-the-course approach" for the administration, the secretary answered, "I think that the course, certainly, that General Petraeus has set has been a successful course. So frankly, I think staying that course is not a bad idea."

By early May 2008, the U.S. intelligence agencies viewed Maliki in a slightly better light than they had in the past, but plenty of problems remained. "He is no longer willing to take direction," said one of the most experienced senior intelligence officials in the U.S. government. "He's his own man." But his governing skills remained weak. "He is still sectarian and he hasn't changed his spots. In his heart of hearts, he hates Sunnis. He has no use for Kurds," the official said. Making political progress still depended on reconciliation. "And he gets an 'F' as far as that goes." A month later, after watching Maliki undertake operations against the Shia militias, the same official said he would raise Maliki's grade to "a solid B."

By the summer of 2008, Cheney was getting ready to move on. After four decades in government, he believed he had had quite a run. He felt the invasion of Iraq had been the right decision. They had planted a democratically elected government in the heart of the Middle East and, he maintained, administered a major defeat to al Qaeda. The Bush antiterrorist policies, in his view, were sound. The Terrorist Surveillance Program, which authorized the National Security Agency to listen in on suspected terrorists in the United States without court-ordered warrants, had been necessary. After all the debate, Congress had finally authorized its essential elements. Despite the controversy and allegations of torture, he believed that the administration had established an effective and necessary interrogation program for high-value detainees, even though harsh techniques such as sleep deprivation and waterboarding, or simulated drowning, had been used against multiple detainees.

Cheney was convinced that the heart and soul of the 2008 presidential campaign would get down to national security—the Iraq War and the aggressive antiterrorism programs. He thought McCain would continue them and that Obama wouldn't.

During Cheney's years in the Bush administration, the official vice presidential residence at the Naval Observatory in northwest Washington had been transformed into a kind of fortress with a hardened bunker in case of another terrorist attack. Armed security guards, multiple barriers, explosive-sniffing dogs, and two fences protected the house, a stately but weathered 19th-century Queen Anne mansion on a hill.

In the summer of 2008, the house needed work. The light-colored carpets and furniture were visibly worn. There was a barren feel to the first-floor rooms, as if the moving out had already commenced. Cheney was proud of his three-foot-long shelf of well-read leather-bound fly-fishing books, many of them classics. He loved to hunt and fly-fish, and after nearly eight years in office, the summer home he and his wife Lynne owned near the winding Snake River in Wyoming beckoned. But a decade earlier they had bought a lot in McLean, the toniest of the Virginia suburbs, and were overseeing the construction of a new house. Come 2009, they would move there. He might prefer just heading back to the Snake River, but Lynne wanted to stay near Washington. They had spent decades in the capital, and their two daughters and six grandchildren lived in the area.

Cheney knew that for much of America, he had become the Darth Vader of his generation, a dark and shadowy villain. He claimed he didn't worry about it, said he had developed a pretty thick skin and just rolled with the punches. He could have settled for the more traditional role, a vice presidency with duties at state funerals and fund-raisers. He had attended more than his share of fund-raisers, where he was always a big draw for red-meat Republicans. But early on, he had set out to make his vice presidency a consequential one. He had been at the center of the action, shaping policy and working to strengthen presidential powers.

Everything had its price. If his chosen path meant leaving office as a symbol of belligerency and excess, he was willing to pay.

Cheney's hard-nosed approach to the vice presidency mirrored his view of the presidency itself. In 2005, I interviewed Cheney in his West Wing office about President Gerald Ford. He had served as Ford's chief of staff and remained a great admirer of the former president. At the end of the interview, I asked a more general question. It was a softball really, an attempt to glean how he viewed the presidency after seeing it up close for three decades.

"What's the definition of the job of president?" I asked. "My definition is to determine what the next stage of good is for the majority of people in the country . . . and then develop a plan to carry it out, and then carry it out."

"That's not the way I think about it," Cheney replied. "I tend to think about it more in terms of there are certain things the nation has to do, things that have to get done. Sometimes very unpleasant things. Sometimes committing troops to combat, going to war. And the president of the United States is the one who's charged with that responsibility . . .

"The stuff you need the president for is the hard stuff. And not everything they have is hard. They do a lot of things that are symbolic, and the symbolic aspects of the presidency are important. And they can inspire, they can set goals and objectives—'Let's go to the moon'— but when they earn their pay is when they have to sit down and make those really tough decisions that in effect are life-and-death decisions that affect the safety and security and survival of the nation, and most especially those people that we send into harm's way to guarantee that we can defeat our enemies, support our friends, and protect the nation.

"That's the way I think of it."

By July 2008, Gates felt that Iraq was better off than he could have dreamed 18 months earlier, when he had moved into the secretary's office. The main problem now was Iraqi overconfidence. Prime Minister Maliki thought he was on a roll after months of waning violence.

But Gates realized the entire endeavor remained fragile. As the presidential election loomed just four months away, Gates felt that if the election somehow became a referendum on Iraq, the American public would still want to end the war faster than he thought would be wise for the long-term position of the United States. For the moment, it looked like the real issue in the campaign, as far as the war was concerned, was not going to be whether to draw down, but rather how quickly. Gates hoped that in their new positions, Petraeus and Odierno would be able to determine the pace of withdrawal as they saw fit. Better to let them dictate the terms than the politics of the moment. In a sense, the two generals could hold public opinion at bay.

When Gates talked privately about the war with both Republicans and Democrats in Congress, he warned, "For those of you who were critical that nobody paid enough attention to the generals at the beginning of the war, has it occurred to you that you don't want to make that mistake at the end of the war?"

Hadley was hopeful by July 2008 that real political progress was taking shape in Iraq. For the first time, the Shia and Sunnis seemed to be working things out nonviolently, though still at a painfully slow pace. The sectarian violence that had raged two years earlier, reaching a peak of more than 2,000 "ethno-sectarian deaths" a month, had now dropped to almost none, according to General Petraeus. Overall, violent attacks were down to about 200 a week from the peak of 1,550.

That was nearly 30 a day—still a lot, but Hadley found the reduction a real measure of success.

He went so far as to say that al Qaeda had done the United States and Iraq a favor. Its brutal tactics and violent, oppressive rule over many local communities had given the Iraqi population a reason to unify against it. Hadley believed that the United States' invasion in 2003 had liberated Iraq, but also had been a humiliation to its citizens. He was convinced that people ultimately had to win their own fight—"self-liberation," as he called it. Al Qaeda had given the Iraqis the opportunity to win their own freedom and construct their own narrative of triumph.

Hadley even handed out copies of a June 28, 2008, Thomas Friedman column in *The New York Times* that discussed the psychological importance of "self-liberation" in the Middle East. But Friedman, who had initially supported the war but later became of strong critic of its management, had ended his column with a warning.

"Iraq is miles away from being healthy," he wrote. "And now that Iraqi's Shiite and Sunni communities are taking more responsibility for their own country, you are also going to see an intense power struggle over who dominates within each community. With oil dollars piling up, there is a lot to fight over. But if we're lucky, this struggle will play out primarily in the political arena. If we're not lucky? Well, let's just hope we're lucky."

"I have believed from day one that Iraq was going to change the face of the Middle East. I've never stopped believing that," Rice said during a meeting at the State Department in May 2008. She acknowledged that, "There were times in '06 when I wondered if it was going to change the face of the Middle East for the better or not."

During those difficult days, when the violence had kept rising and the very fabric of Iraqi society was rending, Rice had thought often about the early days of the Cold War in the late 1940s, and she drew comparisons to that conflict and the present one. Back then, the future of Europe remained uncertain. The United States had undertaken the Marshall Plan to help rebuild countries devastated by World War II, and President Harry Truman had enunciated his doctrine to protect Greece and Turkey, all in the name of stopping the spread of communism. The Soviets exploded a nuclear weapon years before expected, and the communists took over China. The Korean War broke out and became increasingly unpopular.

Despite all that, the Soviet Union had collapsed in 1991, and the Cold War had ended without a shot being fired.

"The long view helps," Rice said. "That's where I went for repose. And I think that's where the president did, too."

Rice rejected the notion that the Middle East had been stable and that the Bush administration had come along and disturbed it by invading Iraq. Anyone who felt that way simply didn't know what they were talking about. "What stability? Saddam Hussein shooting at our aircraft and attacking his neighbors and seeking WMD and starting a war every few years? Syrian forces, 30 years in Lebanon? Yasser Arafat stealing the Palestinian people blind and refusing to have peace?" No, it had been anything but stable, she said, and the malignant politics prevalent in the radical mosques had helped produced al Qaeda. Sure, al Qaeda was now threatening to gain a foothold in Southeast Asia and the Horn of Africa, but the real battleground lay in the Middle East, Rice maintained. "If you defeat them in the Middle East, they can't win.

"There's nothing that I'm prouder of than the liberation of Iraq," she said without hesitation. "Did we screw up parts of it? Sure. It was a big, historical episode, and a lot of it wasn't handled very well. I'd be the first to say that."

But Rice largely absolved herself of accountability for the problems with the war during its first 20 months, when she had been Bush's national security adviser. "It wasn't my responsibility to manage Iraq," she said. "Look, the fact of the matter is, as national security adviser you have a lot of responsibility and no authority."

Rice maintained that one result of the war was a better U.S. posture in the Middle East. Yes, Iran had escalated its involvement in what she called "troubled Arab waters," including backing Hezbollah in Lebanon and increasing its influence in the Palestinian territories. But "on the heels of Iraq, you can structure a Middle East in which Iran is kept at bay," she insisted.

Rice considered the war nothing less than "the realignment of the Middle East. On one side you've got Saudi Arabia, Egypt, Jordan, the Gulf states" supporting nonextremists. "At the other side, you've got the Iranians, Hezbollah, Hamas," with Syria shifting sides, she said. She felt there had never been a greater cohesion of American allies in the Middle East, even if those countries didn't want to be on the front lines supporting the United States publicly.

On Iran, she said, "We're not going to let them use negotiations as a cover while they continued to improve their nuclear capability. . . . Iran is a challenge to our interests because they essentially want to become the dominant regional player. We're not going to sit and talk to them about how they become the other great superpower in the Middle East, which is what they would like.

"You can't let them acquire nuclear capability because that emboldens and strengthens their claim to great-power status in the region." She said the history of the Soviet Union is instructive. "The Soviet Union became nuclear before it became powerful," she said. It had tested the first nuclear weapon on April 29, 1949. "And the fact that it became nuclear made it powerful. And I don't want that to happen with Iran, which is why if I could get them out of that business, we'll have time.

"There is an image of diplomacy that is making deals to stabilize the situation. That set of deals that stabilize the Middle East has now broken down, and good riddance. Now, before we restabilize the Middle East, let's be careful that we don't just lock in bad deals. A month ago, Jaish al-Mahdi [JAM] was holding Basra. Jaish al-Mahdi is no longer holding Basra. Tactically, I would much rather have a conversation with the Iranians today about Iraq than a month ago."

Rice said that a Palestinian state would deprive Iran of chances to meddle. "A strong Iraq, I think, is going to turn out to be their worst nightmare," she added.

"I don't want to make a grand bargain with the Ayatollah Khamenei and [President] Ahmadinejad because that grand bargain is going to be a kind of least-common-denominator view of what the Middle East ought to look like." She again turned to the Soviet model. Maybe in

Iran the "revolutionary fervor" would start to burn out and diminish what she called Iranian "expansionist" goals.

"Let's say that we have to live with the Iranian revolutionary state for some time," she said. "Would I rather live with the Iranian revolutionary state with American forces in Iraq, Afghanistan, the Gulf and Central Asia? You bet. When I hear that the Iranians are just sitting pretty, I think, well, how does their neighborhood look to them? What has really happened is that starting with Gulf War I [in 1991], but really after 9/11, the center of American power has moved." Following World War II, the United States had moved the epicenter of its military power to Europe, but it had taken four decades for the Soviet Union to collapse. Now American power had shifted to the Middle East.

Rice agreed that on inauguration day 2009, no new president, Democrat or Republican, was going to say the Bush administration had fixed the Middle East. But she thought that over time a democratic Iraq would emerge, Iran would be transformed or defeated, Lebanon would be free of Syrian forces, and a Palestinian state would exist. And none of it would be possible without some future victory in Iraq. "This president not just set it in motion," Rice said, "he's put in place now the foundation where it can come out in our favor.

"We didn't come here to maintain the status quo. And the status quo was cracking in the Middle East. It was coming undone. And it was going to be ugly one way or another. And it just might as well have been ugly in a good cause. And now, with the emergence of Iraq as it is, it's going to be bumpy and it's going to be difficult but big. Historical change always is. There are a lot of things if I could go back and do them differently, I would. But the one I would not do differently is, we should have liberated Iraq. I'd do it a thousand times again. I'd do it a thousand times again."

Later, in the Oval Office, I asked the president if he too would do it "a thousand times again."

"The decision to remove Saddam Hussein was the right decision," he said. "And I say it to [everyone] and to the American people often."

What does the president worry about most in the national security area? Iran? Iraq? Afghanistan?

"The rise of radical fundamentalism," Bush said, "that is fueled by nation states and/or carried out by these groups that are buried into, kind of, soft spots around the world, and that these people who are committed to harming America and our allies possess the capacity to use a serious weapon. They used airplanes last time on our soil. The idea of them having, you know, biological or chemical or nuclear capabilities is very frightening."

I told him that Rice had put it this way: "Every day is September 12."

"That's a very poetic way of putting it," Bush said. "But the biggest thing a president must fear—and a citizen must fear—is that our country becomes isolationist, saying it doesn't matter what happens over there. I think about the security of the country all the time.

"Every day, sitting in this chair, you realize your biggest responsibility is to prevent America from being attacked again. It's the safeguard of the people. I also recognize that the long-term security, however, is going to be advanced by helping people realize the blessings of liberty. And to some in America, that sounds Pollyanna-ish. However, if you look at history, it's worked. It's worked. It's a powerful force. Liberty is transformative. And the great debate right now is whether or not, you know, Muslims can self-govern and whether it's worthwhile to try to help them become free societies. I believe strongly that free societies, or hopeful societies, which marginalize these extremists, they just wither, they wither away over time. And that's not to say there won't be killers, there won't be people out there. But there will be a lot less. The public will turn on them. Kind of the ultimate concerned citizens group."

Josh Bolten ducked into the Oval Office and said the president had lunch plans that were being delayed.

"Yeah. Get moving, will you?" Bush said to me. "How many more questions you got?"

"Just a few," I said. Of course, I had hundreds.

"You better hurry. I'm getting less indulgent, as you can tell. One, I'm hungry. And two, I've got a meeting."

"Is there kind of a recentering of American power in the Middle East?"

"Absolutely," the president said. "And it should be. And the reason it should be: It is the place from which a deadly attack emanated. And it is the place where further deadly attacks could emanate. And the idea of Iran having a nuclear weapon is a very dangerous notion. And the idea of people having the capacity, a nuclear capacity, and giving those to terrorist groups that could use them is a very deadly notion, as well."

"And so we have military hegemony in the region, just as a practical matter?"

"We've got freedom hegemony we're pushing. We're trying to get freedom moving," the president answered.

Hadley interrupted, alerting the president to the implications of the word "hegemony," which means dominance or leadership and carries overtones of empire.

"It's a loaded word, as you know very well," the president said.

"It *is* a loaded word," I agreed.

"It's a very tricky, Washington loaded word. It was very tricky, Woodward. Very tricky," Bush said.

"No, no," I protested.

"Yeah, it was. It was a Woodward tactic," Bush said.

"If you listen to Secretary Rice on this subject," I said, "She is absolutely delighted that we have all these troops there."

"Is it hegemonistic to have troops in Korea?" the president said. "I don't think so. Is it hegemonistic to have them in Japan? Was it hegemonistic to have them in Germany? No. The United States has got a troop presence at the invitation of governments to help provide security. Which, by the way, also helps provide the conditions for liberty to advance."

EPILOGUE

The outcome of the Iraq War, now in its sixth year, remains uncertain. General Petraeus has it right when he says that any gains are "fragile and reversible."

Derek Harvey, the defense intelligence expert and early pessimist about the prospects for the war, had nonetheless become a cautious optimist by May 2008. As a strategic adviser reporting directly to Petraeus, Harvey saw much to suggest that the worst might be over.

Prime Minister Maliki had removed 1,400 Shia from the ministry of interior for sectarian actions. Maliki still had a sectarian bent himself, but his actions suggested more evenhandedness. The number of vehicle bombs had dropped from a high of 130 a month in March 2007 to 30 a month in May 2008—still a significant number. Most were detonated at checkpoints and killed far fewer people. Only occasionally did a vehicle bomb penetrate into large markets to inflict the massive casualties reminiscent of 2006–07.

Violence was down so much in a few places that some U.S. soldiers were not receiving combat action badges because there was no fighting in their area. The Mahdi Army, responsible for much of the Shia sectarian violence, was fracturing in Harvey's view. Iran, which the United States was trying to hold at bay, seemed increasingly unpopular in Iraq. Several polls showed that 65 to 70 percent of Iraqis viewed Iran negatively.

Harvey believed that fatigue had overwhelmed Iraq and an increasing number of citizens had simply grown weary of five years of war. Though anti-Americanism and doubts about the U.S. role remained fierce, support for al Qaeda had dropped significantly. He believed that the United States had been hurt in the region but al Qaeda had been hurt more. It was possible, he thought, that the Iraqi insurgency might become like the Irish Republican Army, capable of conducting urban bombings but not potent enough to cripple social, political and economic life.

As always, there were caveats and lingering concerns. The Iraqi elections, scheduled for the end of 2008, could bring about a sea change in the provinces and Baghdad, Harvey believed. For example, the 41-seat Baghdad council had only one Sunni member. That could rise to as many as 18 Sunnis after the elections. Though it might suggest reconciliation, it ran the risk of triggering a Shia backlash.

There was always the possibility of what Harvey called "wildcat hits," unexpected catastrophic events such as the assassination of Maliki or a massive attack on Americans, either on U.S. bases or in the Green Zone. Support for the insurgency continued to flow into Iraq through Syria and Jordan, and the Iranian-Syrian alliance, he believed, was stronger than ever. Iran continued its lethal and carefully calibrated efforts to support and train militias and supply them with advanced IEDs, the Explosively Formed Penetrators (EFPs), which could pierce almost any armored vehicle.

Harvey believed the critical task to defeat the will of the enemy and rebuild communities so that violent elements could not filter back in was monumental and far from complete in Iraq. Reminders that life was still far from normal occurred regularly, such as the June 17, 2008, explosion that killed at least 65 people, the highest-casualty bombing in Baghdad in three months. Uncertainty was more constant than electricity.

The ministries of interior and defense—the two best run in the Iraqi government—had some 2,500 American advisers holding everything together. Without them, Harvey worried, they would increasingly return to their sectarian ways.

Meanwhile, China, Russia, India, and the U.S. partners in Europe were salivating at what seemed like American exhaustion and over-commitment in Iraq. These countries seemed eager to pounce and exploit opportunities in the oil-rich Middle East, further weakening America's standing in the world.

The headline splashed across the top of *The Washington Post* on June 14, 2008, "Key Iraqi Leaders Deliver Setbacks to U.S.," encapsulated the constant uncertainty of the war. Maliki announced that negotiations over the status of U.S. forces in Iraq had "reached a dead end." Though talks would continue, he said, "We could not give amnesty to a [U.S.] soldier carrying arms on our ground. We will never give it." At the same time, Moqtada al-Sadr announced he was setting up a new paramilitary unit to attack U.S. forces, effectively ending his stand-down from the previous year. It was almost as if Maliki and Sadr were competing to see who could more aggressively push the American hand off the bicycle seat.

Even if Iraq turned out well in the end, Harvey did not think it would rescue the Bush legacy. For too many years—from 2003 to the end of 2006—the president had not been frank about the costs, duration, and challenges of what had been undertaken in the Iraq War. As he shuffled from Washington to Baghdad and back, Harvey wondered about the president. "What was he really seeing, and why did it take so long for him to understand?"

As I complete my fourth book on President Bush and his wars, I keep returning to some key questions. Most important, how did Bush perform as commander in chief? Has the president set up and enforced a decision-making system worthy of the sacrifice he has asked of others, particularly the men and women of the U.S. military and their families? Has he been willing to entertain debate and consider alternative courses of action? Was he slow to act when his strategies were not working? Did he make the right changes? And did he make them in time? Was the Bush administration a place where people were held accountable?

The seeds to some of those answers can be found in my 2002 book, *Bush at War,* which provided a detailed account of the months after the September 11, 2001, terrorist attacks.

On the day of the attacks, the president's two public addresses were shaky, but over the next nine days he rallied his war cabinet and the nation. On September 20, he gave one of his finest, most confident speeches as president. Addressing Congress and 80 million Americans watching on television, he pledged to strike back.

"We will direct every resource at our command," he said. "I will not yield; I will not rest; I will not relent in waging this struggle for freedom and security for the American people." The applause inside the Capitol that night was thunderous and praise for the speech almost universal.

Just two weeks after the terrorist attacks, Rice, then Bush's national security adviser, was receiving a briefing at the CIA on covert operations inside Afghanistan when the president called her. He wanted to know if the military was going to be ready to start bombing Afghanistan right away. She explained that there might be a delay.

"Why? That's not acceptable!" the president roared.

Their conversation was cut short by a bad connection. When Rice reached the White House, she sprinted to her office, where Bush was already calling from the residence. She repeated that the military was not fully ready.

"That's unacceptable!" Bush said again. "Why is that?"

Rice explained that the U.S. military didn't have bases close to Afghanistan. The intelligence was weak. Targets were scarce. And the weather was deteriorating.

"I'm ready to go," he later told me. "Sometimes that's the way I am—fiery. . . . I can be an impatient person." On the eve of that first war, he was riddled with impatience.

In another instance, on October 25, 2001, after the bombing in Afghanistan had begun, Rice went to see the president. She reported that several members of his war cabinet were worried that the progress in the initial weeks was too slow. She suggested that he solicit their views at the NSC meeting the next morning. "I'll take care of it," he told her.

At the next day's meeting, Bush said, "I just want to make sure that all of us did agree on this plan, right?" He went around the table asking everyone to affirm allegiance to the plan. He asked if anyone had any ideas, but as I later wrote after interviewing everyone who had been in the room, "In fact the president had not really opened the door a crack for anyone to raise concerns or deal with any second thoughts. He was not really listening."

I first interviewed President Bush in the Oval Office on December 20, 2001, three months after the terrorist attacks. The war in Afghanistan appeared to be going well, with the overthrow of the Taliban regime and promising efforts to deny sanctuary to al Qaeda. Bush was jaunty and full of self-confidence. At 55, he was a young president, filled with certainty. He directed an aide to his desk to pull out three sheets with short biographies of al Qaeda leaders, each with a color photo. He showed how he had crossed through the pictures with a large "X" as each suspected terrorist leader was killed or captured.

"One time early on, I said, 'I'm a baseball fan. I want a scorecard.'" He was going to have a body count.

And he had major goals. "We're going to root out terror wherever it may exist," he said. He talked of achieving "world peace," and of creating unity at home. "The job of the president," he said, "is to unite the nation."

President Bush once said to me of the path he'd chosen, "I know it is hard for you to believe, but I have not doubted what we're doing. I have not doubted . . . There is no doubt in my mind we're doing the right thing. Not one doubt."

It wasn't so hard to believe. He repeatedly told me that his certainty was an asset. "A president has got to be the calcium in the backbone," he said. "If I weaken, the whole team weakens. If I'm doubtful, I can assure you there will be a lot of doubt. If my confidence level in our ability declines, it will send ripples throughout the whole organization. I mean, it's essential that we be confident and determined and united.

"I don't need people around me who are not steady . . . And if there's kind of a hand-wringing going on when times are tough, I don't like it."

He spoke a dozen times about his "instincts" or his "instinctive reactions," summarizing once, "I'm not a textbook player, I'm a gut player."

After I recounted these details in *Bush at War* many readers and a number of reviewers and columnists thought I had portrayed Bush as a strong, inspirational leader. But my account also showed that he didn't want an open, full debate that aired possible concerns and considered alternatives. He was the "gut player," the "calcium-in-the-backbone" leader who operated on the principle of "no doubt."

"His instincts are almost his second religion," I wrote. In the Afghanistan War, he had laid down the marker that his convictions would trump nearly everything and everyone else.

During an interview at his Crawford ranch on August 20, 2002, he had laid out his thinking about an Iraq war, which was still seven months away.

"As we think through Iraq," Bush said, "we may or may not attack. I have no idea yet. But it will be for the objective of making the world more peaceful."

"I will seize the opportunity to achieve big goals," he said, and on his own he brought up North Korea. He had identified it along with Iraq and Iran as an "axis of evil" in his State of the Union address earlier that year. He made it clear that Iraq and North Korea were linked in his mind. Bush leaned forward in his chair and spoke about his gut reaction to the North Korean leader.

"I loathe Kim Jong Il!" the president bellowed, waving his finger. "I've got a visceral reaction to this guy, because he is starving his people. And I have seen intelligence of these prison camps—they're huge—that he uses to break up families, and to torture people. I am appalled . . . It is visceral. Maybe it's my religion, maybe it's my—but I feel passionate about this." He said he'd been advised not to move too fast on North Korea, but he added, "Either you believe in freedom and . . . worry about the human condition or you don't.

"And I feel that way about the people of Iraq, by the way," he said, adding that Saddam Hussein was starving the Shia in outlying areas of Iraq. "There is a human condition that we must worry about."

But the president made it clear that he didn't think much of diplomacy. "You can't talk your way to a solution to a problem," he said, and the United States had the responsibility to lead. That triggered "resentment toward us," and caused people to say, "Bush is a unilateralist; America is unilateral." He added, "I've been to meetings where there's a kind of 'We must not act until we're all in agreement.' Well, we're never going to get people all in agreement about force and use of force." International coalitions or the United Nations were probably not viable ways to deal with dangerous rogue states, he said. "Confident action that will yield positive results provides kind of a slipstream into which reluctant nations and leaders can get behind."

Again, his blind faith in his instincts meant more than the concerns of his war cabinet and the international community.

My second book on Bush, *Plan of Attack*, recounted the president's decision making during the 16 months from November 2001 to the invasion in March 2003. During this period, Rumsfeld and the Central Command commander at the time, General Tommy Franks, gave the president a dozen detailed briefings on the invasion plan. Every meeting was about *how* to go to war. There was no meeting to discuss *whether* to go to war. The president had never questioned its rightness, and its rightness made it the only course.

Bush later acknowledged in interviews with me that he did not seek recommendations from four key people: his father, former President George H. W. Bush, who had overseen the first Gulf War in 1991; Secretary of State Colin Powell; Secretary of Defense Donald Rumsfeld; and CIA Director George Tenet.

When I pressed him a dozen times on what his father's advice on invading Iraq might have been, Bush dodged the questions and told me he couldn't recall. Finally, he said, "He is the wrong father to appeal to in terms of strength. There is a higher Father."

There was a momentum toward war and a lack of caution that the president embraced. His convictions were driving the march to war like a locomotive gaining steam.

In a December 2003 interview, nine months after the Iraq invasion,

Bush told me, "I believe we have a duty to free people." He wanted to liberate the Iraqis from oppression and said he had a "zeal" to do so. In May 2008, I asked if he still believed that.

"I do," he said. "It's very important, though, for you to understand that I have a set of beliefs that are inviolate: faith in the transformative power of freedom and the belief that people, if just given a chance, will choose free societies."

I have never doubted the sincerity of the president's convictions. But convictions alone are not enough. The decision to go to war is momentous. The decision to launch a preemptive war is doubly so and carries with it a great weight of responsibility.

In my 1991 book, *The Commanders,* on the invasion of Panama and the first Gulf War to oust Saddam from Kuwait, I wrote, "The decision to go to war is one that defines a nation, both to the world and, perhaps more importantly, to itself. There is no more serious business for a national government, no more accurate measure of national leadership."

A president must be able to get a clear-eyed, unbiased assessment of the war. The president must lead. For years, time and again, President Bush has displayed impatience, bravado and unsettling personal certainty about his decisions. The result has too often been impulsiveness and carelessness and, perhaps most troubling, a delayed reaction to realities and advice that run counter to his gut.

This was most evident in the three years after the invasion, the period covered in my third Bush book, *State of Denial,* published in September 2006. Bush and his administration had not openly acknowledged the severity of escalating violence and deterioration in Iraq. "With all Bush's upbeat talk and optimism," I wrote in the book's last line, "he had not told the American public the truth about what Iraq had become."

My reporting for this book showed that to be even more the case than I could have imagined.

In some ways, President Bush has changed very little since my first interview with him on December 20, 2001. He remains a man of few doubts, still following his gut, convinced that the path he has chosen is right. But in other ways, the 61-year-old president I encountered in May 2008 was a different man entirely. It wasn't just the inevitable aging. The presidency, not surprisingly, has worn on him. Seven years of war have taken a visible toll. His hair is much grayer, and the lines in his face deeper and more pronounced. Still fit for his age, he has a noticeable paunch and sometimes slouches in his chair.

During the first years of the Iraq War, the president always spoke about "winning" or "victory." By 2008, he seemed to have tempered his expectations. Twice in the interview when he mentioned "win," he immediately corrected himself and said "succeed," a subtle but definite scaling back of his once fiery rhetoric.

Since March 2003, when President Bush ordered the invasion of Iraq, about half a million men and women of the U.S. military have served there. More than 4,100 have died and another 30,000 have been seriously wounded. Tens of thousands of Iraqis have been killed. As I write this in the early summer of 2008, about 140,000 U.S. troops remain there.

In our final interview, the president talked irritably of how he believed there was an "elite" class in America that thought he could do nothing right. He was more guarded than ever, often answering that he could not remember details and emphasizing many times how much he had turned over to Steve Hadley. There was an air of resignation about him, as if he realized how little he could change in the eight months he had left as president.

He alternately insisted that he was "consumed" by the war, "reviewing every day," before adding, "But make sure you know, it's not as though I'm sitting behind the desk and totally overwhelmed by Iraq, because the president's got to do a lot of other things."

By his own ambitious goals of 2001, Bush had fallen short. He had not united the country but had added to its divisions, and he himself had become the nation's most divisive figure. Even the president acknowledged that he had failed "to change the tone in Washington." He had not rooted out terror wherever it existed. He had not achieved world peace. He had not attained victory in his two wars.

• • •

On August 7, 2007, my assistant Brady Dennis and I went to see former Defense Secretary Robert McNamara, one of the architects of the Vietnam War. In his 1995 book, *In Retrospect*, McNamara had owned up to his mistakes and concluded that the United States could have withdrawn from Vietnam much earlier without serious consequence to national security.

We sat with McNamara in the white-carpeted living room of his Watergate apartment. At 91, his mind was still lively, and his blue eyes still flickered with enthusiasm. Throughout the three-hour interview, he kept returning to one theme: The major disagreements about the Vietnam War too often had not been put on the table before President Johnson, especially with all his key advisers present. Too few people had expressed their reservations, and the president hadn't exactly sought them out.

"I am absolutely positive that most leaders wish to avoid confrontation among their senior people, particularly in front of them," McNamara said. "And that's a serious weakness. I think every leader should force his senior people to confront major issues in front of him." Presidents want to maintain harmony. "They steer away from conflict." McNamara believed that was a great disservice.

McNamara said he thought he was being loyal to Lyndon Johnson at the time by going along with the president's policy on the war. "As I look back on it," he said, "I should have been more forceful in forcing Johnson to address these issues." When he announced his resignation in 1967, he said, "I felt at the end very reluctant to expose the differences that existed. I was worried they might get out. And I was worried that they would make the job of the president more difficult, because [internal memos] basically said we're losing."

One final question: Who pays the price of war? I don't mean the billions of dollars spent each year on it. I mean the human cost. That falls to the 140,000 service members and to their loved ones. They are the ones losing limbs, losing lives, and losing years to deployments halfway around the world. A friend of mine labeled this the "ripple of human misery" that disperses slowly, quietly throughout every corner of the country, often unnoticed by the majority of Americans.

Those who serve and their families are the surrogates of all Americans. They bear the risk and the strain of a year or more in a violent foreign land. So many have spent their youth and spilled their blood in a fight far from home. What do we owe them? Everything. And what have we given them? Much less than they deserve.

President Bush has rarely leveled with the public to explain what he was doing and what should be expected. He did not seek sacrifice from most of the country when he had the chance. He did not even mobilize his own party. Republicans often voiced as much suspicion and distrust as Democrats.

The president rarely was the voice of realism on the Iraq War.

There is an encyclopedia of lessons for the next president to learn from Bush's management of the war. The first might be to trust the public with the truth, in all its pain and uncertainty. In the summer and early fall of 2006, when it was obvious the United States was failing in Iraq, the American people most likely would have rejoiced if the president had leveled with them, said he knew the strategy was not working and that he had begun an intensive review.

The president is correct when he says he should not make decisions based on polls or focus groups. But in a democracy, the public is not something just to "game" or "spin." The administration worried too much about a "hothouse" election year story of internal debate and strife and not enough about the war itself. In the decision not to level, the president gave up what could have been his greatest asset—public support.

"When did he decide to become commander in chief?" one of the people involved for years in Iraq War decision making asked me recently. "That is the question."

The answer is that there were moments, but far too few. After ordering the invasion, the president spent three years in denial and then delegated a strategy review to his national security adviser. Bush was intolerant of confrontations and in-depth debate. There was no deadline, no hurry. The president was engaged in the war rhetorically but maintained an odd detachment from its management. He never got a full handle on it, and over these years of war, too often he failed to lead.

As the Bush presidency becomes history, the wars he began will become part of another president's story.

"Most important question, really. There's going to be a new president-elect who will come in here," I asked during our last interview on May 21, 2008. "Not as a Democrat or a Republican, but as the president, what are you going to say to the new leader about what you are handing off in Iraq?"

He thought about it for a moment. "What I'll say is, 'Don't let it fail.'"

Every person has shortcomings. But a president's shortcomings are visited upon an entire nation and, in a major war, they are visited upon the world.

The next president will face a complex set of organizational, military, political and leadership challenges because of the Iraq War. It won't be solved with slogans or party doctrine, or through wishful thinking. When the next president steps into the Oval Office on January 20, 2009, and surveys what he has inherited, I suspect he will be sobered by all that has been left behind.

GLOSSARY

AIF: Anti-Iraqi forces.

Al Qaeda: International terrorist organization headed by Osama bin Laden.

AQI or AQIZ: Al Qaeda in Iraq. Homegrown terrorist organization affiliated with al Qaeda that sprang up after the U.S. invasion in March 2003.

Baath Party: Saddam Hussein's ruling political party in Iraq from 1968 to 2003.

Battalion: U.S. Army or Marine unit normally made up of about 600 to 800 personnel.

Brigade: U.S. Army or Marine unit normally made up of 3,000 or more personnel.

CentCom: Central Command. U.S. military command responsible for the Middle East and South Asia; headquartered in Tampa, Florida.

CPA: Coalition Provisional Authority. Agency responsible for Iraqi occupation from May 2003 to June 2004; led by L. Paul Bremer.

Dawa Party: "The Call"; small Shia party in Iraq that includes Prime Minister Nouri al-Maliki.

DDR: Disarmament, demobilization and reintegration of militias.

DIA: Defense Intelligence Agency. Coordinating intelligence agency in the Defense Department that reports to the secretary of defense but is subject to the coordinating authority of the director of national intelligence.

de-Baathification: Policy of removing Baath Party members from positions of responsibility in government, military and schools.

Defense Policy Board: Group of former officials, retired military officers and other experts who advise the secretary of defense on policy.

DNI: Director of national intelligence. Office established in 2005 that oversees and directs the activities of the various intelligence agencies.

DOD: Department of Defense.

EFP: Explosively formed projectile. A shaped charge capable of penetrating armor that is substantially more lethal than conventional IEDs.

GCC: Gulf Cooperation Council. Regional group made up of the United Arab Emirates, Bahrain, Saudi Arabia, Oman, Qatar, and Kuwait.

Green Zone: Also known as the International Zone. Heavily fortified area of central Baghdad where the Iraqi government and U.S. diplomatic presence are headquartered.

HUMINT: Human intelligence.

IED: Improvised explosive device. A makeshift bomb made of old munitions and other explosives, used by various al Qaeda and insurgent groups on or alongside roads.

ISF: Iraqi security forces.

Iraq Study Group: Bipartisan group formed March 2006, charged with conducting an independent assessment of the situation in Iraq.

J2: Intelligence directorate of the Joint Staff.

J3: Operations directorate of the Joint Staff.

J5: Strategic plans and policy directorate of the Joint Staff.

JAM or Mahdi Army: The Jaish al Mahdi. Militia headed by radical anti-American Shia cleric Moqtada al-Sadr.

JCS: Joint Chiefs of Staff.

JSAT: Joint Strategic Assessment Team. Group that advised General Petraeus in Iraq in early 2007.

JSOC: Joint Special Operations Command.

MCNS: Ministerial Committee on National Security. The high-level Iraqi policy council.

MNSTC-I and/or Minsticky: Multi-National Security Transition Command—Iraq. Training arm of the U.S. Army responsible for forming the new Iraqi army and police force.

NIE: National Intelligence Estimate.

NSA: National Security Agency. Responsible for intercepting foreign communications and protecting the communication and cryptographic systems and codes of the United States.

NSC: National Security Council. The president and his senior foreign policy makers, including the vice president, the secretaries of state and defense, the chairman of the Joint Chiefs of Staff and the director of national intelligence. The NSC staff is headed by the national security adviser.

OIF: Operation Iraqi Freedom. Name of the 2003 invasion and ongoing U.S. military operations in Iraq.

Operation Together Forward: Unsuccessful two-phase security plan to reduce violence in Baghdad that ran from June 2006 to October 2006.

PRT: Provincial Reconstruction Team. State Department civilian teams that coordinate rebuilding and government issues at the provincial level in Iraq.

RFF: Request for Forces. Official request by a battlefield commander for additional troops.

SCIRI or SIIC: Supreme Council for Islamic Revolution in Iraq. The leading Shia party in Iraq, it was renamed the Supreme Islamic Iraqi Council on May 12, 2007.

SecDef: Secretary of Defense.

SVTS or VTC: Secure video teleconference. Video and audio hook-up used between Washington and Baghdad.

Tank: Pentagon conference room designated for use by the Joint Chiefs of Staff.

NOTES

A NOTE ON SOURCES

Almost all of the Bush administration's internal deliberations on the Iraq War have been classified. Early in my reporting, I was able to obtain documents that provided glimpses of how the decision making evolved in 2006 and 2007. The White House agreed to declassify a dozen documents after my initial inquiries, and I was able to independently acquire dozens more.

Most of the information in this book was obtained from interviews with more than 150 people, including the president's national security team, senior deputies and other key players responsible for the intelligence, diplomacy and military operations in the Iraq War. Officials with firsthand knowledge of meetings, documents and events, employed at various levels of the White House staff, the departments of Defense and State, and the intelligence community also served as primary sources.

Most interviews were conducted on "background," meaning that the information provided could be used but the sources would not be identified by name in the book. Many sources were interviewed multiple times by me or my research assistant, Brady Dennis. We interviewed some sources a half-dozen times or more. Nearly everyone allowed us to record the interviews so the story could be told more fully and accurately, with the exact language they used.

I interviewed President Bush on the record in the Oval Office for nearly three hours on May 20–21, 2008. In all, I have interviewed him six times about the wars in Afghanistan and Iraq, for a total of nearly 11 hours. Past interviews from which I drew material for this book are noted.

In addition, critical information came from an array of documents—memos, letters, official notes, personal notes, briefing summaries, PowerPoint slides, e-mails, journals, calendars, agendas and chronologies. Where documents are quoted, we have had access to the originals or to copies.

The use of dialogue in meetings or conversations comes from at least one participant, usually more, as well as from written memos or contemporaneous notes. When thoughts, conclusions or feelings are attributed to a participant, that point of view has been obtained from that person directly, from the written record, or from a colleague whom the person told. Quotation marks are used when I judged the written record or firsthand recollections precise enough to justify their use. Quotation marks were not used when the sources were unsure about the exact wording, or when the documentation was unclear.

I have attempted to preserve the language of the main characters and sources as much as possible, using their words even when they are not directly quoted, reflecting the flavor of their speech and attitudes as best I could.

No reporter can with 100 percent accuracy re-create events that occurred months or even years earlier. The human memory is fallible, and the past often looks different in retrospect. By checking with numerous sources and comparing their accounts to the written record, I have tried to provide as accurate an account as possible.

I realize that because this book provides the first in-depth examination of the deliberations that led to the troop surge in Iraq, it is much closer to the first draft of history than the last. I have tried, as always, to find the best obtainable version of the truth.

PROLOGUE

The information in this chapter comes primarily from background interviews with seven firsthand sources.

7 *In 2005, after Hurricane Katrina:* Spencer S. Hsu and Susan B. Glasser, "FEMA Director Singled Out by Response Critics," *The Washington Post*, September 6, 2005, p. A1.

7 *The day before Bush's conversation:* SECRET Camp David agenda summary dated June 12, 2006, and declassified by the White House in 2008 in response to specific questions asked by the author. Casey's presentation was from 9:30 A.M. to 10:15 A.M.

7 *The plan, classified SECRET:* Author's review and dictated notes of a SECRET document dated June 12, 2006, consisting of a one-page security assessment, a counterinsurgency strategy and a joint campaign plan.

8 *I later read Hadley's statement:* Author interview with President George W. Bush, May 20, 2008.

9   *In his special file:* SECRET statistical review described to the author by a knowledgeable source.

9   *The president himself:* Interview with President George W. Bush, May 20, 2008, and several knowledgeable sources.

10 *As a first step:* SECRET Camp David agenda summary dated June 12, 2006, and declassified by the White House in 2008 in response to specific questions asked by the author.

10 *The morning had begun:* Author's review and dictated notes of a SECRET document dated June 12, 2006, consisting of a one-page security assessment, a counterinsurgency strategy and a joint campaign plan.

10 *Rice's State Department briefing:* SECRET Camp David agenda summary dated June 12, 2006, and declassified by the White House in 2008 in response to specific questions asked by the author. The State Department briefing was from 3:15 P.M. to 3:45 P.M.

12 *And yet, "I sense something":* Presidential Documents, June 14, 2006, p. 1133 (Vol. 42, No. 24), www.gpoaccess.gov/wcomp/v42no24.html.

12 *In an interview two years later:* Interview with President George W. Bush, May 20, 2008.

13 *Bush insisted he understood:* Interview with President George W. Bush, May 21, 2008.

13 *"What frustrated me is that":* Interview with President George W. Bush, May 20, 2008.

13 *"That's one of many questions":* Interview with President George W. Bush, May 21, 2008.

CHAPTER 1

The information in this chapter comes primarily from background interviews with five firsthand sources.

20 *The snowflake sent on October 28, 2003:* Author's review and dictated notes of a SECRET snowflake dated October 28, 2003.

CHAPTER 2

The information in this chapter comes primarily from background interviews with five firsthand sources.

22 *A SECRET analysis showed:* Author's review and dictated notes of a document dated January 8, 2005.

23 *Daily attacks doubled:* Chart of weekly security incidents in Iraq between January 2004 and May 2008.

26 *"With a month to go before elections":* A knowledgeable source's account of the December 2004 document.

28 *When I interviewed the president:* Interview with President George W. Bush, August 20, 2002. See Bob Woodward, *Bush at War,* New York: Simon & Schuster, 2002, p. 342.

CHAPTER 3

The information in this chapter comes primarily from background interviews with five firsthand sources.

30 *On February 10, 2005, Zelikow:* Notes of a SECRET document dated February 10, 2005.

31 *On October 11, 2005, he dashed off:* Author's review and notes of a SECRET snowflake dated October 11, 2005.

31 *Casey replied, "I believe this":* Author's review and notes of a SECRET memorandum.

31 *Rice made it the core:* Federal News Service, "Hearing of the Senate Foreign Relations Committee, Subject: Iraq in United States Foreign Policy," October 19, 2005, www.fnsg.com.

33 *The president said in a speech:* Presidential Documents, October 25, 2005, pp. 1610–1617 (Vol. 41, No. 43), www.gpoaccess.gov/wcomp/v41no43.html.

33 *On November 12, he forwarded:* Author's review and notes of a SECRET summary dated November 12, 2005.

33 *"I also note that on page two":* Author's review and notes of a SECRET snowflake dated November 17, 2005.

34 *On December 2, 2005, a snowflake:* Author's review and notes of a SECRET snowflake dated December 2, 2005.

34 *"I am in general agreement":* Author's review and notes of a SECRET document.

34 *"Attached is a worrisome":* Author's review and notes of a SECRET snowflake dated December 12, 2005, and an attached SECRET report.

35 *"The interesting point here":* CBS News Transcripts, *Face the Nation*, February 26, 2006.

36 *On March 20, the president drew attention:* Presidential Documents, March 20, 2006, pp. 498–516 (Vol. 42, No. 12), www.gpoaccess.gov/wcomp/v42no12.html.

38 *The next day, March 21, a SECRET CIA report:* Author's review and notes of a SECRET document dated March 21, 2006.

38 *Within days, Rumsfeld sent:* Author's review and notes of a SECRET snowflake dated April 3, 2006.

38 *Dated April 16, the SECRET report:* Author's review and notes of a SECRET document dated April 16, 2006.

38 *On April 17, the inevitable snowflake:* Author's review and notes of a SECRET snowflake dated April 17, 2006.

39 *On May 8, Rumsfeld composed:* Author's review and notes of a SECRET snowflake dated May 8, 2006.

CHAPTER 4

The information in this chapter comes primarily from background interviews with 11 firsthand sources and contemporaneous notes by two participants.

43   *On May 18, the last interview:* This study group session with Petraeus is based on dictated notes from the Iraq Study Group's record, dated May 18, 2006.

43   *I first met Petraeus:* Interview with Major David Petraeus, January 31, 1990.

45   *His hair had long ago turned gray:* This study group session with Powell is based on dictated notes from the Iraq Study Group's record, dated May 19, 2006.

CHAPTER 5

The information in this chapter comes primarily from background interviews with 13 firsthand sources and contemporaneous notes by two participants.

53   *Rumsfeld immediately dashed off:* Author's review and notes of a SECRET snowflake dated May 26, 2006.

54   *"I just took a look":* Author's review and notes of a SECRET snowflake dated May 30, 2006.

54   *On June 5, Zelikow and Jeffrey:* Dictated notes of a SECRET memo dated June 5, 2006.

56   *Not long afterward, McChrystal called:* Patrick Quinn and Kim Gamel, "Inside Tip Helped U.S. Take Out Al-Zarqawi," Associated Press, June 8, 2006.

57   *Later, Rumsfeld dictated:* Author's review and notes of a SECRET snowflake dated June 8, 2006.

57   *"I've just returned from Baghdad":* Presidential Documents, June 14, 2006, pp. 1125–1137 (Vol. 42, No. 24), www.gpoaccess.gov/wcomp/v42no24.html.

58   *That same afternoon, the president met:* This study group session with President Bush is from dictated notes from the Iraq Study Group's record, dated June 14, 2006.

59   *"Iraq Update and Way Ahead":* Author's review and notes taken from a SECRET briefing dated June 21, 2006.

60   *"Just so you know":* Interview with President George W. Bush, May 20, 2008.

CHAPTER 6

The information in this chapter comes primarily from background interviews with six firsthand sources.

64   *Al-Qaeda launched:* Joshua Partlow and Naseer Nouri, "Dozens Are Killed in Violence Across Iraq," *The Washington Post,* June 27, 2006, p. A16.

64   *A few days later, on Saturday, July 1:* Edward Wong, "Car Bomb Kills More than 60 in Iraq Market," *The New York Times,* July 2, 2006, p. A1.

64   *A Sunni female member:* "Sunni Female Legislator Kidnapped in Baghdad," Associated Press, July 1, 2006.

65   *All hell broke loose:* Donna Miles, "Leaders Praise Fortitude of Stryker Brigade Families," American Forces Press Service, December 25, 2006, www.defenselink.mil/news/articles. html.

65   *Jennifer Davis:* "172nd Stryker Brigade Tour of Duty in Iraq Extended; Family

Members Speak Out Against the War," MFSO press release, July 28, 2006, www.mfso.org.

66 *Rumsfeld sent a SECRET snowflake:* Author's review and notes of a SECRET document dated August 2, 2006.

66 *Casey waited a week to answer:* Author's review and notes of a SECRET document dated August 9, 2006.

66 *Rumsfeld went to Fort Wainwright:* Rumsfeld made this trip August 26, 2006, according to Robert Burns, "Defense Secretary Praises Soldiers Doing Extra Duty in Iraq, Says Families Should Not Be Angry," Associated Press, August 26, 2006.

66 *One woman asked why her husband:* Michael Hastings, "Straight to the Heart," *Newsweek,* September 18, 2006, p. 36.

66 *In a SECRET snowflake to Pace:* Author's review and notes of a SECRET document dated August 26, 2006.

67 *On July 7, President Bush answered:* Presidential Documents, July 7, 2006, p. 1290 (Vol. 42, No. 27), www.gpoaccess.gov/wcomp/v42no27.html.

67 *On July 19, Hadley called Rumsfeld:* Author's review and notes of a SECRET document.

67 *Rumsfeld snowflaked Casey:* Author's review and notes of a SECRET document.

67 *Instead, Casey said:* Author's review and notes of a SECRET document.

68 *On July 19, she sent:* SECRET document dated July 19, 2006, and declassified by the White House in 2008 in response to specific questions asked by the author.

70 *But other events:* Charles Babington, "Stem Cell Bill Gets Bush's First Veto," *The Washington Post,* July 20, 2006, p. A4; Edward Wong and Michael Slackman, "Iraqi Denounces Israel's Actions," *The New York Times,* July 20, 2006, p. A1.

CHAPTER 7

The information in this chapter comes primarily from background interviews with six firsthand sources.

72 *The Army had a SECRET graphic:* Author's review and notes of a classified chart.

72 *Bush later confirmed:* Interview with President George W. Bush, May 20, 2008.

73 *There were 14 major questions:* Author's review and notes of a SECRET document dated July 22, 2006.

78 *O'Sullivan prepared a SECRET summary:* Author's review and notes of a SECRET summary of the July 22, 2006, SVTS session.

78 *Asked later if this was accurate:* Interview with President George W. Bush on May 20, 2008.

CHAPTER 8

The information in this chapter comes primarily from background interviews with 11 firsthand sources and contemporaneous notes by two participants.

80 *A dozen top congressional Democrats:* Press release, Senator Harry Reid's office, "United House, Senate Democratic Leadership Put Forward Concrete Plan for Change of Course in Iraq," U.S. Federal News, July 31, 2006, accessed via Nexis.

80 *On August 1, a roadside bomb:* Joshua Partlow and Saad al-Izzi, "Attacks Target Iraqi Soldiers and Police; Dozens of People Die in Series of Shootings, Blasts," *The Washington Post,* August 2, 2006, p. A11; Damien Cave, "The Struggle for Iraq: Violence," *The New York Times,* August 3, 2006, p. A13.

81 *Their first session:* This study group session with Frist and McConnell is based on dictated notes from the Iraq Study Group's record, dated August 2, 2006.

81 *The next meeting:* This study group session with Warner and Levin is based on dictated notes from the Iraq Study Group's record, dated August 2, 2006.

83 *The study group members headed:* This study group session with Abizaid is based on dictated notes from the Iraq Study Group's record, dated August 2, 2006.

84 *The next day, August 3, Abizaid testified:* Congressional Quarterly Transcriptions, "U.S. Senator John Warner Holds a Hearing on Iraq, Afghanistan and Counterterrorism," Senate Armed Services Committee, August 3, 2006, accessed via Nexis.

85 *On Friday, August 4, Rice appeared:* State Department transcript, Interview on MSNBC's *Hardball* with David Gregory, August 4, 2006, www.state.gov.

85 *The next morning, Saturday, Rice left:* Author's review and notes of Rice's schedule.

86 *In an interview two years later:* Interview with President George W. Bush, May 20, 2008.

86 *She voiced optimism and disagreed:* State Department transcript, interview on NBC's *Meet the Press* with Tim Russert, August 6, 2006, www.state.gov.

86 *On Monday, Bush and Rice:* State Department transcript, "President Bush and Secretary Rice Discuss the Middle East Crisis," Crawford, Texas, August 7, 2006, www.state.gov.

86 *At a political rally in Lancaster:* Presidential Documents, August 16, 2006, p. 1463 (Vol. 42, No. 33), www.gpoaccess.gov/wcomp/v42no33.html.

CHAPTER 9

The information in this chapter comes primarily from contemporaneous notes by a participant and background interviews with four firsthand sources.

89 *In a recent Gallup poll:* Frank Newport, "Americans Continue to Call Iraq Involvement a Mistake," Gallup News Service, July 28, 2006; Jeffrey M. Jones, "Latest Bush Approval Rating at 37%," Gallup News Service, August 15, 2006, www.gallup.com.

93 *The problem during the Vietnam War:* Interview with President George W. Bush on August 20, 2002; see Bob Woodward, *Bush at War,* p. 168.

99 *Bush later told me:* Interview with President George W. Bush on May 20, 2008.

CHAPTER 10

The information in this chapter comes primarily from background interviews with five firsthand sources.

101 *Bush later confirmed to me:* Interview with President George W. Bush on May 20, 2008.

103 *"Senator, are we winning":* MSNBC Transcript, *Meet the Press,* August 20, 2006, www.msnbc.msn.com/.

104 *The next day, August 21:* Presidential Documents, August 21, 2006, pp. 1480–1493 (Vol. 42, No. 34), www.gpoaccess.gov/wcomp/v42no34.html.

105 *On Thursday, August 24:* David Ignatius, "Returning Some Order to Iraq's Mean Streets," *The Washington Post,* August 25, 2007, p. A17.

105 *The next day, Casey issued:* Author's review and notes of a SECRET document dated August 25, 2006.

105 *I asked President Bush about this August 25 report:* Interview with President George W. Bush, May 20, 2008.

108 *On August 30, in Salt Lake City:* Presidential Documents, August 30, 3006, pp. 1537–1544 (Vol. 42, No. 35), www.gpoaccess.gov/wcomp/v42no35.html.

108 *In the streets of Baghdad:* Edward Wong, "Car Bomb and Rockets Kill 43 in Baghdad's Shiite Strongholds," *The New York Times,* September 1, 2006, p. A6.

108 *The next day, August 31:* Notes of a classified document dated August 31, 2006.

109 *The violence unfolding outside the fortified Green Zone:* Damien Cave, "Violence Grows, Killing 52 Iraqis, in Face of Security Plan," *The New York Times,* August 21, 2006, p. A10.

CHAPTER 11

The information in this chapter comes primarily from background interviews with six firsthand sources and contemporaneous notes by two participants.

110 *Seven members of the Iraq Study Group:* This study group session with Maliki is based on dictated notes from the Iraq Study Group's record, dated August 31, 2006.

112 *On September 1, the morning after:* This study group session with Rubaie is based on dictated notes from the Iraq Study Group's record, dated September 1, 2006.

112 *Later that day the group met:* This study group session with Salih is based on dictated notes from the Iraq Study Group's record, dated September 1, 2006.

113 *Still later that day came a session:* This study group session with Obeidi is based on dictated notes from the Iraq Study Group's record, dated September 1, 2006.

114 *The next morning, September 2:* This study group session with CIA officials is based on dictated notes from the Iraq Study Group's record, dated September 2, 2006.

115 *Later that day, the group met:* This study group session with Jabr is based on dictated notes from the Iraq Study Group's record, dated September 2, 2006.

115 *The members gathered at the U.S. embassy:* This study group session with Chiarelli is based on dictated notes from the Iraq Study Group's record, dated September 3, 2006.

CHAPTER 12

The information in this chapter comes primarily from background interviews with five firsthand sources and contemporaneous notes by two participants.

119 *Next, the study group met:* This study group session with Dempsey and Peterson is based on dictated notes from the Iraq Study Group's record, dated September 3, 2006.

120 *The study group members headed across:* This study group session with Hakim is based on dictated notes from the Iraq Study Group's record, dated September 3, 2006.

120 *Hakim, head of the powerful Shia party:* On May 12, 2007, the Supreme Council for Islamic Revolution in Iraq (SCIRI) was renamed the Supreme Islamic Iraqi Council (SIIC). See Damien Cave, "Changes by Iraqi Shiite Party Signal Distancing from Iran," *The New York Times,* May 13, 2007, p. A6.

123 *On September 5, President Bush addressed:* Presidential Documents, September 5, 2006, pp. 1557–1565 (Vol. 42, No. 36), www.gpoaccess.gov/wcomp/v42no36.html.

123 *The 29-page document:* "National Strategy for Combating Terrorism," The White House, www.whitehouse.gov/nsc/.

124 *On September 11, 2006:* Presidential Documents, September 11, 2006, pp. 1597–1601 (Vol. 42, No. 37), www.gpoaccess.gov/wcomp/v42no37.html.

126 *For the better part of an hour:* Interview with Congressman John Murtha, September 27, 2007, and interviews with other knowledgeable sources.

127 *Several days later, on September 15:* Presidential Documents, September 15, 2006, pp. 1607–1620 (Vol. 42, No. 37), www.gpoaccess.gov/wcomp/v42no37.html.

128 *So he wrote a memo:* Chuck Robb memo to Iraq Study Group members, September 18, 2006.

CHAPTER 13

The information in this chapter comes primarily from background interviews with a firsthand source and contemporaneous notes of a participant.

CHAPTER 14

The information in this chapter comes primarily from background interviews with five firsthand sources.

139 *One Saturday morning in September 1991:* Interviews with several knowledge-able sources. See also Rick Atkinson, *In the Company of Soldiers* (New York: Henry Holt, 2004), pp. 37–38, and Lois Romano, "When Edwards Nips Senate, Dodd Bites Back," *The Washington Post,* May 3, 2007, p. A23.

141 *On September 19, the same day:* Presidential Documents, September 19, 2006, pp. 1638–1639 (Vol. 42, No. 38), www.gpoaccess.gov/wcomp/v42no38 .html.

142 *That same day, September 20:* Author's review and notes of a SECRET intelligence document dated September 20, 2006.

142 *Later, when I asked the president:* Interview with President George W. Bush on May 20, 2008.

142 *He forwarded copies of the report:* Author's review and notes of a SECRET snowflake.

CHAPTER 15

The information in this chapter comes primarily from background interviews with six firsthand sources.

CHAPTER 16

The information in this chapter comes primarily from background interviews with nine firsthand sources.

160 *On September 30, General Casey presented:* SECRET document dated September 30, 2006, declassified by the White House in 2008 in response to specific questions asked by the author.

160 *Lindsey Graham, the South Carolina senator:* Jim Davenport, "McCain Says Mistakes Made in Iraq War," Associated Press, October 25, 2006.

160 *Virginia Senator George Allen:* Tom Raum, "Republicans Worry They'll Pay Heavy Political Price for War," Associated Press, October 23, 2006.

160 *Kay Bailey Hutchison:* Ibid.

161 *In Reno, Nevada, on October 2:* Presidential Documents, October 2, 2006, pp. 1713–1718 (Vol. 40, No. 40), www.gpoaccess.gov/wcomp/v42no40.html.

161 *In Arizona, on October 4:* Presidential Documents, October 4, 2006, pp. 1734–1740 (Vol. 40, No. 40), www.gpoaccess.gov/wcomp/v42no40.html.

CHAPTER 17

The information in this chapter comes primarily from background interviews with nine firsthand sources.

167 *They descended into the secure conference room:* Bernard E. Trainor, "Inside the 'Tank': Bowls of Candy and Big Brass," *The New York Times,* January 11, 1988, p. A16.

169 *At 10:45 A.M. on October 10:* Author's review and notes of a SECRET snowflake dated October 10, 2006.

171 *At 11 A.M. on October 11:* Presidential Documents, October 11, 2006, pp. 1782–1796 (Vol. 42, No. 41), www.gpoaccess.gov/wcomp/v42no41.html.

175 *On the Sunday, October 15, television talk shows:* Nedra Pickler, "Two Republican Senators Call for a New Strategy in Iraq," Associated Press, October 15, 2006.

175 *At 7:40 the next morning:* Author's review and notes of a SECRET summary dated October 16, 2006.

CHAPTER 18

The information in this chapter comes primarily from background interviews with eight firsthand sources.

179 *On Thursday, October 19, in Baghdad:* MNF-I press briefing, October 19, 2006, www.mnf-iraq.com.

180 *A few days later, Rumsfeld sent a snowflake:* Author's review and notes of a SECRET snowflake dated October 23, 2006.

181 *That same afternoon at the White House:* White House press briefing, October 23, 2006, www.whitehouse.gov/news.

182 *As promised, Khalilzad and Casey:* MNF-I press conference, October 23, 2006, www.mnf-iraq.com.

183 *On Wednesday, October 25:* Presidential Documents, October 25, 2006, pp. 1877–1890 (Vol. 42, No. 43), www.gpoaccess.gov/wcomp/v42no43.html.

CHAPTER 19

The information in this chapter comes primarily from background interviews with four firsthand sources.

187 *Satterfield drafted a SECRET/NODIS:* Notes of a SECRET document dated October 31, 2006.

190 *"The outcome will determine":* Presidential Documents, October 25, 2006, pp. 1877–1890 (Vol. 42, No. 43), www.gpoaccess.gov/wcomp/v42no43.html.

190 *She called it "The Way Forward":* SECRET document declassified by the White House in 2008 in response to specific questions asked by the author.

CHAPTER 20

The information in this chapter comes primarily from background interviews with 11 firsthand sources.

196 *Bush later told me:* Interview with President George W. Bush, May 20, 2008.
198 *How did you pick Gates:* Ibid.

200 *The colonels eventually pieced together slides:* According to the notes of a partici-
     pant.

201 *On Sunday, November 5, Bush welcomed Gates:* Sheryl Gay Stolberg and Jim
     Rutenberg, "Rumsfeld Resigns; Bush Vows 'to Find Common Ground';
     Focus Is on Virginia," *The New York Times,* November 9, 2006, p. A1.

202 *"He worked in, you know":* Interview with President George W. Bush, May 20,
     2008.

203 *They debated a list:* According to the notes of a participant.

204 *On November 6, the day before:* "Rumsfeld's Memo of Options for Iraq War," *The
     New York Times,* p. A28. Contents confirmed by a knowledgeable administra-
     tion source in 2008.

206 *When I asked the president two years later:* Interview with President George W.
     Bush, May 20, 2008.

206 *In a five-page SECRET memo:* Michael Gordon, "Bush Adviser's Memo Cites
     Doubts About Iraqi Leader," *The New York Times,* November 29, 2006, p. A1;
     "Text of the National Security Adviser's Memorandum on the Political Situa-
     tion in Iraq," *The New York Times,* November 29, 2006, p. A19. Contents con-
     firmed by a knowledgeable administration source in 2008.

208 *Hadley dispatched a SECRET memo:* SECRET document dated November 11,
     2006, and declassified by the White House in 2008 in response to specific
     questions asked by the author. ·

CHAPTER 21

The information in this chapter comes primarily from background interviews with
ten firsthand sources and contemporaneous notes by two participants.

209 *Just after 8 A.M. on November 13:* This study group session with President Bush
     is based on dictated notes from the Iraq Study Group's record, dated Novem-
     ber 13, 2006.

213 *I later asked the president:* Interview with President Bush, May 20, 2008.

214 *When I spoke to the president later:* Ibid.

214 *After the president left:* This study group session with Casey is based on dic-
     tated notes from the Iraq Study Group's record, dated November 13, 2006.

216 *After the video teleconference:* This study group session with Hayden is based on
     dictated notes from the Iraq Study Group's record, dated November 13,
     2006.

218 *Next up was Khalilzad:* This study group session with Khalilzad is based on
     dictated notes from the Iraq Study Group's record, dated November 13,
     2006.

CHAPTER 22

The information in this chapter comes primarily from background interviews with
seven firsthand sources and contemporaneous notes by two participants.

220 *At 1 P.M., Secretary Rice sat down:* This study group session with Rice is based on dictated notes from the Iraq Study Group's record, dated November 13, 2006.

222 *Rumsfeld and Pace arrived at 2 P.M.:* This study group session with Rumsfeld and Pace is based on dictated notes from the Iraq Study Group's record, dated November 13, 2006.

224 *The next day, November 14:* This study group session with Blair is based on dictated notes from the Iraq Study Group's record, dated November 14, 2006.

225 *At 2:30 that afternoon:* This study group session with President Clinton is based on dictated notes from the Iraq Study Group's record, dated November 14, 2006.

CHAPTER 23

The information in this chapter comes primarily from background interviews with nine firsthand sources.

231 *His SECRET briefing paper had read:* Author's review and notes of a SECRET document dated November 16, 2006.

232 *"The original objectives of America's invasion":* Author's review and notes of "Advancing America's Interests: Preserving Iraq's Independence," a SECRET document dated November 17, 2006.

235 *On November 18, the Defense Department representatives:* Author's review and notes of a SECRET document dated November 18, 2006.

235 *The SECRET paper from the two Joint Staff generals:* Author's review and notes of a SECRET document.

236 *David Gordon, the representative:* Details from the document given to the author by a knowledgeable source.

CHAPTER 24

The information in this chapter comes primarily from background interviews with nine firsthand sources.

240 *Tom Ricks, a well-sourced Pentagon reporter:* Thomas E. Ricks, "Pentagon May Suggest Short-Term Buildup Leading to Iraqi Exit," *The Washington Post,* November 20, 2006, p. A1.

244 *On November 26, the Sunday after Thanksgiving:* Author's review and notes of a SECRET document. A similar document was declassified by the White House in 2008 in response to specific questions asked by the author.

245 *He then presented a chart of nine key assumptions:* Author's review and notes of a SECRET chart. A similar chart was declassified by the White House in 2008 in response to specific questions asked by the author.

252 *Meese recounted how Reagan had made the decision:* Author interview with Edwin Meese, June 15, 2007. The United States invaded the tiny Caribbean island of

Grenada in 1983 after extremists, allegedly supported by Cuba and possibly the Soviet Union, staged a coup and overthrew the government. In addition, about 1,000 Americans were on the island and potentially needed protection or rescue.

CHAPTER 25

The information in this chapter comes primarily from background interviews with four firsthand sources.

255   *"He was proud of his plan":* Interview with President George W. Bush, May 20, 2008.

257   *Later, Bush told me about Maliki in Amman:* Ibid.

257   *In a joint press conference:* Presidential Documents, November 30, 2006, pp. 2104–2121 (Vol. 42, No. 48), www.gpoaccess.gov/wcomp/v42no48.html.

257   *And in a joint statement:* Presidential Documents, November 30, 2006, p. 2112 (Vol. 42, No. 48), www.gpoaccess.gov/wcomp/v42no48.html.

257   *The week before, a barrage of car bombs:* Sudarsan Raghavan, "Sadr Casts a Shadow over Bush-Maliki Meeting," *The Washington Post,* November 30, 2006, p. A19.

258   *About this time, reporter David Sanger:* David Sanger, "Panel to Weigh Overture by U.S. to Iran and Syria," *The New York Times,* November 27, 2006, p. A1; David Sanger, "Iraq Panel to Recommend Pullback of Combat Troops," *The New York Times,* November 30, 2006, p. A1.

259   *On December 5, former President George H. W. Bush:* Peggy Noonan, "A Father's Tears," *The Wall Street Journal,* December 8, 2006.

CHAPTER 26

The information in this chapter comes primarily from background interviews with 13 firsthand sources and contemporaneous notes by two participants.

261   *Bob Gates headed to the Senate:* Congressional Quarterly Transcriptions, "U.S. Senator John Warner Holds a Hearing on the Nomination of Robert Gates to Be U.S. Secretary of Defense," Senate Armed Services Committee, December 5, 2006.

261   *When I later asked the president:* Interview with President George W. Bush, May 21, 2008.

263   *"I just received":* Presidential Documents, December 6, 2006, pp. 2126–2127 (Vol. 42, No. 49), www.gpoaccess.gov/wcomp/v42no49.html.

263   *Bush said later that he understood:* Interview with President George W. Bush, May 20, 2008.

264   *The news media treated:* Michael Abramowitz and Robin Wright, "Iraq Panel Proposes Major Strategy Shift," *The Washington Post,* December 7, 2006, p. A1; David Sanger, "Panel Urges Basic Shift in U.S. Policy in Iraq," *The New York Times,* December 7, 2006, p. A1.

264 *"This was such a sobering report!":* David Montgomery, "Footnote to History: Rituals of Delivering the Iraq Report," *The Washington Post,* December 7, 2006, p. C1.

264 *"There's almost a biblical thing":* Ibid.

266 *One SECRET document:* Document dated December 7, 2006, and declassified by the White House in 2008 in response to specific questions asked by the author.

267 *Another five-page SECRET document:* Document dated December 7, 2006, and declassified by the White House in 2008 in response to specific questions asked by the author.

267 *At the NSC meeting December 8:* Notes of a participant at the December 8, 2006, NSC meeting and interviews with other knowledgeable sources.

269 *In a later interview, Bush told me:* Interview with President George W. Bush, May 20, 2008.

CHAPTER 27

The information in this chapter comes primarily from background interviews with six firsthand sources.

270 *The NSC gathered at 7 A.M.:* Notes of a participant at the December 9, 2006, NSC meeting and interviews with other knowledgeable sources.

274 *Early the next Monday:* Notes of a participant at the December 11, 2006, NSC meeting and interviews with other knowledgeable sources.

CHAPTER 28

The information in this chapter comes primarily from background interviews with eight firsthand sources.

279 *On Monday, December 11:* Notes and several knowledgeable sources' accounts of the meeting held at the White House on December 11, 2006.

282 *At 10:30 that morning:* Presidential Documents, December 11, 2006, pp. 2151–2152 (Vol. 42, No. 50), www.gpoaccess.gov/wcomp/v42no50.html.

283 *The next day, Tuesday, December 12:* Notes of a participant at the December 12, 2006, NSC meeting and interviews with other knowledgeable sources.

283 *He wrote in green pen:* Author's review and notes of a SECRET document.

289 *Of course, Casey had also presented:* Author's review and notes of a SECRET document called "Iraq Security Way Ahead," dated December 12, 2006.

290 *"The tank meeting was a very important meeting":* Interview with President George W. Bush, May 21, 2008.

CHAPTER 29

The information in this chapter comes primarily from background interviews with eight firsthand sources.

294 *Bush was quoted as saying:* Peter Baker, "U.S. Not Winning War in Iraq, Bush Says for 1st Time," *The Washington Post,* December 20, 2006, p. A1.

300 *Typically, 20 counterinsurgents:* United States Army and United States Marine Corps, *The U.S. Army/Marine Corps Counterinsurgency Field Manual,* 2007.

300 *The president later told me:* Interview with President George W. Bush, May 20, 2008.

CHAPTER 30

The information in this chapter comes primarily from background interviews with nine firsthand sources.

305 *"I'm not sure I bought the last card":* Interview with President George W. Bush, May 21, 2008.

305 *At about five the next morning:* Notes and a knowledgeable source's account of the meeting held at President Bush's Crawford ranch on December 28, 2006.

311 *That same Thursday, the new Congress:* Jonathan Weisman and Shailagh Murray, "Democrats Take Control on Hill," *The Washington Post,* January 5, 2007, p. A1.

312 *"The election of 2006":* Press release, "Pelosi Calls for a New America, Built on the Values That Made Our Country Great," January 4, 2007, www.house .gov/pelosi.

CHAPTER 31

The information in this chapter comes primarily from background interviews with five firsthand sources.

313 *On January 6, 2007, Maliki said:* "Iraqi PM Addresses Army on Saddam Execution, Baghdad Security Plan," BBC Monitoring International Reports transcript, January 6, 2007.

314 *On Wednesday, January 10, about 2 P.M.:* "MSNBC Interview with Senator John McCain (R-AZ); Subject: Iraq, Interviewed by Tim Russert," Federal News Service, January 10, 2007, www.fnsg.com.

315 *"The situation in Iraq is unacceptable":* Presidential Documents, January 10, 2007, pp. 19–23 (Vol. 43, No. 2), www.gpoaccess.gov/wcomp/v43no2.html.

315 *Minutes after the president finished speaking:* MSNBC Transcript, *Hardball,* January 10, 2007, www.msnbc.msn.com.

316 *Republican Senator George Voinovich:* Dana Milbank, "The Secretary vs. the Senators," *The Washington Post,* January 12, 2007, p. A1.

316 *Republican senator and Vietnam veteran Chuck Hagel:* Anne E. Kornblut, "Devastating Criticism by Both Parties," *The New York Times,* January 12, 2007, A12.

317 *"Prior to the Samarra bombing":* Interview with President George W. Bush, May 21, 2008.

320 *"If what you're trying to do":* Interview with President George W. Bush, May 20, 2008.

CHAPTER 32

The information in this chapter comes primarily from background interviews with six firsthand sources.

325 *"The commanders on the ground in Iraq"*: Presidential Documents, January 11, 2007, pp. 25–30 (Vol. 43, No. 2), www.gpoaccess.gov/wcomp/v43no2.html.

326 *Susan Collins, the independent-minded:* "Hearing of the Senate Armed Services Committee; Subject: Nomination of Lieutenant General David H. Petraeus, U.S. Army, to Be General and Commander, Multinational Forces Iraq," Federal News Service, January 23, 2007, www.fnsg.com.

327 *Three days later, on January 26:* U.S. Senate Roll Call Votes, 110th Congress, 1st Session, January 26, 2007, www.senate.gov.

327 *On January 30, 2007:* "Hearing of the Senate Armed Services Committee; Subject: The Nomination of Admiral William Fallon for Appointment to the Grade of Admiral and to Be Commander, U.S. Central Command," Federal News Service, January 30, 2007, www.fnsg.com.

328 *He declared the situation:* General David Petraeus's change of command remarks, MNF-I change of command, February 10, 2007, www.mnf-iraq.com.

329 *He sent a short letter to everyone:* Commanding General's Letter to the Troops for February, February 9, 2007, www.mnf-iraq.com.

330 *"With the advantage of hindsight"*: Presidential Documents, February 19, 2007, pp. 182–183 (Vol. 43, No. 8), www.gpoaccess.gov/wcomp/v43no8.html.

331 *"President Truman made clear"*: Press release, "President Delivers Commencement Address at the United States Military Academy at West Point," May 27, 2006, www.whitehouse.gov.

332 *Gates had said during:* "Hearing of the Senate Armed Services Committee; Subject: Defense Department Fiscal Year 2008 Budget and Fiscal Year 2007 Supplemental," Federal News Service, February 6, 2007, www.fnsg.com.

CHAPTER 33

The information in this chapter comes primarily from background interviews with 10 firsthand sources.

335 *By early March, Petraeus and McMaster had assembled:* Included in the group were David Kilcullen, an Australian counterinsurgency expert; Robert Ford, the U.S. ambassador to Algeria; Molly Phee, a seasoned diplomat who'd spent time in Iraq; Rick Waddell, a West Point alumnus and Rhodes Scholar who'd served a stint on the National Security Council; Ylber Bajraktari, a former journalist and Albanian refugee from Kosovo who'd earned a master's degree at Princeton; Colonel Marty Stanton, an author and veteran of the first Gulf War, Bosnia and the Iraq War; P. J. Dermer, a former Army helicopter pilot who worked in Iraq during 2003 and 2004 for the Defense Intelligence Agency; Steve Biddle from the Council on Foreign Relations and the Brook-

ings Institution; Toby Dodge, an Iraq expert from London; Colonel J. R. Martin, a professor at the Army War College and former classmate of Petraeus.

339 *The president later told me:* Interview with President George W. Bush, May 21, 2008.

342 *At 3 P.M. the next day:* Defense Department News Briefing, April 11, 2007, www.defenselink.mil.

CHAPTER 34

The information in this chapter comes primarily from background interviews with ten firsthand sources.

344 *In early April 2007, Petraeus had led McCain:* Kirk Semple, "McCain Wrong on Iraq Security, Merchants Say," *The New York Times,* April 3, 2007, p. A1; "Briefing by Senator John McCain (R-AZ), Representative Mike Pence (R-IN), Representative Rick Renzi (R-AZ); Topic: Their Visit to Iraq," Federal News Service, April 2, 2007, www.fnsg.com; Sudarsan Raghavan, "Sum of Death Statistics: A Perilous Iraq; Merchants, U.S. Officials Take Issue with McCain's Remarks on Security Gains," *The Washington Post,* April 4, 2007, p. A9.

345 *Asked about a suicide bombing:* "Remarks with Senator John McCain After Their Meeting," State Department transcript, April 12, 2007, www.state.gov.

345 *At a press conference:* "Senate Democrats Hold a News Conference on Iraq," Congressional Quarterly Transcriptions, April 19, 2007, accessed via Nexis.

346 *"Could I have couched my words":* Harry Reid, *The Good Fight* (New York: G. P. Putnam's Sons, 2008), p. 20.

346 *I later asked him:* Interview with President George W. Bush, May 21, 2008.

347 *In March, King Abdullah:* Glenn Kessler and Karen DeYoung, "Saudis Publicly Get Tough with U.S.; King's Remarks on Iraq Follow Signs Riyadh Is Distancing Itself from Bush," *The Washington Post,* March 30, 2007, p. A14.

349 *On Wednesday, April 25:* Carl Hulse and Jeff Zeleny, "House Approves War Spending Measure That Requires U.S. to Start Pullout from Iraq," *The New York Times,* April 26, 2007, p. 12.

CHAPTER 35

The information in this chapter comes primarily from background interviews with four firsthand sources.

358 *On May 26, Senate Minority Leader Mitch McConnell:* Michael Abramowitz and Peter Baker, "White House Considers Next Steps in Iraq; Troop Drawdowns and Shift in Mission Are Premised on Successful 'Surge,'" *The Washington Post,* May 27, 2007, p. A5.

358 *"I'm not going to dime that guy":* Interview with President George W. Bush, May 21, 2008.

359 The New York Times *had published:* David E. Sanger and David S. Cloud,

"White House Said to Debate '08 Cut in Troops by 50%," *The New York Times,* May 26, 2007, p. A1.

361 *"Let me make a forecast":* Interview with Bill Perry, June 6, 2007.

362 *Petraeus's forces were beginning:* In June 2008, Petraeus distributed a three-page instruction titled "Multi-National Force—Iraq Commander's Counterinsurgency Guidance" that showed he believed that protecting the Iraqi population involved specific actions by troops on the ground. He listed 22, including:

- *"Live among the people.* You can't commute to this fight. Position Joint Security Stations, Combat Outposts, and Patrol Bases in the neighborhoods we intend to secure. . . .
- *"Promote reconciliation.* We cannot kill our way out of this endeavor. . . .
- *"Foster Iraqi legitimacy.* . . . Legitimacy in the eyes of the Iraqi people is essential to overall success.
- *"Fight for intelligence.* . . . Operate on a 'need to share' rather than a 'need to know' basis. . . .
- *"Walk.* Move mounted, work dismounted. Stop by, don't drive by. Patrol on foot and engage the population. . . .
- *"Build relationships.* Relationships are a critical component of counter-insurgency operations. . . .
- *"Manage expectations.* . . . Avoid premature declarations of success. . . .
- *"Be first with the truth.* . . . Don't put lipstick on pigs. . . . Avoid spin and let facts speak for themselves. . . .
- *"Live our values.* . . . There is no tougher endeavor than the one in which we are engaged. It is often brutal, physically demanding, and frustrating. All of us experience moments of anger, but we can neither give in to dark impulses nor tolerate unacceptable actions by others."

362 *Abu Abed, also known as Saif:* Joshua Partlow, "For U.S. Unit in Baghdad, an Alliance of Last Resort," *The Washington Post,* June 9, 2007, p. A1.

363 *Gates approached a handful of senators:* Interview with Carl Levin, December 6, 2007.

364 *On Friday, June 8, Gates announced:* "News Conference with Secretary of Defense Robert Gates Announcing Recommendation of Admiral Michael Mullen to Be Chairman of Joint Chiefs of Staff, and General James Cartwright to Be Vice Chairman," Federal News Service, June 8, 2007, www.fnsg.com.

CHAPTER 36

The information in this chapter comes primarily from background interviews with nine firsthand sources and the notes of two participants.

365 *On June 13, about 9 A.M.:* John F. Burns, "Revered Mosque in Iraq Is Bombed for Second Time," *The New York Times,* June 14, 2007, p. A1.

368 *On* Fox News Sunday *with Chris Wallace:* General Petraeus on *Fox News Sunday,* Fox News Transcript, June 17, 2007, www.foxnews.com.

372 *"It is the policy of the United States":* Presidential Documents, January 20, 2005, pp. 74–76 (Vol. 41, No. 3), www.gpoaccess.gov/wcomp/v41no03.html.

373 *Hayden had said that:* Hayden's quotes are taken from dictated notes of the Iraq Study Group's record of his testimony on November 13, 2006.

373 *According to Hamilton:* Phone conversation with Lee Hamilton, June 12, 2007.

373 *The* Post *story ran Thursday:* Bob Woodward, "CIA Said Instability Seemed 'Irreversible,'" *The Washington Post,* July 12, 2007, p. A1.

373 *That same day, the president was asked:* Presidential Documents, July 12, 2007, pp. 944–956, (Vol. 43, No. 28) www.gpoaccess.gov/wcomp/v43no28.html.

CHAPTER 37

The information in this chapter comes primarily from background interviews with 11 firsthand sources.

378 *On August 22, Bush spoke:* Presidential Documents, August 22, 2007, pp. 1107–1114 (Vol. 43, No. 34), www.gpoaccess.gov/wcomp/v43no34.html.

378 *Six days later, the president:* Presidential Documents, August 28, 2007, pp. 1124–1131 (Vol. 43, No. 35), www.gpoaccess.gov/wcomp/v43no35.html.

379 *On Thursday, August 24:* NIE, "Prospects for Iraq's Stability: Some Security Progress but Political Reconciliation Elusive," August 2007, www.dni.gov/press_releases/20070823_release.pdf.

381 *"We are the ones who saved our country,":* Interview with Sheikh Ahmed Abu Risha, June 3, 2008. See also Sterling Jensen, "Lessons from an Anbar Sheik," *The Washington Post,* September 29, 2007, p. A19.

CHAPTER 38

The information in this chapter comes primarily from background interviews with four firsthand sources.

383 *On August 29, 2007, Petraeus's aide:* David Kilcullen, "Anatomy of a Tribal Revolt," *Small Wars Journal,* August 29, 2007, www.smallwarsjournal.com.

384 *On Monday morning, September 10:* "General Petraeus or General Betray Us?" MoveOn.org advertisement, *The New York Times,* September 10, 2007, p. A25. See also: http://pol.moveon.org/petraeus.html.

385 *David Gergen, a former adviser:* CNN Newsroom, September 10, 2007, http://transcripts.cnn.com/TRANSCRIPTS.

386 *Throughout a long day that stretched:* "Joint Hearing of the House Armed Services and Foreign Affairs Committees; Subject: The Status of the War and Political Developments in Iraq," Federal News Service, September 10, 2007, www.fnsg.com.

386 *"Petraeus Backs Initial Pullout":* Peter Baker and Jonathan Weisman, "Petraeus Backs Initial Pullout; General Praises Progress, Warns Against 'Rushing to Failure,'" *The Washington Post,* September 11, 2007, p. A1.

386 *Sitting next to the president:* Harry Reid, *The Good Fight,* 2008, p. 10.

388 *That evening, in a nationally televised address:* Presidential Documents, September 13, 2007, pp. 1204–1208 (Vol. 43, No. 37), www.gpoaccess.gov/wcomp/v43no37.html.

389 *At a press conference the next day:* Defense Department news briefing, September 14, 2007, DOD transcripts, www.defenselink.mil.

389 *His comments landed on the front page:* Julian E. Barnes, "Gates Seeks Bigger Troop Cut; The Defense Chief Looks to Reduce the Number in Iraq by Nearly Half Before 2009—a Deeper Trim than Bush Plans," *Los Angeles Times,* September 15, 2007, p. A1.

390 *When I asked the president about it in 2008:* Interview with President George W. Bush, May 21, 2008.

CHAPTER 39

The information in this chapter comes primarily from background interviews with four firsthand sources.

CHAPTER 40

The information in this chapter comes primarily from background interviews with eight firsthand sources.

406 *Maliki overestimated the temporary restraint:* John Affleck, "Al-Maliki Calls on Iraqis to Boost Political Process in Speech Marking Religious Holiday," Associated Press, February 28, 2008.

406 *"This is a defining moment":* Presidential Documents, March 28, 2008, pp. 437–443 (Vol. 44, No. 12), www.gpoaccess.gov/wcomp/v44no12.html.

408 *In early March 2008,* Esquire *magazine published:* Thomas P. M. Barnett, "The Man Between War and Peace," *Esquire,* March 2008.

409 *"I have approved Admiral Fallon's request":* Defense Department news briefing, March 11, 2008, DOD transcripts, www.defenselink.mil.

CHAPTER 41

The information in this chapter comes primarily from background interviews with seven firsthand sources.

415 *On April 8, Petraeus and Crocker:* Lolita C. Baldor, "Petraeus Charts Violence in Iraq," Associated Press, April 8, 2008.

415 *Two weeks later, on April 23, Gates called:* Defense Department news briefing, April 23, 2008, DOD transcripts, www.defenselink.mil.

423 *Later, in the Oval Office, I asked the president:* Interview with President George W. Bush, May 21, 2008.

EPILOGUE

The information in this chapter comes primarily from background interviews with three firsthand sources.

428 *The headline splashed across the top:* Amit R. Paley and Karen DeYoung, "Key Iraqi Leaders Deliver Setbacks to U.S.," *Washington Post,* June 14, 2008, p. A1.

429 *"We will direct every resource":* Presidential Documents, September 20, 2001, pp. 1347–1351 (Vol. 37, No. 38), www.gpoaccess.gov/wcomp/v37no38 .html.

429 *"I'm ready to go," he later told me:* Interview with President George W. Bush, August 20, 2002.

430 *"One time early on," I said:* Interview with President George W. Bush, December 20, 2001.

430 *President Bush once said to me of the path:* Ibid.

431 *"His instincts are almost his second religion":* See Bob Woodward, *Bush at War,* p. 342.

432 *Finally, he said, "He is the wrong father":* Interview with President George W. Bush, December 11, 2003.

432 *In a December 2003 interview:* Ibid.

433 *In May 2008, I asked if he still believed that:* Interview with President George W. Bush, May 20, 2008.

434 *He alternately insisted:* Interview with President George W. Bush, May 20, 2008.

434 *Even the president acknowledged:* Interview with President George W. Bush, May 21, 2008.

ACKNOWLEDGMENTS

_____

While this book is based almost entirely on my own reporting and examination of documents, I offer my deep gratitude to those journalists who have covered the Iraq War. The knowledge and information they've provided have been an indispensable foundation for this book.

In 2007, the Project for Excellence in Journalism concluded that Iraq had become one of the most dangerous wars in American history for reporters to cover, and the Committee to Protect Journalists has documented the killings of more than 125 reporters on assignment in Iraq. We owe them a debt that will never be repaid.

I thank all the sources, named and unnamed, who have patiently sat through session after session of interviews and provided me with documents, both professional and personal. I appreciate their willingness to take the risks inherent in participating in a project like this, especially when the project concerns a controversial war in an election year. It takes guts to let an outsider in, and I hope future historians who study the Iraq War and the swirl of events surrounding it will be grateful for their contribution.

This is my thirty-sixth year and fourteenth book with Alice Mayhew, my editor at Simon & Schuster. She has thrown herself into this project with the same passion, focus, and attention to detail that she has possessed since Carl Bernstein and I first began working with her in 1972 on *All the President's Men.* Unwaveringly fair-minded, an endless source of energy and ideas, Alice seeks the clearest possible view of events as they occurred. She quickly realized that the soul of this book is its verbatim nature, with virtually all of it taken directly from the documents and people involved. Alice shares with me an awareness of the scale of the decision making documented in these pages, as well as a belief in the necessity of impartial reporting and ensuring that all involved receive a chance to have their say.

Carolyn K. Reidy and David Rosenthal at Simon & Schuster run the best publishing house in America. They are hands-on managers and care deeply about their business and their books. They consistently display a commitment to the First Amendment that would make Thomas Jefferson feel good about his early work. Roger Labrie is diligent and meticulous, qualities that have made him a master of thoughtful editing. A great deal of gratitude goes to Elisa Rivlin, senior vice president and general counsel; Victoria Meyer, executive vice president of publicity; Tracey Guest, director of publicity; Jackie Seow, art director and jacket designer; Irene Kheradi, executive managing editor; Michael Szczerban, assistant managing editor; Karen Thompson, associate editor; Paul Dippolito, designer; Lisa Healy, senior production editor; Nancy Inglis, director of copyediting; Lynn Anderson, proofreader; and John Wahler, associate director of production.

Brady Dennis, Evelyn Duffy and I share a deep appreciation for copy editor Fred Chase, who took six days away from his home and family in Texas to travel to Washington and work on his fifth book with me. He is a joy to have around and an integral part of this book. A consummate professional, Fred's observation, insight and sound judgment prove that the best editing is about far more than marks on a page.

Eight years ago, I wrote in *Maestro,* my book on Alan Greenspan and the Federal Reserve, that *The Washington Post* had allowed me to wander on perhaps the longest leash in American journalism. That leash has gotten longer with time, and I am ever grateful for the *Post*'s support. The *Post* continues to play a vital and irreplaceable role in Washington life and politics. Don Graham, the *Post*'s CEO, is a man with a kind soul and a businessman's savvy. He looks out for underdogs and gives voice to the voiceless. He is a generous and compassionate boss, and there is no one else quite like him. Leonard Downie Jr., the *Post*'s executive editor and the best newspaperman in America, is retiring after a spectacular career. The newspaper's 25 Pulitzer Prizes during his tenure are a testament to his determination and skill. The *Post*'s publisher, Katharine Weymouth, shows all the signs of a commitment to independent, aggressive journalism shared by her uncle, Don Graham, and her grandmother, Katharine Graham.

Special thanks to Steve Luxenberg for devoting his time, focus and formidable intellect while helping to excerpt this book for the *Post*.

The work of a number of *Post* reporters who covered the war from both Iraq and Washington provided many key insights. They include but are certainly not limited to Rajiv Chandrasekaran, John Ward Anderson, Ann Scott Tyson, Karen DeYoung, Josh White, Joshua Partlow, Naseer Nouri, Thomas Ricks,

Anne Hull, Amit Paley, Sudarsan Raghavan, Michael Abramowitz, Peter Baker, Ellen Knickmeyer, and Jonathan Weisman. Many of my colleagues again provided help and encouragement, both in the form of their daily coverage and through the informal sharing of advice and ideas. They include Al Kamen, Susan Glasser, David Ignatius, Dana Priest, Glenn Kessler, David Hoffman, Joby Warrick, and Rick Atkinson.

Many thanks also to Michel du Cille and Wendy Galietta at the *Post* for their expert assistance with the photos in this book, and to Laris Karklis for the map.

I thank Carl Bernstein, who has been a friend for 36 years. He is in touch with all that is happening in American politics and he provided many thoughts and insightful analysis on Bush and the war. He and I remain linked for life as friends and colleagues.

My eternal thanks to Ben Bradlee, who raised the bar for all of us and remains a founding father of *The Washington Post*.

No work of this size and scope can be pieced together in a vacuum. I acknowledge the many books and newspaper and magazine articles that added background or detail to my own work. I have drawn on the excellent reporting and analysis of dozens of news organizations, including *The New York Times, The Wall Street Journal,* the *Los Angeles Times, Newsweek* and the Associated Press. The following books were useful points of reference: *The Iraq Study Group Report* by James Baker III, Lee Hamilton, et al.; *In the Company of Soldiers* by Rick Atkinson; *The U.S. Army/Marine Corps Counterinsurgency Field Manual; Fiasco* by Thomas Ricks; *Dead Certain: The Presidency of George W. Bush* by Robert Draper; *Cheney: The Untold Story of America's Most Powerful and Controversial Vice President* by Stephen F. Hayes; *Condoleezza Rice: An American Life* by Elisabeth Bumiller; and *From the Shadows* by Robert Gates. I also found the Web site of the Institute for the Study of War (www.understandingwar.org) and the *Small Wars Journal* weblog (www.smallwarsjournal.com) helpful throughout.

Robert B. Barnett, my agent, attorney and friend, is an institution in Washington. His reach and wisdom know no parallel. Because he represents prominent politicians on both sides of the aisle, including Senators Hillary Clinton and Barack Obama, he was not consulted on the contents of this book and did not see it until it was printed. Thanks also to Brendan Sullivan, a rock of the legal profession, for providing important advice.

Brady, Evelyn and I are deeply grateful for the presence of Rosa Criollo and Jackie Crowe in our lives. They provide guidance, coherence and sustenance in a thousand different ways.

My elder daughter, Tali, spent two weeks reading the manuscript and providing many important insights. She is a brilliant young woman. Her edits and suggestions once again revealed a dedication to making the complexities of national security discussed in this book accessible to as many readers as possible. My younger daughter, Diana, completed a great fifth-grade year and provided endless hours of joy.

My wife, Elsa Walsh, has been unbelievably tolerant of the hours involved in putting together a book like this. She is a calming anchor in my life, an answerer of questions, a settler of debates, and the epitome of a partner in love, life and work.

Finally, as my assistants and I researched and wrote this book in the third-floor offices of my home in Washington, our thoughts have returned often to the many thousands of fellow citizens who volunteer to serve. We have each formed a lasting connection to these men and women. Their example is humbling, and we stand in awe of them and their families.

In November 2006, my colleague and friend Rick Atkinson took me to Arlington National Cemetery. We visited Section 60, where the war dead from Iraq and Afghanistan are buried. In what Atkinson has called "the saddest acre in America," new rows of graves were being added one after another. That day, we met Teresa Arciola, whose 20-year-old son, Michael, had been killed in Iraq. She had brought his favorite childhood book, *Corduroy,* and was reading it aloud at his grave side. Her request to me was the same simple appeal she had made to everyone she told about her son: "Remember . . . respect . . . honor."

PHOTOGRAPHY CREDITS

INDEX

ABOUT THE AUTHOR

Bob Woodward is an associate editor at *The Washington Post*, where he has worked for 37 years. He has shared in two Pulitzer Prizes, first for the *Post*'s coverage of the Watergate scandal, and later for coverage of the 9/11 terrorist attacks. He has authored or coauthored eleven #1 national nonfiction bestsellers, including three on the current administration—*Bush at War* (2002), *Plan of Attack* (2004) and *State of Denial* (2006). He has two daughters, Tali and Diana, and lives in Washington, D.C., with his wife, writer Elsa Walsh.